D0509453

Encyclopedia of
Nutrition & Cooking

Encyclopedia

Culinary Arts Institute Home Economics Staff
Sherrill Corley   Helen Geist   Dee Munson
Ethel La Roche   Ivanka Simatic

Editorial Staff
Jadwiga Lopez   Gerald Pipes   Patricia Westphal
Veronica Lewandowski   Malinda Miller   Margaret Stephens

Art Staff
Richard Nicol   Laurel DiGangi

Book designed by Charles Bozett

of Nutrition &
Cooking

by
the staff of the Culinary Arts Institute

Foreword by Dr. Philip L. White
Director, Department of Foods and Nutrition,
American Medical Association

 Culinary Arts Institute
Chicago

Grosset & Dunlap, Inc., Publishers
New York

Copyright © 1974
by
Processing & Books, Inc.
1727 South Indiana Avenue   Chicago, Illinois 60616

All rights reserved under the International and Pan-American Copyright Conventions.

Library of Congress Catalog Card Number: 74-9182
International Standard Book Number: 0-448-11666-9

Manufactured in the United States of America

FIRST EDITION

PHOTO ACKNOWLEDGMENTS

Alaska King Crab; American Dairy Association; American Spice Trade Association; Diamond Walnut Growers, Inc.; Fleischmann's Yeast; Florida Department of Citrus; Halibut Association of North America; National Broiler Council; National Live Stock and Meat Board; The Olive Administrative Committee; Pacific Bartlett Growers, Inc.; Rice Council; Spanish Green Olive Commission; United Fresh Fruit and Vegetable Association; and Wheat Flour Institute.

Foreword

It is not necessary to know about vitamins, minerals, and proteins in order to assemble an optimum diet—but such knowledge certainly helps. An understanding of the basic concepts of nutrition will assure that proper attention is given to a desirable combination of nutrients through appropriate blends of foods into meals. Most of us eat to satisfy hunger and for the pleasure food brings; all well and good, but we cannot be properly nourished following such simple guidelines as hunger and pleasure.

Nutrition is a very personal science because it is the science of ourselves. Personal well-being and vitality depend upon many interrelated factors—proper food, rest, exercise, relaxation, and good mental health habits. Health, vitality, and that great feeling of well-being are impossible without appropriate attention to nutrition. Nutrition cannot be taken for granted. Nearly half of us do take it for granted and look at the result: overweight, anemia, and other signs of malnutrition.

Surveys of the nutrition status of Americans by the Department of Health, Education and Welfare, such as the Ten-State Nutrition Survey and the Health and Nutrition Examination Survey, reveal that too many Americans of all ages and income levels have faulty diets leading to sub-optimal intake of essential nutrients or the consumption of too few or too many calories. This American experience is confirmed in nearly every other country in the world. There are countries, of course, where some people are poorly nourished because food supplies are limited. But the widespread malnutrition that exists among the affluent is due largely, not to poor food, but to poor food choices. We really ought to be ashamed of our record. I know we can do something to improve it.

Firstly, we must learn to care enough about ourselves to begin moving in the right direction. We need motivation, if you will—motivation to see the information which will enable us to confirm or condemn present food habits.

Secondly, we must learn not to be distracted by foods that taste great or are convenient but that represent only calories. Vast amounts of advertising are devoted to confusing our food needs with food wants. Candy, soft drinks, and frivolous fun foods may have a minor place in the total diet—but they *must* be kept in a *minor* place.

Thirdly, we must learn how to select and prepare nourishing, wholesome foods that combine the excitement of eating with the satisfaction of good nutrition. To do this may require considerable soul-searching and a willingness to develop new food tastes, since most families restrict themselves to menus representing a limited number of foods and combinations of foods.

Finally, we must learn how to safeguard our family's health with proper food-handling techniques. The conservation of nutrients depends upon appropriate management of food from market to table. Home care in food management to eliminate the possibility of food spoilage and bacteria-related poisoning is, of course, extremely important, and it is your responsibility. The food you purchase is yours to do with what you will. First of all, follow instructions on packages—then use common sense. But wait! Common sense is based on the accumulation of experiences and, as we have seen, our eating habits have not always been the most commendable. So maybe they should be reevaluated and our information about nutrition updated. This is where this book comes in—it will help you gain better insight into the nutritional process, aid you in reassessing your needs, and guide you in fulfilling them.

This book is truly an encyclopedia—a very complete one that you will enjoy reading. Keep it handy for quick reference when troubled about something you hear or read about nutrition. Use the meal-planning guides to enlarge your horizons. The recipes have all been tested for performance and assessed for nutritional quality. It's all right here—all you need to know to become a nutrition expert as well as an expert cook.

Dr. Philip L. White

Contents

Nutrition Know-How

Nutrition is one of the most important factors in the achievement of good health. Good health does not only mean being free from disease: it means having a sense of vitality and well-being; it means being able to take pleasure in life because one is physically fit and mentally alert. The proper functioning of our bodies—and minds—is dependent upon proper nourishment. Eating healthfully can make the difference between feeling great and feeling so-so. Good nutrition helps us look better, feel better, think better, work better, and live longer.

Nutrition is the process of eating and using food, and it is the subject of intense study and research. Fortunately for us, practical application of the principles of nutrition does not depend upon a thorough knowledge of food and body chemistry. Rather, we need simply to learn what foods to eat for energy and nourishment. In other words, we must gain an understanding of the body's nutrient requirements, learn how to select foods that will fulfill those requirements, and develop good eating patterns that provide pleasurable and healthful meals.

Unfortunately, our eating habits (the foods we eat, how we get them, and how we eat meals) are often all too careless. Eating patterns have changed dramatically in the past few decades. Great grandmother, for instance, probably never heard of pizza, nor did she dream of buying it ready-made from a freezer in a supermarket. No longer do we consume large quantities of food in several courses at the set hours of eight, twelve, and six. Life styles have changed, and although many of us eat three meals a day, those meals may be rushed, and the in-between hours are filled with snacks—we may, in fact, eat six or seven "meals" a day. Often we give little thought to variety or nourishment, pausing to munch on what is available or appealing when the fancy or hunger strikes.

In addition, many people interested in good health are too often swayed by the words of self-styled food experts who persuasively guarantee us good health if we follow their special diets; if we eat certain "magic" foods; if we shun processed, packaged, or manufactured foods; or if we load up on vitamins or exotic and expensive substances. Do not count on these specious promises of an easy way to good health. No esoteric diet regimen, augmented by handfuls of vitamin supplements, can set you and your family on a magical road to good health and vitality. Nor can one single food, method, or diet fulfill the body's nutritional needs. Indeed, the effects on one's health of these diet fads are sometimes disastrous.

Our philosophy of good nutrition,

endorsed by medical authorities, is simple: a variety of foods from common sources, eaten in moderation. Proper nourishment does not depend upon following a rigid dietary regimen—there is a wide world of foods and food combinations to choose from. A variety of foods, carefully prepared and attractively presented, helps create lifelong good eating habits that will help insure good health.

The importance of developing good eating habits cannot be overemphasized. Fatigue, listlessness, and minor ailments frequently plague the poorly nourished. Moreover, improper eating habits invite serious health problems such as tooth decay, obesity, cardiovascular disease, calcium deficiency, and anemia. Poor eating habits that start early in childhood, are likely to last a lifetime--so nutrition education should begin early, at home. Children should be encouraged, by example, to eat healthfully. Good eating habits, begun early in childhood, will also last a lifetime.

Becoming knowledgeable about nutrition and developing proper eating habits may seem an enormous task, but the purpose of this book is to provide the information you need to make the job easier. This book will give you the know-how to plan, purchase, store, and prepare a variety of good, nourishing foods. It will help you figure out how to include good foods in the mini-meal snack pattern that has developed for our busy back-and-forth way of life. And it will provide you with recipes designed to combine and take advantage of the nutritional value of a variety of foods. You do not need to wonder what nutrients a recipe supplies: we tell you right along with the recipe. The glossary at the back of the book is a quick reference which supplements the nutrition know-how provided in the following sections with condensed information about foods and nutrition.

Cooking nutritious meals can be both challenging and rewarding. Arm yourself with the basic nutrition know-how provided in this book; then let planning, shopping, storing, cooking, and serving become a pleasure. You and your family will be rewarded with delicious meals and good health.

THE INDIVIDUAL NUTRIENTS

Nutrients are the individual substances that combine to make foods and to supply us with all that we need to move, to grow, to live. At least fifty separate nutrients have been identified, and there may be many more just waiting to be discovered. Because foods may contain unknown nutrients, for good health we are safer eating a variety of foods, rather than consuming pills composed only of the known nutrients.

Nutrients are usually grouped in five categories: proteins, carbohydrates, fats, vitamins, and minerals. Another substance important to nutrition is water. Sections on each of these follow.

Protein

Ask anyone to name a nutrient and a likely answer will be protein. We are indeed protein-conscious. We might be better off if we were a little more protein-knowledgeable.

Proteins are the body builders and body maintainers; they help in the development of muscles; they create a feeling of well-being and fitness. In addition, proteins help make hemoglobin, the blood protein that delivers oxygen to and removes carbon dioxide from cells. Proteins are part of hormones (which regulate growth and body functions), of enzymes (which produce chemical changes in the body), and of genes (which determine the development of hereditary characteristics). Proteins help form antibodies to fight infections, and they are an energy source.

Amino acids, twenty-two of them, are the building blocks of protein. Eight of these twenty-two cannot be manufactured by our bodies. They must be obtained from food eaten daily.

Proteins are classified as high-quality or low-quality according to how much of each of the eight essential amino acids they contain. A high-quality protein is one that supplies all the eight essential amino acids in proper amounts. *Adequate* or *efficient* are words also used to describe these proteins. Proteins from animal sources are high in quality. These sources include beef, lamb, pork, poultry, fish, shellfish, eggs, and milk.

A low-quality protein has too little of some of the eight essential amino acids. Vegetable proteins are generally of low value. Sources of low-quality proteins are lentils and the legumes—dried beans and peas (soy, lima, and kidney beans, chickpeas or garbanzos, split and black-eye peas). Peanuts and peanut butter also supply protein. Larger quantities of low-quality protein foods must be eaten to get the same nutritive value that high-quality protein foods provide. Because of their protein content, these particular vegetables are called meat alternates and are of great interest now as we search for meat substitutes. Cereal grains, some fruits, and several other vegetables also contain some protein. More attention should be paid in our diets to the vegetable protein sources. They are usually cheap, plentiful, and filling.

In meal planning, vegetable or plant proteins ought to be supplemented with small amounts of high-quality animal protein in order to provide the body with enough of the eight essential amino acids. Certain combinations of vegetable and/or animal proteins are popular dishes in themselves and provide a good protein mix as well: macaroni and cheese, beans and rice, cereal and milk, rice and fish, spaghetti and meatballs, baked beans and brown bread, peanut butter and bread. Many vegetarians manage their protein needs by carefully teaming vegetable proteins with each other to provide the eight amino acids in proper amounts. Most people, however, will opt for the simple protein insurance policy of eating both vegetable and animal proteins.

Because our bodies cannot store amino acids (amino acid reserves are depleted in a matter of hours), we need small amounts of protein daily, preferably at each meal. When we consume protein foods, the protein is separated into the various amino acids by the digestive process. These separated amino acids come together again in new combinations to form special human proteins. This explains why eating animal and vegetable proteins together at each meal is such a good policy—it assures the body enough of all eight amino acids. If we eat a variety of foods, including the vegetable proteins, we will be safe from protein deficiency.

How much protein we actually need is greatly overestimated by many Westerners. The amount of protein any individual needs is determined by several factors: by the individual's size, age, activity, and by the type of protein he regularly consumes.

Nutritionists recommend that protein comprise about 15 percent of a day's calorie intake. In other terms, about one gram of protein for each kilogram of body weight (or, to be exact, 0.424 grams per pound of body weight) is the figure generally accepted as a wise level for protein intake. That is fifty-five grams for the average woman and sixty-five for the average man. Most adults in the United States regularly consume eighty to ninety grams per day. The extra protein is used for energy—there are cheaper places to get food energy than from protein.

Eating large quantities of animal proteins is also a wasteful use of the

PICK A PROTEIN

Food Group	Portion	Protein Grams	Food Group	Portion	Protein Grams
Milk			Pork, cooked, lean to medium-fat	3 oz.	18
Milk			Salmon, pink, canned	3 oz.	17
Whole	1 cup	9	Sardines, canned, drained	3 oz.	20
2% (nonfat milk solids added)	1 cup	10	Shrimps, canned	3 oz.	21
Skim	1 cup	9	Tuna, canned, drained	3 oz.	24
Buttermilk	1 cup	9	Veal, cooked, lean to medium-fat	3 oz.	23
Nonfat dry, reconstituted	1 cup	8	**Fruit and Vegetable**		
Cheese			Apricots, dried	½ cup	4
American	1 slice (1 oz.)	7	Beans, lima	½ cup	6
Blue or Roquefort	¼ cup (1 oz.)	6	Brussels sprouts	½ cup	4
Camembert	1 wedge (1⅓ oz.)	7	Corn	½ cup	3
Cheddar	1 slice (1 oz.)	7	Peas, green	½ cup	4
Cottage, creamed	½ cup	16	Potato	1 medium	3
Cream cheese	3 oz.	7	**Bread and Cereal**		
Swiss	1 slice (1 oz.)	8	Bagel	1	6
Ice cream, vanilla	½ cup	3	Bread		
Yogurt, plain	1 cup	8	Rye	2 slices	4
Meat			White	2 slices	4
Bacon, crisp	2 slices	5	Whole wheat	2 slices	6
Beans, baked, with pork	1 cup (8 oz.)	16	Cereal, cooked	1 cup	4
Beans, dried, cooked	1 cup (5 oz.)	14	Corn muffin, plain	1	3
Beef, cooked, lean to medium-fat	3 oz.	23	Macaroni, cooked	1 cup	6
Bologna or lunch meat	2 slices (1 oz.)	3	Noodles, cooked	1 cup	7
Chicken, broiled, boneless	3 oz.	20	Pancakes (4-inch)	2	4
Clams, canned, meat and liquid	3 oz.	7	Rice, cooked	1 cup	4
Clams, raw meat	3 oz.	11	Waffle (7-inch)	1	7
Crabmeat, canned	3 oz.	15	**Miscellaneous**		
Egg	1 large	6	Cream, dairy sour	1 cup	7
Fish, breaded, fried	3 oz.	17	Custard, baked	½ cup	7
Frankfurter	1 (2 oz.)	7	Danish pastry	1	5
Ham	1 slice (1 oz.)	6	Eclair, chocolate	1	8
Lamb, cooked, lean to medium-fat	3 oz.	21	Gelatin dessert	1 cup	4
Liver, beef, fried	3 oz.	22	Pie	⅙ of 9-inch	
Nuts, shelled, roasted	¼ cup (1 oz.)	6	Custard		9
Oysters, raw meat	3 oz.	7	Fruit		3
Peanut butter	2 tablespoons	8	Pecan		7
Pea soup, canned	1 cup (8 oz.)	9	Pizza	⅛ of 14-inch	7
Peas, split, dried, cooked	1 cup	20	Pudding		
			Chocolate	½ cup	4
			Rice, with raisins	½ cup	5
			Vanilla	½ cup	5

world's food supplies. It takes three pounds of grain to produce one pound of poultry, five pounds of grain to produce one pound of pork, and ten pounds of grain to produce one pound of beef. Over 1,600 pounds of grain are consumed per person per year in the United States and Canada. Eighty percent of this grain is consumed indirectly through meat. Only an awareness of these facts and a change in eating patterns among the affluent will reduce the demand for certain foods and release food sources to a larger, and more needy, number of people

One typical diet mistake is that we forget that protein foods have calories. We often ignore the calorie cost of high-protein foods, erroneously assuming that protein is "thinning." Six ounces of sirloin steak will indeed give you, among other things, forty grams of protein, but at a cost of 660 calories.

Planning, selection, and moderation are all important when it comes to putting protein in your meals. The Pick a Protein chart gives you an idea of the protein content of several foods. Foods in the list provide, in a normal serving, at least three grams of protein.

Carbohydrates

Just as proteins are often overemphasized in our diets, so is the value of carbohydrates suprisingly underestimated. Many dieters cut out carbohydrates in the belief that they are fattening. That belief is partially true, but partial truths can be dangerous.

Carbohydrates are essential because they provide energy, and they are necessary for the processing of fatty acids in the body. Furthermore, the grain products, fruits, and vegetables which supply our bodies with carbohydrates also provide many essential vitamins and minerals.

Carbohydrates is the name of a group of organic substances that are made up of carbon, hydrogen, and oxygen. Carbohydrates include simple sugars, or monosaccharides, such as glucose, fructose, and galactose; disaccharides, such as table sugar; and complex carbohydrates (starches and cellulose). The special chemical structure of cellulose gives it a very different character than other carbohydrates. Cellulose does not provide us with energy because the human body is not equipped to break it down. But we do need cellulose, as fiber or bulk, to assist in digestion.

Starches and sugars are two of our major energy sources. Starches are bunches of simple sugars chemically combined. Because they are more complex than sugars, they digest slightly more slowly.

Sugars are the simplest carbohydrates and, whatever their form, are all basically the same. One difference among honey, table sugar, maple syrup, corn syrup, raw sugar, and brown sugar is flavor. Honey and brown sugar contain small amounts of other nutrients besides carbohydrates, but these amounts are insignificant. The important factor in a healthful diet is how much sugar is used, not which sugar.

Generally, researchers indicate that we might be better off eating less sugar, which provides energy but little else, and getting our carbohydrate intake instead from other foods which also supply vitamins and minerals. The familiar carbohydrate sources are readily available and inexpensive: all grains and the products made from them (flour, baked goods, macaroni, spaghetti, noodles, bread, and breakfast cereals), potatoes, sweet potatoes, and beans and peas. Some of these carbohydrate sources add protein, too (see the Pick a Protein chart). Most other fruits and vegetables supply smaller amounts of carbohydrates, the vegetables giving starches and the fruits sugars.

Carbohydrates are broken down after

digestion into three simple sugars: glucose, fructose, and galactose. After absorption, the simple sugars are carried to the liver, where fructose and galactose are changed to glucose. Glucose is used by the body in different ways. It may be released into the blood stream as blood sugar and used by cells as energy for physical activity or as energy for the metabolism of other compounds. It may be stored in the liver as glycogen and released as needed as blood sugar. Or it may be converted to fat and stored in cells.

Although carbohydrates have been blamed for tooth decay, it is not the carbohydrates we eat that affect our teeth. It is the bacteria that feed on them that are the villains because they produce an acid that damages teeth. Keeping the mouth and the teeth clean helps to cut down the food supply of these busy bacteria, and thus lessens tooth decay.

Eliminating carbohydrates from the diet is downright dangerous. Both carbohydrates and fats together are necessary for proper fuel chemistry. Without carbohydrates, fats are not completely broken down, and substances called ketones are formed. If ketones are allowed to build up, they become poisonous and produce a serious and sometimes fatal condition called ketosis.

Carbohydrates comprise about 45 to 50 percent of the calories in the average American diet. Carbohydrate intake can go as high as 55 percent of the calories in a healthful diet. Unfortunately, in more affluent societies, carbohydrates tend to be slighted and fat intake increased. Many Americans may consume more than 50 percent of their daily calorie intake in the form of fat. Nutrition experts recommend limiting fat in the diet to 30 to 35 percent. Wise food selection and moderation are essential in balancing fat and carbohydrate intake.

Fats

Fat is probably the most controversial item in our diet. How much fat do we need, and what kind of fat? You've heard fats described as saturated, unsaturated, polyunsaturated, and hydrogenated. What do these terms mean?

Fats are a concentrated source of energy. Gram for gram, ounce for ounce, fats supply more than twice as much energy (or calories) as proteins or carbohydrates. Proteins provide 112 calories per ounce or 4 calories per gram; carbohydrates, the same; fat supplies 252 calories per ounce or 9 calories per gram.

Fat, as already mentioned, is a concentrated energy source. In addition, fat carries the fat-soluble vitamins A, D, E, and K. Fat makes up a part of the cell structure within every one of us; it forms protective cushions around our vital organs; it lets protein go about its work of building and repair by providing food energy; and, in a thin layer under the skin, it insulates the body and prevents loss of heat.

We all need some fat in our diets. Just as we need the essential amino acids to make protein, we must take in certain essential fatty acids from fat sources. These essential fatty acids number three: linoleic, linolenic, and arachidonic. Since our bodies can make the last two from the first, all we need concern ourselves with is linoleic acid. We need linoleic acid for growth, for healthy skin, and for the proper use and storage of fats in our bodies. Natural oils supply goodly amounts of linoleic acid. A tablespoon of corn, cottonseed, or soy oil, or two of peanut oil, plus the fat that is in other foods, usually takes care of our daily needs.

Fats are classified according to the amounts of certain kinds of fatty acids they contain. Fats which contain predominantly *saturated* fatty acids are of animal origin, and they are usually solid or plastic at room temperature. They include the fat on and in meat, butterfat from and in whole milk products, and lard.

Unsaturated and polyunsaturated fatty acids are found in liquid oils from plant sources: corn, cottonseed, safflower, sesame, soy, or wheat germ. Margarines, salad dressings, mayonnaise, and cooking oils are usually made from one or more of these oils.

Hydrogenated fatty acids are unsaturated or polyunsaturated fatty acids to which hydrogen has been added. Some oils are hydrogenated to change them from liquids into solids or semisolids (fat). Also, some oils are lightly hydrogenated to reduce the amounts of very reactive fatty acids to prevent oxidation and the development of off flavors.

The controversy about the effect of fats upon our health rages on; unless otherwise instructed by your physician, we suggest you follow the advice of the United States Department of Agriculture: "In choosing daily meals, it is well to keep the total amount of fat at a moderate level and to include some foods that contain polyunsaturated fats."

Cholesterol

Cholesterol is an organic substance found in foods of animal origin. In the human body, cholesterol is an important part of nerve tissue (and therefore of the brain) and of digestive juices, and it plays a significant role in the formation of steroid hormones.

Although our bodies produce cholesterol, the cholesterol level in the blood is dependent to an extent on the foods we eat. Cholesterol is found in foods of animal origin, especially organ meats, shellfish, egg yolks, and animal fats. Fruits, vegetables, cereal grains, legumes, nuts, oil, or anything else coming from plants have no cholesterol content.

In spite of cholesterol's usefulness in our bodies, too much cholesterol in the blood may be dangerous. Medical research has shown that persons with high cholesterol levels are more susceptible to arteriosclerosis (hardening of the arteries), strokes, heart disease, and heart attacks. However, it has not been proven that a high cholesterol level is the cause of heart disease. Other factors, too, contribute to heart disease. Among them are inherited tendencies, obesity, cigarette smoking, high blood pressure, and hypertension.

The question posed by medical authorities is whether decreasing the consumption of animal foods and saturated fats (and thereby lowering the level of cholesterol in the blood) will diminish the possibility of heart disease and related conditions. The American Heart Association believes that a diet low in cholesterol, low in saturated fats (animal fats, butter, fats found in whole milk, etc.) and higher in polyunsaturated fats (vegetable oils) can decrease the risk of heart disease.

If you have questions concerning your cholesterol level, consult your doctor. If he advises you to take steps to change your diet, the American Heart Association is a good source of information and assistance.

Vitamins

Even though man has been eating and somehow surviving for thousands of years, it is only within the last fifty years that he has started to learn about vitamins. Vitamins are essential to life and well-being. They are necessary for the proper functioning of many of our body processes. Moreover, we cannot manufacture vitamins in our bodies and must obtain them from a variety of foods or from synthetic sources. Fortunately, vitamins are vitamins, whatever their source—natural or synthetic. Vitamins help the body utilize nutrients; they promote the normal growth of tissue; they are necessary for the proper functioning of nerves and muscles; they are a necessary part of the reproductive and digestive processes; and they may help the body resist infections.

Lack of vitamins causes deficiency diseases. Each of the better-known vitamins is related to an equally well-known disease. The remarkable thing about these diseases is that the cure is usually simple and immediately effective. Start eating foods rich in the vitamin that was deficient and it won't be long before you are well, providing your diet continues to supply proper amounts of the vitamin. Interestingly enough, the food "cures" for some of the vitamin-deficiency diseases were discovered long before the vitamins themselves were isolated and identified. For example, the British navy realized that limes and lemons prevented scurvy years before the remedy was known as vitamin C. A word of warning here—vitamin deficiency diseases *can* be cured by certain foods. Other diseases *cannot* be cured by certain foods.

Scientists and nutritionists have identified a dozen or so major vitamins that are necessary for good health. These vitamins will be available in a well-chosen, varied diet made up of foods from your neighborhood grocery store. You *do not* have to wander from health-food store to organic-produce market to find healthful, nutritious foods.

Vitamin pills and supplements are not necessary additions to a varied, balanced diet. If you want extra insurance for children, pregnant or nursing women, or if you feel your appetite and eating habits are below par, then check with your doctor and take a vitamin pill containing United States Recommended Daily Allowances (U.S. RDA) and *no more than those recommended amounts*. Taking massive doses of vitamins or megavitamins is unwise and dangerous. Few people realize that excesses of some vitamins can be poisonous and even fatal. Excesses of vitamin A, for instance, can cause blurred vision, hair loss, diarrhea, nausea, loss of appetite, and dry skin. Toxicity may be reached if 50,000 International Units (IU) are consumed daily for several months. An excess of vitamin D may produce some of the same symptoms as an overdose of vitamin A, and in addition it may cause high levels of calcium in the blood and calcium deposits in soft tissues, including the lungs, kidneys, and blood vessels.

Vitamin overdoses are rarely due to food intake, but rather to the addition of vitamin supplements to the diet. Since popping vitamin pills can become just as dangerous as any other drug abuse, therapeutic vitamin intake must be supervised by a physician.

Vitamin C (Ascorbic Acid)

Many people are aware that not enough vitamin C can cause gums to bleed and eventually produce the disease known as scurvy. And many people have heard the remarkable claims recently made for this vitamin. One claim under study is that ascorbic acid can cure or prevent the common cold. But few know any more than that. Read on and put yourself among those who know more.

C is a water-soluble vitamin that is not stored in the body. C (ascorbic acid) performs a number of vital functions. It has a part in forming and maintaining the material that holds living cells together and that strengthens the walls of blood vessels. C, a handy helper in normal tooth and bone formation, also helps build resistance to bacterial infection and hastens healing.

Natural vitamin C and commercially produced ascorbic acid are chemically the same substance. It is possible to get the daily requirement of C from fortified drinks. However, such products add a great deal of vitamin C and sugar to the diet but little else. Natural sources of vitamin C, such as cantaloupe, orange juice, or strawberries, add other nutrients besides C and provide bulk, necessary for good digestion. Citrus fruits, tomatoes, white potatoes, sweet potatoes, and green leafy vegetables are good sources of vitamin C. A more extensive list of C-rich foods is on page 23.

Vitamin C is elusive and fragile, so foods high in vitamin C must be handled with care. Check pages 40–41, under Cooking to Conserve Nutritive Values, to learn how to handle C-rich foods.

How much vitamin C is needed each day? One-half grapefruit (or six ounces of orange juice) plus a serving of a vegetable high in C will meet the daily requirement. As the body does not store this vitamin, moderate amounts of C-rich foods must be eaten daily.

The B Vitamins

There are many vitamins in the B-family complex known to be important in the daily diet. All of them are vital to normal metabolism and good health. There is a little bit of each B vitamin in every body cell. All the B vitamins are water-soluble, like vitamin C, which means they are not stored in the body and must be taken daily. The B's work together in the task of metabolizing carbohydrates and providing our bodies with energy. Each of the B vitamins has additional special functions.

Thiamine—Thiamine plays an important part in carbohydrate metabolism (call it energizing, if you like) and in the functioning of the nervous system. Good digestion and a normal appetite are unlikely without proper amounts of thiamine. A deficiency of thiamine causes beriberi, fortunately little known today in our part of the world. The enrichment of bread and flour with thiamine has considerably raised this vitamin's content in our food supply. Pork and liver are particularly good sources of thiamine.

Riboflavin—Like thiamine, riboflavin plays a part in converting sources of energy in the body into energy itself. A deficiency of riboflavin causes sore lips, tongue, and mouth, and rough scaly skin. The eyes are also affected by lack of riboflavin. Meat, milk, and enriched or whole grain bread and cereal products provide riboflavin in our meals. Liver is an excellent source of this vitamin.

Niacin—Niacin helps the body metabolize the nutrients in food. Pellagra is the disease caused by niacin deficiency and its symptoms include inflammation of the skin, diarrhea, and mental disorders. Untreated pellagra may be fatal. Niacin is available to the body from tryptophan, which is present in protein foods and can be changed by the body into niacin. Thus, proper amounts of protein give us the niacin we need. Enriched and whole grain bread and cereal products add niacin, too.

Pyridoxine—B_6 is a part of the enzyme system that helps us use and build protein. It also helps convert tryptophan into niacin. Meat, whole grain cereals, dried beans, potatoes, and dark green leafy vegetables are good B_6 providers.

Pantothenic Acid—Pantothenic acid is another of the B vitamin complex that plays a part in the chemical processes that keep us moving and working. Foods that supply the other B's are good sources of pantothenic acid: liver and organ meats, eggs, muscle meats, legumes, and cereals.

Biotin—Biotin is available in organ or variety meats, muscle meats, milk, vegetables, egg yolks, grains, and some fruits. This vitamin works in several enzyme systems. There isn't much need to worry about biotin deficiency, unless you eat a lot of raw egg white, which prevents biotin absorption by the body.

Folacin and B$_{12}$—Folacin and B$_{12}$ are particularly important in preventing anemia. Both are needed in formation of red blood cells and participate in enzyme systems. Green leafy vegetables, liver, legumes, meat, whole grains, and other vegetables give us folacin. Organ and muscle meats, milk, cheese, and eggs take care of our B$_{12}$ needs.

Choline—Probably not a true B vitamin, choline is made in the body from an amino acid with the help of B$_{12}$ and folacin. Choline is available in a variety of foods, and if meals are varied, there is not much chance of a deficiency.

Vitamin A

Vitamin A is a fat-soluble vitamin. It facilitates normal bone growth, it helps the eyes adjust to dim light, and it helps provide healthy, infection-resistant skin and mucous membranes.

Since vitamin A is fat-soluble, it can be stored in the body and it need not be consumed every day, as do the water-soluble vitamins. It is wise to eat A-rich foods every other day, though. Foods that are good sources of A are such flavorful and colorful additions to meals that working them into menus should not be a problem.

Vitamin A is found in animal foods only, such as liver, eggs, butter, whole milk, and cheese. A precursor or provitamin of A, carotene, changes into the vitamin form after digestion. Dark green and deep yellow vegetables and deep yellow fruits are good carotene sources. See the Fruit and Vegetable Group on page 23 for a list of A-rich fruits and vegetables.

Vitamin D

Vitamin D is known as the sunshine vitamin because direct action of sunlight on the skin converts precursors to active vitamin D. Vitamin D helps the body to use calcium and phosphorus—strong bones and teeth are the result.

Rickets is the soft-bone disease caused by deficiencies of vitamin D, calcium, and phosphorus. Cod-liver oil, rich in vitamin D, was recognized many years ago as an inhibitor of rickets, but it was not until 1922 that the vitamin itself was discovered.

Some D is found in egg yolk, butter, and liver; but some fish, particularly sardines, salmon, herring, and tuna, are more abundant sources of vitamin D. Milk that has been fortified with D is the most common source of this vitamin.

Vitamin K

Another of the fat-soluble vitamins, K is best known for its work in the normal clotting of blood and functioning of the liver.

Several foods—green leafy vegetables, egg yolks, and organ meats—supply vitamin K. Some vitamin K is produced by bacteria in the intestinal tract.

Vitamin E

Vitamin E is a fat-soluble vitamin whose most important feature is its antioxidant properties. It prevents the unwanted oxidation of polyunsaturated fatty acids. Were these nutrients to oxidize in the body, they could not be used properly in body chemistry. (Because of its antioxidant properties, E is also used as a food additive to prevent spoilage.)

Vitamin E is stored in the body in muscles and in fat deposits. Deficiencies of this vitamin are unknown in the United States and other developed countries. E is found in many common foods: unsaturated fats, wheat germ and wheat germ oil, leafy vegetables, legumes, whole grains, liver, butter, milk, and eggs.

Recently, enthusiastic reports have circulated claiming that large doses of vitamin E will improve one's sexual potency and inhibit pregnancy disorders, rheumatic fever, and circulatory diseases. There is virtually no scientific support for these claims. All vitamins in moderate amounts are "wonder" vitamins. Not one of them can do everything, but each performs a special function that is vital for good health.

Minerals

Certain minerals are necessary for the proper functioning of the human body. They give strength and rigidity to certain body tissues and help with a number of bodily functions. Minerals are originally found in the soil and are made available to us in the plants and animals we eat.

We need more of some minerals than of others. Our bodies require significant amounts of calcium, phosphorus, chlorine, magnesium, potassium, sodium, and sulphur. Elements needed in small amounts include iron, chromium, cobalt, copper, fluorine, iodine, manganese, molybdenum, selenium, and zinc. The tiny amounts of minerals required by the body have definite limits. Excesses can be toxic.

Minerals, like vitamins, work with each other in many different combinations. Each is described as having a specific purpose, but a mineral seldom acts all by itself.

Calcium

Ninety-nine percent of the calcium in the body is in the skeleton—98 percent in the bones, 1 percent in the teeth. Calcium also works as a part of the mechanism that helps blood clot and helps nerves and muscles react normally. One of these muscles is especially important—the heart.

Bones act as a storehouse for calcium, 20 percent of which is reabsorbed and replaced each year—thus our need for calcium is lifelong. Children and pregnant or nursing women need more calcium than other people.

Milk and milk products are our greatest sources of calcium. Fish bones such as those eaten in sardines also provide calcium. Dark green leafy vegetables (collards, mustard, turnip, kale, and dandelion greens) are sources of calcium, too. Most of the daily requirement of calcium for an average adult is provided by just two glasses of milk a day. Other foods that provide calcium can be substituted for milk.

Iron

Television commercials have probably done more to give iron an "image" than legions of nutritionists, physicians, home economists, and dietitians.

Iron combines with protein to make hemoglobin, the red substance in blood which carries oxygen from the lungs to the muscles, brain, and elsewhere. Iron helps cells use oxygen. Lack of iron can cause iron-deficiency anemia which, in turn, can cause lack of sleep, energy, and appetite. Studies have proven that iron deficiencies are indeed a problem in the United States today, particularly for infants, children, and the elderly. Women need extra iron to replace that lost in blood during childbirth and menstruation. Extra iron is essential during pregnancy and lactation, too. The Food and Drug Administration is considering tripling the amount of iron in enriched bread to help assure adequate iron intake.

Wise food planning can help assure sufficient iron. Organ meats (liver, kidney, heart) and red meats are great iron sources. Oysters, eggs, whole grain and enriched cereals, dried fruits (especially raisins and prunes), dark green leafy vegetables, dried beans, peas, and nuts supply some iron, too. Milk, nutritious though it is, comes up short on iron.

Phosphorus

Ninety percent of the body's phosphorus is deposited as inorganic phosphate in the bones and teeth. The other 10 percent is located in cells as organic phosphorus. Besides functioning as a component of bones and teeth, phosphate plays other important roles in the body. It is intimately involved in the release of chemical energy, it helps transport fatty acids in the blood, and it helps maintain the balance of acid and alkali in the blood. Phosphorus is found in many of the same foods that provide calcium, and it is found in protein foods as well. Thus, a diet that supplies calcium and protein will take care of phosphorus needs.

Iodine

The thyroid gland needs iodine to make thyroxin, the regulator of certain body processes. Iodine shortages can cause goiter (enlarged thyroid). Anyone who has lived in the American Midwest knows that, among other names, it is called the "Goiter Belt." This is because of its great distance from the sea, the major source of iodine.

The addition of iodine to salt has helped prevent goiter. In fact, the iodization of salt is looked upon as a great step forward for public health. But iodized salt has become so commonplace, and goiter so unusual, that shoppers forget and buy ordinary salt.

Fluorine

Like iodine, fluorine is naturally available in certain areas of the country, usually in water supplies. Common foods contain only small amounts of fluorine, although fish and soybeans do provide some.

Fluorine is the name of the pure element. When in solution or combination with other materials, it is called fluoride, and that is how we refer to it. Fluoride helps prevent tooth decay, and it also helps develop stronger bones. Many of us may have missed the benefits of fluoridation, but our children can enjoy strong teeth and bones.

Fluoridation of community water supplies has been endorsed by the American Dental Association and leading medical groups. Dentists can also apply a fluoride compound directly to the teeth. If you aren't sure whether there is fluoride in your water supply, check with your dentist.

Sodium, Potassium, Chlorine

These three minerals help in the transport of fluids in and out of cells and in the maintenance of a normal balance of water between fluids and cells.

Sodium and potassium are vital to normal nerve responses and muscle contractions (including the heart). Sodium, potassium, and chlorine are essential in maintaining the balance of acid and alkali of the blood.

There is seldom need to worry about deficiencies of these three minerals. A *moderate* amount of table salt will take care of our sodium needs. Excesses of sodium may cause water retention. Any concern about sodium should, of course, be directed to your doctor. Potassium and chlorine are present in so many foods that we get enough of these minerals without any special effort.

Sulfur

Sulfur is active in every cell of the body and is an integral part of sulfur-containing amino acids. An adequate protein intake will meet the body's sulfur needs.

Copper

Copper works hand in hand with iron to make hemoglobin in the blood. Iron needs copper to work with. Fortunately, enough copper is supplied in a normal diet to meet our requirements.

Cobalt, Molybdenum, Manganese, Selenium, and Zinc

All of these elements are in adequate supply in the normal diet. Supplementation, other than under a doctor's care, could be dangerous.

Water

The human body is one half to two thirds water—ten gallons in an adult male. Water is absolutely necessary for life. Lack of it for even a few days can be fatal. We can live many days longer without food than without water.

Water is the river of life to our bodies. It is the solvent for everything that we digest, it holds nutrients in solution and carries them through to the blood stream. Water is an important part of every cell structure. It carries away waste materials, controls the body's temperature by evaporation from the skin, aids digestion, and sustains the health of all cells.

Water is provided largely by the fluids we drink, whether it is water itself, or other liquids such as coffee, tea, juices, milk, or soft drinks. Many foods contain a lot of water, too—celery and lettuce, for example. Nutritionists recommend drinking two quarts of water a day.

Although water supplies no energy and no vitamins, it does contain some minerals (see Fluorine). You never see or hear a commercial for it, but water is a terrific thirst quencher! It is low in calories (0) and does not contribute to tooth decay. Try some today.

FOUR FOOD GROUPS

Now that you understand a little of the what, why, and how of nutrients, how do you apply that information to daily eating patterns? The Four Food Groups classification system is meant to provide a simple and straightforward guide to what foods are needed daily for good nutrition. Developed simultaneously by Harvard's Department of Nutrition and the United States Department of Agriculture, the "Basic Four" classification is now the basis of most nutrition education in the United States.

In this classification, foods are divided into four categories according to their similarity in nutrient content. The groups are the Milk Group, the Meat Group, the Fruit and Vegetable Group, and the Bread and Cereal Group. Other foods that fall outside these four categories are included in an additional or Other Group. These foods are largely fats and sugars, necessary for proper metabolism and energy, and they are generally not lacking in normal American diets.

In the next few pages, each food group is described in terms of what foods belong in the group, what nutrients the group supplies, what these foods do for you, and how many servings from the group are needed each day. Following the descriptions, a chart called the Daily Food Guide (page 24) presents in a simple form the daily servings needed from each group for children, teens, adults, and the elderly.

Milk Group

The Milk Group includes all types of milk and milk products except butter and cream. These products are ice cream, cheese, and yogurt.

Milk is our main source of calcium. It also supplies phosphorus, protein, riboflavin, and vitamins A and D. Lowfat milks are fortified with vitamin A, and all milk you buy should be fortified with vitamin D. Foods from the milk group help promote the development of strong bones and teeth, healthy skin and tissue, good night vision, and a well-running nervous system.

Remember that cheese, ice cream, and milk used in cream soups, sauces, puddings, or in other cooking all count towards the daily number of servings of milk.

A serving of milk is one cup (eight ounces) of milk, buttermilk, skim milk,

2 percent milk, reconstituted nonfat dry milk, reconstituted whole or skim evaporated milk, chocolate-flavored milk drink, and homemade cocoa. One cup of yogurt or custard is the nutritional equivalent of a serving of milk, as is a one-ounce slice of Swiss cheese or two one-ounce slices of process American cheese.

The following will provide the equivalent of one-third cup of milk: one-half cup creamed cottage cheese, one-half cup of milk-based pudding, one-half cup of ice milk or ice cream. Two tablespoons of cream cheese or Neufchâtel cheese are comparable to one tablespoon of milk.

The dairy case and shelves at your supermarket are full of a variety of milks and milk products. Read the labels to be sure what you are getting.

Whole milk has 3.5 percent milk fat (sometimes called butterfat) and over 8 percent total milk solids. Whole milk is pasteurized and usually homogenized. Choose milk that is fortified with vitamin D. One quart of fortified whole milk has 400 IU units of vitamin D, which is the recommended daily allowance of that vitamin.

Two-percent milk has 2 percent milk fat. One-percent milk has 1 percent milk fat and usually has some nonfat milk solids added for flavor and body. Skim milk has no fat. Nonfat dry milk is skim milk with the water removed. This is the budget watcher's favorite because it is inexpensive. All these milks should be fortified with vitamins A and D. Read the label to be sure that you are getting fortified milk.

Evaporated milk is milk reduced to half its volume, homogenized, fortified with vitamin D, and canned. Sweetened condensed milk has had 60 percent of the water removed and sugar added. It is canned.

Although cream supplies about the same amounts of protein and minerals as does milk, its high fat content disqualifies it from being a member of the Milk Group. Different kinds of cream contain different amounts of butterfat. Half-and-half is 10 to 12 percent butterfat. Light cream or coffee cream is 18 to 30 percent fat, and whipping or heavy cream is 30 to 40 percent. Dairy sour cream is 18 to 20 percent fat and dairy sour half-and-half is 10 to 12 percent fat. Creams should be considered, along with butter, as part of the Other Group.

Meat Group

The Meat Group includes beef, lamb, veal, pork, variety meats (liver, kidney, brains, and heart), poultry, eggs, fish, and shellfish. Meat alternates or substitutes are dried beans and peas (soy, pinto, navy, lima, kidney beans, chickpeas, split or black-eye peas), lentils, nuts, and peanut butter.

Foods from the Meat Group supply protein, iron, and the B vitamins (especially thiamine, niacin, and riboflavin). The section on protein (pages 10–13) has more information on proteins and their use in the body.

Two or more servings of meat a day are recommended. Preferably, something from the meat group should be included at each meal.

Two to three ounces of lean boneless cooked meat, poultry, or fish make a serving. That's two hot dogs; a three-inch hamburger patty; two slices of chicken; a medium fillet of fish; two postcard-sized slices of roast beef; half of a seven-ounce can of tuna; eighteen medium shrimp; a thick pork chop, lamb chop, or veal cutlet; or two slices of bologna. Two eggs, one-fourth cup peanut butter, one cup baked beans, or one cup cooked dried peas or lentils also equals a serving from the Meat Group. See the Pick a Protein chart on page 12.

Fruit and Vegetable Group

All fruits and vegetables fall in this group, but special emphasis goes to those that are good sources of vitamins C and A. Look below for a list of fruits and vegetables high in these vitamins.

Vitamins A and C help to make skins glow, eyes bright, and gums and body tissues firm and healthy. Fruits and vegetables also supply other vitamins, minerals, and carbohydrates—all at little calorie cost. In addition, they add bulk, which is important for good digestion.

Plan meals and snacks to include four or more servings from this group every day. One of those four must be a good source of vitamin C (or two servings of foods containing lesser amounts of C). One serving every other day should be a good source of vitamin A.

A serving is usually one-half cup of the fruit or vegetable. Equivalent amounts are one medium-sized fruit or vegetable, such as an apple, orange, pear, peach, banana, or potato; two small fruits, such as plums; one-half cantaloupe or grapefruit; one cup of fresh berries; one cup of raw leafy vegetables; or one-half cup of fruit juice.

Fruits and vegetables high in vitamin C include grapefruit or grapefruit juice, orange or orange juice, cantaloupe, fresh strawberries, papaya, mango, guava, broccoli, Brussels sprouts, and sweet green or red pepper.

Other fruits and vegetables which supply lesser amounts of vitamin C are: honeydew melon, lemon, lime, tangerine, raspberries, watermelon, asparagus, cabbage, cauliflower, collard greens, mustard greens, turnip greens, kale, kohlrabi, potatoes (both white and sweet, cooked in jackets), rutabaga, spinach, tomatoes or tomato juice, and cranberry juice. Two servings of these foods will provide as much vitamin C as one serving of those foods high in vitamin C.

Fruits and vegetables high in vitamin A are dark green and deep yellow vegetables and deep yellow fruits. These include cantaloupe, mango, carrots, pumpkin, spinach, broccoli, sweet potato, winter squash, collard greens, mustard greens, turnip greens, and other dark green leafy vegetables.

Lesser amounts of vitamin A are provided by apricots, persimmon, watermelon, and beet greens.

Some fruits and vegetables, such as cantaloupe, greens, and broccoli, do a great job of providing both vitamins A and C. One serving of these can count as a serving of both an A and a C fruit or vegetable.

Bread and Cereal Group

Enriched, whole grain, or restored breads, cooked or dry cereals, cornmeal, crackers, flour, grits, macaroni, spaghetti, noodles, rice, rolled oats, baked goods, bulgur, or parboiled rice or wheat are all members of the Bread and Cereal Group. Check labels to be sure products other than whole grain are enriched.

Breads and cereals are an excellent source of carbohydrates (see page 13 for their purposes), iron, and those important B vitamins (thiamine, niacin, and riboflavin). Small amounts of protein are also supplied by breads and cereals. The nutrients in breads and cereal products give us energy as well as assistance in regulating body processes and in converting food into energy.

Three to four servings should be eaten daily. Products that are not enriched, not whole grain, nor restored don't count! If one of the servings is not a cereal, have an extra serving of enriched or whole grain bread or baked goods.

A serving is one slice bread; one ounce (about a cup) ready-to-eat cereal; one-half to three-quarter cup cooked cereal, corn-

DAILY FOOD GUIDE

By Food Groups	child	pre-teen & teen	adult	aging adult
MILK GROUP cups of milk or equivalents (see pages 21–22 under Milk Group)	3–4	4 or more	2	2
MEAT GROUP 3 oz. serving meat, fish, shellfish or poultry; 2 eggs; 1 cup cooked dried beans, peas or lentils; ¼ cup peanut butter	1–2	3 or more	2	2
FRUIT AND VEGETABLE GROUP servings of C-rich fruits and vegetables	1	1–2	1	1–2
servings of A-rich fruits and vegetables	1	2	1	1
servings of potatoes, other fruits and vegetables	2	1	2	0–1
BREAD AND CEREAL GROUP servings of whole grain or enriched bread or cereal, baked goods, macaroni	3–4	4 or more	3–4	2–3
OTHER tablespoons of fat (oil, butter, margarine)	2	2–4	2–3	1–2

Water or liquid equivalent to make 3 to 5 cups total daily intake.

See pages 25–26 for amounts for pregnant and nursing women.

(Chart adapted from American Medical Association and reprinted with permission.)

meal, grits, macaroni, noodles, rice, or spaghetti; three tablespoons flour; one doughnut; one roll, biscuit, or muffin; one pancake, waffle, popover, or bagel; two tortillas; the crust of one wedge of pizza; or one square gingerbread or cake.

Other Group

The Other Group is the gathering place for those foods not included in the Four Food Groups. Many of the foods in the Other Group are fun foods. Examples of foods that belong outside the Four Food

Groups are sugars (candy, soft drinks, gelatin desserts, alcoholic beverages, and syrup), salad dressings, cream, butter, margarine, oils, and other fats.

These foods contribute fat, sugar, seasoning, and calories to our diets. They add flavor to other foods and help us meet our energy needs. We must remember, though, that these foods are luxury bonuses and, except for the recommended amounts of fat, they are not essential to a healthy diet. Dieters know that this is the first group to be cut when calorie intake must be reduced. The Other Group foods are often ingredients in a recipe or are added at the table. Use them in moderate amounts. Two or three tablespoons of fat each day is enough.

Many foods, such as pizza, casseroles, spaghetti with meat sauce, creamed vegetable soups, and sandwiches, do not belong to any one particular food group because they are made up of foods from two or more of the groups. Remember this when you are shopping and planning meals—you may well be able to prepare dishes that count as a serving from two or more food groups. Check the list of ingredients on packaged or convenience foods to see which food groups are represented.

SPECIAL NEEDS FOR SPECIAL PEOPLE

Everybody needs the same nutrients, but some people need more than others because of special demands on their bodies at various times in their lives. Pregnant and nursing women, infants, children, teenagers, the elderly, and persons on special diets all have special nutritional needs.

Pregnant Women

The health of an expectant mother has a great deal to do with the health of her baby. Teen-age mothers particularly have a tendency to give birth to undernourished babies. The pregnant teen-ager must meet the special nutritional needs of her age group as well as those of a pregnant woman. If the mother-to-be is healthy and has followed the Daily Food Guide suggestions before she became pregnant, she may not have to make any changes in her diet during the first three months of pregnancy. If her diet has been deficient in certain nutrients, her need for those nutrients should be met right away. The expectant mother's nutritional needs will increase as her child gets larger. Her doctor is the one, and the only one, qualified to tell a pregnant woman what she should eat and how much she should eat.

During the last three months of pregnancy, the baby will triple in weight. During this period, not only must the mother's diet help the baby's growth, but it must also provide nutrients for the mother's milk supply. Now the pregnant woman will need half again as much calcium, one-third more vitamin C, two-thirds more protein, one-fourth more riboflavin and vitamin A, and more thiamine and vitamin D. Although a pregnant woman's nutritional needs are greater than before, her calorie needs are not, except in this last three-month period of pregnancy. Even then, her caloric needs will be only 10 to 20 percent greater than before pregnancy. Thus she must pick foods that will provide all those extras at little calorie cost. More milk (A and D fortified skim milk is just as wholesome and has fewer calories than whole milk), more selections from the Meat Group, more servings of A- and C-rich foods from the Fruit and Vegetable Group, and wise choices from the Bread and Cereal Group will do it. The obstetrician may prescribe vitamin supplements for the period of pregnancy and nursing. There is a lot of new information, along with a lot of old wives' tales, about weight gain during pregnancy. Weight gain depends on the expectant mother's size, eating habits, and general health. Her doctor will set the ground rules for safe weight gain. His guidelines should be followed and will result in a more comfortable pregnancy, a safer delivery, a healthier baby, and a more rapid return from shapeless to shapely.

Nursing Mothers

The best food for a human infant is, not surprisingly, human milk. Food manufacturers have yet to come up with a product as readily available and as foolproof for safety, sanitation, and convenience. Fortunately, breast feeding is coming back into fashion, and mothers who wish to nurse are surrounded with encouragement.

A woman who breast feeds her baby must eat to provide nutrients for herself and for her infant. She needs 50 percent more calcium and vitamin A, 40 percent more protein and riboflavin, 33 percent more vitamin C and thiamine, and 25 percent more calories than a woman who is not pregnant or nursing. This means two servings of fruits or vegetables rich in vitamin C and one A-rich fruit or vegetable every day. She will require four cups of milk (six if she is a teen-ager) and plenty of water and other liquids.

Infants

Both mother's and cow's milk provide all the nutrients that an infant needs during his or her first few months. A baby is born with a three-month supply of iron, copper, and vitamin A tucked away in his liver (provided the mother ate healthfully during pregnancy). The baby's pediatrician may suggest supplements of vitamins C and D. He's the one (and the only one) to set the diet for the baby. An infant's needs are indeed special, so let the specialist handle them.

Children

The daily needs of preschool, school-age, and preteen children for protein and for most vitamins and minerals are not so great as adult needs because children's bodies are smaller. But preteens and teens do need more calcium and phosphorus than adults. To fulfill their nutritional needs, a five-, ten-, and fifteen-year old will need to eat, respectively, small, medium, and large portions from those foods recommended from the Four Food Groups. See the chart on page 29 for the Recommended Daily Dietary Allowances of nutrients for children and teens.

Studies have shown that, in spite of their lesser nutritional needs, many children's diets are low in vitamins A and C and iron. Proper amounts of fruits and vegetables are often conspicuously missing from many children's diets, while sweets, fried snack foods, bakery goods, and soft drinks comprise too large a part of the foods they eat. Plenty of milk and milk products will fulfill children's needs for calcium, phosphorus, and vitamin D. Increasing the number of deep green and yellow vegetables and fruits will give them the vitamins they need. Be certain that flour and baked goods are enriched to provide B vitamins and iron.

Children eat smaller meals than do adults—their appetites are smaller and their smaller stomachs cannot handle the same amounts of food. Although young children's meals and nutritional needs are smaller than adults', their calorie needs are just as great (see the Recommended Daily Dietary Allowances chart on page 29). Therefore, children may be hungry more frequently than grown-ups. At mealtime, serve small portions of good food and let them come back for seconds. If they are hungry between meals, let them eat healthful snacks like fruit, small sandwiches, milk, or baked goods made with enriched flour.

Healthy children can judge how much they want to eat, but they can't judge the quality of foods, To get the extra calories they need, children can be allowed to eat more "junk," or nutritionally weak, foods than can adults. But too much sugar, starch, and fat is never wise—regulate their snacks carefully. Stock up on good foods, and limit the supply of sweets—if sweets aren't available, they can't be eaten.

The preschooler should get a good start on good eating habits. Poor eating habits established in childhood will be difficult to alter later, and may affect the child's health for years to come. Introduce the child to a variety of foods, and present them in an interesting and pleasant manner. Studies have proved that children with varied diets tend to be better nourished than those with narrow, limited diets.

Breakfast is a must. School children who skip breakfast are often tired and listless during the morning hours at school. If your child carries his lunch to school, pack a good one. Plan for snacks, too. Recipes for Sandwiches and Snacks begin on page 87 and some breakfast and lunch ideas are given on pages 33–34.

Use food as nourishment, not as a reward or punishment. Children constantly promised and rewarded with sweets develop the wrong ideas about food, learn incorrect eating habits, invite tooth decay, and probably develop a weight problem.

Children will eat healthfully if they are provided good foods to eat and if parents set the right example by eating healthfully themselves. Indeed, parents' eating patterns are the single most important factor in the development of their children's eating habits.

Teen-agers

In general, the older children get, the worse their diets become. Teen-agers, who generally have more freedom in food choices than younger children, tend especially to make poor food choices and to ignore their special nutritional needs. Therefore, parental supervision of their eating habits is still important. Refer to the chart on page 29 for the nutritional needs of teenagers and to the Daily Food Guide (page 24) for amounts of foods they need daily.

Teen-age boys generally do better at meeting their nutritional needs than girls, largely because they eat more. But they still slight the Milk Group and the Fruit and Vegetable Group. They should be encouraged to eat foods from these groups to fulfill their special needs for calcium, iron, and vitamins. Milk shakes, ice cream or yogurt with fruit, a plate of interesting cheeses and fruit, or raw vegetables and dips are snacks that could help fill the nutritional gaps in a teen-ager's diet.

Teen-age girls in particular tend to make food choices unwisely and they are susceptible to unwise dieting fads. Teen-age girls need all the nutrients (and more iron) than their male counterparts do, but they require fewer calories. They must select foods carefully to keep calories down and to fulfill all their nutritional needs.

Teens should be fed well-balanced meals every day, and the importance of good nutrition should be impressed upon them.

The Elderly

Attaining the golden years does not change one's needs for protein, carbohydrate, or any of the other nutrients. Total calorie intake is the only area where the needs of elderly persons differ from those of other adults. The minimum number of calories required per day for the body to function properly decreases in the elderly. As a result, 5 to 10 percent less food energy is needed, but the same amounts of nutrients are required. This means foods must be selected wisely to get foods full of nutritional value but low in calorie cost.

Older people tend not to eat very well,

and for a variety of reasons—poor appetite, ignorance of their real nutrition needs, lack of interest, or a generally low intake of food. Although limited income is often thought to be a reason for poor eating habits among the elderly, studies have shown that this is not true. The wealthy senior citizen often makes poorer food choices than the less affluent elderly person. A small budget may be a limiting factor in food purchasing, but it is the consumer who decides what he will spend his money on.

Promises of renewed health and wonder cures are particularly appealing to those who are growing older. Food faddists make bundles of money selling promises to the elderly. But good foods work better than expensive, but empty, promises.

In foods consumed by the elderly, breads, cereals, and fats are rarely lacking, but appropriate amounts of milk, meat, fruits, and vegetables are often missing, resulting in deficiencies of calcium, iron, vitamins, and protein. A little extra effort in selecting nutritious foods and preparing appealing meals will pay off in better health and greater pleasure in life.

Special Diets

Your physician is the one to decide if you do need a special diet. Self-diagnosis and self-treatment are dangerous.

When your doctor tells you that you must eat in a certain fashion, ask him to explain the why, what, and how of your particular needs.

You don't have to be a stick-at-home on a special diet. If you're going to dinner in someone else's home, explain your needs to your hostess. If she's gracious, she'll be happy to fit your needs into her plans. If you are going to a restaurant, check ahead to see if the menu there can fill your needs. Take a positive approach to your special diet. Its purpose is to help you.

U.S. RDA AND NUTRITION LABELING

U.S. RDA is a set of initials that will probably become familiar to everyone interested in nutrition and good health. U.S. RDA stands for "United States Recommended Daily Allowances." The U.S. RDAs were developed by the Food and Drug Administration (FDA) for its nutrition labeling and dietary supplement programs, and were derived from the Recommended Daily Dietary Allowances of the Food and Nutrition Board of the National Academy of Sciences. The U.S. RDAs represent amounts of protein, vitamins, and minerals that will fully satisfy a healthy adult's daily needs for these nutrients. Many adults may need only three fourths of the U.S. RDA for several nutrients, and children may need only about one half. Thus the U.S. RDAs are only a guideline for good nutrition and are intended primarily for use in nutrition labeling.

The initials *U.S. RDA* will appear on the new nutrition labels required on many foods. They replace the initials *MDR* you may remember seeing on cereal boxes. MDR stands for Minimum Daily Requirements. They represent the minimum amount of nutrients needed to maintain good health, and they used to be the yardstick for rating the nutrient value of certain foods.

The U.S. RDAs that appear on the new nutrition labels are for adults and children over four. U.S. RDAs have also been established for infants and children under four years of age and for pregnant and nursing women. These allowances are listed on the labels of vitamins and mineral supplements.

Nutrition labeling is a new program sponsored by the FDA to provide consumers with nutrition information on many foods, and nutrition information

RECOMMENDED DAILY DIETARY ALLOWANCES (Abridged),* Revised 1973

| | Years | | Weight | | Height | | Energy | Protein | Vitamins | | | | | Minerals | |
	From	Up to	(kg)	(lbs)	(cm)	(in)	(calories)	(g)	Vitamin A (IU)	Ascorbic Acid (mg)	Niacin (mg)	Riboflavin (mg)	Thiamine (mg)	Calcium (mg)	Iron (mg)
Infants	0.0–0.5		6	14	60	24	kg × 117	kg × 2.2	1,400	35	5	0.4	0.3	360	10
	0.5–1.0		9	20	71	28	kg × 108	kg × 2.0	2,000	35	8	0.6	0.5	540	15
Children	1–3		13	28	86	34	1300	23	2,000	40	9	0.8	0.7	800	15
	4–6		20	44	110	44	1800	30	2,500	40	12	1.1	0.9	800	10
	7–10		30	66	135	54	2400	36	3,300	40	16	1.2	1.2	800	10
Males	11–14		44	97	158	63	2800	44	5,000	45	18	1.5	1.4	1200	18
	15–18		61	134	172	69	3000	54	5,000	45	20	1.8	1.5	1200	18
	19–22		67	147	172	69	3000	52	5,000	45	20	1.8	1.5	800	10
	23–50		70	154	172	69	2700	56	5,000	45	18	1.6	1.4	800	10
	51+		70	154	172	69	2400	56	5,000	45	16	1.5	1.2	800	10
Females	11–14		44	97	155	62	2400	44	4,000	45	16	1.3	1.2	1200	18
	15–18		54	119	162	65	2100	48	4,000	45	14	1.4	1.1	1200	18
	19–22		58	128	162	65	2100	46	4,000	45	14	1.4	1.1	800	18
	23–50		58	128	162	65	2000	46	4,000	45	13	1.2	1.0	800	18
	51+		58	128	162	65	1800	46	4,000	45	12	1.1	1.0	800	10
Pregnant							+300	+30	5,000	60	+2	+0.3	+0.3	1200	18+
Lactating							+500	+20	6,000	60	+4	+0.5	+0.3	1200	18

* The allowances are amounts of nutrients recommended by the Food and Nutrition Board, National Academy of Sciences—National Research Council. They are intended to provide for individual variations among most normal persons as they live in the United States under usual environmental stresses. Diets should be based on a variety of common foods in order to provide other nutrients for which human requirements have been less well defined. The Recommended Daily Dietary Allowances, which in unabridged form cover 16 vitamins and minerals, are revised from time to time in accordance with newer knowledge of nutritional needs.

panels are already on some of your favorite products. Nutrition labeling is voluntary for most foods. But by 1975 all fortified foods (those to which a nutrient has been added) and all foods for which a nutrition claim is made on the label or in advertising will have nutrition information on their labels. This means that you can pick up a can or a box and find out, in addition to the product's name, weight, and ingredients, the nutritional value of the contents.

Listed will be the number of calories and amounts of protein, carbohydrate, and fat. The amounts will be given in grams for single servings, with the serving size and number of servings indicated on the panel. Also included on the nutrition labels will be percentages of nutrients given in terms of the U.S. RDAs. Information on fat and cholesterol content may be on the label, too, in case you or someone in your family has special needs. The nutrients *not* provided by that particular food will also be listed, so that you will have all the strong and weak points right there in black and white.

The information given on nutritional labels will help you plan more nutritious meals, help you compare nutritive values of different brands and help you in selecting foods for special diets.

FOOD ADDITIVES

Most of us have seen the initials *BHA* or *BHT* on the labels of some food items, or obscure chemical names such as *potassium citrate* and *monosodium phosphate*, or the more understandable words *artificial coloring* or *gum arabic*. All of these are food additives. A food additive is any substance added to foods during processing or packaging. Most additives are in chemical form, derived from natural substances. About 10,000 additives are available to food processors for use in foods and packaging.

Additives play an important role in the foods we eat. They add or enhance flavor, they stabilize and thicken, they neutralize or alter acidity or alkalinity, they hinder oxidation and spoilage, they retain moisture, they add nutrients, they improve texture, they add leavening, they add color, and they sterilize.

Food additives are nothing new. Salt and pepper have been used for centuries for the preservation of meat. Spices and herbs are also additives. Other food additives may be found on your own shelves and used regularly in food preparation—monosodium glutamate, cream of tartar, artificial sweeteners, meat tenderizers. "Pectin" is often seen on the labels of certain foods, and it is used frequently in the home in making jams and jellies.

In order to be used as a food additive, a substance must be safe in the quantity used, it must perform its intended function, and it must not jeopardize the nutritional value of the food. In the United States the Food and Drug Administration (FDA) enforces an extensive program for testing and regulating the use of food additives.

Without additives our foods would cost more and probably be less wholesome. Furthermore, the laws in the United States governing food quality and the use of food additives are the strictest in the world. Nevertheless, since some food additives remain insufficiently tested, many questions regarding their safety have yet to be answered.

WEIGHT CONTROL

Library shelves and bookstores are filled with books about weight control, because many people are concerned with overweight. This concern is justified. Obesity, the condition in which too much of the body is composed of fat, is a serious health problem and can contribute to cardio-

CALORIES FOR ACTIVITIES

Type of Activity	Calories per hour
Sedentary activities, such as: Reading; writing; eating; watching television or movies; listening to the radio; sewing; playing cards; and typing, miscellaneous officework, and other activities done while sitting that require little or no arm movement	80 to 100
Light activities, such as: Preparing and cooking food; doing dishes; dusting; handwashing small articles of clothing; ironing; walking slowly; personal care; miscellaneous officework and other activities done while standing that require some arm movement; and rapid typing and other activities done while sitting that are more strenuous.	110 to 160
Moderate activities, such as: Making beds; mopping and scrubbing; sweeping; light polishing and waxing; laundering by machine; light gardening and carpentry work; walking moderately fast; other activities done while standing that require moderate arm movement; and activities done while sitting that require more vigorous arm movement.	170 to 240
Vigorous activities, such as: Heavy scrubbing and waxing; hand-washing large articles of clothing; hanging out clothes; stripping beds; other heavy work; walking fast; bowling; golfing; and gardening.	250 to 350
Strenuous activities, such as: Swimming; playing tennis; running; bicycling; dancing; skiing; and playing football.	350 and more

vascular disease (disease of the heart and blood vessels), which is a major cause of death in the Western world. Even being just ten pounds overweight, or simply "out of shape," can reduce one's physical capabilities and affect one's enjoyment of life.

Some weight-loss programs are dangerous, some are safe. If you are overweight and serious about losing extra pounds, the solution is simple—consume fewer calories and get more exercise. It takes 3,500 calories to make one pound of body fat, so by wise cutting down of only 500 calories a day, a dieter can lose one pound in a week. This is a safe amount to lose and an effective way to diet.

Cutting down on calories does not mean cutting down on nutrition. The trick to losing weight while maintaining good health is to carefully select foods that provide the maximum amount of nutrients for the minimum number of calories. Eat less but make that less go further when it comes to supplying nutrients.

A wise weight-control diet, which will

school lunch, and *if* they eat it. The responsibility for packed lunches falls closer to home. Milk is a must, unless it is available at school. Put representatives from the Meat, Bread and Cereal, and Fruit and Vegetable Groups into the lunch box or bag. Choose enriched or whole grain bread as the basis for sandwiches with protein-rich fillings. Add carrot sticks, green pepper slices, cauliflower, or broccoli flowerets to make a good meal. Fresh fruits are obvious dessert choices, but enriched or whole grain baked goods are acceptable also. Brown bags, as well as their contents, can get pretty dull. Check the recipes in the Sandwiches and Snacks chapter for new ideas.

Packed lunches may wait for twelve o'clock under less than ideal conditions, so keep food safety in mind. (More on food safety appears on pages 38–40). Mayonnaise sandwich mixtures are safer if you pack them separately in insulated containers to stay cool, and spread the sandwich at lunchtime. You can wrap lettuce leaves separately too, and they will stay a little crisper than if added to the sandwich in the morning. There are many handy new wraps and containers that can make lunches away from home a little brighter.

Dinner

Usually the evening meal is planned around a main dish, whether it be a roast, casserole, soup, or sandwich. A green or yellow vegetable, rich in vitamins, will complement any main dish, but keep color and texture contrasts in mind. Refer to the recipes in the Vegetables chapter for some new ideas for serving vegetables. Salads and breads are frequent accompaniments to dinners and suppers. Vary the greens you use in tossed salads. Try fresh spinach leaves for a change, or a bit of escarole. When a tossed salad doesn't seem to fit the bill, offer fruit salad, cole slaw, or a relish tray. Muffins, biscuits, or French bread can add a special touch to a meal, too. Desserts should be chosen to complement the dinner. Choose a light dessert, such as sherbet or fruit, to follow a heavy meal.

When planning dinner menus, save the quick-to-prepare main dishes, such as hamburger, meat loaf, or omelet, for those evenings you know will be busy. Brown-and-serve breads, make-ahead molded salads, and simmered vegetables dressed up with bacon bits, nuts, or cheese, will help you fit a tight timetable. Convenience foods may also offer relief on busy evenings, but choose them carefully for variety, nutrition, and cost.

More complicated meals should be saved for those evenings when you have time to prepare them. Check the recipe section for a variety of dinner-time main dishes, vegetables, soups, and salads. Make a selection and then build around it, keeping the Four Food Groups and the daily requirements in mind.

Snacks

You may never have control over the opening and closing of the refrigerator door, but you can determine what will be waiting inside that door. Hard-cooked eggs, cold cuts, celery ribs to fill with cheese or peanut butter, cauliflowerets, and green pepper slices to dip in packaged or homemade dips, milk and all the fixings for flavored or fruit shakes, and fruits of the season are all good-tasting, nutritious snacks for a mid-afternoon pick-up or late-night refresher.

Check the Sandwiches and Snacks chapter beginning on page 87. That is where you'll discover how to bring nutritional value into favorite foods and snacks.

Shopping

Concentrate on your shopping. For the time that you are in the store it is your profession. Bring along the list of foods you plan to buy for use during the week. Remember the purpose of the list so you will stick to it. Ignore those sudden impulses, remember the time you spent planning, and go by that plan. It is a good idea to eat before you go to the market. If you shop hungry, you may be tempted to buy more than you need, especially snack-type foods.

Go grocery shopping by yourself, if possible. If the children are with you, take the opportunity to teach them some shopping and nutrition know-how. Turn them into your assistants and send them on a search for particular sizes and brands of products.

As a professional shopper, learn the dating codes and select products that are the freshest. Unless you have a specific use in mind (over-ripe bananas for banana bread, for example), pick foods that are as nearly perfect as you can get. Your eyes and nose are good guides to quality. Good fresh foods are blemish-free, fresh-smelling, and bright in color. Packages or cans should be clean, unopened, and unmarred.

Read labels, check unit pricing, and buy grades to match you purposes. Private or "house" brands are usually less expensive than name brands. Compare costs and forms (fresh, frozen, canned, dried) and pick what is best for your needs. Select package sizes that are appropriate to your family and your uses. A five-pound bag of rice may seem a great bargain. But if your family seldom eats rice and your cupboard space is at a premium it hasn't saved you anything.

While we are on the subject of packages, remember that you are shopping for food, not for beauty. You want what is inside, not the wrapper or the box. That doesn't mean that you should ignore the package. Read the label: the new nutritional labels are more informative than ever. (See the section on Nutrition Labeling on page 28.)

Calculate costs per serving, unit prices, and your ever-mounting total. If you haven't a mathematical mind, there are handy booklets, converters, charts, and inexpensive hand-sized adding devices to help you know just how much and what you are buying.

A USDA publication, *Your Money's Worth in Foods* (to order, see References), is a helpful reference for budgeting, menu planning, and shopping. It includes charts and tables of costs per serving and per pound, and cost-weight tables to compare costs of foods from different-sized containers. Knowing the cost per serving is especially important when meat shopping. Figuring the cost per pound may include bone, fat, and gristle, none of which is part of a serving.

Buy only enriched, whole grain, or restored flour, bread, baked goods, macaroni products, and cereals. Read the label or ask at the bakery. If it is not enriched, it doesn't count toward a serving from the Bread and Cereal Group.

You can save money on milk, too. Fortified nonfat dry milk costs only one third to one half as much as whole milk, but it is every bit as nutritious and is lower in calories. Mix it up to use in cooking, baking, and for drinking. Your family may prefer it mixed with whole milk. Buy the largest package you can use and store without waste. Bigger packages of anything are usually cheaper, as long as you can store them properly.

Creamers and whipped toppings may be strictly nondairy products and will not count toward any of the Four Food Groups, except the Other Group. Read the label.

Convenience foods are likely to be expensive, and high cost does not mean high nutritive value. Read labels on convenience food items to be sure what you are getting. Remember that ingredients are listed on labels in descending order of predominance by weight. Some packaged and/or frozen dinners, for example, are much higher in carbohydrates and fats than in protein, even though they are meant to be main dishes. The new nutritional labeling will show you nutrient percentages, so read and see. Some convenience foods are healthful, inexpensive, and well worth buying. Refrigerated biscuits and orange juice concentrate are two good examples. But other products can be duplicated in your kitchen with less expense and probably with more nutritional value.

Once you are past the check-out counter, the care of food products is up to you. Sad to say, the losses of freshness and nutritive value between the store and the dinner table are greater than those anywhere else along the line. Manufacturers and processors try to assure that as few nutrients as possible are lost during their trip to the supermarket. You are responsible for losses on the trip *from* the supermarket. A little thought, a lot of common sense, and a constant awareness of the investment you have just made in nutrition should help you keep these losses to a minimum.

After shopping, go directly home. Do nonfood errands before you get to the supermarket. It should be your last stop. Perishables lose food value quickly if they are not promptly and properly cared for.

Storing

Unpack, sort, and store foods carefully. Nonperishables in unopened packages are best kept in cool, dark places. Pretty though it may be, a sunny spot on the kitchen counter isn't a good place to leave foods because light and heat can be damaging. After opening, certain items must be refrigerated—the label will tell. Other foods, such as macaroni, nuts,

flour, and sugar, may be transferred to containers with tight-fitting lids.

Your refrigerator should be cold—35° to 45°F. Foods to be stored in the refrigerator should be covered or wrapped to protect flavor and moisture. Whole fruits and vegetables and covered packages may be stored as is. You probably have a refrigerator with special sections—crisper drawers for fruits and vegetables, colder spots for meats, etc. Use these special areas.

Your freezer should be at 0°F, and you should rotate the items kept there. Keep track of what is in your freezer. A note pad hung on the handle (or a more sophisticated inventory) is important. Remember—first in should be first out. Wrap foods properly for freezing: airtight in moisture-proof wrapping, packages, or containers. Different shapes and types of food require different containers and wrappings. You will find several good freezer wraps on the market such as aluminum freezer foil, coated cartons and freezer papers. Label clearly. Today you may be sure that you'll remember what the package is. But in six months, when you remove an odd-shaped bundle covered with frost, its contents will probably be a mystery.

Storing food is more than just setting it aside for later use. Storing improperly can waste nutritive values, so follow these tips:

Meat—Store prepackaged fresh meat unopened in the meat-keeper or in the coldest part of refrigerator, where the temperature is as low as possible without freezing. Do not store ground meat or small cuts such as steaks or chops in the refrigerator longer than one to two days, or large cuts (roasts) more than four days. Meat can be frozen in store wrappings and kept for up to two weeks. For longer freezer storage, overwrap with moisture-proof material and seal. If properly wrapped and stored in the freezer, recommended maximum storage time for beef is six to twelve months; lamb and veal, six to nine months; pork, three to six months; poultry, six to seven months; smoked meats, two months; ground beef, veal, and lamb, three to four months; ground pork, one to three months; variety meats, three to four months; and leftover cooked meat, two to three months.

Fish and Shellfish—Prepacked fresh or frozen seafood may be stored as is in the refrigerator or freezer. Fresh fish wrapped in butcher-paper should be rewrapped in moisture-proof material for both refrigerator and freezer storage. Thawed fish should be used as soon as possible and never refrozen. Cooked seafood should be in a covered container for the refrigerator and in moisture-proof wrapper or container for the freezer. Fresh seafood can wait a day or two in the refrigerator, four to six months in the freezer. Cooked seafood can stay in the refrigerator three to four days or be frozen two to three months.

Poultry—Remove giblets and wrap separately. Wrap poultry loosely for refrigerator storage, and use within one to two days. For freezer storage, wrap in moisture-proof material and use in six to seven months. Cooked poultry should have stuffing removed to refrigerate separately. Wrap loosely and use within one or two days. *Never* refrigerate a bird with stuffing in it, because stuffing is an excellent environment for bacteria growth, especially if it has picked up raw meat juices. Remove stuffing right after dinner and refrigerate it separately. Always prepare stuffing and put it in the bird just before it goes into the oven. If desired, poultry can be roasted without stuffing.

Eggs—As soon as possible after purchasing, store eggs in the refrigerator in their own egg container to keep them upright, or store on the egg shelf of the refrigerator door, small ends down. Remove only as many eggs as needed at one time. If separating egg yolks from egg whites, it is quicker and easier if done soon after eggs are removed from refrigerator. Leftover egg yolks may be placed in a tightly covered container and stored in the refrigerator two or three days. Leftover egg whites may be stored the same way for one week. Freeze them for longer storage periods. Do not forget to label the contents, amount, and date.

Dairy Products—All dairy products must be refrigerated. Butter can be stored in the original wrappings or in a covered container. If your refrigerator has a butter-storage compartment, keep only the amount of butter to be used in two or three days. Overwrap in moisture-proof material for freezer time. Unsalted butter is more susceptible to change during storage than salted butter. Its delicate flavor can be insured by limiting storage time to a week or two. Cheese should be tightly covered. Most cheeses should be allowed to come to room temperature for serving because they are then at their most flavorful. Soft cheeses, such as cottage cheese, cream cheese, or ricotta, should stay in the refrigerator until you are ready to use them. Milk and cream must always be kept chilled, in opaque, tightly covered containers. Unopened cans of evaporated or sweetened condensed milk may be stored at room temperature, but once opened they must be refrigerated. Nonfat dry milk should be stored in a cool, dry place. Ice cream, ice milk, and sherbet should be kept in tightly closed containers at 0°F. For long storage, ice cream products should be overwrapped.

Fruits—Wash, dry, and keep fruits at room temperature until ripe, then refrigerate and use them within a few days. Citrus fruits should be refrigerated.

Vegetables—Wash vegetables, drain well, and sort out bruised or soft items for immediate use. Remove tops from beets, carrots, and radishes. Refrigerate vegetables in plastic bags or in the crisper drawer. Dry onions are best kept at room temperature or cooler, in a mesh bag or open to the air. Potatoes like a cool, dark, dry, and well-ventilated spot.

Frozen Foods, Fruits, and Vegetables— Put frozen foods right into the 0°F freezer and keep there until ready to cook.

Canned Goods—A cool, dark place is best. Try the basement or garage if your kitchen storage space is at a premium.

Fats and Oils—Vegetable shortening can stay on the shelf for a few months. For longer periods of time, it should be stored in the refrigerator. Lard must be refrigerated. Let fats warm up to room temperature before measuring. Oils should be tightly capped; storage at room temperature is fine for them.

Flours and Cereals—Tuck grain products into tightly covered containers and store in dry places at room temperature. Whole grain and wheat germ flours should be stored in tight containers in the refrigerator. If opened and stored at normal room temperature, the natural oil of the wheat germ may cause rancidity after about a month.

Bread—Unless it is hot and humid, keep bread out of the refrigerator, because it stales more rapidly when cold than at room temperature. A well-ventilated bread box is the best spot for storage. Bread can be frozen for a week or two in its original wrapper. Overwrap for longer freezer storage.

Spices, Herbs, Leavening Agents—Keep these products tightly covered and stored in a cool, dry place. Although it is handy to have these items near the range, hot spots shorten their flavor-life.

Sugars, Syrups—Granulated sugar is best kept in a covered container in a dry place. Brown sugar needs an airtight container. Adding a slice of bread or chunk of apple will help to keep brown sugar moist. Opened syrups and honey need not be refrigerated.

Nuts—Keep nuts tightly covered in a cool, dry place.

Macaroni Products—Keep macaroni and noodles tightly covered or well wrapped. They like it cool, dry, and dark, too.

Many foods, especially frozen and canned fruits and vegetables, tend gradually to lose their nutritional value when stored for long periods of time (several months to a year). To get the full vitamin content of these foods, plan to use them within a month or so of their purchase. Fresh fruits and vegetables should be used as soon as possible.

Nutrition is lost when foods spoil, and poor planning is the cause of waste. Try to cook just the right amounts of food, and if you do have leftovers, use them right away.

Food Safety

How you handle food is important. Careful handling of food can help prevent sickness and can even be a matter of life or death. Reports of cases of botulism poisoning remind us of the dangers inherent in food preparation. Most food poisoning is the result of inadequate sanitary precautions in the kitchen.

A clean, dry kitchen and a clean cook are the best precautions you can take. Tuck away your hair and wear clean clothes. Hands should be clean and dry. Wash them after touching nonfood items, after handling each particular food, and especially after handling each raw food. If you have a cut or infection on your hands, wear rubber or plastic gloves. No coughing or sneezing near food, please. If you are sick you shouldn't be cooking.

Bacteria like warm, moist, cozy spots to grow and reproduce. Bacteria are likely to be found wherever food is or has been. Sometimes bacteria just spoil food, but sometimes they create toxins that can spoil us.

To control bacteria and their growth, wash foods before preparing them. This includes poultry, meat, fruits, vegetables, and eggs in the shell. Do not use cracked or dirty eggs. Keep *everything* clean—can-opener cutting blades, small and large appliances, utensils, cords, countertops, windowsills, floors, drawers, cabinets, corners, and crevices.

It may be efficient to use utensils, bowls, pots, or pans more than once while you have them out, but please wash and rinse them after each use. Wash dishes with hot suds and rinse with hot water. Remember that a serving spoon and a tasting spoon are two separate utensils. Never put a spoon to your mouth and then back to the pot. Cracked cups, bowls, or other containers should be thrown out— they are dangerous to use and the cracks will harbor food particles and bacteria.

Wooden cutting boards are favorites in many kitchens. Bacteria love them, too —all those snug little cracks to nestle into. They may be disturbed by a quick rinse or a speedy scrape off, but that remedy is only temporary. Food safety specialists don't mince words about wooden cutting boards. They say to throw them out and use nonwood cutting surfaces instead. If that's too radical a change for you, remember you *must* keep your cutting surfaces clean. Scrub the board or block with hot suds and rinse, not after you're done with all your chopping, but after *each* type of food you chop. Otherwise you're spreading germs from one food to another.

A clean refrigerator is not only a safer place to keep food, but keeping it clean helps you to keep track of and use what otherwise might be forgotten. There is an old saying, "When in doubt, throw it out." It applies to items in the refrigerator as well as to those stored at room tempera-

ture. Molds that grow on breads and cheese are usually not harmful, but the moldy portion should be discarded. Cut off the spoiled portion well away from where the mold is visible, because adjacent parts of the food are likely to be affected, also. Other foods that have begun to mold should be thrown away in their entirety, so that neither humans nor animals can eat it. Pets may have stronger stomachs than we do, but bacteria can make them just as sick.

Any food that looks, smells, or tastes bad is definitely for the garbage. But if it looks and smells bad, *do not* taste it! Many people who tasted haven't lived to describe the looks and smells.

Never buy or use bulged cans of anything. That bulge is a sure sign that trouble has brewed inside.

Unfortunately, some bacteria don't give themselves away with obvious signs. So know-how and discretion are important. Keeping foods at proper temperatures is one way to hinder bacteria growth. Keep hot foods hot, at temperatures about 140°F, and cold foods cold, at temperatures below 40°F. Letting foods stand at lukewarm temperatures can mean danger. A meat thermometer will let you know the doneness of meats and let you check other foods for safe temperatures, too. Always cook pork to 170°F on your meat thermometer.

Prepared convenience foods must be handled carefully and package directions followed closely. All home-canned foods should be brought to boiling and held there for several minutes to destroy any toxins and insure safety—and this means before you taste them. Nearly all cases of botulism poisoning stem from improperly processed home-canned foods. Pressure-cooker processing is the safest method for home preserving of all foods, and is the only method for preserving low-acid vegetables.

Cookbooks specializing in canning and freezing are available, and the USDA and state extension services, as well as jar and container manufacturers, can help with information. Follow their instructions exactly.

It is unwise to eat or taste raw meat, fish, poultry, eggs, or home-canned goods. Sample them after they have been cooked.

Thaw foods in the refrigerator or under cool running water. Foods allowed to thaw on the counter all day may begin to spoil. Quick thawing should be used only in an emergency, as it tends to alter the texture of meats, fish, and vegetables. Use all foods as quickly as possible after thawing.

Cool foods in the refrigerator, not on the counter. With today's refrigerators and modern containers and plastic wraps, hot foods can go directly into the refrigerator to cool. Arrange the food so it can all get cold quickly. A huge bowl of chicken salad will take a long time to chill, especially the center. Spread it out on a tray to chill, then transfer it to a more compact container.

Leftovers should be chilled quickly. An hour spent on the counter in a cozy kitchen can give bacteria a real head start. As mentioned under Poultry (page 37), stuffing for turkey or other birds should be prepared immediately before cooking, and leftover dressing should be removed immediately from the bird and stored in the refrigerator.

All food items taken from the refrigerator for meal preparation or for snacks should be returned to the refrigerator promptly.

Picnic foods, especially egg, chicken, meat, or potato salad, are particular favorites of bacteria. If you must have these foods on your outing, have all the ingredients for the salad well-chilled, separately wrapped, and packed for the journey in a prechilled ice chest or cooler. Mix them up at the picnic spot, not before.

Picnic leftovers that are likely to spoil are better left behind. They can't be kept cold enough or hot enough for them to be safe. The same tips apply to packed lunches, too.

A final note—bugs do not belong in your kitchen. Check packages and bags you bring in from the store—you may have carried home some unwanted guests. Wiping off cans and boxes before you put them away may seem persnickety, but it could protect you. If you do have bugs in the kitchen, or anywhere else, use a pesticide, following label directions exactly. Children and pets should be far away. Foods and utensils should be out of the way and covered. Scrub up after using the pesticide and put down clean shelf paper.

Cooking to Conserve Nutritive Values

Sensible storage can save nutrients; careful preparation and cooking can, too. Happily, cooking to save nutrients not only gives you the best of the food, but is the easiest of all methods—simple and short. By cooking quickly, with a minimum of preparation, you save time, steps, and nutrients. As a bonus, you get food that looks, tastes, feels, and *is* better.

Some foods, such as whole fruits or vegetables that can be eaten raw, need no preparation, so you don't lose nutrients along that route. But for other foods, cooking is necessary. Cooking helps break down complex starches and prepare protein for easy digestion. It also makes the food safer to eat, because raw meats and fish are unwise food choices. Cooking has little effect on fats, although over-cooking can reduce their nutritive value.

Special precautions are needed to prevent loss of vitamins.

Vitamin C is the fragile flower of the vitamin family, so C-rich foods should be treated with care. Vitamin C will combine with oxygen, becoming useless to us. Heat, alkalies, certain metals, and enzymes within the C foods themselves are other vitamin thieves to be reckoned with. Follow these tips to safeguard vitamin C. Do not crush or peel C-rich foods far in advance of use or cooking. Tear greens for salad just before dinner; slice berries at the last minute.

Rush C foods from farm to table, the quicker the better. Cover and refrigerate foods if they are not to be used right away. There will be some vitamin loss at refrigerator temperatures, but not nearly as much as at room temperature or warmer. Whole, uncut citrus fruits and tomatoes keep their vitamin C at room temperature, but it's safer to chill them. Citrus juices should be covered tightly, kept chilled, and used promptly. Heat C-rich foods only enough to cook them to bring them to serving temperature. Don't let them sit around, but serve and eat right away. Cook in a minimal amount of water, because vitamin C is water soluble. Save any cooking water for use in stocks and soups. Cook only what you need—reheating leftovers can drive off C. Don't add baking soda to cooking water. It destroys the vitamin. Iron and copper (unlined) cooking vessels are C thieves, so save them for uses other than preparing C-rich foods.

These same rules apply to canned and frozen foods as well as fresh foods. The canning process does drive off some C, but conditions are controlled so that the loss is controlled. Heat canned foods only to serving temperature and eat right away. Don't forget to use the liquid, too. There's a lot of the vitamin there.

B vitamins are also water soluble, so to conserve thiamine, niacin, and riboflavin (the best-known of the B's), follow those same C principles: cook quickly, in little water, and serve right away.

Thiamine does go into cooking water, so use that liquid for food. Soups, stews, and gravies made from cooking liquids make use of dissolved thiamine and taste good, too. Heat can destroy thiamine, so cook only as long as is necessary and at low temperatures—for meat that is usually 325°F. Bread has thiamine to give, so when toasting bread, preserve as much thiamine as possible by toasting lightly. Careful handling is the watchword.

Riboflavin is a little more resistant to heat and water than thiamine, but light is its enemy. Milk, an important source of riboflavin, is safer packed in cartons or opaque plastic containers than in clear glass bottles. It then follows that pretty, clear containers are not the best type for storing dried beans, peas or legumes, baked goods, noodles or macaroni. They should be stored in dark glass or opaque containers. Some riboflavin may be lost by cooking foods uncovered, so pop the top on the pot.

Niacin is the sturdiest of the B vitamins. If you follow the basic principles to conserve the water-soluble vitamins you will preserve most of the niacin in foods.

Freezing preserves all three of these B's, so you can feel confident that frozen foods are as high in the B's as their fresh counterparts.

Vitamins A and D are fat soluble and thus less fragile than the water soluble vitamins (C and the B's). A and its precursor, carotene, are sensitive to light and oxygen, though. Covered and refrigerated are the watchwords for preserving vitamin A. D is hardly lost at all in ordinary processing and preparation. E and K do not require any special precautions.

Careful handling and cooking of foods will help meet the nutrition needs—and help protect the health—of you and your family. It's our hope that, using the Nutrition Know-How information provided in these pages and the recipes that follow, you'll find planning and preparing nutritious meals easy and rewarding.

Soups

A flavorful homemade soup is an exciting accompaniment to any meal and a rewarding addition to any cook's repertoire. Serve a steaming mug of soup on a cold day, or serve it chilled on those hot summer evenings. Soup provides a friendly and appetizing welcome to guests, and it can be an elegant introduction to the entree. Soup is also a wonderful main dish in itself, served with bread, cheese, or salad on the side. Anyone from beginner to experienced cook can create delicious soups easily and from simple ingredients—from the traditional *Fresh Vegetable Beef Soup* to the unusual *Creamy Brussels Sprouts Soup*, made with sour cream and chicken broth, or the exotic *Mixed Fruit Soup*.

Soups make use of a wide variety of nutritional foods. Hearty bean, pea, or lentil soups are rich in vegetable protein, thiamine, riboflavin, and iron. Soups with a milk or cream base, such as *Oyster Soup* or *Cream of Fresh Mushroom Soup*, provide protein, riboflavin, niacin, and calcium. The many vegetables used in soups, from cabbage and carrots to tomatoes and zucchini, are excellent sources of vitamins and minerals. Meat, chicken, or fish soups are rich in protein, niacin, and riboflavin.

There is nothing complicated about preparing the stocks for these soups. In many of the following recipes the stocks are created during the cooking of the meat or vegetables. Others use milk or cream as the base. In those recipes calling for broth or bouillon, you may use homemade stock, canned broth, or bouillon cubes.

The judicious use of herbs, spices, and other flavorings will enhance the taste of any soup. Nutmeg, cayenne pepper, rosemary, mustard, parsley, and pimiento are some of the seasonings called for in the following recipes. You might like to experiment with herbs of your own choosing to add an exotic touch to your soups. Many soups can be given special treatment with the addition of sherry (to fish and cream soups) or red wine (to meat or vegetable soups).

Garnishes are an attractive final touch to a serving of soup and add intriguing flavor contrasts. Top your soups with tarragon, dill, chopped hard-cooked eggs, parsley, chives, watercress, lemon, sour cream, bacon, cheese, or nuts, and you will also enhance the soup's nutritional value.

So pick a favorite soup or experiment with a new recipe—a homemade soup is always a welcome and healthful treat.

Baked Ripe Olive Minestrone

Prepare this crowd-pleaser in the oven and treat your family and friends to a really delicious meat-and-vegetable blend that offers protein, riboflavin, niacin, iron, and an assortment of other nutrients.

1½ **pounds lean beef for stew, cut in 1¼-inch cubes**
1 **cup coarsely chopped onion**
1 **teaspoon minced garlic**
1 **teaspoon salt**
¼ **teaspoon ground black pepper**
2 **tablespoons olive oil**
3 **cans (10½ ounces each) condensed beef broth**
2 **soup cans water**
1½ **teaspoons herb seasoning**
1 **can (16 ounces) tomatoes (undrained)**
1 **can (15¼ ounces) kidney beans (undrained)**
1 **can (6 ounces) pitted ripe olives (undrained)**
1½ **cups thinly sliced carrots**
1 **cup small seashell macaroni**
2 **cups sliced zucchini Grated Parmesan cheese**

1. Mix beef, onion, garlic, salt, and pepper in a Dutch oven or saucepot. Add olive oil and stir to coat meat evenly.
2. Set in a 400°F oven about 40 minutes, stirring once or twice.
3. Reduce heat to 350°F. Add broth, water, and herb seasoning; stir. Cover; cook 1 hour, or until meat is almost tender.
4. Remove from oven and stir in tomatoes and kidney beans with liquid, ripe olives with liquid, carrots, and macaroni. Put sliced zucchini on top. Cover Dutch oven and return to oven 30 to 40 minutes, or until carrots are tender.
5. Ladle hot soup into bowls. Serve with grated cheese.

About 3½ quarts soup

Creamy Brussels Sprouts Soup

A minimum of cooking helps retain the vitamin content of the Brussels sprouts in this easy-to-make soup, which offers vitamins A and C and iron.

1 **cup dairy sour cream**
1 **package (10 ounces) frozen Brussels sprouts, defrosted and cut in halves**
½ **teaspoon salt**

1. Put sour cream, Brussels sprouts, salt, and pepper into an electric blender container. Blend. Add chicken broth; blend.
2. Pour into a saucepan and heat thoroughly (do not boil).

¼ teaspoon ground black
 pepper
1¾ cups chicken broth
 Parsley or watercress
 (optional)

3. Ladle into soup bowls and, if desired, garnish with parsley or watercress.

About 1 quart soup

Potato Soup

Potatoes never let us down, and in this savory soup they build us up. Here, in combination with other ingredients, they provide vitamins A and C in a dish that's just right for a winter's day.

6 medium (about 2 pounds)
 potatoes, pared and cut in
 ¼-inch slices
5 cups cold water
1 carrot, pared and cut in
 pieces
1 leek, washed thoroughly
 and thinly sliced (white
 part only)
1 stalk celery, cut in pieces
1 medium onion, cut in slices
2 teaspoons salt
¼ teaspoon ground white
 pepper
¼ teaspoon ground thyme
¼ teaspoon ground marjoram
1 bay leaf
1 beef bouillon cube
2 tablespoons butter or
 margarine
3 tablespoons flour
 Fresh parsley, snipped

1. Put potatoes and water into a large heavy saucepan. Cover and bring to boiling. Reduce heat to medium and add carrot, leek, celery, onion, salt, pepper, thyme, marjoram, and bay leaf. Cover; bring to boiling, reduce heat, and simmer about 1 hour, or until vegetables are tender.
2. With a slotted spoon, remove the carrot, leek, celery, onion, and bay leaf; discard. Remove 1 cup of the potato broth and add beef bouillon cube; stir until dissolved.
3. Force remaining potato mixture through a fine sieve into saucepan.
4. Heat butter in a saucepan. Blend in flour. Heat until bubbly. Add the 1 cup of potato broth gradually, stirring constantly. Pour into the soup and blend well. Bring to boiling, reduce heat, and simmer 5 to 10 minutes.
5. Ladle hot soup into bowls. Garnish with parsley.

About 2½ pints soup

Fresh Vegetable Beef Soup

This large recipe may be cut in half if desired, or part of it may be frozen for future use. Either way, in addition to its delicious taste, the fresh vegetables in the recipe provide vitamins A and C, calcium, and other minerals.

Beef broth (about 4½ quarts):

- 3 tablespoons butter or margarine
- 3 pounds beef shank cross cuts
- 1 clove garlic, peeled
- 2 onions, peeled and cut in quarters
- 4 pieces celery with leaves
- 4 tomatoes, cut in wedges
- 2 carrots, pared and cut in pieces
- 1 bay leaf
- 1½ teaspoons thyme leaves
- 2 parsley sprigs
- 4 beef bouillon cubes
- 6 peppercorns
- 1 tablespoon salt
- 4½ quarts water

Vegetables for soup:

- 1½ cups sliced celery
- 1½ cups sliced pared carrots
- 3 cups chopped cabbage
- 2 cups fresh green beans, cut in 1-inch pieces
- 4 tomatoes, peeled and chopped
- 4 large potatoes, pared and cut in 1-inch cubes
- 1½ cups fresh corn kernels
- 1 tablespoon salt

1. For broth, heat butter in a large kettle. Add beef shank and brown on all sides. Add garlic, onions, celery, tomatoes, carrots, herbs, bouillon cubes, peppercorns, salt, and water. Cover; bring to boiling, reduce heat, and simmer about 2 hours.

2. Remove meat. Strain broth and return broth to kettle. Cut meat into small pieces and add to broth.

3. For soup, add celery, carrots, cabbage, green beans, tomatoes, potatoes, corn, and salt to broth. Cover; bring to boiling, reduce heat, and simmer 30 minutes, or until vegetables are tender.

4. Ladle hot soup into bowls.

About 5½ quarts soup

Cream of Fresh Mushroom Soup

A homemade treat that provides protein, riboflavin, and niacin, mushroom soup is a classic that rates high among good cooks the world over.

¼ cup butter or margarine
2 tablespoons chopped onion
½ cup enriched flour
½ teaspoon salt
⅛ teaspoon ground pepper
 Few grains cayenne pepper
3 cups chicken broth
 (homemade, canned, or
 from bouillon cubes)
8 ounces fresh mushrooms,
 cleaned and sliced
 lengthwise
2 cups milk, scalded
2 tablespoons sherry
 Fresh parsley, snipped

1. Heat butter in a saucepan. Mix in onion and cook until crisp-tender. Mix in flour, salt, and peppers. Add chicken broth gradually, stirring constantly. Continue to stir, bring to boiling, and cook 1 minute. Stir in mushrooms. Cover; cook over low heat 30 minutes, stirring occasionally.
2. Remove cover and stir in scalded milk. Cook, uncovered, over low heat 5 to 10 minutes.
3. Just before serving, mix in the sherry. Garnish with parsley.

About 2½ pints soup

Easy Vegetable Soup

Quick and delicious, this vegetable soup has an unusual look and taste. The cabbage gives it a vitamin C and calcium content.

1 can (15½ ounces) green
 beans (undrained)
1 package (10 ounces)
 frozen chopped broccoli,
 defrosted and separated
4 cups shredded cabbage
2 cups chopped celery
4½ cups beef broth
 (homemade, canned, or
 from bouillon cubes)
2 tablespoons instant
 minced onion
2 cups tomato juice

1. Put green beans with liquid, broccoli, cabbage, celery, beef broth, and onion into a large saucepan or Dutch oven.
2. Cover; bring to boiling, reduce heat, and simmer 15 minutes, or until vegetables are tender. Stir in tomato juice. Heat thoroughly.
3. Ladle hot soup into bowls.

About 2½ quarts soup

Lima Soy Bean Soup

Fabulous flavor is not the only good thing about this unusual soup, which combines both meat and vegetable protein and also provides riboflavin, niacin, calcium, and iron.

1 pound dried baby lima beans, rinsed
6 cups water
1 cup dried soy beans, rinsed
¾ cup water
3 medium onions, peeled and chopped
1 pound smoked shoulder roll (butt) or smoked ham (with skin and fat trimmed and reserved), cut in small cubes
4 cups water
1 teaspoon salt
¼ teaspoon pepper
2 tablespoons prepared mustard

1. Put lima beans into a large saucepot or Dutch oven. Add 6 cups water. Bring to boiling and boil rapidly 2 minutes. Cover tightly, remove from heat, and set aside about 1 hour.

2. Put soy beans into a saucepan and add enough water to cover. Cover saucepan; bring to boiling, reduce heat, and cook 30 minutes.

3. Drain and rinse soy beans. Return beans to saucepan and add water to cover. Bring to boiling and cook 30 minutes. Drain and rinse beans.

4. Put beans into an electric blender container with ¾ cup water. Cover; blend until puréed. Set aside.

5. Put onions, meat cubes, skin, fat, and 4 cups water into saucepot with lima beans. Cover; bring to boiling and simmer 1 hour, stirring as necessary.

6. Mix in the soy bean purée, salt, pepper, and prepared mustard. Cook 30 minutes, or until lima beans are tender. Remove and discard meat skin and fat.

7. Ladle hot soup into bowls.

About 4 quarts soup

Lentil Soup

Here's a hearty favorite that needs no meat for flavor or nutrition. Lentils are high in protein and offer thiamine, riboflavin, niacin, and iron as well.

¼ cup olive oil
1 cup chopped onion
1 cup diced green pepper

1. Heat olive oil in a Dutch oven or saucepot. Add onion, green pepper, and pimiento; cook, stirring occasionally, until soft. Blend in flour

¼ **cup diced pimiento**
2 **tablespoons flour**
1 **pound dried lentils, rinsed**
1 **can (16 ounces) tomatoes (undrained)**
2 **cups diagonally sliced carrots**
1 **cup diagonally sliced celery**
1 **tablespoon salt**
8 **cups water**

and heat until bubbly. Add lentils, tomatoes with liquid, carrots, celery, salt, and water; stir.

2. Cover; bring to boiling, reduce heat, and simmer 2 hours, stirring as necessary.

3. Ladle hot soup into bowls.

About 3 quarts soup

Blender Pea Soup

Don't miss this quickie soup that provides protein and vitamin A from ingredients you probably have on hand. Try lemon pepper marinade for a little zing!

1 **can (17 ounces) green peas (undrained)**
1½ **cups milk**
2 **tablespoons butter or margarine**
2 **teaspoons flour**
½ **teaspoon salt**
½ **teaspoon monosodium glutamate**
½ **teaspoon ground nutmeg**
¼ **teaspoon sugar**
1 **small onion, quartered Lemon pepper marinade (optional)**

1. Put green peas with liquid, 1 cup milk, butter, flour, salt, monosodium glutamate, nutmeg, and sugar into an electric blender container. Cover and blend thoroughly. Remove cover and add onion, a quarter at a time, continuing to blend.

2. Pour mixture into a heavy saucepan.

3. Use the remaining ½ cup milk to rinse out blender (cover blender and turn on, then off). Pour into the saucepan. Bring to boiling, stirring occasionally.

4. Ladle hot soup into mugs. Sprinkle, if desired, with lemon pepper marinade.

About 1 quart soup

Split Pea Vegetable Soup

Split peas combine with other vegetables to add flavor interest and extra nutrition. Protein, thiamine, riboflavin, niacin, and iron are the big plusses.

1 **pound green split peas, rinsed**

4 **leeks, washed thoroughly and cut in large pieces**

2 **large dry onions, peeled and cut in large pieces**

1 **bunch green onions, diced**

4 **large carrots, pared and diced**

2 **teaspoons salt**

⅛ **teaspoon ground black pepper**

4 **quarts water**

1 **package (10 ounces) frozen cut okra**

1 **package (10 ounces) frozen whole kernel corn**

2 **cans (10½ ounces each) condensed beef broth**

2 **cans (about 13 ounces each) chicken broth**

½ **cup butter or margarine**

½ **pound fresh mushrooms, cleaned and diced**

Dairy sour cream

Fresh parsley, snipped

1. Put split peas into a large saucepot or Dutch oven. Add leeks, dry onions, green onions, carrots, salt, pepper, and water; stir. Cover; bring to boiling, reduce heat, and simmer about 2 hours, stirring occasionally.

2. Add okra, corn, beef broth, and chicken broth; stir. Bring to boiling and simmer, covered, about 1 hour, stirring occasionally.

3. Meanwhile, heat butter in a skillet. Add mushrooms and cook until lightly browned, stirring occasionally.

4. Mix mushrooms into soup. Simmer, covered, about 30 minutes.

5. Ladle hot soup into bowls. Top with sour cream and parsley.

About 4 quarts soup

Peanut Butter Soup

Peanut butter, famous for its high protein content, gives fabulous flavor to this un-usual soup. The addition of soy protein supplies even more body-building nutrients.

2 tablespoons butter or
  margarine
1/4 cup finely chopped onion
1/3 cup finely chopped celery
1 tablespoon flour
1/4 teaspoon salt
2 cups milk
3/4 cup chicken broth
  (homemade, canned, or
  from bouillon cube)
1/2 cup peanut butter
  Crisp bacon, crumbled; or
  prepared baconlike pieces
  (a soy protein product)

1. Heat butter in a saucepan. Add onion and celery; cook about 5 minutes. Blend in flour and salt; heat until bubbly. Add milk and chicken broth gradually, stirring until smooth. Bring to boiling; cook and stir 1 to 2 minutes.
2. Add the sauce gradually to peanut butter, stirring until blended. Return to saucepan; heat thoroughly.
3. Ladle hot soup into bowls and spoon bacon or baconlike pieces on top.

About 1 1/2 pints soup

Frosty Cucumber-Yogurt Soup

Here's a chilled soup you make ahead of time for summer entertaining. Yogurt supplies protein, riboflavin, and calcium.

1 large firm unpared
  cucumber, scored
  lengthwise with a fork
1/2 clove garlic
1/4 teaspoon salt
1/8 teaspoon ground pepper
1 1/2 cups chilled yogurt
1 1/4 cups cold water
1/2 cup (about 2 ounces)
  walnuts, ground in an
  electric blender
2 cloves garlic, minced

1. Halve cucumber lengthwise and cut cross-wise into very thin slices. Rub inside of a large bowl with cut surface of a half clove of garlic. Turn cucumber into the bowl, sprinkle with salt and pepper, and toss with a fork to mix. Cover and chill.
2. Blend yogurt and water, pour over chilled cucumber, and mix well. Chill thoroughly.
3. Meanwhile, mix walnuts and minced garlic; set aside for topping.
4. Ladle chilled soup into bowls. Serve with walnut topping.

About 1 quart soup

Chilled Rosemary Vegetable Garden Soup

Here's a hot-weather refresher, cool to make and cool to eat. No cooking means that all the nutrients of the raw vegetables—especially vitamin C—are retained. It's also rich in vitamin A and calcium.

3 large firm ripe tomatoes
1 clove garlic, peeled
1 small cucumber (unpared)
1 green pepper, seeded
½ cup chopped green onions, including tops
¼ cup chopped onion
¼ cup chopped parsley
1 tablespoon rosemary, crushed
¼ teaspoon basil, crushed
1 teaspoon monosodium glutamate
¼ cup olive oil
¼ cup salad or cooking oil
2 tablespoons lemon juice
2 cups strong chicken broth (3 bouillon cubes dissolved in 2 cups boiling water)

1. Chop tomatoes, garlic, cucumber, and green pepper finely; put into a large bowl. Add the green onions, chopped onion, parsley, rosemary, basil, and monosodium glutamate; stir until thoroughly mixed.

2. Mix oils and lemon juice; pour over vegetables. Stir in chicken broth. Refrigerate until thoroughly chilled.

3. Ladle into chilled soup bowls.

About 3½ pints soup

Mixed Fruit Soup

This spicy fruit soup will warm you in the winter, cool you in the summer, and supply niacin, calcium, and iron whenever you serve it. It makes a romantic late-night snack.

1¼ cups (½ pound) dried prunes
¾ cup (¼ pound) dried apricots
1 cup (about 5 ounces) seedless raisins

1. Rinse dried fruits and put into a large saucepan with 6 cups water. Cover; set aside to soak overnight. Put tapioca and 2 cups water into a small saucepan. Cover; set aside to soak overnight.

2. The next day, bring tapioca to boiling and

8 cups water
¼ cup pearl tapioca
1 cup sugar
¼ teaspoon salt
2 pieces stick cinnamon
(about 4 inches)
3 large apples, cored and cut
in pieces
1 lemon, sliced and cut in
half slices
1 orange, sliced and cut in
half slices
¼ cup maraschino cherries

cook, uncovered, stirring frequently, about 45 minutes, or until the pearls are clear.

3. Stir cooked tapioca, sugar, salt, cinnamon, apple, lemon, and orange pieces into the soaked fruit. Bring to boiling and cook until fruit is soft, about 5 minutes, stirring occasionally. Remove from heat; stir in maraschino cherries.

4. Serve soup either hot or chilled.

About 3 quarts soup

Oyster Soup

Whether you call it "oyster soup" or "oyster stew," this soup is loaded with nutrients. Oysters provide protein, niacin, riboflavin, and calcium while the dairy products add more of the same, plus vitamins A and D.

6 tablespoons butter or
margarine
2 tablespoons flour
2 teaspoons salt
2 cups milk
4 small carrots, pared and
finely diced
2 small turnips, pared and
finely diced
4 celery stalks, finely diced
1 pint oysters (undrained)
¼ teaspoon ground black
pepper
2 cups cream, heated just
until hot
1 teaspoon Worcestershire
sauce
Fresh parsley, snipped

1. Heat 2 tablespoons butter in a saucepan. Blend in flour and ½ teaspoon salt. Heat until bubbly. Add milk gradually, stirring constantly. Bring to boiling; cook 1 to 2 minutes. Set aside and keep warm.

2. Heat 2 tablespoons butter in a skillet. Add carrots, turnips, and celery and cook until just tender, stirring frequently. Remove from heat and set aside.

3. Heat 2 tablespoons butter in a saucepan. Add oysters with liquor, 1½ teaspoons salt, and pepper. Simmer 3 minutes, or until oysters are plump and edges begin to curl.

4. Blend cream with the white sauce. Stir in Worcestershire sauce, vegetables, and oyster mixture.

5. Ladle hot soup into bowls. Sprinkle with parsley.

About 2 quarts soup

Tuna Chowder

Canned salmon (which contains calcium) can be substituted for tuna here. In either case the flavor is delicious, and the chowder is rich in protein and niacin.

3 tablespoons butter or margarine

½ cup chopped onion

2 tablespoons chopped green pepper

1 can (10½ ounces) condensed cream of celery soup

3 cups milk

2 cans (6½ or 7 ounces each) tuna, drained and flaked

1½ cups diced pared potatoes, cooked

1 cup diced pared carrots, cooked

1 can (16 ounces) tomatoes, drained

1 teaspoon salt

½ teaspoon monosodium glutamate

¼ teaspoon ground black pepper

1. Heat butter in a large saucepan. Add onion and green pepper; cook, stirring occasionally, until tender.

2. Add condensed soup, then milk, blending well. Add tuna, cooked potatoes and carrots, drained tomatoes, salt, monosodium glutamate, and pepper; stir. Heat thoroughly, stirring occasionally (do not boil).

3. Ladle hot soup into bowls.

About 2 quarts soup

Breads

Everybody loves homemade bread, whether it's a batch of blueberry-studded muffins, a crusty loaf right out of the oven, or an elegant braided coffee cake. And breads are so easy to make that every cook will enjoy baking and serving them to family or guests.

Breads are generally divided into two groups: quick breads and yeast breads. The quick breads, which include muffins, biscuits, and many kinds of nut and fruit breads, are made with fast-working leaveners such as baking powder, baking soda, or eggs. They are quick to mix up—indeed, the one rule for quick breads is not to overmix—and quick to disappear once served. The second group of breads uses the slower-working yeast as a riser. These breads take a bit more time to prepare than the quick breads, but they demand hardly any more effort—just a little elbow grease for the kneading!

The key word for breads is variety. *Whole Wheat Bread* will be a sure success for beginning bakers; or try the *Potato Bread*, a delicious variation of the traditional white bread. Popovers can be filled with creamed chicken or seafood as a main dish, or served for dessert filled with ice cream or fresh fruit. Nut or fruit breads are delicious served warm with butter, or sliced when chilled and spread with a mild cheese. Try the *Steamed Boston Brown Bread* or the *Apricot-Sesame Puffs* for a real treat!

Homemade breads are valuable sources of vitamins and minerals. Many of the following recipes call for enriched all-purpose flour, available in all supermarkets. Whole wheat flour and bran make frequent appearances in these recipes and, as both are packed with B vitamins and iron, they will add some nutrition points to your recipes. Rye, oats, wheat germ, and wheat flakes are other healthful grain products found in some of these breads. Other ingredients, too, add to the nutritious value of homemade breads. Milk, cream, cheese, yogurt, and eggs supply protein, calcium, and vitamins. The many fruits and nuts that give a special touch to a wide array of breads are another source of vitamins and minerals.

A wide variety of flours and grain products is becoming readily available in supermarkets. Keep a supply on hand and you'll always be ready to make up that fresh loaf of bread that is sure to please everyone in the house!

Muffins /
Nut Muffins and Whole Wheat Muffins

Convenient individual servings are just one of the reasons that muffins remain popular. These homemade variations using nuts and whole wheat provide calcium and B vitamins, as well as good taste.

2 cups sifted enriched all-purpose flour
¼ cup sugar
4 teaspoons baking powder
½ teaspoon salt
1 egg, well beaten
1 cup milk
¼ cup shortening, melted

1. Sift flour, sugar, baking powder, and salt together into a bowl.
2. Combine egg, milk, and melted shortening. Add liquid mixture to flour mixture; stir only enough to moisten flour.
3. Cut against the side of bowl with spoon for enough batter at one time to fill each greased 2½ x 1¼-inch muffin-pan well two-thirds full. Place spoon in well; push batter off with a rubber spatula.
4. Bake at 400°F 25 minutes. Immediately loosen muffins and tip slightly in wells. Serve warm.

About 1 dozen muffins

Nut Muffins: Follow recipe for Muffins; mix **½ cup chopped nuts** into batter.

Whole Wheat Muffins: Follow recipe for Muffins; substitute **1 cup whole wheat flour** for 1 cup all-purpose flour.

Corn Pocket Rolls

In this delicious roll, cornmeal and dairy sour cream combine to provide protein, vitamin A, the B vitamins, and calcium.

1½ cups sifted enriched all-purpose flour
2 tablespoons sugar
2½ teaspoons baking powder

1. Sift flour, sugar, baking powder, baking soda, and salt together into a bowl; mix in cornmeal.
2. Blend egg and sour cream; stir into flour

¼ teaspoon baking soda
½ teaspoon salt
½ cup enriched yellow
   cornmeal
 1 egg, well beaten
¾ cup dairy sour cream
   Butter or margarine,
   melted

mixture. Turn dough onto a lightly floured surface and roll about ⅛ inch thick. Brush dough with melted butter and cut with a lightly floured 2½-inch round cutter.

3. Using the handle of a wooden spoon, make a slightly off-center crease on each round of dough; fold top (larger side) over bottom. Press edges together at each end of crease.

4. Place rolls about 1 inch apart on lightly greased cookie sheets.

5. Bake at 425°F about 12 minutes.

About 2 dozen rolls

Popovers /
Whole Wheat Popovers

Serve these puffy and beautiful show-stoppers hot from the oven, and reap the benefits of vitamins A and B, calcium, and iron. Fill them with creamed chicken or ham salad for an impressive lunch.

 1 cup sifted enriched all-
   purpose flour
½ teaspoon salt
 2 eggs
 1 cup milk
 1 tablespoon vegetable oil or
   melted shortening

1. Mix flour and salt in a bowl. Mix eggs, milk, and oil; add to flour and beat just until blended.

2. Pour batter into generously greased 6-ounce custard cups, filling each about one-half full.

3. Bake at 450°F 15 minutes; reduce to 350°F and bake 35 minutes. Remove immediately from cups. Serve hot.

6 popovers

Whole Wheat Popovers: Follow recipe for Popovers; substitute ⅓ **cup whole wheat flour** for ⅓ cup all-purpose flour.

Baking Powder Biscuits / Buttermilk Biscuits

Real homemade biscuits are not a thing of the past. You'll get raves when you serve these, and you'll be adding calcium and B vitamins to your family's diet.

2 cups sifted enriched all-purpose flour
1 tablespoon baking powder
1 teaspoon salt
⅓ cup lard or other shortening
¾ cup milk
Milk for brushing tops

1. Sift flour, baking powder, and salt together into a bowl. Add lard and cut in with a pastry blender or two knives until mixture resembles coarse cornmeal. Add milk and stir with a fork until a dough is formed.
2. Turn dough onto a lightly floured surface. Shape into a ball and knead lightly 10 to 15 times. Gently roll dough ½ inch thick. Cut with a floured biscuit cutter or knife, using an even pressure to keep sides of biscuits straight.
3. Place on ungreased cookie sheet, close together for soft-sided biscuits or 1 inch apart for crusty sides. Brush tops lightly with milk.
4. Bake at 450°F 10 to 15 minutes.

About 1 dozen biscuits

Buttermilk Biscuits: Follow recipe for Baking Powder Biscuits; decrease baking powder to 2½ teaspoons and add ¼ **teaspoon baking soda** to dry ingredients. Substitute **buttermilk** for milk.

Refrigerator Bran Muffins

Be ready for the unexpected. Mix the batter for these bran muffins and store in the refrigerator for up to three weeks. Bake and serve for generous portions of protein, vitamins A and B-complex, calcium, and iron.

3 cups whole bran cereal
1 cup boiling water
½ cup shortening

1. Put bran cereal into a bowl. Pour in boiling water. Set aside until cool.
2. Put shortening and sugar into a large

1½ cups sugar
2 eggs
2 cups buttermilk
3 cups sifted enriched all-purpose flour
2½ teaspoons baking soda
½ teaspoon salt

mixer bowl. Beat until thoroughly blended. Beat in eggs one at a time. Alternately mix in the soaked bran and buttermilk.

3. Sift flour, baking soda, and salt together; add to the bran mixture and mix gently until ingredients are thoroughly moistened (do not overmix).

4. Pour batter into well-greased 2½ x 1¼-inch muffin-pan wells, filling each about two-thirds full.

5. Bake at 400°F 15 to 18 minutes. Immediately loosen and tip muffins in wells. Serve warm.

6. Batter may be stored in tightly covered jars in a refrigerator as long as 3 weeks; when ready to bake, pour batter into muffin-pan wells and proceed as above.

About 3 dozen muffins

Prune and Wheat-Flake Muffins

Prunes and whole wheat flakes give a new twist to the wheat muffin, and supply vitamins A, C, and D, niacin, thiamine, and riboflavin.

¾ cup sifted enriched all-purpose flour
⅓ cup sugar
1 tablespoon baking powder
½ teaspoon salt
¾ cup snipped dried prunes
⅓ cup chopped walnuts
1 egg, well beaten
¾ cup milk
3 tablespoons butter or margarine, melted
2 teaspoons grated lemon peel
1½ cups ready-to-eat whole wheat flakes

1. Sift flour, sugar, baking powder, and salt together into a bowl; add prunes and walnuts, but do not mix in.

2. Combine egg, milk, butter, and lemon peel. Add liquid mixture to flour mixture; stir only enough to moisten flour. Quickly and lightly stir in wheat flakes, using about 10 strokes.

3. Cut against the side of bowl with spoon for enough batter at one time to fill each greased 2½ x 1¼-inch muffin-pan well two-thirds full. Place spoon in well; push batter off with a rubber spatula.

4. Bake at 425°F about 15 minutes. Immediately loosen muffins and tip slightly in wells. Serve warm.

About 1 dozen muffins

Cornbread / Crisp Corn Sticks

Enriched yellow cornmeal gives vitamin A and the B vitamins to cornbread. Here's a nutritious treat for any meal.

1 **cup sifted enriched all-purpose flour**
¼ **cup sugar**
1 **tablespoon baking powder**
¾ **teaspoon salt**
1 **cup enriched yellow corn-meal**
¼ **cup melted shortening, butter, or margarine**
1 **egg, well beaten**
1 **cup milk**

1. Sift flour, sugar, baking powder, and salt together into a bowl; mix in cornmeal.
2. Combine melted shortening, egg, and milk. Add liquid mixture to flour mixture; beat just until smooth. Turn batter into a greased 8 x 8 x 2-inch pan and spread to corners.
3. Bake at 425°F about 20 minutes. Cut into squares and serve warm.

9 servings

Crisp Corn Sticks: Follow recipe for Cornbread. Spoon batter into 12 greased hot corn-stick pan sections, filling each three-fourths full. Bake 10 to 15 minutes.

Bran Gems

The bran muffin remains a favorite for the best of reasons—it is loaded with nutrients. These particular beauties provide protein, vitamins A, C, and D, niacin, thiamine, riboflavin, calcium, and iron.

1 **cup sifted enriched all-purpose flour**
⅓ **cup sugar**
1 **tablespoon baking powder**
½ **teaspoon salt**
1 **cup whole bran cereal**
1 **egg, well beaten**
⅔ **cup milk**
3 **tablespoons butter or margarine, melted**

1. Sift flour, sugar, baking powder, and salt together into a bowl; stir in bran cereal.
2. Combine egg, milk, and melted butter. Add to flour mixture and stir quickly and lightly only enough to moisten. Spoon batter equally into greased 1¾ x 1-inch muffin-pan wells.
3. Bake at 400°F 25 to 30 minutes. Immediately loosen and tip muffins in wells. Serve warm.

About 10 muffins

Waffles /
Buttermilk and Wheat Germ Pecan Waffles

All you need is a waffle baker for any of these fun-to-make and hearty variations of an old family favorite. The wheat germ version adds thiamine, riboflavin, and iron.

2 cups sifted enriched all-purpose flour
1 tablespoon sugar
1 tablespoon baking powder
½ teaspoon salt
3 eggs, well beaten
2 cups milk
½ cup butter or margarine, melted

1. Sift flour, sugar, baking powder, and salt together into a bowl.
2. Combine eggs, milk, and melted butter. Add liquid mixture to flour mixture; beat just until batter is smooth.
3. Heat waffle baker. Pour enough batter into waffle baker to allow spreading to within 1 inch of edges. Lower cover and bake waffle; do not raise cover during baking. Lift cover and loosen waffle with a fork.
4. Serve hot.

About 4 large waffles

Buttermilk Waffles: Follow recipe for Waffles; substitute **buttermilk** for milk. Decrease baking powder to 2 teaspoons and add **1 teaspoon baking soda** to dry ingredients.

Wheat Germ Pecan Waffles: Follow recipe for Waffles; decrease flour to 1½ cups. Stir **½ cup toasted wheat germ** into the flour mixture. Sprinkle **3 tablespoons coarsely chopped pecans** onto the batter before baking each waffle.

Pancakes /
Buttermilk, Cornmeal, and Rye Pancakes

Pancakes made from scratch are a nutritious and delicious treat, well worth the effort. These variations give you the B vitamins and calcium.

1½ cups sifted enriched all-purpose flour

1 tablespoon sugar

1½ teaspoons baking powder

¼ teaspoon salt

2 egg yolks, beaten

1⅓ cups milk

2 tablespoons butter or margarine, melted

2 egg whites

1. Start heating griddle or heavy skillet over low heat.

2. Sift flour, sugar, baking powder, and salt together into a bowl.

3. Combine egg yolks, milk, and butter. Add liquid to flour mixture and beat until smooth.

4. Beat egg whites until rounded peaks are formed. Spread beaten egg whites over batter and fold gently together.

5. Test griddle; it is hot enough for baking when drops of water sprinkled on surface dance in small beads. Lightly grease griddle if so directed by manufacturer.

6. Pour batter onto griddle from a pitcher or large spoon into pools about 4 inches in diameter, leaving at least 1 inch between cakes. Turn pancakes as they become puffy and full of bubbles. Turn only once.

7. Serve hot.

About 12 pancakes

Buttermilk Pancakes: Follow recipe for Pancakes; substitute ½ **teaspoon baking soda** for the baking powder and **buttermilk** for the milk. Do not separate eggs. Beat eggs with buttermilk and proceed as in step 3 above.

Cornmeal Pancakes: Follow recipe for Pancakes. Decrease flour to ¾ cup. Mix ¾ **cup enriched yellow cornmeal** into dry ingredients.

Rye Pancakes: Follow recipe for Buttermilk Pancakes. Decrease flour to ¾ cup and mix in ¾ **cup rye flour**. Blend **3 tablespoons molasses** into buttermilk-egg mixture.

Lemony Apple Nut Bread

Here's a bread with a definite lemony flavor plus the interesting taste and texture of apples and walnuts. It provides vitamin A, calcium, protein, thiamine, niacin, and iron.

¼ **cup butter or margarine**
⅔ **cup sugar**
2 **eggs, well beaten**
2 **cups sifted enriched all-purpose flour**
1 **teaspoon baking powder**
1 **teaspoon baking soda**
1 **teaspoon salt**
2 **cups coarsely grated pared cooking apples**
⅔ **cup chopped walnuts**
1 **tablespoon grated lemon peel**

1. Cream butter in a bowl; add sugar gradually, mixing until light and fluffy. Beat in eggs.
2. Sift flour, baking powder, baking soda, and salt together. Add flour mixture alternately with apples to creamed mixture, mixing until blended after each addition. Stir in walnuts and grated lemon peel. Turn into a greased 9 x 5 x 3-inch loaf pan and spread evenly.
3. Bake at 350°F 45 to 50 minutes.
4. Cool bread 10 minutes in pan on wire rack; remove from pan and cool completely before slicing or storing.

1 loaf bread

Fig-Walnut Loaf

Here's an elegant bread you'll enjoy serving as a treat at coffee or snack time, and you'll be offering protein, thiamine, niacin, and iron to your family and guests.

2 **cups sifted enriched all-purpose flour**
⅓ **cup sugar**
4 **teaspoons baking powder**
1 **teaspoon salt**
1 **cup whole wheat flour**
1 **egg, beaten**
1½ **cups milk**
1 **cup chopped walnuts**
½ **cup chopped dried figs**

1. Sift all-purpose flour, sugar, baking powder, and salt together into a bowl. Mix in whole wheat flour.
2. Combine egg and milk and add to flour mixture; stir only enough to moisten dry ingredients. Stir in walnuts and figs. Turn into a greased 9 x 5 x 3-inch loaf pan; spread evenly.
3. Bake at 350°F 50 minutes.
4. Cool bread 10 minutes in pan on wire rack; remove from pan and cool completely before slicing or storing.

1 loaf bread

Apricot Bran Bread

The contrast of tastes here makes an excitingly different bread which is as good a snack as it is a table bread. Whole bran cereal is high in the B vitamins.

1 cup finely snipped dried apricots
¾ cup sugar
1½ cups whole bran cereal
1 cup milk
2 eggs, slightly beaten
⅓ cup vegetable oil
1½ cups sifted enriched all-purpose flour
1 tablespoon baking powder
1 teaspoon salt

1. Pour enough boiling water over apricots to cover; let stand 10 minutes. Drain well; combine apricots and sugar.
2. Mix cereal and milk in a large bowl. Let stand until almost all of the milk is absorbed, about 2 minutes. Add eggs and oil; beat well.
3. Sift flour, baking powder, and salt together. Add flour mixture to cereal mixture and stir only enough to moisten flour. Gently mix in apricots. Turn into a greased 9 x 5 x 3-inch loaf pan and spread evenly.
4. Bake at 350°F 60 to 65 minutes.
5. Cool bread 10 minutes in pan on wire rack; remove from pan and cool completely before slicing or storing.

1 loaf bread

Cranberry-Orange Nut Bread

The versatile cranberry, combined with nuts and orange flavor, makes a tasty quick bread you'll be glad to add to your collection of favorites. It provides vitamins A and C.

2 cups sifted enriched all-purpose flour
1 cup sugar
1½ teaspoons baking powder
½ teaspoon baking soda
1 teaspoon salt
1¼ cups cranberries, cut in pieces
½ cup coarsely chopped walnuts

1. Sift flour, sugar, baking powder, baking soda, and salt together into a bowl. Mix in cranberries and walnuts.
2. Combine egg, orange peel, orange juice, and melted butter. Add liquid mixture to flour mixture; stir only enough to moisten flour. Turn into a greased 9 x 5 x 3-inch loaf pan and spread evenly.
3. Bake at 350°F 40 to 45 minutes.
4. Cool bread 10 minutes in pan on wire rack;

1 egg, well beaten
1 teaspoon grated orange peel
¾ cup orange juice
2 tablespoons butter or
   margarine, melted

remove from pan and cool completely before slicing or storing.

1 loaf bread

Whole Wheat Pear Bread

An assortment of vitamins and minerals, plus a lot of good taste, are given to this bread by the fresh pears it contains.

2 to 3 fresh Bartlett pears
2 tablespoons shortening
1 teaspoon grated lemon peel
⅔ cup firmly packed light
   brown sugar
½ cup honey
2 tablespoons lemon juice
⅓ cup water
1 egg, beaten
1 cup sifted enriched all-
   purpose flour
1 teaspoon baking soda
1 teaspoon salt
½ teaspoon ground cinnamon
¼ teaspoon ground cloves
1 cup whole wheat flour
1 cup chopped walnuts

1. Core pears, but do not peel. Cut lengthwise slices from one pear and reserve to decorate top. Dice enough remaining pears to measure 1 cup.
2. Mix shortening, grated lemon peel, and brown sugar in a bowl. Add honey, lemon juice, water, and egg; mix well.
3. Sift all-purpose flour, baking soda, salt, cinnamon, and cloves; stir in whole wheat flour. Add flour mixture to liquid mixture; stir just enough to moisten flour. Mix in walnuts and diced pears. Turn into a greased 9 x 5 x 3-inch loaf pan and arrange reserved pear slices crosswise along center.
4. Bake at 325°F 70 to 75 minutes.
5. Cool bread 10 minutes in pan on wire rack; remove from pan and cool completely before slicing or storing.

1 loaf bread

Blueberry Pinwheel Rolls

Blueberries provide small amounts of vitamins and minerals. If fresh berries aren't available, feel free to use canned ones for the same results.

2 cups all-purpose biscuit
   mix
2 tablespoons sugar
2 teaspoons grated orange
   peel
½ cup plus 2 tablespoons milk
¼ cup butter or margarine,
   melted
⅓ cup firmly packed brown
   sugar
½ teaspoon ground cinnamon
⅓ cup chopped pecans
1 cup fresh blueberries,
   rinsed and drained

1. Combine biscuit mix, sugar, and orange peel in a bowl. Add milk; stir with a fork until a dough is formed.
2. Turn dough onto a lightly floured surface. Shape into a ball and knead until dough is smooth. Roll dough into a rectangle, 18 x 10 inches. Brush dough with melted butter. Mix brown sugar, cinnamon, pecans, and blueberries and spoon over dough. Roll up jelly-roll fashion and cut into 12 equal pieces.
3. Put each piece cut side up into a well-greased muffin-pan well or paper baking-cup-lined muffin-pan well.
4. Bake at 425°F 15 to 20 minutes. Remove from muffin pans. Serve warm.

1 dozen rolls

Banana Nut Bread

It's nice to know that this familiar favorite provides some of the nutrients you want to plan for in your menus. Count on some vitamin A and the B vitamins from ripe bananas.

2 cups sifted enriched all-
   purpose flour
¾ cup sugar
1 tablespoon baking powder
¼ teaspoon baking soda
½ teaspoon salt
1 cup chopped pecans
1 egg, well beaten
1½ cups (3 to 4) mashed ripe
   bananas
¼ cup buttermilk

1. Sift flour, sugar, baking powder, baking soda, and salt together into a bowl; mix in pecans.
2. Combine egg, bananas, buttermilk, melted shortening, and vanilla extract; blend thoroughly. Add liquid mixture to flour mixture; stir only enough to moisten flour. Turn into a greased 9 x 5 x 3-inch loaf pan and spread evenly.
3. Bake at 350°F about 50 minutes.
4. Cool bread 10 minutes in pan on wire

⅓ **cup shortening, melted**
1 **teaspoon vanilla extract**

rack; remove from pan and cool completely before slicing or storing.

1 loaf bread

Steamed Boston Brown Bread

In addition to all the good things supplied by the rye and whole wheat flours and the cornmeal, the dark molasses gives you calcium and iron.

1 **cup rye flour**
1 **cup whole wheat flour**
1 **cup enriched yellow corn-meal**
1½ **teaspoons baking powder**
¾ **teaspoon baking soda**
1 **teaspoon salt**
2 **cups buttermilk**
¾ **cup dark molasses**
1 **cup dark or golden raisins**

1. Mix flours, cornmeal, baking powder, baking soda, and salt in a large bowl.
2. Combine buttermilk, molasses, and raisins. Add liquid mixture to flour mixture; stir only enough to moisten flour.
3. Spoon batter into 3 well-greased 16-ounce fruit or vegetable cans, filling each about two-thirds full. Cover cans tightly with aluminum foil.
4. Place filled cans on a trivet in a steamer or saucepot with a tight-fitting cover. Pour boiling water into the steamer to no more than one half the height of the cans. Tightly cover steamer. Steam 3 hours. Keep water boiling gently at all times. If necessary, add more boiling water during the steaming period.
5. Remove cans from steamer; remove foil. Run a knife around inside of cans to loosen loaves and unmold onto wire rack. Serve warm. Or cool, wrap, and store loaves; resteam to serve.

3 loaves bread

Toasted Filbert Coffee Cake

Protein, thiamine, calcium, and iron are the main nutrients in this treat for breakfast or for an afternoon snack.

Topping:
- 1 **cup finely chopped toasted filberts (see Note)**
- ⅓ **cup firmly packed light brown sugar**
- ¼ **cup sugar**
- 1 **teaspoon ground cinnamon**

Batter:
- ½ **cup butter or margarine**
- 1 **teaspoon vanilla extract**
- 1 **cup sugar**
- 2 **eggs**
- 2 **cups sifted enriched all-purpose flour**
- 2 **teaspoons baking powder**
- ½ **teaspoon baking soda**
- ½ **teaspoon salt**
- 1 **cup dairy sour cream**

1. For filbert topping, mix filberts, sugars, and cinnamon. Set aside.

2. For coffee cake batter, cream butter and vanilla extract. Add sugar gradually, beating constantly until thoroughly creamed. Add eggs, one at a time, beating until light and fluffy after each addition.

3. Sift flour, baking powder, baking soda, and salt together.

4. Alternately add dry ingredients and sour cream to creamed mixture, beating only until blended after each addition.

5. Spoon half of the batter into a greased and floured 9 x 9 x 2-inch pan. Evenly sprinkle half of the filbert topping over batter. Spoon on remaining batter and top with filbert mixture.

6. Bake at 325°F about 40 minutes. Cut into squares and serve warm.

9 servings

Note: To toast filberts, spread them in a pan and set in a 400°F oven 10 to 15 minutes, or until browned, stirring occasionally.

Kumquat Coffee Cake

Kumquats add not only a delicious taste, but a smattering of vitamins and minerals to this crumb-topped coffee cake.

Topping:
- ¼ **cup all-purpose biscuit mix**
- ¼ **cup sugar**
- ½ **teaspoon ground cinnamon**

1. For topping, blend biscuit mix, sugar, cinnamon, and nutmeg in a bowl. Using a pastry blender or two knives, cut in butter until crumbly. Set aside.

½ teaspoon ground nutmeg
2 tablespoons butter or
  margarine

Batter:

2 cups all-purpose biscuit mix
⅓ cup sugar
¼ cup butter or margarine,
  softened
1 egg
½ cup milk
1 teaspoon orange extract
1 teaspoon lemon extract
2 tablespoons kumquat syrup
¼ cup finely chopped
  preserved kumquats
⅓ cup finely chopped pecans

2. For batter, blend biscuit mix and sugar in a bowl. Add butter, egg, and ¼ cup milk; stir until blended. Beat vigorously 1 minute.

3. Combine extracts, kumquat syrup, and remaining ¼ cup milk; add to batter and blend. Beat about ½ minute. Mix in kumquats and pecans. Turn batter into a greased 8 x 8 x 2-inch pan and spread evenly. Spoon topping evenly over batter.

4. Bake at 350°F 35 to 40 minutes.

5. Remove from oven and place on wire rack. Cut into squares and serve warm.

9 servings

Graham-Fig Bread

Graham crackers and figs and nuts combine to provide small amounts of several nutrients, but the B vitamins are the main contribution this unusual bread makes to your nutritional regimen.

¾ cup sifted enriched all-
  purpose flour
¾ cup sugar
3½ teaspoons baking powder
1 teaspoon salt
3 cups graham cracker crumbs
1½ cups coarsely chopped
  walnuts
1½ cups chopped dried figs
  (stems removed)
2 eggs, well beaten
1 cup milk
¼ cup vegetable oil
1 teaspoon vanilla extract

1. Sift flour, sugar, baking powder, and salt together into a bowl. Add graham cracker crumbs, walnuts, and figs; mix well.

2. Combine eggs, milk, oil, and vanilla extract. Add liquid mixture to flour mixture; stir only enough to moisten flour. Turn batter equally into three greased 5 x 3 x 2-inch loaf pans and spread evenly.

3. Bake at 350°F 45 to 50 minutes.

4. Cool loaves 10 minutes in pans on wire racks; remove from pans and cool completely before slicing or storing.

3 small loaves bread

Wheat-Germ Yogurt Braid

Show your skill in braiding these large and luscious loaves. The wheat germ and yogurt combine to provide protein, riboflavin, thiamine, calcium, and iron.

9 to 10 cups sifted enriched all-purpose flour
¾ cup instant nonfat dry milk
5 teaspoons salt
1 package active dry yeast
2¾ cups water
1 cup plain yogurt
¼ cup honey
2 tablespoons butter or margarine
1 cup toasted wheat germ
1 egg, beaten
1 tablespoon water
Toasted wheat germ

1. Mix 4 cups flour, dry milk, salt, and undissolved yeast thoroughly in a large bowl.
2. Combine water, yogurt, honey, and butter in a saucepan. Set over low heat until very warm (butter does not need to melt).
3. Add the liquid mixture to dry ingredients while beating at low speed of electric mixer. Beat at medium speed 2 minutes, scraping bowl occasionally. Add 1 cup flour. Beat at high speed 2 minutes, scraping bowl occasionally. Stir in 1 cup wheat germ, then beat in enough of the remaining flour to make a stiff dough.
4. Turn dough onto a lightly floured surface. Knead 8 to 10 minutes, or until dough is smooth, elastic, and shows small blisters under surface when drawn tight.
5. Form dough into a ball and place in a greased deep bowl; turn to bring greased surface to top. Cover; let rise in a warm place until double in bulk (about 1 hour).
6. Punch dough down and divide in half. Divide each half into 3 equal portions. Shape each into a 16-inch rope. Braid 3 ropes together; pinch ends to seal. Place on a greased cookie sheet. Cover; let rise again until double in bulk (about 30 minutes).
7. Brush loaves lightly with a mixture of egg and water. Sprinkle with wheat germ.
8. Bake at 350°F about 35 minutes. Remove loaves from cookie sheets and place on wire racks to cool.

2 large loaves bread

Potato Bread

Here's the trusty potato again, this time adding its wealth of vitamin C to the other good nutrients that are basic to bread.

2½ cups water
1 medium potato, scrubbed, pared, and cut in pieces
1 package active dry yeast
2 tablespoons shortening
2 tablespoons sugar
1 tablespoon salt
6 to 6½ cups sifted enriched all-purpose flour

1. Bring water to boiling in a saucepan. Add potato, cover, and cook until tender. Reserve ¼ cup liquid; cool to warm.
2. Mash the potato in the remaining liquid; add enough water to make 2¼ cups liquid.
3. Soften yeast in the reserved ¼ cup liquid.
4. Put shortening, sugar, and salt into a bowl; add the potato liquid, and stir until smooth. Beat in about half of flour. Stir in the yeast. Beat in enough of the remaining flour to make a stiff dough.
5. Turn dough onto a lightly floured surface. Knead about 8 minutes, or until dough is smooth, elastic, and shows small blisters under surface when drawn tight.
6. Form dough into a ball and put into a greased deep bowl; turn to bring greased surface to top. Cover; let rise in a warm place until double in bulk (about 1½ hours).
7. Punch dough down and divide in half. Shape into loaves and place in well-greased 9 x 5 x 3- or 8 x 4 x 2-inch loaf pans. Cover; let rise again until double in bulk (about 30 minutes).
8. Bake at 375°F 35 to 40 minutes. Remove from pans and cool on wire racks.

2 loaves bread

Molasses-Oatmeal Bread

Oats, long a breakfast favorite, give this hearty bread a rich flavor that is welcome at the breakfast table or at dinnertime. Whenever you enjoy it, it supplies protein, niacin, riboflavin, and thiamine.

> 1 **package active dry yeast**
> ¼ **cup warm water**
> ½ **cup uncooked oats, quick**
>   **or old-fashioned**
> ¾ **cup boiling water**
> ¼ **cup dark molasses**
> 1 **teaspoon salt**
> 3 **tablespoons butter or**
>   **margarine**
> 2¾ **cups sifted enriched all-**
>   **purpose flour**
> 1 **egg, beaten**
>   **Butter or margarine,**
>   **melted (optional)**

1. Soften yeast in warm water. Set aside.
2. Combine oats, boiling water, molasses, salt, and butter in a large mixer bowl. Cool until lukewarm.
3. Mix into the oat mixture 1 cup of flour, then the yeast and egg, beating vigorously with an electric beater until batter is smooth. Beat in only enough remaining flour to make a soft, smooth dough. (Dough will be slightly sticky.)
4. Scrape down sides of bowl with a rubber spatula. Cover bowl; refrigerate until dough is almost double in bulk (at least 2 hours).
5. Turn dough onto a lightly floured surface and shape into a smooth loaf. Place in a greased 9 x 5 x 3-inch loaf pan.
6. Cover with waxed paper; let rise in a warm place until double in bulk (about 1 hour).
7. Bake at 375°F about 35 minutes. Remove immediately from pan, place on a wire rack, and, if desired, brush top and sides of loaf with melted butter.

1 loaf bread

Yeast Rolls

The classic dinner roll is a perennial favorite, building us up with protein, B vitamins, vitamin D, calcium, and iron. Here's your chance to rediscover good eating.

> 2 **packages active dry yeast**
> 1 **cup warm water**
> ½ **cup butter or margarine**

1. Soften yeast in warm water. Set aside.
2. Combine butter, sugar, salt, and milk in a large bowl; stir until butter is melted. Beat in

¼ cup sugar
2½ teaspoons salt
2 cups milk, scalded
8¼ cups sifted enriched all-
    purpose flour
2 eggs, slightly beaten

about 1 cup flour. Stir in the yeast. Add about half of remaining flour, beating until smooth. Beat in eggs, then enough of the remaining flour to make a stiff dough.

3. Turn dough onto a lightly floured surface; cover and let rest 10 minutes. Knead about 10 minutes, or until dough is smooth, elastic, and shows small blisters under surface when drawn tight.

4. Form dough into a ball and place in a greased deep bowl; turn to bring greased surface to top. Cover; let rise in a warm place until double in bulk.

5. Punch dough down; turn onto lightly floured surface.

6. Shape as desired (see Shaping).

7. Lightly grease tops. Cover; let rise until double in bulk.

8. Bake at 425°F 10 to 12 minutes.

About 5 dozen rolls

Shaping

Pan Rolls: With hands, shape dough into rolls 1 inch thick. Cut off equal pieces; form into balls. Put into greased round pans.

Cloverleaf: See Pan Rolls for shaping of balls only. Place 3 balls in each greased muffin-pan well.

Crescents: Roll dough into 8-inch rounds about ¼ inch thick. Brush surface with melted butter. Cut into wedge-shaped pieces. Roll up each piece, starting at wide end. Place on greased cookie sheet about 1 inch apart with points underneath. Curve ends.

Golden Bran Bread

Coffee cans with plastic covers make dandy containers for this yeast bread to rise in, and the two delicious loaves yield vitamins A, C, and D, plus niacin, thiamine, riboflavin, and iron.

3 cups sifted enriched all-purpose flour
2 teaspoons salt
1 package active dry yeast
½ cup water
½ cup milk
½ cup vegetable oil
⅓ cup honey
2 eggs
1 cup whole bran cereal
½ cup toasted wheat germ

1. Mix 1½ cups flour, salt, and undissolved yeast thoroughly in a large bowl.
2. Combine water, milk, oil, and honey in a saucepan. Set over low heat until warm. Add liquid to flour mixture and beat until smooth. Stir in eggs, bran cereal, wheat germ, and remaining flour; beat thoroughly until smooth.
3. Divide mixture into 2 well-greased 1-pound coffee cans. Cover with plastic lids and let rise in a warm place until dough rises almost to top of cans (about 35 minutes). Remove lids.
4. Bake at 350°F 35 minutes. Remove from oven and place on wire racks. Cool loaves slightly, then remove from cans and place on racks to cool.

2 loaves bread

Yeast Rolls Distinctive

These crescent rolls have a flavor so unusual that you'll be getting lots of requests for more. They are high in vitamins A and C, too.

¾ cup milk, scalded
⅓ cup butter or margarine
⅓ cup sugar
1 teaspoon salt
1 cup sieved cooked potatoes
½ cup orange juice
1 tablespoon grated lemon peel
1 package active dry yeast
¼ cup warm water

1. Mix scalded milk, butter, sugar, and salt in a large bowl; stir in potatoes, orange juice, and lemon peel. Cool to lukewarm.
2. Meanwhile, soften yeast in warm water.
3. Add 1 cup flour to the cooled milk mixture and beat until smooth. Stir in the yeast. Add about half of the remaining flour and beat vigorously. Add eggs and beat until smooth. Beat in enough of the remaining flour to make a soft dough. Cover; let rise in a warm place

6 to 6½ cups sifted
enriched all-purpose flour
2 eggs, beaten
Butter or margarine,
melted

until dough is double in bulk (about 1 hour).
4. Stir dough down and let rise again until double in bulk (about 45 minutes).
5. Turn onto a lightly floured surface. Divide dough into fourths. Roll each fourth into a 9-inch round, ¼ inch thick. Brush with melted butter. Cut into 8 wedges. Roll up each wedge, starting from the wide end.
6. Place rolls, points down, on greased cookie sheets. Curve to form crescents. Brush with melted butter. Let rise again until double in bulk (about 30 minutes).
7. Bake at 375°F about 18 minutes. Remove from oven and brush with melted butter. Serve piping hot.

32 rolls

Whole Wheat Bread

A classic favorite for the best of reasons: whole wheat bread gives you good flavor, the B vitamins, and iron.

2 packages active dry yeast
1 cup warm water
½ cup butter or margarine
⅓ cup dark molasses
4 teaspoons salt
1½ cups milk, scalded
4 cups whole wheat flour
3½ cups sifted enriched all-purpose flour

1. Soften yeast in warm water. Set aside.
2. Combine butter, molasses, salt, and milk in a large bowl; mix well. Cool to lukewarm.
3. Mix 1 cup whole wheat flour, then yeast, into liquid mixture. Add remaining whole wheat flour, 1 cup at a time, mixing after each addition. Add all-purpose flour gradually, beating until a stiff dough is formed.
4. Turn dough onto a lightly floured surface. Knead 10 minutes, or until dough is smooth and elastic. Cover; let rest 20 minutes.
5. Punch dough down and divide in half. Shape into loaves and place in greased 9 x 5 x 3-inch loaf pans. Cover; let rise in a warm place until double in bulk (1 hour).
6. Bake at 375°F 40 to 45 minutes. Remove from pans and place on wire racks to cool.

2 loaves bread

Date Nut Bread

This delicious bread, rich in niacin, calcium, and iron, is perfect for company meals because you can prepare it a day ahead and bake it an hour or so before mealtime.

½ cup warm water
2 packages active dry yeast
1¾ cups warm milk
2 tablespoons sugar
1 tablespoon salt
3 tablespoons margarine
5 to 5½ cups sifted enriched all-purpose flour
1 cup whole wheat flour
1 cup chopped dates
½ cup chopped pecans
1 teaspoon ground cinnamon
Peanut oil
Margarine (optional)

1. Measure warm water into a warm large bowl. Sprinkle in yeast; stir until dissolved. Add warm milk, sugar, salt, and margarine. Stir in 2 cups all-purpose flour. Beat with rotary beater until smooth (about 1 minute). Add 1 cup all-purpose flour; beat with rotary beater until smooth (about 1 minute). Add 1 cup all-purpose flour; beat vigorously with a wooden spoon until smooth (about 150 strokes). Stir in whole wheat flour, dates, pecans, cinnamon, and enough of the remaining all-purpose flour to make a soft dough.

2. Turn dough onto a lightly floured surface. Knead 8 to 10 minutes, or until dough is smooth, elastic, and shows small blisters under surface when drawn tight. Cover with plastic wrap, then a towel. Let rest 20 minutes.

3. Punch dough down. Divide into 3 equal portions. Roll each into a 12 x 7-inch rectangle. Shape into loaves. Place in 3 greased 7 x 4 x 2-inch loaf pans. Brush loaves with oil. Cover pans loosely with plastic wrap. Refrigerate 2 to 24 hours.

4. When ready to bake, remove loaves from refrigerator. Uncover dough carefully. Let stand uncovered 10 minutes at room temperature. Puncture with a greased wooden pick or metal skewer any gas bubbles which may have formed.

5. Bake at 400°F about 35 minutes. Remove from pans immediately, place on wire racks to cool, and, if desired, brush with margarine.

3 loaves bread

Bran Rolls

Vitamins A, C, and D, niacin, thiamine, riboflavin, and iron are all found in these fabulous dinner rolls. Serve them warm and don't tell anybody how nutritious they are.

¾ cup whole bran cereal
⅓ cup sugar
1½ teaspoons salt
½ cup margarine
½ cup boiling water
½ cup warm water
2 packages active dry yeast
1 egg, beaten
3¼ to 3¾ cups sifted enriched all-purpose flour
Margarine, melted

1. Combine bran cereal, sugar, salt, and margarine in a bowl. Add boiling water; stir until margarine is melted. Cool to lukewarm.

2. Measure warm water into a warm large bowl. Sprinkle in yeast; stir until dissolved. Mix in lukewarm cereal mixture, egg, and enough of the flour to make a stiff dough.

3. Turn dough onto a lightly floured surface; knead 8 to 10 minutes, or until smooth and elastic. Form dough into a ball and place in a greased deep bowl; turn to bring greased surface to top. Cover; let rise in a warm place until double in bulk (about 1 hour).

4. Punch dough down; divide in half. Divide each half into 12 equal pieces. Form each piece into a smooth ball. Place in greased muffin-pan wells, 2½ x 1½ inches, or in 2 greased 8-inch round cake pans. Brush rolls with melted margarine. Cover; let rise again until double in bulk (about 30 minutes).

5. Bake at 375°F 20 to 25 minutes. Remove from pans and place on wire racks. Serve warm.

2 dozen rolls

Piquant Cheese Loaf

Spiced by a touch of ham, this cheese-flavored bread is enriched by the unusual combination of yogurt and muenster cheese. It provides protein, vitamin A, riboflavin, and calcium.

7 to 7¼ cups sifted enriched all-purpose flour
1 teaspoon sugar
1 tablespoon salt
2 packages active dry yeast
1 cup plain yogurt
½ cup water
2 tablespoons margarine
6 eggs (at room temperature)
½ pound muenster cheese, shredded (about 2 cups)
2 cups julienne cooked ham (optional)
1 egg, slightly beaten
1 tablespoon milk

1. Mix 1½ cups flour, sugar, salt, and undissolved yeast thoroughly in a large mixer bowl.

2. Combine yogurt, water, and margarine in a saucepan. Set over low heat until very warm (120–130°F); margarine does not need to melt. Add liquid mixture gradually to dry ingredients while beating at low speed of electric mixer. Beat at medium speed 2 minutes, scraping bowl occasionally. Add 6 eggs, 1 cup flour, and 1½ cups shredded cheese. Beat at high speed 2 minutes, scraping bowl occasionally. Stir in enough of the remaining flour to make a stiff dough.

3. Turn dough onto a lightly floured surface. Knead 8 to 10 minutes, or until dough is smooth, elastic, and shows small blisters under surface when drawn tight.

4. Form dough into a ball and place in greased deep bowl; turn to bring greased surface to top. Cover; let rise in a warm place until double in bulk (about 1 hour).

5. Punch down dough; turn onto lightly floured surface. Divide in half. If using ham, knead 1 cup ham strips into each half. Shape each half into a ball and place on a greased cookie sheet. Cover; let rise again until double in bulk (about 1 hour).

6. Combine egg and milk; brush over loaves. Sprinkle with remaining ½ cup cheese.

7. Bake at 350°F about 30 minutes. Remove from cookie sheets and place on wire racks to cool.

2 loaves bread

Petite Cheese Loaves

Cheddary and good, these practical little loaves will feed a crowd or keep their freshness for several days of family meals. The cheese adds protein, vitamin A, and calcium.

1 **package hot roll mix**
1 **cup (about 4 ounces) finely shredded sharp Cheddar cheese**
2 **teaspoons butter**
2 **tablespoons instant onion flakes**
   Egg white, slightly beaten (optional)

1. Prepare dough, following package directions; add cheese to dry ingredients.
2. Turn dough onto lightly floured surface and knead lightly about 3 minutes. Form dough into a ball and put into a greased deep bowl; turn to bring greased surface to top. Cover; let rise in a warm place until double in bulk (about 1 hour).
3. Punch dough down and turn onto a lightly floured surface. Divide into fourths, shape into loaves, and put into greased 5 x 3 x 2-inch loaf pans.
4. Melt butter in a small saucepan or skillet. Mix in onion flakes and cook over low heat just until soft. Spoon mixture over the loaves. Let rise again until double in bulk (about 45 minutes).
5. Bake at 375°F 30 to 35 minutes. If a glazed crust is desired, brush tops of loaves lightly with egg white 3 minutes before bread is done. Turn loaves onto wire racks.

4 small loaves bread

Raised Cornmeal Muffins

Here's a variation of the corn muffin that comes out light and delicious, adding vitamin A and the B vitamins to your nutritional intake.

5 **to 5¼ cups sifted enriched all-purpose flour**
½ **cup sugar**
1 **tablespoon salt**
2 **packages active dry yeast**
2¼ **cups milk**
½ **cup shortening**
2 **eggs**
1 **cup enriched yellow cornmeal**
   Butter or margarine, melted

1. Mix 2¾ cups flour, sugar, salt, and undissolved yeast thoroughly in a large mixer bowl.
2. Put milk and shortening into a saucepan. Set over low heat until very warm (120–130°F). Add liquid mixture gradually to dry ingredients while mixing until blended. Beat 2 minutes at medium speed of electric mixer, scraping bowl occasionally. Mix in eggs and 1¾ cups flour, or enough to make a batter. Beat at high speed 2 minutes, scraping bowl occasionally. Blend in cornmeal and enough of the remaining flour to make a smooth, thick batter.
3. Cover; let rise in a warm place until double in bulk (1 to 1½ hours).
4. Beat batter down. Cut against side of bowl with a large spoon enough batter at one time to fill each greased 2½- or 3-inch muffin-pan well two-thirds full, pushing batter with a rubber spatula directly into well. Cover; let rise again until almost double in bulk (about 30 minutes).
5. Bake at 400°F about 20 minutes. Brush tops with melted butter. Remove from pans and serve piping hot.

1½ to 2 dozen muffins

Note: If desired, mix 1 teaspoon crushed herb, such as chervil, oregano, rosemary, or thyme with flour before adding to batter.

Black Bread

Rye flour adds B vitamins and rich taste to this black bread, and a few surprise ingredients help boost the color and flavor.

3¾ cups rye flour
3¾ cups sifted enriched all-
      purpose flour
  2 packages active dry yeast
  ½ cup warm water
  ½ cup unsweetened cocoa
  ¼ cup sugar
  3 tablespoons caraway seed
  2 teaspoons salt
  1 tablespoon instant coffee
  2 cups water
  ¼ cup vinegar
  ¼ cup dark molasses
  ¼ cup butter or margarine
      Butter or margarine,
      melted, or milk for brushing
      (optional)

1. Combine flours in a large bowl; set aside 3 cups of mixture.

2. Soften yeast in warm water. Set aside.

3. Put reserved 3 cups flour mixture into a large bowl. Add cocoa, sugar, caraway seed, salt, and instant coffee; mix well.

4. Combine 2 cups water, vinegar, molasses, and butter in a saucepan. Set over low heat until warm (butter does not need to melt). Add liquid mixture to cocoa mixture and blend well. Mix in softened yeast. Beat in enough of the remaining flour mixture, 1 cup at a time, to make a stiff dough.

5. Turn dough onto a lightly floured surface; cover and let rest 10 minutes. Knead about 10 minutes, or until dough is smooth and elastic. Form dough into a ball and place in a greased deep bowl; turn to bring greased surface to top. Cover; let rise in a warm place until double in bulk (about 1 hour).

6. Punch dough down and turn onto lightly floured surface. Divide in half. Shape each half into a ball and place in center of a greased 8-inch round cake pan. Cover; let rise again until double in bulk (about 1 hour).

7. Bake at 350°F about 45 minutes. Remove from pans, place on wire racks to cool, and, if desired, brush with melted butter or milk.

2 loaves bread

Raisin-Filled Bread / Raisin Bread

Here's a nutritious raisin bread recipe that gives you an option. Whether you heap the raisins into the bread or make a raisin filling, you'll be adding niacin, calcium, and iron.

Dough:
   Yeast Rolls (page 72)

Filling:
- ⅔ **cup fine dry bread crumbs**
- ⅓ **cup sugar**
- 4 **teaspoons grated orange peel**
- 2 **to 3 teaspoons ground cardamom**
- ½ **cup butter or margarine**
- 2½ **cups dark seedless raisins, snipped**

Glaze:
- 1 **egg yolk**
- 1 **teaspoon water**

1. For dough, follow Yeast Rolls recipe through step 5.

2. For filling, mix bread crumbs, sugar, orange peel, and cardamom in a bowl. Add butter and cut in with pastry blender or two knives until pieces are about the size of small peas. Mix in raisins.

3. Divide dough in half. Roll each half into a 14 x 9-inch rectangle. For glaze, blend egg yolk and water. Brush over dough. Spoon filling over dough almost to edges and tightly roll up, beginning at 9-inch side. Pinch to seal. Place, sealed side down, in greased 9 x 5 x 3-inch loaf pan. Proceed as directed in step 7 of Yeast Rolls.

4. Bake at 375°F about 45 minutes. Remove from pans and place on wire racks to cool.

2 loaves bread

Raisin Bread: For dough, follow Yeast Rolls recipe through step 5; mix in **1½ cups dark seedless raisins** after eggs. Shape loaves, place in pans, and proceed as directed in steps 3 and 4 above.

Prune-Wheat Coffee Cake

Whole wheat flour and prunes combine to add B vitamins, calcium, and iron to your diet, while you enjoy a delightful new taste.

Filling:
- 1 **cup snipped dried prunes**
- ¾ **cup water**

1. For filling, put prunes and water into a small saucepan. Bring to boiling. Reduce heat and simmer 10 to 15 minutes, or until mixture

¼ teaspoon ground allspice
¼ teaspoon ground cinnamon
½ teaspoon lemon juice
¼ cup honey
⅓ cup firmly packed brown sugar
½ cup sliced almonds

Dough:

1 package active dry yeast
½ cup warm water
2 tablespoons oil or melted shortening
⅓ cup honey
1¼ teaspoons salt
¾ cup milk
3½ to 4 cups whole wheat flour
½ cup finely chopped almonds

Topping:

Confectioners' sugar (optional)

becomes mushy. Turn contents of saucepan into an electric blender container. Add the spices, lemon juice, honey, and brown sugar; cover and blend until smooth. Pour into a bowl and mix in sliced almonds. Cool.

2. For dough, soften yeast in warm water in a large bowl. Add oil, honey, salt, and milk. Stir in 1 cup whole wheat flour and ground almonds. Beat vigorously 2 minutes. Beat in enough of the remaining flour to make a stiff dough.

3. Turn dough onto a surface lightly floured with whole wheat flour. Knead about 10 minutes, or until dough is smooth, elastic, and shows small blisters under surface when drawn tight.

4. Form dough into a ball and put into a greased deep bowl; turn to bring greased surface to top. Cover; let rise in a warm place until double in bulk (about 1¼ hours).

5. Punch dough down and turn onto a lightly floured surface. Divide in half. Roll each half into a 12 x 4-inch rectangle. Spread with half of cooled filling. Roll up jelly-roll fashion, starting with a 12-inch side, and shape into a half circle. Place seam side down on greased cookie sheet. Cut dough with kitchen scissors at 1-inch intervals about three quarters of the way through roll. Turn each section on its side. Cover and let rise again until double in bulk (about 45 minutes).

6. Bake at 425°F 10 minutes. Reduce to 350°F and bake 20 to 25 minutes.

7. Remove from oven and place on wire racks. If desired, sift confectioners' sugar over coffee cakes.

2 coffee cakes

Apricot-Sesame Puffs

The filling alone contributes vitamin A, niacin, and iron to these puffy treats. Serve them warm and delight your family and guests.

Dough:
- 1 package active dry yeast
- 1½ cups warm water
- ¼ cup sugar
- ½ cup instant nonfat dry milk
- ½ teaspoon salt
- 4½ cups sifted enriched all-purpose flour
- ½ cup butter or margarine, melted
- 2 eggs, well beaten
- 1 tablespoon vanilla extract

Filling:
- 1 cup dried apricots, coarsely snipped
  Hot water
- 2 tablespoons butter or margarine
- ⅔ cup sugar
- ½ teaspoon ground cinnamon

Topping:
- Butter or margarine, melted
- Toasted sesame seed

1. Soften yeast in the warm water in a large bowl. Beat in sugar, dry milk, salt, and 2 cups of flour. Continue beating while adding butter, eggs, and vanilla extract. Add the remaining flour gradually, beating thoroughly. Scrape down sides of bowl. Cover; let rise in a warm place until double in bulk (about 1 hour).

2. Meanwhile, for filling, put apricots into a saucepan, add hot water to almost cover, and cook, covered, over low heat 15 minutes. Stir in butter, sugar, and cinnamon. Bring to boiling; cook 5 minutes, stirring occasionally.

3. Stir dough down with spoon; drop by spoonfuls into lightly greased 1¾ x 1-inch muffin-pan wells, half filling each well. Spoon about 1 teaspoon filling onto each, then spoon dough into each well until two-thirds full.

4. Brush tops with melted butter and sprinkle with sesame seed.

5. Bake at 375°F 20 to 25 minutes. Remove from wells and serve warm.

About 3 dozen rolls

Fresh Plum Coffee Cake

Discover what a "plumb good" coffee cake is, and add a variety of vitamins and minerals to your nutritional count at the same time.

Coffee cake:
- 1 package active dry yeast
- 2 tablespoons warm water

1. For coffee cake, soften yeast in warm water.

2. Put butter, ¼ cup sugar, and salt in a

¼ cup butter or margarine
½ cup sugar
½ teaspoon salt
½ cup milk, scalded
2½ to 3 cups sifted enriched
all-purpose flour
1 egg
¼ teaspoon ground cinnamon
⅛ teaspoon ground cloves
2 tablespoons butter or
margarine, softened
2 cups halved purple plums
Glaze:
3 tablespoons confectioners'
sugar
2 teaspoons lemon juice

bowl; pour milk over all and stir until butter is melted. Beat in about 1 cup flour. Stir in the yeast.

3. Gradually add 1 cup flour, beating until smooth. Beat in egg. Beat in enough of the remaining flour to make a soft dough.

4. Turn dough onto a lightly floured surface. Cover and let rest about 10 minutes. Knead until dough is smooth, elastic, and shows small blisters under surface when drawn tight.

5. Form dough into a ball and place in a greased deep bowl; turn to bring greased surface to top. Cover; let rise in a warm place until double in bulk (about 1 hour).

6. Meanwhile, blend remaining ¼ cup sugar, cinnamon, and cloves; set aside.

7. Punch dough down; turn onto a lightly floured surface and roll into a 15 x 10-inch rectangle. Spread with softened butter; arrange plum halves, cut side down, over the center third of dough. Sprinkle the spiced sugar over plums.

8. Overlap the longer sides of dough onto plums, sealing well. Seal opposite ends. Place on a well-greased cookie sheet; make crosswise cuts, 1 inch apart, over top. Let rise again until double in bulk (about 45 minutes). Make cuts again.

9. Bake at 350°F about 20 minutes.

10. For glaze, blend confectioners' sugar and lemon juice. While coffee cake is hot, spread with glaze.

1 coffee cake

Sweet Potato Rolls

Sweet potatoes add vitamin A to the other good things found in these unusual rolls.
You'll notice a difference in color, texture, and taste, too.

1¼ cups milk, scalded
3 tablespoons sugar
¾ teaspoon salt
1½ tablespoons vegetable oil
1 cup mashed cooked sweet potato
2 teaspoons ground coriander
1 package active dry yeast
¼ cup warm water
4 cups sifted enriched all-purpose flour

1. Combine scalded milk, sugar, salt, and oil in a large mixer bowl. Mix sweet potato and coriander; add to milk mixture and beat on medium speed of mixer until blended. Cool to lukewarm.

2. Meanwhile, soften yeast in warm water.

3. Add 1 cup flour to cooled sweet potato mixture and beat until smooth. Mix in yeast. Beat in enough of the remaining flour to make a stiff dough.

4. Turn dough onto a lightly floured surface. Knead until dough is smooth, elastic, and shows small blisters under surface when drawn tight.

5. Form dough into a ball and place in a greased deep bowl; turn to bring greased surface to top. Cover; let rise in a warm place until double in bulk (about 1 hour).

6. Punch dough down; turn onto a lightly floured surface. Shape dough into balls, about 2 inches in diameter. Place in greased 2½-inch muffin-pan wells. Cover; let rise again until double in bulk (about 30 minutes).

7. Bake at 350°F about 25 minutes. Remove from wells and serve hot.

About 2 dozen rolls

Sandwiches and Snacks

Tired of the limp bologna sandwich routine? Try something new for a change. Sandwiches can be full of visual appeal, good eating, and good health, and they are a great way to make use of a wide variety of foods in delicious and imaginative combinations. Broiled sandwiches, such as the superb *Canadian Mushroom Sandwiches* or *The Apple Special*, make an entire meal when accompanied by a beverage or soup. For an easy-going Saturday night supper, serve a sandwich loaf or a sandwich baked in the oven, such as the *Asparagus Sandwich Puff*. Cold sandwiches travel well in picnic basket or lunch box—the *Onion-Liver Sausage on Rye*, spread with blue cheese, is especially good. Tasty fillings and spreads can be prepared ahead of time to spark up a bag lunch, or adapted for main-dish attractions or party-time canapés and appetizers.

Here are new ideas for festive nibblers and appetizers, too. They can be great fun to eat, a delight to both eye and palate, and a nutritious introduction to an evening meal or party. With the following recipes on hand, there's no need to get trapped in the chip-and-dip habit! These appetizers, whether hot or cold, are bite-size, easy to handle, and full of color. They also make use of intriguing flavor and texture contrasts—crunchy and creamy, sweet and tart, spicy and mild. Serve a well-flavored cheese dip with crisp vegetables, for instance, or with slices of apple or pear. *Tiny Tomato Toppers* or *Hot Mushroom Appetizers* are sure to please, or serve the *Sauerkraut-Sausage Pizza* for a vitamin-packed evening snack.

The delicious sandwiches and snacks in this section combine nutritious ingredients from the basic four food groups. Milk and cheese products are valued for their calcium, protein, and vitamin A content. The foods from the meat group that star in many of these recipes supply protein, iron, and B vitamins. Cereal products such as breads and crackers provide B vitamins and iron. Fruits and vegetables are important sources of vitamins and minerals. Cheese, eggs, meat, fish, poultry, breads, crackers, fruits, and vegetables— each recipe is a mix-and-match combination of many of these ingredients. Nutrition-wise cooks will enjoy finding occasions to serve these tempting snacks and sandwiches.

Hot Flank Steak Sandwiches

Great taste is just one of the good things you'll get from this hearty sandwich. The others are protein, niacin, riboflavin, and iron.

¼ cup olive oil
¼ cup red wine vinegar
2 cloves garlic, crushed in a garlic press or minced
6 peppercorns, crushed
½ teaspoon salt
½ teaspoon sugar
½ teaspoon chili powder
1 flank steak (about 1¼ pounds), scored
¼ cup butter or margarine
1 large sweet onion, thinly sliced
6 slices rye bread with caraway seed, or dark rye, toasted
1 can beef gravy, heated
Fresh parsley, finely snipped

1. Combine olive oil, vinegar, garlic, peppercorns, salt, sugar, and chili powder. Beat or shake to blend. Pour marinade over flank steak in a shallow dish. Cover and marinate in refrigerator at least 4 hours, turning meat occasionally.
2. Remove meat from marinade and place on broiler rack. Broil about 3 inches from heat 4 to 5 minutes on each side, or until desired degree of doneness; turn once.
3. Meanwhile, heat butter in a skillet and add onion; cook about 5 minutes, stirring occasionally.
4. Thinly slice meat diagonally across the grain. Place on toasted bread. Cover with cooked onion and spoon hot gravy over all. Garnish top with parsley. Serve immediately.

6 servings

Baked Chicken Sandwich

Sandwiches you bake in the oven! Everybody loves them, and they add protein, niacin, and iron to your diet.

¼ cup butter or margarine, softened
2 teaspoons prepared mustard
12 slices enriched white sandwich bread, trimmed
1 cup (about 4 ounces) shredded Cheddar cheese
2 cups coarsely chopped cooked chicken

1. Blend ¼ cup butter and prepared mustard. Spread on one side of bread slices.
2. Arrange 6 slices, buttered side up, in a greased shallow 3-quart baking dish.
3. Reserve 2 tablespoons cheese. Combine remaining cheese, chicken, peas, onion, pimiento, salt, and pepper. Spread chicken mixture evenly over bread in baking dish.
4. Cut remaining 6 bread slices in half

1 cup drained cooked green peas
¼ cup chopped onion
2 tablespoons chopped pimiento
½ teaspoon salt
¼ teaspoon ground pepper
Butter or margarine, softened
4 eggs, beaten
1 can (10½ ounces) condensed cream of mushroom soup
1½ cups milk
Parsley sprigs

diagonally. Place over chicken filling, mustard-butter side down. Butter bread.

5. Blend eggs, soup, and milk. Pour evenly over sandwiches. Sprinkle with reserved cheese.

6. Bake at 325°F about 1 hour and 10 minutes, or until set and browned.

7. Garnish with parsley. Serve at once.

6 servings

Canadian Mushroom Sandwiches

Open-faced and delicious, this combination of Canadian-style bacon and mushrooms supplies protein, niacin, riboflavin, and thiamine.

6 enriched kaiser rolls
Butter or margarine, softened
1 tablespoon chopped uncooked bacon
2 tablespoons chopped onion
1 jar (2 ounces) sliced mushrooms, drained
1 teaspoon snipped parsley
18 slices (about 1 pound) Canadian-style bacon, cut ⅛ inch thick
6 slices (1 ounce each) Swiss cheese
6 thin green pepper rings
Paprika
Cherry tomatoes
Pimiento-stuffed olives

1. Split rolls; if desired, reserve tops to accompany open-faced sandwiches. Spread roll bottoms with butter.

2. Combine bacon, onion, mushrooms, and parsley in a skillet and cook about 5 minutes.

3. Arrange 3 slices Canadian-style bacon on each buttered roll and top with mushroom mixture and 1 slice cheese. Place 1 green pepper ring on each cheese slice; sprinkle paprika inside ring.

4. Place sandwiches on a cookie sheet and broil 6 inches from heat until cheese melts (3 to 5 minutes). Garnish each with a cherry tomato and an olive on a skewer.

6 open-faced sandwiches

Asparagus Sandwich Puff

Right before your eyes these open-faced beauties puff up and fairly burst with protein, vitamin A, niacin, thiamine, riboflavin, calcium, and iron.

6 slices enriched white bread
Butter or margarine
1 can (6½ or 7 ounces) tuna, drained and flaked
6 slices pasteurized process pimiento cheese
1 can (about 15 ounces) green asparagus spears, drained
3 egg yolks
½ teaspoon salt
Few grains pepper
1 tablespoon salad dressing or mayonnaise
3 egg whites

1. Toast bread and spread with butter. Arrange on a cookie sheet.
2. Spoon tuna over toast and cover with cheese slices. Top with asparagus spears (about 4 per sandwich).
3. Beat egg yolks until thick and lemon colored. Add salt, pepper, and salad dressing.
4. Beat egg whites until stiff, not dry, peaks are formed; fold into egg yolk mixture. Spoon egg mixture over asparagus.
5. Bake at 350°F 15 to 18 minutes, or until lightly browned.

6 open-faced sandwiches

The Apple Special

Ham and fruit are a traditional combination of tastes, but here's an idea that might be new to you. The sandwich provides protein, vitamin A, the B vitamins, calcium, and iron.

12 slices enriched white sandwich bread
Mayonnaise or salad dressing
Prepared mustard
12 slices (1 ounce each) cooked ham
36 to 48 slices apple (such as Jonathan or McIntosh), pared, if desired
24 slices (1 ounce each) pasteurized process American cheese

1. Spread bread slices lightly with mayonnaise, then with prepared mustard. Cover each slice with 1 slice ham, 3 or 4 slices apple, and 2 slices cheese.
2. Place sandwiches on cookie sheets and broil 4 inches from heat until cheese is lightly browned (about 3 minutes). Serve hot.

12 open-faced sandwiches

Note: If desired, toast bread on one side, turn, and spread untoasted side.

Sardine-Pizza Sandwiches

Sardine lovers will really appreciate these unusual open-faced sandwiches, broiled in a pizzalike sauce. Protein, niacin, vitamin D, calcium, and iron are the nutrients you get.

1 **can (6 ounces) tomato paste**
½ **teaspoon seasoned salt**
⅛ **teaspoon garlic powder**
1 **teaspoon oregano, crushed**
4 **small enriched English muffins, split and toasted**
¾ **cup (about 3 ounces) shredded sharp Cheddar cheese**
1 **can sardines, drained (reserve oil)**
Green pepper strips
Pimiento strips

1. Blend tomato paste, seasoned salt, garlic powder, and oregano. Spread about 1½ tablespoons on each toasted muffin half.
2. Sprinkle cheese over the tomato spread and arrange about 3 sardines on each muffin half. Place two green pepper strips crossing the sardines and place a pimiento strip between them. Brush top with some of the reserved sardine oil.
3. Place sandwiches on a cookie sheet and broil 3 to 4 inches from heat about 3 minutes. Serve hot.

8 open-faced sandwiches

Saucy Beef 'n' Buns

Spoon this tasty mixture over toasted buns, and you'll also spoon protein, niacin, riboflavin, iron, vitamin A, and vitamin C into your diet.

2 **tablespoons fat**
½ **cup finely chopped onion**
1 **pound ground beef**
1 **teaspoon salt**
½ **teaspoon monosodium glutamate**
¼ **teaspoon ground black pepper**
¾ **cup chopped celery**
¾ **cup chopped green pepper**
1 **cup chili sauce**
1 **cup ketchup**
Enriched hamburger buns, buttered and toasted

1. Heat fat in a large skillet. Add onion and cook until soft, stirring occasionally. Add beef, salt, monosodium glutamate, and pepper; cook until meat is lightly browned, separating it into pieces with a fork or spoon.
2. Add celery, green pepper, chili sauce, and ketchup; mix well. Simmer, uncovered, about 25 minutes; stir frequently.
3. To serve, spoon over toasted buns.

About 6 servings

Wonderful Western Heroes

You'll be a hero too, when you serve these hunger-busters that provide protein, vitamins A and D, thiamine, riboflavin, calcium, and iron.

4 brown-and-serve style enriched French rolls
2 cans (4½ ounces each) deviled ham
8 eggs
¼ cup milk
½ teaspoon seasoned salt
½ teaspoon crushed thyme
¼ cup minced onion
¼ cup minced green pepper
1 teaspoon vegetable oil
  Onion rings
  Green pepper rings

1. Bake rolls following package directions. Split into halves lengthwise; spread cut sides with deviled ham. Keep rolls warm.
2. Meanwhile, using a fork or rotary beater, mix eggs, milk, seasoned salt, and thyme in a bowl. Stir in onion and green pepper.
3. Heat oil in a 10-inch skillet over medium heat and pour in egg mixture. As mixture thickens, lift with fork or spatula from bottom and sides of skillet, allowing uncooked portion to flow to bottom; do not stir. When bottom is browned, cut egg mixture into four strips and turn each strip. Cook until browned.
4. Cut each egg strip in half and place each half strip on a roll half. Top each sandwich with onion and green pepper rings. Serve hot.

8 open-faced sandwiches

Turkey in Buns

Leftover turkey is no problem at all, thanks to this easy and delicious recipe. You can expect protein, niacin, and iron to be added to your store of nutrients.

¾ cup ketchup
1 cup currant jelly
¼ cup finely chopped onion
2 tablespoons Worcestershire sauce
1 teaspoon salt
¼ teaspoon garlic salt
3 cups diced cooked turkey
  Enriched buns, split, buttered, and toasted

1. Combine ketchup, jelly, onion, Worcestershire sauce, salt, and garlic salt in a saucepan. Set over low heat and bring to boiling, stirring occasionally. Reduce heat and simmer about 20 minutes. Stir in turkey. Heat thoroughly.
2. Spoon turkey mixture into buns.

8 to 10 servings

Grilled Peanut Butter Sandwiches / French Toast Sandwiches

These peanut butter delights can be made with plain bread or French toast. Either way they are high in protein and niacin.

8 slices enriched firm-type white bread
½ cup crunchy peanut butter
¼ cup apple butter
Butter or margarine

1. Spread 4 bread slices with peanut butter and then apple butter. Close sandwiches. Spread both sides with butter.
2. Heat enough butter in a skillet to cover bottom. Put in as many sandwiches at one time as will fit in skillet. Brown on both sides over medium heat.

4 sandwiches

French Toast Sandwiches: Follow recipe for Grilled Peanut Butter Sandwiches, step 1. Beat **1 egg** in a shallow dish and mix in **½ cup milk, 2 teaspoons sugar,** and a **few grains salt.** Dip both sides of sandwiches in egg mixture. Proceed as directed in step 2.

Sauerkraut-Peanut Butter Burgers

Whether you think of them as a way of stretching your meat budget with protein-rich peanut butter, or just as a flavorful new type of hamburgers, these broiled patties provide protein, niacin, vitamin C, and calcium.

¼ cup crunchy peanut butter
¼ cup dairy sour cream
1 egg, fork beaten
½ teaspoon salt
Few grains black pepper
1 cup sauerkraut, thoroughly drained and finely chopped
1 pound ground beef
Enriched hamburger buns

1. Beat peanut butter, sour cream, egg, salt, and pepper together until blended. Mix in sauerkraut, then lightly mix in beef.
2. Shape mixture into 6 burgers about ¾ inch thick.
3. Place burgers on a broiler rack and broil 4 to 5 minutes. When patties are browned on one side, turn and broil second side about 3 minutes, or until desired degree of doneness.
4. Serve in buns.

6 burgers

Chickpea Salad Sandwiches

Here's a salad sandwich that is different, combining chickpeas and bean sprouts and providing protein, calcium, and iron.

12 slices whole wheat bread
   Butter or margarine
1 can (15½ ounces) chickpeas (garbanzos), drained and chopped
⅓ cup chopped green onion
3 tablespoons mayonnaise
1 tablespoon lemon juice
1½ teaspoons dried basil leaves, crushed
½ teaspoon salt
⅛ teaspoon ground black pepper
6 lettuce leaves
1 can (16 ounces) bean sprouts, drained
12 tomato slices
   Seasoned salt, seasoned pepper, or lemon pepper marinade
   Carrot curls

1. Spread bread slices with butter.
2. Combine chickpeas, green onion, mayonnaise, lemon juice, basil, salt, and pepper in a bowl.
3. Place lettuce leaves on buttered side of 6 slices of bread. Top evenly with chickpea mixture and bean sprouts. Sprinkle sprouts and tomato slices with desired seasoning. Place 2 tomato slices on top and close sandwiches. Cut diagonally in half.
4. Garnish with carrot curls.

6 sandwiches

Paul Bunyan Tuna Hobos

One of these is a meal, unless you really are a Paul Bunyan. The nutritional benefits are large too, with protein, niacin, riboflavin, and iron heading the list.

Smoked Beef Butter (see recipe)
Tuna Salad (see recipe)
1 loaf enriched Italian bread (about 15 inches long), cut in half lengthwise

1. Prepare Smoked Beef Butter and Tuna Salad.
2. Spread beef butter on cut surface of each bread half. Cover with lettuce. Top with tuna salad, tomato, onion, luncheon meat, and then cheese.

Lettuce leaves
Sliced tomato
Sliced sweet onion
8 ounces assorted luncheon meat
4 ounces sliced pasteurized process American cheese
Cherry tomatoes
Pimiento-stuffed olives

3. Impale cherry tomatoes and pimiento-stuffed olives on picks and use to garnish sandwiches. Cut sandwiches into serving-sized pieces.

8 servings

Smoked Beef Butter: Cream ½ **cup butter or margarine** until softened. Mix in **1 cup chopped smoked sliced beef, 2 tablespoons ketchup, 1 teaspoon prepared mustard,** and ½ **teaspoon Worcestershire sauce.**

Tuna Salad: Mix the contents of **2 cans (6½ or 7 ounces each) tuna,** drained and flaked, ¼ **cup sweet pickle relish,** and **6 tablespoons mayonnaise.**

Swiss 'n' Tuna Buns

Here's still another recipe that will encourage your family to enjoy tuna as a source of nutrients; in this case protein, vitamin A, niacin, and calcium.

¼ cup mayonnaise-type salad dressing
2 tablespoons minced onion
1 teaspoon lemon juice
½ teaspoon salt
1 can (6½ or 7 ounces) tuna, drained and flaked
3 to 4 ounces Swiss cheese, shredded
4 enriched buns, split and buttered

1. Combine salad dressing, onion, lemon juice, and salt. Mix in tuna and cheese.
2. Spoon into buns. Wrap each in aluminum foil.
3. Heat in a 350°F oven 20 minutes. Remove from oven, unwrap, and serve immediately.

4 servings

Scrumptious Tunaburgers

A delicious way to get the protein and niacin that tuna provides, these broiled beauties can be served in a variety of imaginative ways.

2 eggs
¼ cup ketchup
1 tablespoon lemon juice
2 tablespoons capers
2 teaspoons instant minced onion
¾ teaspoon lemon pepper marinade
1½ cups soft enriched bread crumbs
3 cans (6½ or 7 ounces each) tuna, drained and flaked
2 tablespoons butter or margarine
6 enriched hamburger buns, halved, buttered, and toasted

1. Beat eggs slightly in a bowl. Add ketchup, lemon juice, capers, onion, lemon pepper marinade, bread crumbs, and tuna; mix thoroughly.
2. Heat butter in a large skillet.
3. Meanwhile, shape tuna mixture into 6 patties (mixture will not be smooth). Put patties into hot butter as each is shaped. Cook over medium heat until browned. Using a large spatula, carefully turn patties to brown other side. Immediately transfer to toasted buns.

6 burgers

Note: If desired, serve tunaburgers with any of the following: ketchup, sweet onion slices, avocado wedges, tomato slices, green pepper rings, cucumber spears, lemon wedges, Cheddar or Swiss cheese slices.

Triple-Decker Chivey Beef Krautwich

Before you finish explaining the name of this one, they'll be asking for seconds. Besides an unusual flavor, you'll be supplying protein, vitamin A, niacin, riboflavin, and iron.

3 packages (3 ounces each) cream cheese
2 tablespoons milk
3 tablespoons fresh or frozen chopped chives
2 cups well-drained sauerkraut
18 slices pumpernickel

1. Mix 1 package cream cheese with milk and 1 tablespoon chives. Stir in kraut and chill.
2. Beat remaining cream cheese and chives. Set aside.
3. Cover 6 slices of the bread with the kraut-cheese mixture, using about ⅓ cup per slice. Spread chive-cream cheese mixture on 6 slices (about 2 tablespoons per slice), put

2 **packages (3 ounces each)
smoked sliced beef
Butter or margarine**

several slices of smoked beef on top, and place on kraut mixture, meat side up. Spread remaining bread slices with butter and complete sandwiches.

6 sandwiches

Note: If desired, omit 1 package cream cheese and use the sauerkraut alone as the bottom layer. Spread the bottom slice of bread with a favorite seasoned butter or spread.

Chicken Fiesta Buns

This spicy chicken sandwich has a south-of-the-border flavor plus protein, niacin, and iron.

3 **tablespoons butter or margarine**
⅓ **cup finely chopped green pepper**
⅓ **cup finely chopped celery**
⅓ **cup finely chopped onion**
1 **clove garlic, minced**
½ **cup tomato paste**
2 **tablespoons Worcestershire sauce**
2 **tablespoons cider vinegar**
1 **tablespoon brown sugar**
½ **teaspoon chili powder**
½ **teaspoon salt**
¼ **teaspoon seasoned pepper**
1½ **cups chopped cooked chicken or turkey**
¼ **cup chopped pimiento-stuffed olives**
8 **enriched frankfurter buns, split and heated**

1. Heat butter in a skillet and add green pepper, celery, onion, and garlic; cook about 3 minutes.
2. Mix tomato paste, Worcestershire sauce, vinegar, brown sugar, chili powder, salt, and seasoned pepper. Add to skillet along with chicken and olives; stir well. Bring to boiling, reduce heat, and simmer about 10 minutes to blend flavors, stirring occasionally.
3. To serve, spoon hot chicken mixture into buns.

8 servings

Onion-Liver Sausage on Rye

This zesty combination containing blue cheese and onions gives you protein, vitamins A and D, riboflavin, and iron.

¼ cup lemon juice
1½ teaspoons sugar
1 red onion, cut in 4 slices
8 slices rye bread
  Whipped butter
2 ounces blue cheese, softened
4 ounces liver sausage

1. Blend lemon juice and sugar in a bowl. Add onion slices and allow to marinate 30 minutes, carefully turning onion slices from time to time. Drain.
2. Spread each slice of bread with butter. Spread buttered sides of 4 bread slices with liver sausage and put onion slice over sausage. Spread other 4 bread slices with blue cheese, and put these, cheese side down, over the first bread slices. Cut each sandwich diagonally into halves.

4 sandwiches

Note: For an appetizer, chop onion before marinating. Use small rye bread rounds (about 1½ inches in diameter). Toast on one side; turn and brush with melted butter. Toast in oven until crisp. Spread with blue cheese, then liver sausage; top with a spoonful of marinated chopped onion.

French Toast Triple Decker

This recipe could be the basis for an unforgettable Sunday brunch. It's definitely a basic ingredient for good nutrition, providing protein, vitamins A and D, the B vitamins, calcium, and iron.

3 eggs
1 cup milk or cream
1 tablespoon sugar
¼ teaspoon salt
2 to 3 tablespoons butter or margarine

1. To prepare French toast, beat eggs slightly in a shallow dish. Blend in milk, sugar, and salt.
2. Heat butter in a large skillet.
3. Dip bread slices, one at a time, into the egg mixture, turning to coat each side well.

12 slices enriched white bread,
    cut about ¼ inch thick
1 tablespoon dry mustard
2 tablespoons cold water
4 slices cooked ham
4 slices cooked chicken
4 slices Swiss cheese
4 slices tomato
    Ripe olives
    Fresh parsley, finely
    snipped
    Bacon curls

Put into the hot skillet and lightly brown on one side; turn with spatula to brown other side. If necessary, add more butter to keep slices from sticking.

4. Blend dry mustard with water and set aside.

5. To assemble sandwiches, put 4 French toast slices on a flat surface. Cover each with a slice of ham and brush generously with some of the mustard mixture. Add a chicken slice and brush with mustard; then another slice of toast, a slice of Swiss cheese, and a third slice of toast; finally a tomato slice. Garnish with olives, parsley, and bacon.

4 sandwiches

Note: If desired, the coated bread slices may be placed on a well-greased cookie sheet and browned in a 450°F oven 8 to 10 minutes.

Egg Salad Sandwiches with Bacon Flavor

Bacon and eggs, an unbeatable combination, make an unbeatable sandwich too. Spread on this bacon-flavored egg salad and gain protein, vitamins A and D, thiamine, riboflavin, calcium, and iron.

4 hard-cooked eggs, chopped
    Seasoned pepper
3 to 4 tablespoons mayonnaise
8 slices enriched white bread,
    buttered
    Baconlike pieces (a soy
    protein product)

1. Sprinkle eggs lightly with seasoned pepper and moisten with mayonnaise.

2. Spread egg mixture on buttered bread and top with desired amount of baconlike pieces. Close sandwiches.

4 sandwiches

Hearty Sardine Sandwiches

If this sounds like a full-course dinner, that's because it comes about as close to a complete meal as a sandwich can, providing protein, vitamins A and D, calcium, and iron.

1 package (3 ounces) cream cheese, softened
2 tablespoons mayonnaise
1 tablespoon prepared mustard
1 tablespoon pasteurized process cheese spread
1 teaspoon chopped capers
½ teaspoon lemon juice
2 drops Tabasco
  Few grains turmeric
5 tablespoons butter or margarine
1 clove garlic, crushed in a garlic press or minced
2 diagonally cut pieces enriched French bread (8 inches each)
2 cans (3¾ ounces each) sardines, drained
6 thin slices Bermuda onion
6 tomato slices

1. Blend cream cheese, mayonnaise, prepared mustard, cheese spread, capers, lemon juice, Tabasco, and turmeric thoroughly; set aside.
2. Cream butter and garlic together. Cut bread in half horizontally and toast the cut sides. Spread with garlic butter, then with the cream cheese mixture. Top each bottom piece with half the sardines, onion, and tomatoes. Close sandwiches.
3. Cut each sandwich diagonally in half and secure each piece with a pick.

4 sandwiches

Super Sandwich Loaf

This is a great party-type sandwich. Try it and you'll see how much fun protein, vitamin A, thiamine, calcium, and iron can be!

1 loaf (1 pound) enriched French bread
½ cup butter or margarine
1 cup (about 4 ounces) shredded sharp Cheddar cheese

1. Cut loaf of bread into 1½-inch slices almost through to bottom. Using a sharp-pointed knife, remove alternate slices, leaving ¼ inch of the crust at bottom of loaf. Store alternate slices for other use.
2. Blend butter and cheese; mix in dry mus-

½ teaspoon dry mustard
2 tablespoons ketchup
¼ cup finely chopped onion
2 tablespoons chopped parsley
1 teaspoon prepared horseradish
8 slices salami
8 slices mozzarella cheese
8 thin lengthwise slices dill pickle
8 thin green pepper rings
8 thin slices cooked ham

tard, ketchup, onion, parsley, and horseradish.

3. Place loaf on a large piece of aluminum foil or a cookie sheet. Spread cheese mixture generously over the surface of each cutout section.

4. Arrange vertically in each cavity: one slice salami, folded in half, one slice mozzarella cheese, one slice pickle, one green pepper ring, and one slice ham, folded in thirds.

5. Set loaf in a 400°F oven about 10 minutes.

6. To serve, use a very sharp knife to divide the 1½-inch slices of bread in half, cutting through bottom crust to separate each sandwich.

8 servings

Yard-Long Sandwich

Here's a variation of the Super Sandwich Loaf that provides protein and the B vitamins. Serve both sandwiches and you will have an extra big, nutritious party.

1 loaf (1 pound) enriched French bread
⅓ cup butter or margarine, softened
2 tablespoons chopped parsley
1 teaspoon prepared mustard
2 teaspoons prepared horseradish
8 slices bologna
8 slices pasteurized process American cheese
2 medium tomatoes, sliced
3 small dill pickles, sliced lengthwise

1. Cut loaf of bread into 1½-inch slices almost through to bottom. Using a sharp-pointed knife, remove alternate slices, leaving ¼ inch of the crust at bottom of loaf. Store alternate slices for other use.

2. Blend butter, parsley, prepared mustard, and horseradish. Spread mixture over surfaces of each cutout section.

3. Arrange vertically in each cavity: one slice bologna, rolled, one slice cheese, folded in half, one slice tomato, and one slice dill pickle. Place loaf on a long piece of heavy-duty aluminum foil or a cookie sheet.

4. Set loaf in a 400°F oven about 10 minutes.

5. To serve, use a very sharp knife to divide slices of bread in half, cutting through bottom crust to separate each sandwich.

8 servings

Pickle-Baked Bean Sandwich Filling

Serve this one either hot or cold on rye bread. It's a good way to enjoy protein, niacin, thiamine, and iron.

1 can (14 to 17 ounces) pork and beans with tomato sauce
¼ cup chili sauce
⅔ cup chopped sweet pickles
2 tablespoons chopped onion
¼ cup prepared baconlike pieces (a soy protein product)

1. Mix pork and beans, chili sauce, chopped pickles, onion, and baconlike pieces.
2. Serve filling hot or cold.

About 3 cups filling

Favorite Salmon Sandwich Filling

Whole wheat bread enhances the combined flavors in this tasty sandwich. It's a quickie to make, yet it's full of protein, riboflavin, niacin, vitamins C and D, and calcium.

¾ cup flaked canned salmon
½ cup finely chopped cabbage
3 tablespoons chopped ripe olives
1 tablespoon olive liquid
¼ teaspoon paprika
2 or 3 drops Tabasco
3 tablespoons mayonnaise or salad dressing

Put salmon, cabbage, and ripe olives into a bowl. Add olive liquid, paprika, Tabasco, and mayonnaise; mix well.

About 1½ cups filling

Cream Cheese-Peanut Sandwich Filling

Especially good on whole wheat or rye bread, this creamy crunchy spread provides protein, vitamin A, niacin, riboflavin, thiamine, and iron.

1 package (8 ounces) cream cheese, softened

Combine cream cheese, milk, onion, Tabasco, and Worcestershire sauce in a small bowl.

2 to 3 tablespoons milk or cream

¼ teaspoon instant minced onion

2 or 3 drops Tabasco

¼ teaspoon Worcestershire sauce

¼ cup Spanish peanuts, chopped

¼ cup chopped pimiento-stuffed olives

Beat with an electric beater until the consistency of whipped cream, adding more milk, if necessary. Stir in peanuts and olives.

About 1½ cups filling

Note: If desired, substitute ¼ cup chopped ripe olives for the stuffed olives and mix in 2 to 4 tablespoons flaked coconut.

Sardine-Cucumber Sandwich Filling

Spread this one on thinly sliced enriched white bread and you'll be treating yourself to protein, niacin, vitamin D, calcium, and iron.

1 package (3 ounces) cream cheese, softened

1 tablespoon mayonnaise

2 teaspoons lemon juice

6 drops Tabasco

3 tablespoons finely chopped onion

1 tablespoon minced chives

8 to 10 sardines (3¾-ounce can), drained and mashed

½ cup finely chopped cucumber, well drained

Blend cream cheese, mayonnaise, lemon juice, Tabasco, onion, and chives. Mix in sardines and cucumber. Chill thoroughly.

About 1¼ cups filling

Fruit-Cottage Cheese Sandwich Filling

Served on whole wheat bread, this different sandwich gives you protein, vitamin A, niacin, riboflavin, calcium, and iron.

1 cup creamed cottage cheese

¼ cup pitted dates, finely snipped

¼ cup raisins, finely snipped

⅛ teaspoon salt

Combine cottage cheese, dates, raisins, and salt in a bowl; mix well. Chill thoroughly. Stir before using.

About 1½ cups filling

Sauerkraut-Sausage Pizza

Here's an entirely different variation on the pizza theme, and it's bound to be a hit. It scores nutritionally too, providing protein, vitamin C, calcium, and some B vitamins.

1 **package hot roll mix**
Olive oil
½ **pound sweet Italian sausage**
½ **cup chopped onion**
¼ **teaspoon basil leaves, crushed**
2 **cans (8 ounces each) tomato sauce with onions**
2 **cups drained sauerkraut**
6 **green pepper rings**
8 **ounces mozzarella cheese, sliced**
¼ **cup shredded Parmesan cheese**

1. Prepare hot roll mix following package directions for pizza dough. Divide dough into two equal portions and form each into a ball. Place one ball in center of a 12-inch pizza pan; freeze second ball for later use, or see note.

2. Push dough down in center with hand and spread dough with fingers to cover bottom of pan. Shape edge by pressing dough between thumb and forefinger to make a ridge. Brush lightly with oil and set aside.

3. Cut half of sausage into about 12 slices; dice remaining half. Turn sausage and onion into a skillet and cook until meat is browned, spooning off excess fat as it accumulates. Remove the cooked sliced sausage from skillet and transfer to absorbent paper; set aside.

4. Add basil to skillet and blend. Stir in tomato sauce and kraut. Cook, stirring occasionally, until mixture is thoroughly heated.

5. Remove from heat and turn kraut mixture onto pizza dough, spreading evenly to cover entire surface. Arrange the sliced cooked sausage, green pepper rings, and mozzarella cheese over kraut mixture. Sprinkle with Parmesan cheese.

6. Bake at 450°F 15 to 20 minutes, or until cheese is melted and crust is browned. Cut into wedges and serve hot.

One 12-inch pizza

Note: If desired, prepare 2 pizzas, doubling the filling ingredients.

Tomato and Cheese Pizza / Mushroom Pizza

You'll be amazed at the really authentic-tasting pizza you can make at home with a minimum of effort. This recipe gives you protein, vitamins A and C, and calcium.

1 package active dry yeast
¾ cup warm water
2½ cups all-purpose biscuit mix
1 can (28 ounces) Italian style tomatoes, drained and sieved
1 can (6 ounces) tomato paste
8 ounces mozzarella cheese, thinly sliced
½ cup olive oil
¼ cup shredded Parmesan cheese
2 teaspoons oregano
1 teaspoon salt
½ teaspoon ground black pepper

1. Soften yeast in warm water. Add biscuit mix; beat until well mixed. Turn onto a lightly floured surface. Knead until smooth (about 20 times).

2. Divide dough into halves. Roll each half into a 15-inch round. Put each round of dough onto an ungreased large cookie sheet; shape edge by pressing dough between thumb and forefinger to make ridge.

3. Combine sieved tomatoes and tomato paste. Spread half of mixture over each round of dough; top each with half of mozzarella cheese. Sprinkle half of olive oil, Parmesan cheese, oregano, salt, and pepper over each round.

4. Bake at 425°F 15 to 20 minutes, or until crust is browned. To serve, cut in wedges.

2 large pizzas

Mushroom Pizza: Follow recipe for Tomato and Cheese Pizza. Before baking, top each pizza with **1 cup (8-ounce can) drained mushrooms.**

Nibblers

Keep this easy mixture on hand for unexpected occasions. Protein, niacin, ribo-flavin, thiamine, and iron are the nutritional benefits.

½ **cup butter or margarine**
3 **cups ready-to-eat crisp oat cereal**
2 **cups ready-to-eat bite-size shredded rice biscuits**
1½ **cups stick pretzels**
1 **cup salted peanuts or other nuts**
¾ **teaspoon Worcestershire sauce**
¾ **teaspoon salt**
¾ **teaspoon garlic salt**

1. Put butter into a small saucepan and set over low heat to melt.
2. Meanwhile, mix oat cereal, shredded rice biscuits, pretzels, and peanuts in a large bowl.
3. Mix Worcestershire sauce, salt, and garlic salt with butter and pour over cereal mixture; toss lightly to coat evenly. Turn into a 15 x 10 x 1-inch jelly-roll pan and spread evenly.
4. Set in a 250°F oven 2 hours, stirring mixture occasionally with a spoon.
5. Cool. Serve as a snack. Store in a tightly covered container.

About 2 quarts nibblers

Pickled Biscuit Roll with Vegetable-Cheese Spread

This hot biscuit roll with a creamy vegetable spread makes a wonderful hot snack or appetizer, and it is loaded with vitamin A.

Pickled Biscuit Roll:
4 **cups all-purpose biscuit mix**
1 **cup cold water**
1 **cup drained sweet pickle relish**

Vegetable-Cheese Spread:
1 **package (8 ounces) cream cheese, softened**
1½ **teaspoons grated lemon peel**
¼ **teaspoon salt**

1. Using biscuit mix and water, prepare biscuit dough, following directions on package. Divide dough in half. Roll one half into a rectangle, about 14 x 11 inches. Spread dough evenly with ½ cup relish. Roll up lengthwise, beginning at one end; press long edge to seal, and put sealed edge down, at one side of a large ungreased cookie sheet. Repeat procedure with remaining dough and relish.

⅛ teaspoon seasoned pepper
2 tablespoons milk
½ cup finely shredded carrot
⅓ cup chopped green pepper
¼ cup thinly sliced green onion with tops

2. Bake at 450°F about 15 minutes.
3. Meanwhile, prepare Vegetable-Cheese Spread. Put cream cheese into a bowl. Add lemon peel, salt, seasoned pepper, and milk; mix well. Stir in carrot, green pepper, and green onion.
4. Remove baked rolls from oven to wire rack and cool on cookie sheet about 10 minutes. Immediately transfer to a cutting board, cut diagonally into ¾-inch slices, and serve warm. Accompany with a bowl of Vegetable-Cheese Spread.

2 biscuit rolls; 1½ cups spread

Hot Mushroom Appetizers

Two distinctive flavors combine here to make a memorable hot appetizer which provides protein, vitamin A, niacin, riboflavin, thiamine, and iron.

1 pound large mushrooms
3 tablespoons butter or margarine
½ teaspoon fresh onion juice
½ pound chicken livers
1 cup crushed wheat wafers
½ cup strong chicken broth (1 chicken bouillon cube dissolved in ½ cup boiling water)
½ teaspoon salt
⅛ teaspoon tarragon leaves, crushed
Butter or margarine, melted
Garlic powder
Hard-cooked egg yolk, sieved

1. Remove stems from mushrooms and chop them. Set caps aside.
2. Heat butter in a skillet. Combine chopped mushroom stems with onion juice and chicken livers; cook in heated butter 10 minutes, stirring occasionally. Remove livers; chop and return to skillet with crushed wheat wafers, chicken broth, salt, and tarragon. Blend thoroughly.
3. Brush mushroom caps generously, inside and out, with butter and sprinkle lightly with garlic powder. Fill caps with the chicken-liver mixture. Place in a shallow baking pan.
4. Bake at 375°F 20 minutes. Garnish with sieved egg yolk. Serve hot.

About 1½ dozen appetizers

Cheddar-Stuffed Celery

Here's another one-handed appetizer—the kind you'll particularly want to serve a stand-up crowd—and it delivers protein, vitamin A, and calcium.

1 teaspoon dry mustard
6 tablespoons cream
2 tablespoons dairy sour cream
1 tablespoon minced onion
½ teaspoon Worcestershire sauce
¼ teaspoon seasoned salt
1 small clove garlic, crushed in a garlic press
2 cups (8 ounces) shredded very sharp Cheddar cheese
  Crisp celery, cut in diagonal lengths, rinsed, dried, and chilled

1. Measure dry mustard into a bowl and gradually add cream, stirring until mustard is diluted. Blend in sour cream, onion, Worcestershire sauce, seasoned salt, and garlic. Using an electric hand mixer, add cheese gradually, beating until blended.
2. Stuff celery lengths.

About 1½ cups cheese stuffing for celery

Note: Mixture may be used as an appetizer spread for crackers and toasted cocktail rye bread slices. Or, thin with additional cream or sour cream for a cheese dip.

Nutty Popcorn Cups

If you prefer tiny treats, shape these delicious balls in small muffin-pan wells. Either way they provide protein, niacin, riboflavin, thiamine, and iron.

1½ quarts unsalted popped popcorn
1 cup dry-roasted peanuts
½ cup golden raisins
½ cup sugar
½ cup light corn syrup
½ cup creamy peanut butter
½ teaspoon vanilla extract

1. Combine popcorn, peanuts, and raisins in a large bowl.
2. Combine sugar and corn syrup in a heavy 1½-quart saucepan. Bring to a full boil, stirring constantly. Remove from heat and blend in peanut butter and vanilla extract. Pour syrup evenly over popcorn mixture and quickly toss lightly to coat evenly.
3. Press into well-buttered muffin-pan wells, 2½ x 1¼ inches. Let stand until firm.
4. Serve in paper baking cups, if desired.

About 1½ dozen popcorn cups

Cranberry-Cucumber Cups

A perfect summer appetizer, this one is sure to awaken sleeping taste buds. It's loaded with vitamin C.

36 scored unpared cucumber slices, about ½ inch thick
Seasoned salt
1 envelope unflavored gelatin
1 cup cranberry juice cocktail
¾ cup water
1 teaspoon instant chicken bouillon
1 tablespoon lemon juice
1 teaspoon prepared horseradish
6 drops Tabasco
⅛ teaspoon dill weed

1. Scoop out the cucumber slices, leaving a thin layer on bottom. Invert onto absorbent paper to drain. Sprinkle seasoned salt on the inside of each cup; chill.

2. Soften gelatin in ½ cup cranberry juice; set aside.

3. Combine the remaining cranberry juice, water, bouillon, lemon juice, horseradish, Tabasco, and dill weed in a small saucepan. Bring to boiling, stirring until bouillon is dissolved; reduce heat and simmer about 2 minutes. Immediately stir softened gelatin into hot liquid until gelatin is completely dissolved.

4. Strain through a double thickness of clean cheesecloth; cool. If desired, add a few drops of red food coloring to tint gelatin mixture the desired shade of red.

5. Pour into a lightly oiled 8-inch square pan. Chill until firm.

6. Cut gelatin into tiny cubes. Fill cucumber cups with cubes and garnish with tiny lemon wedges.

3 dozen appetizers

Note: If desired, substitute ⅛ teaspoon tarragon leaves, crushed, for the dill weed.

Mandarin Orange-Avocado Appetizer

This lush and easy-to-prepare appetizer is high in vitamins A and C, as well as exotic good taste.

1 cup dairy sour cream
¼ cup grapefruit juice
½ teaspoon ground ginger
¼ teaspoon tarragon
   leaves, crushed
¼ teaspoon salt
1 teaspoon cider vinegar
¼ teaspoon Tabasco
   Lettuce leaves
2 ripe small avocados,
   halved
1 can (11 ounces) mandarin
   orange segments, drained
   and chilled

1. Mix sour cream, grapefruit juice, ginger, tarragon, salt, vinegar, and Tabasco in a bowl. Chill at least 1 hour to allow flavors to blend.
2. To serve, line small plates with lettuce and put an avocado half on each. Mix mandarin orange segments lightly into sour cream mixture. Spoon into avocado halves.

4 servings

Apricot-Nut Chews

Easy and delicious, these chewy treats are a combination of dried fruits and nuts that add niacin, calcium, and iron to your diet.

1 cup dried apricots
1 cup pitted dates or dried
   figs (stems removed)
1 cup raisins
½ cup almonds or walnuts,
   chopped
½ cup maple-blended syrup
⅛ teaspoon salt
   Coconut, flaked or finely
   chopped
   Finely chopped nuts

1. Put apricots and dates through coarse blade of food chopper. Mix and grind once more. Put into top of double boiler with raisins, almonds, syrup, and salt. Cook over boiling water until fruit softens slightly. Stir until well blended. Set aside to cool.
2. Shape mixture into balls, about 1¼ inches in diameter. Roll some in coconut and some in nuts.
3. To store, wrap in waxed paper and keep in a cool place.

About 2 dozen balls

Carrot-Cottage Cheese Dip

This nutritious appetizer dip tastes great and will be especially appreciated by the weight watchers among your guests.

¾ cup creamed cottage cheese
3 tablespoons mayonnaise
½ teaspoon salt
⅛ to ¼ teaspoon pepper
2 to 3 teaspoons caraway seed
2 medium carrots, pared and finely shredded
3 radishes, finely chopped
3 cups fresh cauliflower or broccoli flowerets, chilled

1. Sieve cottage cheese into a bowl. Mix in mayonnaise, salt, pepper, caraway seed, carrots, and radishes. Turn into a small serving dish and chill.
2. Serve the dip in the center of a platter with cauliflower or broccoli flowerets around the edge.

About 1¼ cups dip

Crunchy Honey Granola

Here's a chance to test your creativity while providing protein, niacin, riboflavin, thiamine, calcium, and iron. It can be served as a snack with snipped dried apricots, or as a cereal with milk; the mixture can be sprinkled on peanut butter sandwiches or on top of yogurt, pudding, or ice cream.

2 cups uncooked old-fashioned oats
1 cup toasted wheat germ
½ cup almonds or filberts, chopped
2 tablespoons sesame seed
¼ cup vegetable oil
½ cup honey

1. Put oats, wheat germ, almonds, sesame seed, oil, and honey into a bowl. Stir until well mixed. Turn into a 15 x 10 x 1-inch jelly-roll pan and spread evenly.
2. Bake at 275°F 1¼ to 1½ hours, stirring occasionally.
3. Remove from oven and while still hot turn into a bowl. Cool completely. Break into pieces. Store in a tightly covered container.

About 3½ cups granola

Rumaki

Skewered and wrapped in bite-size portions, these broiled beauties are another crowd-pleaser. Let your guests enjoy the taste and don't bother to mention the protein, vitamin A, niacin, riboflavin, thiamine, and iron they contain.

½ **pound chicken livers**
1½ **tablespoons honey**
1 **tablespoon soy sauce**
2 **tablespoons vegetable oil**
½ **clove garlic, crushed in a garlic press**
1 **can (5 ounces) water chestnuts, drained and cut in quarters**
Bacon slices, cut in halves or thirds

1. Rinse chicken livers with running cold water and drain on absorbent paper; cut into halves and put into a bowl.
2. Pour a mixture of honey, soy sauce, oil, and garlic over the liver pieces. Cover. Let stand about 30 minutes, turning pieces occasionally. Remove from marinade and set aside on absorbent paper to drain.
3. Wrap a piece of bacon around a twosome of liver and water chestnut pieces, threading each onto a wooden pick or small skewer.
4. Put appetizers on rack in broiler pan with top of appetizers about 3 inches from heat and broil about 5 minutes. Turn with tongs and broil until bacon is browned. Serve hot.

About 1½ dozen appetizers

Spinach Crescents

Hot appetizers such as this are as popular at cocktail parties as they are with the after-school set. Whoever you serve them to will be getting vitamin A and iron.

1 **package refrigerated fresh dough for crescent rolls**
Italian salad dressing
Grated Parmesan-Romano cheese
1 **cup finely snipped fresh spinach**
5 **tablespoons prepared baconlike pieces (a soy protein product)**

1. Divide roll dough into triangles; cut each lengthwise in half. Brush dough with Italian salad dressing. Sprinkle with grated cheese. Mix spinach and baconlike pieces; spoon over triangles and press into dough. Roll up and place on a cookie sheet, curving to form crescents.
2. Bake at 375°F 10 to 15 minutes.

16 rolls

Tiny Tomato Toppers

Bite-size appetizers are easy to serve when you have a crowd. These will be a special favorite because they have good taste plus vitamins A, C, and calcium.

  1 package (3 ounces) cream cheese, softened
⅓ cup minced cooked chicken
¼ cup finely chopped walnuts
1½ tablespoons finely chopped apple
1½ teaspoons lemon juice
½ teaspoon Worcestershire sauce
½ teaspoon grated onion
 18 cherry tomatoes, rinsed and cut in halves

1. Beat cream cheese in a bowl until fluffy. Add chicken, walnuts, apple, lemon juice, Worcestershire sauce, and onion; mix thoroughly.
2. Spoon about ½ teaspoon of the chicken mixture onto each tomato half. Chill.

3 dozen appetizers

Shrimp Cocktail Seviche Style

Do-aheads are easy on the cook, and this shrimp cocktail must be made at least eight hours before serving to allow the flavors to mix and mingle. The shrimp gives you protein, calcium, and iron.

1½ pounds cooked shrimp, shelled, deveined, and chilled
  1 firm ripe tomato, peeled and diced
¼ cup thinly sliced green onions with tops
¼ cup thinly sliced celery
½ cup lime juice
1½ teaspoons salt
  2 to 3 teaspoons soy sauce
¼ teaspoon Worcestershire sauce
½ clove garlic, minced
 Leaf lettuce

1. Dice chilled shrimp into a bowl and combine with tomato, green onion, celery, lime juice, salt, soy sauce, Worcestershire sauce, and garlic; toss lightly to mix well. Chill, covered, about 8 hours, or overnight.
2. Serve very cold on cocktail sea shells lined with leaf lettuce.

6 servings

Sweet-Tart Meatball Appetizer

Don't be surprised when this one draws a crowd around the buffet, for these saucy meatballs are delicious as well as nutritious. Count on protein, vitamins A and C, niacin, riboflavin, calcium, and iron.

Meatballs:

1½ **pounds ground beef**

1½ **tablespoons instant minced onion**

2 **teaspoons Worcestershire sauce**

1 **egg**

⅓ **cup fine dry enriched bread crumbs**

1 **teaspoon salt**

¼ **teaspoon ground black pepper**

Sauce:

2 **cups water**

1 **can (6 ounces) tomato paste**

1 **medium onion, cut in pieces**

1 **medium carrot, cut in pieces**

1 **medium tart apple, cut in pieces**

½ **cup apricot preserves**

¼ **cup firmly packed brown sugar**

1 **teaspoon salt**

1 **teaspoon lemon juice**

1 **teaspoon instant beef bouillon**

1. For meatballs, combine beef, instant minced onion, Worcestershire sauce, egg, bread crumbs, salt, and pepper in a bowl. Mix lightly with a fork until well blended. Shape into balls about 1 inch in diameter. Put in a single layer in a shallow 3-quart baking dish.

2. For sauce, combine water, tomato paste, onion, carrot, apple, apricot preserves, brown sugar, salt, lemon juice, and bouillon in an electric blender; purée. Pour mixture over meatballs. Cover tightly with aluminum foil.

3. Bake at 325°F 45 minutes. Serve warm.

About 3½ dozen appetizers

Meat

In most homes a meat dish, whether it's a flavorful meat loaf, a classic crown roast of lamb, or an exotic curry, is the main attraction at dinner. Nutritionally speaking, meat well deserves to be the center of attention at mealtime, as it is one of the most important sources of protein and iron in our diets. Thiamine, riboflavin, and niacin are also found in meats. Numerous meat dishes achieve their special character in combination with fruits or vegetables, which are valuable sources of additional nutrients, especially vitamins. Lima beans and dried fruits, often combined with lamb or pork, are noted for the small but significant amounts of iron they contain.

With the following recipes, even everyday suppers can be exciting and healthful eating adventures. Many of the recipes take traditional stand-bys such as ground beef, pork chops, or spareribs, and dress them up with a fruity sauce or herbs and vegetables. *Fresh Pear and Pork Chop Skillet* or *Parsleyed Oven Pot Roast* are two such dishes you'll love to serve. Working people will appreciate the many quickly prepared meat dishes in this section. Mix up tarragon and white wine in the morning, and you can serve delicious *Veal Glacé* in less than thirty minutes at night. Or bring a touch of Greece to your table with *Topnotch Lamb Bake*, a quick-to-make blend of lamb, cheese, eggplant, tomato, and allspice. Do-aheads, too, are real time-savers. Meat cubes can be marinated ahead of time for broiled shish kabobs, or a luscious stew can be prepared on a lazy Sunday afternoon for easy reheating on those busy week nights.

Meat purchases are likely to take a sizeable portion of the weekly food budget, and preparing healthful but economical meals is the concern of every cook. Look for economical cuts of meat when you shop, and take advantage of special bargains. Don't forget variety meats, either. Liver, for instance, is less expensive than many meats and can't be beaten for its vitamin A and iron content. You'll find in these recipes many ideas for creative use of a variety of meat cuts. *Oxtail Stew*, *Lamb Kidney Kabobs*, and *Polynesian Supper*, made with ground beef, are only a few of them. Meat can be stretched to fit your budget and feed a small crowd when you make a one-pot meal with meat and beans or rice, such as *Short Ribs, Western Style*.

Whether it's dinner for two or for ten, prepare one of these nutrition-packed meat dishes soon!

Oxtail Stew

Make a generous amount of this dish, for your family will be almost sure to ask for seconds. You'll be giving them vegetable and meat protein combined, plus vitamins A and C, and calcium.

½ cup enriched all-purpose flour
1 teaspoon salt
¼ teaspoon ground black pepper
3 oxtails (about 1 pound each), disjointed
3 tablespoons butter or margarine
1½ cups chopped onion
1 can (28 ounces) tomatoes, drained (reserve liquid)
1½ cups hot water
4 medium potatoes, pared
6 medium carrots, pared
2 pounds fresh peas, shelled
1 tablespoon paprika
1 teaspoon salt
¼ teaspoon ground black pepper
¼ cup cold water
2 tablespoons flour

1. Mix ½ cup flour, 1 teaspoon salt, and ¼ teaspoon pepper in a plastic bag; coat oxtail pieces evenly by shaking two or three at a time.

2. Heat butter in a 3-quart top-of-range casserole. Add onion and cook until soft. Remove onion with a slotted spoon and set aside.

3. Put meat into casserole and brown on all sides. Return onion to casserole. Pour in the reserved tomato liquid (set tomatoes aside) and hot water. Cover tightly and simmer 2½ to 3 hours, or until meat is almost tender when pierced with a fork.

4. When meat has cooked about 2 hours, cut potatoes and carrots into small balls, using a melon-ball cutter. Cut the tomatoes into pieces.

5. When meat is almost tender, mix in potatoes, carrots, peas, paprika, 1 teaspoon salt, and ¼ teaspoon pepper. Cover and simmer 20 minutes. Stir in tomatoes and cook 10 minutes, or until meat and vegetables are tender. Put meat and vegetables into a warm dish.

6. Blend cold water and 2 tablespoons flour; add half gradually to cooking liquid, stirring constantly. Bring to boiling; gradually add only what is needed of remaining flour mixture for desired gravy consistency. Bring to boiling after each addition. Cook 3 to 5 minutes after final addition. Return meat and vegetables to casserole and heat thoroughly.

6 to 8 servings

Short Ribs, Western Style

Simmer up a batch of short ribs with lima beans, spicy and loaded with protein, B vitamins, and iron.

4 **medium onions, peeled and quartered**
2 **teaspoons salt**
¼ **teaspoon ground black pepper**
½ **teaspoon rubbed sage**
1 **quart water**
1 **cup dried lima beans**
3 **tablespoons flour**
1 **teaspoon dry mustard**
2 **to 3 tablespoons fat**
2 **pounds beef rib short ribs, cut in serving-size pieces**

1. Combine onions, salt, pepper, sage, and water in a large heavy saucepot or Dutch oven. Cover, bring to boiling, reduce heat, and simmer 5 minutes. Bring to boiling again; add lima beans gradually and cook, uncovered, 2 minutes. Remove from heat, cover, and set aside to soak 1 hour.
2. Meanwhile, mix flour and dry mustard and coat short ribs evenly.
3. Heat fat in a large heavy skillet and brown short ribs on all sides over medium heat. Add meat to soaked lima beans. Bring to boiling and simmer, covered, 1½ hours, or until beans and meat are tender.

About 6 servings

London Broil

A classic meat dish that they probably never heard of in London (ever try to get a hamburger in Hamburg?), the London Broil is simplicity itself and gives you protein, niacin, riboflavin, and iron.

1 **beef flank steak (about 2½ pounds)**
Salt and pepper
3 **tablespoons butter or margarine**
2 **teaspoons bottled exotic sauce**

1. Place flank steak on broiler rack and broil about 3 inches from heat 2 to 3 minutes on each side. Season with salt and pepper before turning the steak.
2. Meanwhile, brown butter in a skillet, add exotic sauce, and blend thoroughly.
3. Brush both sides of steak with sauce; place on a heated platter. To serve, cut steak diagonally across grain into very thin slices.

6 to 8 servings

Liver and Onions

Here's a variation of a classic which will appeal to liver fanciers everywhere. In addition to the good nutrients that liver provides, onions contribute small amounts of vitamins and minerals.

1 **medium onion, thinly sliced**
½ **cup beef broth**
½ **teaspoon Worcestershire sauce**
¼ **teaspoon caraway seed**
1 **pound sliced calf's or beef liver (4 slices ½ inch thick)**

1. Put onion, broth, Worcestershire sauce, and caraway seed into a skillet. Bring to boiling, reduce heat, and simmer, covered, until onion is just tender; stir occasionally.
2. Meanwhile, if necessary, remove tubes and outer membrane from liver slices.
3. Remove onion from broth with a slotted spoon and reserve. Add liver to broth and simmer about 2 minutes. Turn slices and spoon onion over top. Continue cooking about 2 minutes, or until liver is just tender.

4 servings

Company Beef and Peaches

Here's a tasty dish fit for any company. And if your guests knew you were giving them protein, vitamin A, niacin, riboflavin, and iron, they'd probably be pleased about that, too!

1 **can (8 ounces) tomato sauce with onions**
1 **can (8 ounces) sliced peaches, drained; reserve syrup**
¾ **cup beef broth**
2 **tablespoons brown sugar**
2 **tablespoons lemon juice**
1 **tablespoon prepared mustard**
1 **teaspoon Worcestershire sauce**
1 **clove garlic, minced**

1. Turn the tomato sauce with onions into a bowl. Mix in the peach syrup (set peaches aside), beef broth, brown sugar, lemon juice, prepared mustard, Worcestershire sauce, and garlic. Set aside.
2. Cut meat across the grain into 6 to 8 slices, about ¾ inch thick.
3. Heat oil in a large skillet. Add the meat slices and brown on both sides. Sprinkle with salt and seasoned pepper. Pour the sauce mixture over the meat. Bring to boiling, reduce heat, and simmer, covered, about 1½ hours, or until meat is fork-tender; turn meat

1 beef round bottom round
roast or eye round roast,
boneless (2 to 3 pounds)
Vegetable oil
Salt and seasoned pepper
2 tablespoons cold water
2 teaspoons cornstarch
Watercress or parsley

slices occasionally.

4. Overlap meat slices to one side of a heated serving platter.

5. Blend water and cornstarch; stir into sauce in skillet. Bring to boiling; cook about 1 minute. Mix in sliced peaches and heat thoroughly; spoon to the side of meat on the platter. Cover meat with sauce. Garnish with watercress.

6 to 8 servings

Italian-Style Meat Stew

Spices, flavorings, and vegetables impart an Italian touch to this delicious lamb-and-beef stew, which provides, protein, niacin, riboflavin, thiamine, and iron.

¼ cup olive oil
1 pound lean beef for stew
(1½-inch cubes)
1 pound lean lamb for stew
(1½-inch cubes)
1 can (28 ounces) tomatoes
(undrained)
1½ cups boiling water
1½ cups chopped onion
1 cup diced celery
2 teaspoons salt
½ teaspoon ground black
pepper
4 large potatoes, pared and
quartered (about 3 cups)
5 large carrots, pared and
cut in strips (about 2 cups)
1 teaspoon basil, crushed
¼ teaspoon garlic powder
½ cup cold water
¼ cup enriched all-purpose
flour

1. Heat oil in a large saucepot or Dutch oven; add meat and brown on all sides.

2. Add undrained tomatoes, boiling water, onion, celery, salt, and pepper to saucepot. Cover and simmer 1 to 1½ hours, or until meat is almost tender.

3. Add potatoes, carrots, basil, and garlic powder to saucepot; mix well. Simmer 45 minutes, or until meat and vegetables are tender when pierced with a fork.

4. Blend cold water and flour; add gradually to meat-and-vegetable mixture, stirring constantly. Bring to boiling and continue to stir and boil 1 to 2 minutes, or until sauce is thickened. (Leftover sauce may be served the following day on mashed potatoes.)

8 to 10 servings

Sauerbraten Moderne

This easy-on-the-cook version of the old German favorite tastes as good as if you'd spent the day preparing it, and supplies protein, niacin, riboflavin, and iron.

1 cup wine vinegar
1 cup water
1 medium onion, thinly sliced
2 tablespoons sugar
1 teaspoon salt
5 peppercorns
3 whole cloves
1 bay leaf
2 pounds beef round steak (¾ inch thick), boneless, cut in cubes
1 lemon, thinly sliced
2 tablespoons butter or margarine
1 can (10¾ ounces) beef gravy
1 can (3 ounces) broiled sliced mushrooms (undrained)
6 gingersnaps, crumbled (about ⅔ cup)
Cooked noodles

1. Combine vinegar, water, onion, sugar, salt, peppercorns, cloves, and bay leaf in a saucepan. Heat just to boiling.
2. Meanwhile, put meat into a large shallow dish and arrange lemon slices over it. Pour hot vinegar mixture into dish. Cover and allow to marinate about 2 hours.
3. Remove and discard peppercorns, cloves, bay leaf, and lemon slices; reserve onion. Drain meat thoroughly, reserving marinade.
4. Heat butter in a skillet over medium heat. Add meat and brown pieces on all sides. Stir 1 cup of the reserved liquid and the onion into skillet. Cover, bring to boiling, reduce heat, and simmer about 45 minutes.
5. Blend beef gravy and mushrooms with liquid into mixture in skillet. Bring to boiling and simmer, loosely covered, about 20 minutes longer, or until meat is tender.
6. Add the crumbled gingersnaps to mixture in skillet and cook, stirring constantly, until gravy is thickened. Serve over noodles.

6 to 8 servings

Blue Ribbon Meatball Stew

This one could easily become a family favorite. It's easy on the cook and heavy on the nutrients, including protein, vitamins A, B, and C, calcium, and iron.

1½ pounds lean ground beef
1 egg, beaten
⅓ cup fine dry enriched bread crumbs

1. Combine meat, egg, bread crumbs, instant minced onion, Worcestershire sauce, salt, and pepper; shape into 16 balls. Arrange in a single layer in a shallow 3-quart baking dish;

1½ tablespoons instant minced onion

1½ tablespoons Worcestershire sauce

1 teaspoon salt

¼ teaspoon ground black pepper

¼ cup enriched all-purpose flour

3 large potatoes, pared and cut in 6 pieces each

4 carrots, pared and cut in 1-inch diagonal slices

1 medium onion, sliced

1 can (16 ounces) tomatoes (undrained)

2 cups beef broth

1 teaspoon vegetable bouquet sauce

sprinkle with flour. Cover with fresh vegetables. Pour tomatoes, broth, and bouquet sauce over all. Cover tightly with aluminum foil.

2. Cook in a 350°F oven 1½ hours, or until vegetables are tender. If necessary, spoon off excess fat before serving.

About 6 servings

Beef Liver with Rice

Wine and spices make this liver dish really special, and of course protein, B vitamins, vitamins A, C, and D, and iron are all there.

2 tablespoons vegetable oil

1 clove garlic, minced

1½ pounds sliced beef liver (½ to ¾ inch thick), cut in strips about 2½ inches

⅓ cup dry white wine

1 can (16 ounces) tomatoes (undrained)

1 teaspoon basil

1 teaspoon salt

¼ teaspoon seasoned pepper

3 cups hot cooked rice

1. Heat oil with garlic in a large skillet. Add the liver strips and brown over medium heat, turning occasionally.

2. Add wine and lower the heat; simmer, uncovered, about 5 minutes.

3. Add tomatoes with liquid, basil, salt, and seasoned pepper. Cover skillet and cook slowly until liver is tender (about 20 minutes). Remove cover the last few minutes of cooking to allow sauce to thicken slightly.

4. Mound the hot rice on a heated serving plate and top with the liver and sauce.

6 servings

Parsleyed Oven Pot Roast

This appealing combination of beef, unusual vegetables, and wine provides protein, vitamins A and C, niacin, riboflavin, calcium, and iron.

1½ teaspoons salt
¼ teaspoon ground black pepper
1 beef round bottom round roast (4½ to 5 pounds)
1 can (28 ounces) tomatoes, cut in pieces
¾ cup dry red wine
¼ cup instant minced onion
½ teaspoon instant minced garlic
2 tablespoons parsley flakes
1 bay leaf
1 teaspoon salt
6 medium carrots, pared and sliced
1½ pounds zucchini squash, sliced
2 cups cherry tomatoes, pricked with fork

1. Rub 1½ teaspoons salt and pepper over surface of meat.
2. Place meat, fat side down, in a heavy ovenproof casserole or Dutch oven. Brown well on all sides in a 450°F oven (about 1 hour). Drain off fat.
3. Combine tomatoes, wine, onion, garlic, parsley flakes, bay leaf, and salt. Pour over meat. Cover; turn oven control to 350°F and cook 2 hours. Mix in carrots and cook 30 minutes, then mix in zucchini and cook 20 minutes. Finally, mix in cherry tomatoes and continue cooking 10 minutes, or until meat and vegetables are tender.
4. Serve meat and vegetables on a heated platter.

8 to 10 servings

Note: If desired, serve pot roast with Old-Fashioned Cauliflower Pickles (page·358) and mashed potatoes topped with freeze-dried chives.

Beef-Corn Casserole

Quick yet tasty, this casserole retains the slight natural sweetness of the corn and is rich in protein, B vitamins, and iron.

1 pound ground beef
1 cup chopped onion
½ cup chopped green pepper
1 can (16 ounces) cream style corn

1. Put meat into a heated skillet, separate with a fork, and cook until meat is no longer pink. Mix in onion and green pepper; cook until tender. Drain off any excess fat. Stir in corn, salt, and pepper.

1 teaspoon salt
⅛ teaspoon ground black pepper
½ cup buttered bread crumbs

2. Turn mixture into a 1-quart casserole. Top with crumbs.
3. Heat in a 350°F oven 25 to 30 minutes.

About 4 servings

Polynesian Supper

Here's an easy-to-bake Polynesian treat your family will really appreciate, and it gives them protein, vitamin A, niacin, riboflavin, vitamin C, calcium, and iron.

1 pound lean ground beef
1 egg, beaten
½ cup fine dry enriched bread crumbs
¼ cup chopped onion
¼ cup water
2 tablespoons prepared mustard
1 teaspoon salt
1 can (8 ounces) unsweetened sliced pineapple
4 tomato slices
4 green pepper rings
⅓ cup firmly packed brown sugar
2 tablespoons flour
½ cup chopped onion
¼ cup cider vinegar
Cooked rice

1. Combine meat, egg, bread crumbs, ¼ cup chopped onion, water, prepared mustard, and salt. Shape into 4 patties.
2. Drain pineapple, reserving juice. Arrange pineapple slices in a shallow 9-inch square casserole; top with patties, tomato slices, and green pepper rings.
3. Blend brown sugar and flour. Stir reserved pineapple juice into sugar mixture. Add ½ cup chopped onion and vinegar; mix well. Pour over contents of casserole; cover casserole tightly with its cover or aluminum foil.
4. Cook in a 350°F oven 30 minutes. Serve on hot fluffy rice.

4 servings

Kidney Bean Rice Olympian

Served over rice and shredded lettuce and topped with chopped onion, this kidney bean and beef combination seems to have a touch of Mexico, and provides protein, niacin, riboflavin, thiamine, iron, and vitamin A.

2 tablespoons olive oil
1½ pounds beef round steak, boneless, cut in 1-inch cubes
2 teaspoons salt
¼ teaspoon ground black pepper
2 large cloves garlic, crushed in a garlic press
2 cups beef broth
1 cup sliced celery
1 can (16 ounces) tomatoes, cut in pieces (undrained)
2 cans (16 ounces each) kidney beans (undrained)
1 large green pepper, diced
3 cups hot cooked rice
1 large head lettuce, finely shredded
3 medium onions, peeled and coarsely chopped

1. Heat olive oil in a large heavy skillet. Add meat and brown on all sides. Add salt, pepper, and garlic; pour in beef broth. Bring to boiling, reduce heat, and simmer, covered, about 1 hour.

2. Stir celery and tomatoes and beans with liquid into beef in skillet; bring to boiling and simmer, covered, 30 minutes. Add green pepper and continue cooking 30 minutes.

3. To serve, spoon rice onto each serving plate, cover generously with shredded lettuce, and spoon a generous portion of the bean mixture over lettuce. Top each serving with about 3 tablespoons chopped onion.

About 8 servings

Steak Diane

Who would believe steaks with this unusual flavor could be turned out so quickly, and give you protein, niacin, riboflavin, vitamin C, and iron as well?

¼ cup butter or margarine, softened
1 clove garlic, crushed in a garlic press
8 thin slices beef loin tenderloin (1 pound)
Salt

1. Blend butter and garlic; set aside 20 minutes.

2. Heat about 1 tablespoon of the garlic butter in a large heavy skillet. When very hot, add as many steaks at a time as will fit uncrowded; brown quickly on both sides.

3. Transfer steaks to a hot serving platter

Freshly ground black pepper
½ **teaspoon Worcestershire sauce**
½ **lemon**
Chives, snipped

and season with salt and pepper on both sides.

4. Add remaining butter and Worcestershire sauce to pan; heat until bubbly and lightly browned.

5. Holding the cut lemon over the skillet, squeeze it and drizzle in some juice. Insert the tines of a fork through the peel and use to quickly blend in the juice (rubbing sides and bottom of skillet with cut side).

6. Immediately pour hot sauce over steak and sprinkle with chives.

4 servings

Red-Topper Meat Loaf

Recipes like this have put the meat loaf on many a company dinner table. This one provides protein, B vitamins, iron, and a sensational taste.

Meat loaf:
2 **tablespoons butter or margarine**
¾ **cup finely chopped onion**
¼ **cup chopped green pepper**
1½ **pounds lean ground beef**
½ **pound bulk pork sausage**
1 **cup uncooked oats, quick or old fashioned**
2 **eggs, beaten**
¾ **cup tomato juice**
¼ **cup prepared horseradish**
2 **teaspoons salt**
1 **teaspoon dry mustard**
½ **teaspoon monosodium glutamate**
Topping:
2 **to 3 tablespoons brown sugar**
1 **teaspoon dry mustard**
¼ **cup ketchup**

1. For meat loaf, heat butter in a skillet. Mix in onion and green pepper; cook about 5 minutes, or until onion is soft.

2. Meanwhile, lightly mix beef, sausage, and oats in a large bowl. Combine eggs, tomato juice, horseradish, salt, dry mustard, and monosodium glutamate; add to meat mixture and mix lightly. Turn into a 9 x 5 x 3-inch loaf pan and press lightly.

3. For topping, mix brown sugar with dry mustard and blend in ketchup. Spread over meat loaf.

4. Bake at 375°F about 1 hour. Remove from oven and allow meat to stand several minutes before slicing.

About 8 servings

Liver-Apple Bake

Meat and fruit always make an interesting taste combination, and usually give a nutritional bonus, too. This liver-and-apple dish offers protein, vitamin A, niacin, riboflavin, thiamine, vitamins C and D, and iron.

1 pound sliced beef liver (about ¼ inch thick)
2 cups chopped apple
½ cup chopped onion
2 teaspoons seasoned salt
⅛ teaspoon ground black pepper
4 slices bacon, cut in thirds
Parsley sprigs

1. Remove tubes and outer membrane from liver, if necessary. Put liver slices into a greased shallow baking dish.
2. Combine apple, onion, seasoned salt, and pepper; toss to mix. Spoon over liver. Arrange bacon pieces over top. Cover dish.
3. Cook in a 325°F oven 1 hour. Remove cover and continue cooking about 15 minutes.
4. Garnish with parsley.

4 servings

Potato-Frosted Lamb Loaf / Crusty Individual Lamb Loaves

Here are two appetizing ideas from one basic recipe; with either you'll be serving up generous amounts of protein, B vitamins, vitamin C, and calcium.

1½ pounds ground lamb
¾ cup uncooked oats (quick or old-fashioned)
½ clove garlic, minced
¼ cup minced onion
2 tablespoons minced parsley
1 can (10¾ ounces) condensed tomato soup
2 eggs, beaten
1½ teaspoons salt
¾ teaspoon monosodium glutamate
¼ teaspoon ground black pepper

1. Combine lamb, oats, garlic, onion, parsley, and condensed soup in a large bowl. Add eggs, salt, monosodium glutamate, and pepper; mix well. Turn into a greased 9 x 5 x 3-inch loaf pan and press lightly.
2. Bake at 350°F about 1½ hours.
3. Meanwhile, prepare potatoes.
4. Unmold loaf onto a heat-resistant platter or baking dish. Spread mashed potatoes over top and sides of loaf. Brush with melted butter. Return to oven 15 to 20 minutes, or until potatoes are lightly browned. Remove from oven and sprinkle chives over top.

6 to 8 servings

Mashed potatoes (about 4 cups)
Butter or margarine, melted
2 tablespoons snipped chives

Crusty Individual Lamb Loaves: Follow recipe for Potato-Frosted Lamb Loaf. Lightly grease a shallow baking pan instead of the loaf pan. Divide unbaked mixture into 6 portions and shape each into a loaf. Gently roll loaves in **crushed corn flakes** (about 1 cup). Place loaves in the baking pan and bake at 350°F about 45 minutes. Omit potatoes, chives, and second baking period.

Lamb Kabobs

Fun to serve and fun to eat, lamb kabobs are appropriate for any size group. In addition to the nutrients already listed for lamb, the potatoes and tomatoes in this recipe contribute vitamins A and C and calcium.

1½ pounds lamb (leg, loin, or shoulder), boneless, cut in 1½-inch cubes
½ cup vegetable oil
1 tablespoon lemon juice
2 teaspoons sugar
½ teaspoon salt
½ teaspoon paprika
¼ teaspoon dry mustard
⅛ teaspoon ground black pepper
¼ teaspoon Worcestershire sauce
1 clove garlic, cut in halves
6 small whole cooked potatoes
6 small whole cooked onions
Butter or margarine, melted
6 plum tomatoes

1. Put lamb cubes into a shallow dish. Combine oil, lemon juice, sugar, salt, paprika, dry mustard, pepper, Worcestershire sauce, and garlic. Pour over meat. Cover and marinate at least 1 hour in refrigerator, turning pieces occasionally. Drain.
2. Alternately thread lamb cubes, potatoes, and onions on 6 skewers. Brush pieces with melted butter.
3. Broil 3 to 4 inches from heat about 15 minutes, or until lamb is desired degree of doneness; turn frequently and brush with melted butter. Shortly before kabobs are done, impale tomatoes on ends of skewers.

6 servings

Topnotch Lamb Bake

Topnotch for flavor and economy, and perfect for any occasion, this casserole dish contains protein, vitamin A, niacin, riboflavin, thiamine, and calcium.

2 tablespoons bacon drippings
¾ pound ground lamb
1 teaspoon salt
⅛ teaspoon ground black pepper
⅛ teaspoon ground allspice
3 tablespoons butter or margarine
1 small onion, thinly sliced
1 eggplant (about 1 pound), pared and diced
½ teaspoon salt
2 large tomatoes, peeled and sliced
1 can (4 ounces) mushrooms, drained
1 cup (about 4 ounces) shredded Cheddar cheese
1 cup soft enriched bread crumbs
2 tablespoons butter or margarine, melted

1. Heat bacon drippings in a large heavy skillet. Add lamb, separate into small pieces, and cook until lightly browned. Put meat into a greased 1½-quart casserole. Mix 1 teaspoon salt, pepper, and allspice; sprinkle over meat.
2. Heat butter in skillet. Add onion slices and cook until golden. Put onion slices over meat in casserole.
3. Add eggplant to skillet and cook until lightly browned, turning frequently. Sprinkle with ½ teaspoon salt. Put half of the eggplant over onions and arrange tomato slices over eggplant. Cover with mushrooms and remaining eggplant. Sprinkle with cheese. Toss bread crumbs with melted butter and spoon over top.
4. Set in a 400°F oven 20 minutes, or until mixture is thoroughly heated.

4 to 6 servings

Oven Lamb Stew

Good eating and good nutrition are combined in this unusual lamb-and-vegetable stew. The ingredients contain the nutrients protein, vitamin A, B vitamins, vitamin C, and calcium.

2 pounds lean lamb shoulder, boneless, cut in 2-inch cubes
1¾ teaspoons salt
¼ teaspoon thyme, crushed

1. Put lamb into a Dutch oven. Season with salt, thyme, bay leaf, allspice, parsley, and garlic. Add cabbage, leeks, sliced onions, and potatoes. Pour in water. Cover tightly and bring rapidly to boiling.

1 bay leaf
4 whole allspice
2 tablespoons chopped parsley
1 clove garlic, minced
1/4 small head cabbage, shredded
2 leeks, thinly sliced
2 medium onions, sliced
1 cup sliced raw potatoes
4 cups water
8 small onions
4 carrots, cut in 2-inch pieces
2 white turnips, quartered

2. Cook in a 350°F oven about 1½ hours, or until meat is tender.

3. About 30 minutes before cooking time is ended, cook whole onions, carrots, and turnips separately in boiling salted water until tender. Drain.

4. Turn contents of Dutch oven into a food mill set over a large bowl. Return meat to the Dutch oven and add the cooked onions, carrots, and turnips. Discard bay leaf and allspice; force the vegetables through food mill into the bowl containing cooking liquid (or purée vegetables in an electric blender). Heat with meat and vegetables.

6 to 8 servings

Lamb Crown Roast with Mint Stuffing

This elegant company roast is unbelievably easy to prepare—even with the stuffing. Besides impressing your guests, you will be giving them important protein, B vitamins, and iron.

8 slices enriched white bread, toasted and cubed
1 unpared red apple, cored and diced
1½ tablespoons coarsely chopped mint or 1½ teaspoons dried mint flakes
3/4 teaspoon poultry seasoning
1/2 teaspoon salt
6 tablespoons butter
1/2 cup chopped celery
1/4 cup chopped onion
1/2 cup water
1 lamb rib crown roast (5 to 6 pounds)

1. Combine toasted bread cubes, apple, mint, poultry seasoning, and salt in a large bowl.

2. Heat butter in a saucepan. Mix in celery and onion and cook about 5 minutes. Pour over bread mixture along with water; toss lightly.

3. Place lamb on a rack, rib ends up, in a shallow roasting pan. Fill center with stuffing.

4. Roast in a 300°F oven about 2½ hours, or until a meat thermometer registers 175° to 180°F (depending on desired degree of doneness).

5. Place roast on a heated serving platter. Prepare gravy, if desired. Accompany with Parsley-Buttered New Potatoes (page 254) and Butter-Sauced Asparagus (page 232).

About 8 servings

Honey-Lemon Lamb Shoulder Roast

Lemon pepper marinade and a honey glaze add flavor excitement to the nutritional benefits of protein, niacin, riboflavin, and thiamine in lamb.

1 **lamb shoulder square cut, whole (4 to 6 pounds)**
Lemon pepper marinade
¼ **cup chopped parsley**
1 **lemon, sliced and slices halved**
Brown sugar
⅓ **cup honey**
Parsley sprigs

1. Cut 5 crosswise slits in fat side of roast. Rub roast and inner sides of slits with lemon pepper marinade. Place roast, fat side up, on rack in a shallow roasting pan. Insert meat thermometer in the largest muscle so it does not rest in fat or touch bone. Sprinkle chopped parsley over top.

2. Roast in a 325°F oven 2½ to 3½ hours, allowing about 35 minutes per pound. About 30 minutes before roast is done, remove from oven and discard cord. Sprinkle roast with lemon pepper marinade. Dip lemon half-slices in brown sugar and insert in slits. Spoon honey over entire surface of roast. Return to oven and roast until thermometer registers 175°F for medium or 180°F for well done.

3. Remove meat thermometer and bone. Place roast on a hot platter and garnish with parsley.

6 to 8 servings

Glazed Rolled Leg of Lamb

Cranberries and oranges make a delicious main dish of this rolled lamb roast, which contributes protein, vitamin A, niacin, riboflavin, thiamine, and vitamin C to your diet.

1 **lamb leg, whole (5½ to 6 pounds), boned and rolled**
2 **teaspoons salt**
¼ **teaspoon ground pepper**
1 **cup whole cranberry sauce**
1 **cup orange juice**
½ **teaspoon ground ginger**
2 **medium oranges, quartered, seeded, and ground**

1. Rub lamb with salt and pepper. Place lamb on a rack in a shallow roasting pan.

2. Combine cranberry sauce (reserving some berries for garnish), orange juice, and ginger in a saucepan; stir in ground orange. Simmer over low heat 5 to 8 minutes, stirring occasionally during cooking.

3. Spoon half of the orange-cranberry sauce over lamb.

1 cup double-strength
vegetable broth (2 vegetable
bouillon cubes dissolved in
1 cup boiling water)
Orange slices, notched
Curly endive

4. Roast in a 325°F oven 3½ to 4 hours, allowing 40 to 45 minutes per pound. (A meat thermometer should register 175°F for medium-done lamb.) Baste lamb with broth after each 30 minutes of roasting time. About 20 minutes before lamb is done, baste the meat with the remainder of the orange-cranberry sauce.

5. Place roast on a heated platter and garnish with orange slices, reserved cranberries, and curly endive.

8 to 10 servings

Fruited Lamb Stew Deluxe

Dried fruit adds a piquant touch not found in an ordinary stew, and supplements the lamb nutrients with niacin, calcium, and iron.

½ cup enriched all-purpose
flour
4 teaspoons salt
¼ teaspoon ground black
pepper
½ teaspoon ground allspice
1½ pounds lamb for stew
(1- to 1½-inch pieces)
2 tablespoons butter or
margarine
1 tablespoon brown sugar
3 medium onions, coarsely
chopped
¾ cup dried apricots
½ cup pitted dried prunes
4 slices lemon, cut in
quarters
3 cups beef broth
3 packages (10 ounces each)
frozen Brussels sprouts,
partially defrosted to
separate
Cooked noodles

1. Mix flour, salt, pepper, and allspice; coat lamb pieces. Set remaining flour aside.

2. Heat butter in a Dutch oven or a large saucepot. Add meat and brown on all sides.

3. Add brown sugar, onions, dried fruit, lemon, and 2½ cups broth to lamb. Cover and bring to boiling. Reduce heat and simmer about 1 hour.

4. Add Brussels sprouts to Dutch oven and continue cooking 15 to 20 minutes, or until sprouts are just tender.

5. Blend remaining ½ cup broth and reserved seasoned flour; add gradually to boiling stew, stirring constantly. Bring to boiling; cook and stir until thickened (1 to 2 minutes). Serve with noodles.

6 to 8 servings

Curry Superbe

Curried lamb, a combination of flavors that has proved its appeal to millions, is also rich in protein, niacin, riboflavin, thiamine, calcium, and iron.

¼ cup vegetable oil
1 medium onion, chopped
1 clove garlic, minced
¼ cup enriched all-purpose flour
1 tablespoon curry powder
2 teaspoons salt
2 cups beef broth
2 tablespoons lemon juice
1½ pounds lamb shoulder, boneless, cut in 1-inch cubes
1 teaspoon sugar
1 medium apple, sliced
⅓ cup seedless raisins
¼ cup chutney
¼ cup slivered almonds
Cooked rice

Curry accompaniments:
pimiento-stuffed olives, chutney, kumquats, sieved egg yolk, sliced green pepper, toasted flaked coconut

1. Heat oil in a heavy saucepan. Add onion and garlic and cook until onion is almost tender (about 5 minutes). Mix flour, curry powder, and salt; blend in. Stirring constantly, heat until bubbly. Add broth and lemon juice gradually, continuing to stir. Return to heat and cook until thickened, stirring constantly. Remove from heat.

2. Sprinkle lamb with sugar and brown on all sides in a large heavy skillet. Add apple slices; cover and cook 5 minutes.

3. Add the curry sauce to skillet and stir in raisins, chutney, and almonds. Cover; cook 1 hour.

4. Serve over rice with desired curry accompaniments.

6 servings

Broiled Lamb Chops and Mushrooms

Besides making a meal that will be talked about for days, these broiled chops with mushrooms furnish protein, the B vitamins, and iron.

6 lamb rib chops, cut about 1½ inches thick
Vegetable oil
Salt and lemon pepper marinade

1. Brush chops with oil and set on rack of a broiler pan. Broil 6 to 7 inches from heat 10 to 12 minutes on each side, or until desired doneness. After turning chops, season with salt and lemon pepper marinade.

18 medium mushrooms, cleaned
½ cup butter or margarine
1 large clove garlic, minced
1¼ to 1¾ cups coarse dry enriched bread crumbs
¼ cup chopped parsley

2. Meanwhile, remove stems from mushrooms and chop them. Sprinkle inside of caps with salt and set aside.

3. Heat ¼ cup butter in a skillet. Mix in garlic and chopped mushroom stems; cook about 5 minutes, stirring occasionally. Blend in remaining ¼ cup butter; stir until melted. Mix in bread crumbs and parsley until crumbs are well coated.

4. Fill mushroom caps and top broiled chops with crumb mixture. Set caps on broiler rack with chops. Broil 2 to 3 minutes, or until crumbs are golden brown.

6 servings

Roast Leg of Lamb

A classic dish, roast leg of lamb is a treat for company dinners as well as for family meals. Seasoned and spiced, this dressed-up beauty provides protein, niacin, riboflavin, and thiamine.

1 teaspoon salt
½ teaspoon monosodium glutamate
½ teaspoon ground black pepper
1 teaspoon seasoned salt
½ teaspoon ground marjoram
¼ teaspoon dry mustard
⅛ teaspoon ground cardamom
1 lamb leg, whole (about 6 pounds)
2 cloves garlic, cut in slivers
½ teaspoon ground thyme
Orange peel, cut in slivers
Fresh mint sprigs (optional)

1. Mix salt, monosodium glutamate, pepper, seasoned salt, marjoram, dry mustard, and cardamom; rub over lamb. Cut about 16 deep slits in roast. Toss garlic and thyme together. Insert garlic in each slit along with a sliver of orange peel.

2. Place lamb, fat side up, on a rack in a shallow roasting pan. Insert meat thermometer in center of thickest portion of meat.

3. Roast, uncovered, in a 325°F oven 2½ to 3 hours. Meat is medium done when thermometer registers 175°F and is well done at 180°F.

4. Remove meat thermometer. Place roast on a warm serving platter. Put a paper frill around end of leg bone and garnish platter with mint, if desired.

About 10 servings

Lamb Kidney Kabobs

Look for lamb kidneys at your meat market. This often overlooked meat, which provides protein, riboflavin, and thiamine, also stretches your meat budget when you make these flavorful kabobs.

Marinade (see recipe)
1½ **pounds lamb kidneys**
  3 **slices bacon, cut in fourths (12 pieces)**
 12 **large mushroom caps**
    Butter or margarine, melted
 ½ **teaspoon salt**
 ½ **teaspoon monosodium glutamate**
 ⅛ **teaspoon ground black pepper**

1. Prepare marinade.
2. Split kidneys and remove membrane (if not done at the market). Using scissors, remove tubes. Rinse kidneys clean with cold water and cut into 1½-inch cubes. Put into a bowl, pour in marinade, and toss to mix. Refrigerate, covered, at least 24 hours.
3. Using six 8-inch skewers, thread onto each skewer: a piece of bacon, kidney, and a mushroom cap; repeat. (Do not crowd pieces.) Brush kidneys and mushrooms with melted butter. Arrange skewers on broiler rack.
4. Place under broiler about 3 inches from heat. Broil 10 to 15 minutes, or until kidneys are tender; turn occasionally and, if desired, brush with butter. Mix salt, monosodium glutamate, and pepper; sprinkle over kabobs.

6 servings

Marinade: Thoroughly mix ¾ **cup tarragon vinegar, ½ cup vegetable oil, 2 teaspoons salt, ¾ teaspoon monosodium glutamate, ½ teaspoon ground black pepper, 1 bay leaf,** and ½ **clove garlic,** minced.

Curried Veal and Vegetables

Curry again, this time in a delicious savory veal-and-vegetable mixture to be served over rice. Protein, vitamin A, the B vitamins, and iron are the main nutrients.

 1 **pound veal for stew (1-inch cubes)**
 2 **cups water**
 1 **teaspoon salt**

1. Put veal into a large saucepan with water and 1 teaspoon salt. Cover, bring to boiling, reduce heat, and simmer 1 hour. Add carrots, green beans, and celery. Cover, bring to

3 medium carrots, pared and cut in quarters
½ pound green beans
2 large stalks celery, cut in ½-inch slices
3 tablespoons butter or margarine
2 tablespoons flour
½ teaspoon curry powder
¼ teaspoon salt
Cooked rice
Fresh parsley, snipped

boiling, and simmer 1 hour, or until meat is tender.

2. Remove meat and vegetables from broth with a slotted spoon; set aside. Reserve broth.

3. Heat butter in a saucepan. Blend in flour, curry powder, and ¼ teaspoon salt. Heat until bubbly. Add reserved broth gradually, stirring until smooth. Bring to boiling, stirring constantly, and cook 1 to 2 minutes. Mix in meat and vegetables. Heat thoroughly.

4. Serve over rice. Sprinkle with parsley.

About 6 servings

Veal Glacé

These veal cutlets, cooked in wine and consommé, lend an elegant touch to your meal, even if you don't have much time to spend in the kitchen. Protein, niacin, riboflavin, and iron are the nutritional benefits.

1 cup dry white wine
1½ teaspoons tarragon leaves
1½ pounds veal cutlets (about ¼ inch thick)
3 tablespoons butter
½ teaspoon salt
⅛ teaspoon ground black pepper
½ cup condensed consommé (undiluted)
½ cup dry vermouth

1. Stir tarragon into white wine. Cover; allow to stand several hours, stirring occasionally.

2. Cut meat into pieces about 3 x 2 inches. Heat butter in skillet until lightly browned. Add meat and brown lightly. Season with salt and pepper. Reduce heat and pour in tarragon wine mixture with the consommé and vermouth. Simmer uncovered, about 10 minutes, or until veal is tender.

3. Remove veal to a heated dish and cover. Increase heat under skillet and cook sauce until it is reduced to a thin glaze (about 10 minutes), stirring occasionally.

4. Pour glaze over meat, turning meat to coat evenly. Serve hot.

About 6 servings

Note: If desired, accompany with buttered fluffy rice tossed with chopped parsley and toasted slivered almonds.

Roast Stuffed Veal Breast

Veal stuffed with spinach is as good in taste as it is high in nutrition, and it offers protein, vitamin A, the B vitamins, and iron.

1 veal breast with pocket (3 to 4 pounds)	1. Rub roast with 1½ teaspoons salt. Set aside.
1½ teaspoons salt	2. Wash spinach thoroughly. Put spinach into a saucepan with only the water that clings to leaves. Cover and boil until just tender (3 to 10 minutes); drain.
1 pound spinach	
3 cups soft enriched bread cubes	
½ cup (about 2 ounces) shredded Cheddar cheese	3. Mix the cooked spinach with bread cubes, cheese, milk, butter, parsley, ½ teaspoon salt, and pepper. Spoon mixture lightly into veal pocket. Skewer or sew to hold in stuffing.
¼ cup milk	
2 tablespoons butter or margarine	4. Put meat, rib side down, on rack in a shallow roasting pan. Place the bacon slices over top of roast.
½ teaspoon minced parsley	
½ teaspoon salt	5. Roast in a 300°F oven about 2½ hours, or until meat is tender.
⅛ teaspoon ground black pepper	
4 slices bacon	*4 to 6 servings*

Skillet Veal Loaf

The distinctive flavors of veal and ham combined with vegetables and spices make this a most unusual main course, which provides vitamin A, niacin, riboflavin, thiamine, vitamin C, and iron.

1 pound ground veal	1. Have meat retailer grind veal and ham together three times. Set the meat aside.
¼ pound ham	
½ teaspoon salt	2. Add salt, pepper, cinnamon, and lemon peel to beaten eggs; blend well. Lightly mix in meat. Turn onto waxed paper or aluminum foil and gently shape mixture into a large patty. Coat with flour; set aside.
⅛ teaspoon ground black pepper	
⅛ teaspoon ground cinnamon	
1 teaspoon grated lemon peel	
3 eggs, beaten	3. Heat oil and butter in a 10-inch skillet. Add onion, carrot, celery, and parsley; cook about 5 minutes, stirring occasionally. Add meat and brown on both sides.
2 tablespoons flour	
¼ cup olive or vegetable oil	
2 tablespoons butter or margarine	4. When meat is browned, add about half of the vegetable broth to the skillet. Cover
1 medium onion, chopped	

1 **medium carrot, finely chopped**
1 **stalk celery, finely chopped**
2 **tablespoons finely chopped parsley**
1 **cup vegetable broth (1 vegetable bouillon cube dissolved in 1 cup boiling water)**

and simmer about 25 minutes, or until meat is cooked. If necessary, add a little more hot broth to keep meat from sticking. Place meat on a hot platter; set aside and keep hot.

5. Add remaining broth to skillet; force the mixture through a coarse sieve, or purée in an electric blender. Heat the sauce; pour some over meat loaf and serve the remaining sauce in a gravy boat.

6 servings

Savory Sweetbreads

Protein and the B vitamins are derived from this delicacy that isn't usually prepared at home, but that has enhanced the reputation of many fine restaurants.

1½ **pounds sweetbreads**
 Cold water
¼ **cup lemon juice**
1 **teaspoon salt**
1½ **cups beef broth**
2 **stalks celery with leaves, cut in 1-inch pieces**
2 **sprigs parsley**
¼ **teaspoon savory**
¼ **teaspoon thyme**
⅛ **teaspoon ground allspice**
⅛ **teaspoon ground nutmeg**
⅓ **cup butter or margarine**
2 **tablespoons flour**
2 **teaspoons dry mustard**
1 **teaspoon monosodium glutamate**
⅛ **teaspoon ground black pepper**
1 **tablespoon vinegar**
¼ **cup coarsely snipped parsley**
 Melba toast (optional)

1. Rinse sweetbreads with cold water as soon as possible after purchase. Put sweetbreads into a saucepan. Cover with cold water and add lemon juice and salt. Cover saucepan, bring to boiling, reduce heat, and simmer 20 minutes. Drain sweetbreads; cover with cold water. Drain again. (Cool and refrigerate if sweetbreads are not to be used immediately.) Remove tubes and membrane; reserve. Separate sweetbreads into smaller pieces and slice; set aside.

2. Pour broth into a saucepan. Add the tubes and membrane, celery, parsley, savory, thyme, allspice, and nutmeg. Bring to boiling and simmer, covered, 30 minutes. Strain broth reserving 1 cup.

3. Heat butter in a skillet. Blend in flour, dry mustard, monosodium glutamate, and pepper. Heat until bubbly. Add the reserved broth and vinegar while stirring until smooth. Bring to boiling, stirring constantly, and cook until thickened. Add the sweetbreads and parsley. Heat thoroughly.

4. Serve over Melba toast, if desired.

About 6 servings

Prune-Stuffed Pork Roast

Really a show-off dish you can build any dinner party around, this prune-stuffed pork roast provides protein, niacin, thiamine, calcium, and iron.

15 to 20 prunes
¾ to 1 teaspoon salt
  Few grains black pepper
1½ teaspoons ground ginger
1 pork loin roast (3 to 4 pounds)
  Prune Gravy (see recipe)

1. Rinse prunes, cut into halves, and remove and discard pits.
2. Mix salt, pepper, and ginger; rub onto fat side of roast. Lightly mark the fat at about ½-inch intervals to indicate slices. Cut 2 or 3 pockets along each line and insert prunes so they are completely embedded in meat. (Some prunes will come to the top of the meat by the end of roasting period.)
3. Insert meat thermometer in roast so that bulb rests in center of largest muscle, not in fat or on bone. Place roast, fat side up, on a rack in a shallow roasting pan.
4. Roast in a 325° to 350°F oven about 1½ to 2 hours, or until thermometer registers 170°F; allow about 40 to 45 minutes per pound.
5. Transfer roast to heated serving platter and keep warm while preparing gravy. Pour off all but ¼ cup drippings (to be used for gravy). Drizzle some of remaining drippings over roast. Prepare Prune Gravy.
6. To serve, carve roast so that prune design will appear on cut surface of each slice. Accompany with gravy.

About 6 servings

Prune Gravy: Add about **2 cups hot water** to the ¼ cup drippings in roasting pan; bring to boiling, stirring constantly to loosen brown residue. Blend ½ **cup cold water** and ¼ **cup enriched all-purpose flour**; stir into boiling mixture. Season with about ¾ **teaspoon salt**. Bring to boiling and boil 1 to 2 minutes, stirring constantly. Mix in ½ **cup chopped prunes**; heat thoroughly.

Fresh Ham with Exotic Stuffing

The stuffing contributes to the nutritional value of this fresh ham roast as it does to the taste. You will be getting protein, B vitamins, calcium, and iron, as well as compliments from your family and guests.

1 pork leg (fresh ham) roast, boneless (6 to 8 pounds)
¼ cup butter or margarine
1 cup uncooked enriched white rice
1½ cups chopped onion
1 can (10½ ounces) condensed beef broth
1 teaspoon salt
2 cups chopped celery
3 cups small enriched bread cubes
1 can (13¼ ounces) pineapple tidbits, drained; reserve syrup
½ cup seedless raisins
½ to 1 teaspoon curry powder
½ teaspoon garlic powder
½ teaspoon marjoram
1 teaspoon seasoned salt
1 teaspoon salt
¼ teaspoon ground black pepper
2 teaspoons ground ginger
Pineapple slices and spiced crab apples for garnish (optional)

1. Have meat retailer bone the pork leg and cut it almost through to bottom so it will lie flat. Have wooden skewers available.

2. Heat butter in a large skillet. Add rice and onion and cook over medium heat, stirring occasionally, until rice is light brown. Stir in condensed broth and 1 teaspoon salt; cover tightly and cook over very low heat 15 minutes. Combine with celery, bread cubes, pineapple, and raisins. Mix curry powder, garlic powder, marjoram, and seasoned salt. Sprinkle over rice mixture and blend thoroughly by tossing together lightly with a fork.

3. Rub inside surface of flattened leg with 1 teaspoon salt and pepper.

4. Spread stuffing over meat; roll lengthwise, secure firmly with skewers, and lace tightly. (Any leftover stuffing may be baked in a greased casserole; place in oven about 1 hour before meat is done.)

5. Rub meat with ginger, then place on rack in a large shallow roasting pan.

6. Roast in a 325°F oven 4½ to 5½ hours (allow about 45 minutes per pound), or until a meat thermometer inserted in meat, not in stuffing, registers 170°F. During last 30 minutes of roasting, occasionally spoon reserved pineapple syrup over roast.

7. Remove from oven and let stand at least 20 minutes before slicing. Place on a warm platter and, if desired, garnish with pineapple and crab apples. Gravy can be made with drippings in roasting pan.

12 to 16 servings

Spicy Pork with Herbs

This spicily seasoned pork dish, prepared right in the skillet, provides protein, vitamin A, niacin, thiamine, vitamin C, calcium, and iron for as many as twelve people.

1 tablespoon fat
3 pounds lean pork, boneless, cut in 1½-inch cubes
2 medium onions, peeled and cut in wedges (8 from each)
2 green peppers, cut in 1-inch pieces
1 clove garlic, minced
1 can (16 ounces) tomatoes
2 teaspoons seasoned salt
½ teaspoon oregano
⅛ teaspoon ground black pepper
2 teaspoons cider vinegar
¼ cup water
2 tablespoons flour

1. Heat fat in a large heavy skillet. Add pork and brown lightly on all sides. Remove browned meat from skillet with a slotted spoon and set aside. Add onions, green peppers, and garlic to drippings in skillet. Cook until onion and green pepper are just tender. Spoon off any excess fat.
2. Return meat to skillet, add tomatoes, seasoned salt, oregano, pepper, and vinegar, and mix well. Cover and cook over low heat about 1 hour, or until meat is tender.
3. Push meat mixture to sides of skillet. Blend water and flour until smooth. Pour into center of skillet, bring to boiling, and cook, stirring constantly until thickened. Stir with meat mixture.

10 to 12 servings

Saucy Ribs / Saucy Ribs from the Oven

Protein, niacin, thiamine, vitamin C, calcium, and iron are the nutrients contained in these spicy ribs. Save the leftover sauce. It is wonderful when brushed onto broiled or baked chicken.

6 pounds pork spareribs or pork loin back ribs, cut across ribs and in 3-inch lengths
¼ cup firmly packed dark brown sugar
2 teaspoons dry mustard
2 tablespoons seasoned salt

1. Brown ribs on both sides in Dutch oven, heavy skillet, or saucepot, pouring off fat as it accumulates.
2. Meanwhile, prepare the sauce. Blend brown sugar, dry mustard, and seasoned salt and pepper in a saucepan; stir in ketchup, water, lemon juice, Worcestershire sauce, vinegar, onion, horseradish, and Tabasco. Bring to

½ teaspoon seasoned pepper
2 cups ketchup
2 cups water
6 tablespoons lemon juice
6 tablespoons Worcestershire
sauce
¼ cup cider vinegar
½ cup instant minced onion
2 teaspoons prepared
horseradish
6 drops Tabasco

boiling, cover, and simmer about 10 minutes.
3. Pour hot sauce over ribs. Bring to boiling and cover tightly. Simmer 1 to 1½ hours, or until tender, basting and turning ribs frequently.

About 6 servings

Saucy Ribs from the Oven: Follow recipe for the sauce in Saucy Ribs. Brown the ribs in a jelly-roll pan or shallow roasting pan in a 350°F oven; pour off fat. Spoon sauce over ribs, cover tightly with aluminum foil, and cook about 1 hour, or until tender.

Supper Sausage Squares

These sausage links baked in a flavorful batter are always crowd pleasers. Protein, vitamin A, niacin, riboflavin, thiamine, vitamins C and D, and iron are the nutrients.

1½ pounds small pork sausage
links (about 24)
1¾ cups sifted enriched
all-purpose flour
1½ tablespoons sugar
4 teaspoons baking powder
1 teaspoon salt
Milk
1 can (12 ounces) whole
kernel corn, drained;
reserve liquid
½ cup whole bran cereal
1 tablespoon instant minced
onion
3 eggs
Maple-blended syrup

1. Put sausage links into a large cold skillet. Add a small amount of water; cover and cook over low heat 5 minutes. Remove cover and pour off liquid. Continue cooking, turning to brown on all sides. Drain on paper toweling. Reserve ¼ cup drippings.
2. Sift flour, sugar, baking powder, and salt together; set aside.
3. Add enough milk to reserved corn liquid to measure 1½ cups. Combine with drippings, bran cereal, onion, corn, and eggs in a large bowl; beat well. Add dry ingredients and beat until batter is smooth.
4. Turn batter into a greased 15 x 10 x 1-inch jelly-roll pan. Arrange sausage links in batter in a pattern.
5. Bake at 450°F about 20 minutes, or until golden brown. Cut into squares and serve warm with syrup.

8 servings

Pork Loin Roast

Pork is rich in protein, niacin, thiamine, and iron, and this classic roast containing all these nutrients tastes so good you'll wonder why you don't serve it more often.

1 pork loin roast (4 to 6 pounds)
Salt and pepper
Spiced crab apples

1. Have the meat retailer saw across the rib bones of roast at base of the backbone, separating the ribs from the backbone. Place roast, fat side up, on a rack in an open roasting pan. Season with salt and pepper. Insert meat thermometer in roast so the bulb is centered in the thickest part and not resting on bone or in fat.

2. Roast in a 350°F oven about 2½ to 3 hours, or until thermometer registers 170°F; allow 30 to 40 minutes per pound.

3. For easy carving, remove backbone, place roast on platter, and allow roast to set for 15 to 20 minutes. Garnish platter with spiced crab apples, heated if desired. Accompany with Hash Brown Potatoes au Gratin (page 258).

8 to 10 servings

Canadian Style Bacon and Peaches

Spicy cold peaches and hot Canadian bacon make an exciting combination of tastes while they supply protein, vitamin A, niacin, thiamine, and iron.

Roast Canadian Style Bacon:
2 pounds smoked pork loin Canadian style bacon (in one piece)
10 whole cloves

Orange-Spiced Peaches:
½ cup firmly packed brown sugar
⅓ cup red wine vinegar
1 tablespoon grated orange peel

1. Remove casing from the meat and place, fat side up, on a rack in a shallow roasting pan. Stud with cloves. Insert a meat thermometer into bacon so bulb is centered. Roast, uncovered, at 325°F about 2 hours, or until thermometer registers 160°F.

2. For Orange-Spiced Peaches, stir brown sugar, wine vinegar, orange peel, orange juice, cloves, allspice, and peach syrup together in a saucepan. Bring to boiling; reduce heat and simmer 5 minutes. Mix in peaches

2 tablespoons orange juice
1 teaspoon whole cloves
½ teaspoon whole allspice
1 can (29 ounces) peach halves, drained; reserve 1½ cups syrup
Mustard Sauce (see recipe)

and heat 5 minutes.

3. Remove from heat and allow peaches to cool in syrup. Refrigerate until ready to serve.

4. Shortly before meat is roasted, prepare Mustard Sauce.

5. Remove meat from oven and place on a heated serving platter. Remove thermometer. Arrange peaches on platter. Accompany with Mustard Sauce in a bowl.

About 8 servings

Mustard Sauce: Mix **1 cup firmly packed brown sugar, 2 tablespoons prepared mustard, 1 tablespoon butter or margarine, 3 tablespoons cider vinegar** in a saucepan. Stir over low heat until sugar is dissolved; heat thoroughly, stirring occasionally.

⅔ cup sauce

Fresh Pear and Pork Chop Skillet

Pork and fruit always work well together, and here the combination comes from the skillet to give you protein, niacin, thiamine, vitamin C, and iron.

6 pork loin chops, cut ¾ to 1 inch thick
½ teaspoon salt
⅛ teaspoon ground black pepper
6 thin lemon slices
12 thin onion slices
3 Anjou pears, halved and cored
¾ cup firmly packed brown sugar
½ cup lemon juice
½ cup water
⅓ cup soy sauce
½ teaspoon ground ginger

1. Brown pork chops on both sides in a skillet. Drain off excess fat.

2. Season chops with salt and pepper. Put a lemon slice and two onion slices on each chop. Place pear halves cut-side down in skillet around chops.

3. Combine brown sugar, lemon juice, water, soy sauce, and ginger; pour over all. Cover; basting frequently with sauce, cook over low heat about 20 minutes, then turn pears cut-side up and cook 20 minutes longer, or until pork is tender.

6 servings

Ham in Orange Sauce

Leftover ham seldom gets such royal treatment as in this delicious dish that offers protein, vitamin A, thiamine, vitamin C, and iron as well as economy.

⅓ **cup butter or margarine**
1 **cup chopped celery**
½ **cup chopped green pepper**
½ **cup chopped onion**
1 **can (13¼ ounces)
pineapple chunks, drained;
reserve ⅓ cup syrup**
1 **tablespoon cornstarch**
1 **can (6 ounces) frozen
orange juice concentrate,
thawed**
1 **tablespoon soy sauce**
1 **pound fully cooked boneless
ham, cut in strips
(about 3 cups)**
1 **cup packaged enriched
precooked rice**
2 **tablespoons butter or
margarine**
¼ **cup grated Parmesan
cheese**
Toasted chopped almonds

1. Heat butter in a large skillet. Mix in celery, green pepper, and onion and cook about 10 minutes, or until vegetables are crisp-tender.
2. Meanwhile, blend the pineapple syrup with cornstarch in a saucepan. Bring to boiling, stirring constantly; cook 1 minute. Blend in orange juice concentrate, soy sauce, and pineapple chunks. Heat thoroughly.
3. Mix sauce and ham with vegetables in skillet. Cover; heat before serving.
4. Cook rice following package directions. Add butter and cheese and toss lightly.
5. Spoon the hot ham mixture over rice in a serving dish. Top with almonds.

About 6 servings

Apple 'n' Kraut Pork Pie

Once you've served this unusual pie, expect it to be high on your request list. Also expect protein, vitamin A, niacin, thiamine, calcium, and iron from the combination of ingredients.

1½ **pounds ground lean pork**
2 **teaspoons salt**
¼ **teaspoon seasoned pepper**
¼ **teaspoon crushed rosemary
leaves**

1. Combine pork, salt, ¼ teaspoon seasoned pepper, and rosemary in a bowl. Mix in ketchup, eggs, and bread crumbs.
2. Turn mixture into a 10-inch pie plate and press lightly against the bottom and sides,

⅓ cup ketchup
2 eggs, slightly beaten
1 cup enriched bread crumbs (½ cup soft and ½ cup fine dry)
¼ cup butter or margarine
1 medium onion, halved and sliced
3¼ cups well-drained sauerkraut
½ cup apple cider
3 cups cubed apple
¼ teaspoon seasoned pepper
¼ teaspoon thyme leaves
¼ teaspoon rubbed sage
4 to 5 ounces Swiss cheese, cut in strips

shaping into a shell. Bake at 350°F 35 to 40 minutes, or until browned. Remove from oven and spoon off any excess fat.

3. Meanwhile, heat butter in a large saucepan. Stir in onion and cook, stirring occasionally, until crisp-tender. Mix in sauerkraut, apple cider, apple, ¼ teaspoon seasoned pepper, thyme, and sage. Simmer, covered, 20 to 25 minutes, or until apple is tender.

4. Spoon kraut mixture onto hot meat shell. Arrange Swiss cheese strips in a lattice pattern over top. Set under broiler with top about 3 inches from heat about 3 minutes, or until cheese is bubbly. Serve hot.

6 to 8 servings

Pork and Succotash Skillet

Here's a quick meal that's a nutritional powerhouse, containing both meat and vegetable protein, vitamins A and C, niacin, riboflavin, thiamine, calcium, and iron.

2 tablespoons fat
1 medium onion, halved and thinly sliced
1 green pepper, cut in long thin strips
2 cups cubed roast pork
1 can (17 ounces) green lima beans, drained
1 can (12 ounces) whole kernel corn, drained
¾ cup beef broth
½ teaspoon seasoned salt
¼ teaspoon marjoram leaves
¼ teaspoon ground black pepper

1. Heat fat in a large skillet. Add onion and green pepper; cook about 5 minutes. Stir in pork and heat several minutes.

2. Add lima beans, corn, broth, seasoned salt, marjoram, and pepper to mixture in skillet; mix well. Cover and simmer 10 to 15 minutes.

About 6 servings

Saucy Ham Loaf

This recipe calls for a little more work than an ordinary meat loaf, but it is worth the effort. Your nutritional rewards will be protein, vitamin A, niacin, riboflavin, thiamine, calcium, and iron.

Meat loaf:

1½ pounds ground cooked ham
½ pound ground veal
½ pound ground pork
2 eggs, fork beaten
½ teaspoon salt
⅛ teaspoon ground black pepper
½ teaspoon ground nutmeg
½ teaspoon dry mustard
¼ teaspoon ground thyme
¼ cup finely chopped onion
½ cup finely chopped green pepper
2 tablespoons finely chopped parsley
¾ cup soft enriched bread crumbs
¾ cup apple juice

Sauce:

⅔ cup packed light brown sugar
2 teaspoons cornstarch
1 teaspoon dry mustard
1 teaspoon ground allspice
⅔ cup apricot nectar
3 tablespoons lemon juice
2 teaspoons vinegar

1. Combine ham, veal, and pork with eggs, salt, pepper, nutmeg, dry mustard, and thyme in a large bowl. Add onion, green pepper, and parsley and toss to blend. Add bread crumbs and apple juice; mix thoroughly but lightly. Turn into a 9 x 5 x 3-inch loaf pan and flatten top.

2. Bake at 350°F 1 hour.

3. Meanwhile, prepare sauce for topping. Blend brown sugar, cornstarch, dry mustard, and allspice in a small saucepan. Add apricot nectar, lemon juice, and vinegar. Bring rapidly to boiling and cook about 2 minutes, stirring constantly. Reduce heat and simmer 10 minutes to allow flavors to blend.

4. Remove meat loaf from oven; pour off and reserve juices. Unmold loaf in a shallow baking pan. Spoon some of the reserved juices and then the sauce over loaf. Return to oven 30 minutes.

5. Place loaf on a warm platter and garnish as desired.

8 to 10 servings

Poultry

Poultry dishes are popular round the world and reflect the special cuisines of many nations. Chicken in particular is an international favorite, and with the following recipes any cook can enjoy preparing chicken with a foreign flavor. Garlic, oregano, and tomatoes spell Italian, and combined with chicken the result is *Chicken, Cacciatore Style.* Curry brings the flavor of India to your table—try the *Country Captain* or the *Spicy Skillet Chicken*, with its make-your-own curry powder. From the islands of the Pacific comes *Chicken Polynesian Style.* Almonds, cloves, and raisins bring a Middle Eastern touch to *Skillet Chicken à l'Orange.* Or try one of the versions of typical American dishes such as *Chicken and Dumplings* or *Lemon-Broiled Chicken.*

Duck and goose are also international favorites and are frequently accompanied by a fruit sauce or stuffing to complement the richness of their meat. Turkey, a bird native to the Americas, is always popular roasted to a rich brown and served with a savory stuffing. For an unusual treat with the flavor of the American seaboard, try the *Turkey-Oyster Casserole.*

You'll also find in this section delicious recipes for one-pot meals, such as *Chicken in a Garden*, and great ideas for leftovers, such as *Turkey Biscuit Pinwheel with Fresh Mushroom Sauce* or *Hot Curried Chicken in Tomato Shells.*

Budget-conscious gourmets will enjoy serving a variety of poultry dishes often. Poultry is one of the most readily available meats, and although prices tend to fluctuate, chicken and turkey are almost always economical buys in comparison with other items on the meat counter. To judge how much you should buy for a meal, allow about ¾ of a pound of chicken or turkey for each serving. Goose and duck have a higher ratio of bone to meat than do chicken or turkey; 1½ pounds of goose will be an ample serving for one person, while a single duck of 4 to 6 pounds is usually quartered, serving four people.

Poultry is popular not only for its low cost and adaptability to many flavor combinations but also because of its nutritional value. High in protein and low in fat, chicken and turkey are always welcome among those who must watch their intake of calories. A significant amount of niacin is also found in poultry, as are smaller quantities of iron, thiamine, and riboflavin.

With so many deliciously different and nutritious ways to serve poultry, make it a regular attraction at your dinner table.

Penny-Wise Chicken Casserole

Penny-wise yet nutritious, this recipe gives you not only the protein and other benefits of the chicken, but also vitamins A and C and calcium from the apple-cabbage combination.

1 **head cabbage, cut in 1-inch wedges**
2 **teaspoons flour**
1 **teaspoon caraway seed**
4 **tart red apples, cored and cut in ½-inch rings**
2 **tablespoons brown sugar Broiler-fryer chicken pieces (about 2½ pounds)**
2 **tablespoons butter, melted**
½ **cup cider vinegar**
1 **tablespoon salt Paprika**

1. Put cabbage wedges on bottom of a shallow 2-quart casserole. Sprinkle with 1 teaspoon flour and caraway seed. Top with apple rings. Mix brown sugar and remaining 1 teaspoon flour; sprinkle over apples.
2. Arrange chicken pieces, skin side up, in casserole. Mix melted butter, vinegar, and salt; pour over all. Cover.
3. Cook in a 350°F oven 45 minutes. Remove cover; cook 30 minutes, or until chicken is tender. Sprinkle with paprika.

4 to 6 servings

Chicken in a Garden

Chicken, raisins, and vegetables are combined in this savory dish to give you protein, niacin, calcium, iron, and small amounts of other vitamins and minerals.

1 **roasting chicken (about 5 pounds)**
1½ **to 2 teaspoons salt**
¼ **teaspoon ground black pepper**
½ **teaspoon crushed rosemary**
1 **medium onion, peeled and quartered**
2 **stalks celery with leaves, cut in pieces**
1 **lemon, cut in half (remove seeds)**
2 **tablespoons butter or margarine, melted**

1. Rinse chicken with cold water, drain and pat dry. Mix salt, pepper, and rosemary. Season cavity of chicken with some of mixture; reserve remainder. Put onion and celery into cavity. Skewer openings and tie legs together with cord. Place breast side up in a large deep Dutch oven or roasting pan having a cover.
2. Rub cut lemon over chicken and then squeeze halves over all to drizzle with juice; reserve lemon halves. Brush chicken with melted butter and sprinkle with reserved seasoning mixture.
3. Bake at 425°F 30 minutes, or until chicken

⅔ **cup dark seedless or golden raisins**
2 **cups chicken broth (3 chicken bouillon cubes dissolved in 2 cups boiling water)**
8 **large whole fresh mushrooms, cut in halves**
1 **tablespoon cornstarch**
1 **tablespoon cold water**
   Garden vegetables (such as carrots, onions, potatoes, and zucchini), cooked and seasoned

is delicately browned.

4. Finely chop half of the raisins; set remaining raisins aside. Add chopped raisins, broth, mushrooms, and the reserved lemon halves to the chicken in the Dutch oven or roasting pan. Cover tightly.

5. Turn oven control to 375°F and cook 1 hour. Remove and discard lemon halves. Continue cooking until chicken is tender (1 to 1½ hours).

6. Remove chicken to heated serving platter and keep hot. Remove skewers and cord.

7. For gravy, skim fat from liquid in pan. Measure liquid. If less than 2 cups, add chicken broth to fill. Return liquid to pan. Blend cornstarch and cold water. Stir into liquid, blending thoroughly. Bring rapidly to boiling and boil 3 minutes, stirring as necessary. Stir in reserved raisins.

8. To serve, surround chicken with desired vegetables. Spoon a small amount of gravy over the chicken. Accompany with remaining gravy.

About 6 servings

Potato-Coated Chicken

Two of the staples of our daily diet combine to make a truly different taste surprise. It is highly nutritious, too, as it gives you protein, niacin, vitamin C, and iron.

1 **broiler-fryer chicken, quartered or cut in pieces**
   Seasoned salt
2 **eggs, slightly beaten**
1½ **cups mashed potato flakes**
½ **cup butter or margarine**

1. Sprinkle chicken pieces generously with seasoned salt and rub in. Dip each piece into beaten eggs, then coat with mashed potato flakes.

2. Melt butter in a shallow baking pan; arrange chicken pieces in a layer.

3. Bake at 350°F for 30 minutes; turn pieces and continue baking 30 minutes longer, or until tender.

About 4 servings

Hot Curried Chicken in Tomato Shells

A few spicy touches help make diced chicken a new eating experience. This recipe provides protein, niacin, vitamins A and C, calcium, and iron.

4 **medium firm ripe tomatoes, rinsed**
2 **tablespoons butter or margarine**
3 **tablespoons flour**
1 **teaspoon minced onion**
¼ **to ½ teaspoon curry powder**
1 **cup milk**
1½ **teaspoons salt**
⅛ **teaspoon ground black pepper**
⅛ **teaspoon garlic powder**
1 **cup finely diced cooked chicken**
1 **tablespoon butter or margarine, melted**
Chopped peanuts, coconut, and chutney

1. Cut a slice from the stem end of each tomato. Scoop out the pulp. Invert tomatoes and set aside to drain thoroughly.
2. Heat 2 tablespoons butter in a saucepan. Blend in flour, onion, and curry powder. Heat until bubbly. Add milk gradually, stirring constantly; cook 1 to 2 minutes. Mix in salt, pepper, garlic powder, and then cooked chicken.
3. Fill tomato shells with chicken mixture; set in a greased baking dish. Brush tops lightly with melted butter.
4. Set in a 350°F oven about 20 minutes, or until thoroughly heated.
5. To serve, accompany with small bowls of peanuts, coconut, and chutney.

4 servings

Chicken with Mushrooms

Chicken, mushrooms, and wine are a well-established taste combination. Nutrition-wise, they give you protein, niacin, riboflavin, and iron.

1 **broiler-fryer chicken, about 3 pounds, cut in pieces**
1 **teaspoon salt**
¼ **teaspoon ground white pepper**
⅓ **cup enriched all-purpose flour**
2 **tablespoons butter or margarine**

1. Sprinkle chicken pieces with salt and pepper; coat with flour.
2. Heat butter and olive oil in a large skillet. Add the coated chicken pieces and brown on one side. Add garlic and brown chicken on other side. Discard garlic. Push chicken pieces to side of skillet. Add onion and mushrooms to skillet and cook until onion is tender, stirring occasionally. Add wine, cover, and

2 tablespoons olive oil
1 clove garlic
1 onion, chopped
½ pound mushrooms, quartered
½ cup dry white wine
3 tablespoons tomato sauce
2 tablespoons water
   Fresh parsley, finely snipped

cook slowly about 10 minutes.

3. Mix in tomato sauce and water; continue cooking, covered, until chicken is tender (about 15 minutes). Sprinkle top with parsley before serving.

About 4 servings

Lemon-Chicken Bake

Marinated and basted in a tasty sauce, this dish provides a spicy blend of flavors, plus protein, vitamins A and C, niacin, and iron.

3 broiler-fryer chickens, 2½ to 3 pounds each, split lengthwise
1 tablespoon monosodium glutamate
1 can (8 ounces) tomato sauce
¾ cup water
½ cup vegetable oil
⅓ cup lemon juice
3 tablespoons Worcestershire sauce
1 teaspoon prepared mustard
1 teaspoon Tabasco
3 tablespoons brown sugar
2 teaspoons salt
½ cup minced onion
1 clove garlic, minced
   Parsley sprigs
   Lemon wedges

1. Sprinkle chicken with monosodium glutamate and arrange pieces one layer deep in a large shallow baking pan. Let stand 15 minutes.

2. Meanwhile, combine tomato sauce, water, oil, lemon juice, Worcestershire sauce, prepared mustard, Tabasco, brown sugar, salt, onion, and garlic. Beat to blend thoroughly; pour over chicken. Cover and marinate overnight in the refrigerator, turning chicken occasionally.

3. Drain, reserving marinade for basting sauce. Turn chicken, skin-side down.

4. Bake at 350°F 30 minutes, basting frequently with the marinade. Turn chicken; bake 1 hour, or until thickest part can be easily pierced with a fork; baste frequently with the marinade.

5. Serve chicken on a hot platter garnished with parsley and lemon wedges. If desired, thicken the remaining marinade slightly and serve hot with the chicken.

6 servings

Chicken, Cacciatore Style

The Italian way with spices and flavorings never fails to please. This example of the Italian magic provides protein, vitamin A, niacin, vitamin C, calcium, and iron.

¼ cup vegetable oil
1 broiler-fryer chicken (about 2½ pounds), cut in serving-size pieces
2 medium onions, sliced
2 cloves garlic, crushed in a garlic press or minced
3 tomatoes, sliced
2 medium green peppers, sliced
1 small bay leaf
1 teaspoon salt
¼ teaspoon ground black pepper
½ teaspoon celery seed
1 teaspoon crushed oregano or basil
1 can (8 ounces) tomato sauce
¼ cup sauterne
8 ounces spaghetti, cooked

1. Heat oil in a large heavy skillet. Add chicken and brown on all sides. Remove chicken from skillet.
2. Add onions and garlic to oil remaining in skillet and cook until onion is tender but not brown; stir occasionally to cook evenly.
3. Return chicken to skillet and add the tomatoes, green peppers, and bay leaf.
4. Mix salt, pepper, celery seed, and oregano with tomato sauce; pour over all.
5. Cover and cook over low heat 45 minutes. Blend in sauterne and cook, uncovered, 20 minutes. Discard bay leaf.
6. Put cooked spaghetti onto a warm serving platter and top with the chicken pieces and sauce.

About 6 servings

Chicken and Broccoli au Gratin

Protein, vitamin A, niacin, thiamine, vitamin C, calcium, and iron are all there in this ever-popular vegetable-and-chicken combination.

2 packages (10 ounces each) frozen broccoli spears
¼ cup butter or margarine
¼ cup enriched all-purpose flour
½ teaspoon salt

1. Cook broccoli until crisp-tender. Drain.
2. Meanwhile, heat butter in a saucepan. Blend in flour, salt, and pepper. Heat until bubbly. Add milk and chicken broth gradually, stirring until smooth. Bring to boiling, stirring constantly, and cook 1 to 2 minutes.

Few grains pepper
1 cup milk
1 cup chicken broth
2 tablespoons lemon juice
2 teaspoons Worcestershire sauce
3 chicken breasts, cooked, skinned, boned, and sliced
½ cup grated Parmesan cheese
½ cup crushed ready-to-eat cereal flakes

Remove from heat and stir in lemon juice and Worcestershire sauce. Keep hot.

3. Arrange chicken in a greased 2-quart shallow baking dish. Cover chicken with drained broccoli. Sprinkle with half of cheese. Pour the hot sauce over all. Mix the remaining cheese with cereal flakes and spoon over sauce.

4. Bake at 350°F 20 to 25 minutes, or until topping is lightly browned and sauce is bubbly.

About 6 servings

Chicken Pie with Sweet Potato Crust

In this variation of an all-time chicken favorite, the sweet potato crust adds vitamins A and C and calcium to a dish already bursting with basic nutrients.

3 cups cooked chicken pieces
1 cup diced cooked carrots
6 cooked small white onions
1 tablespoon chopped parsley
2 tablespoons flour
1 teaspoon salt
⅛ teaspoon ground black pepper
1 cup undiluted evaporated milk
1 cup chicken broth
Sweet Potato Crust (see recipe)

1. Put chicken into a shallow 1½-quart baking dish; top with carrots, onions, and parsley.

2. Mix flour, salt, and pepper in a saucepan. Add evaporated milk and broth gradually, stirring constantly. Bring to boiling and boil 1 to 2 minutes. Pour over chicken mixture.

3. Top with Sweet Potato Crust; flute edges.

4. Bake at 350°F about 40 minutes, or until crust is lightly browned.

About 6 servings

Sweet Potato Crust: Blend **1 cup sifted enriched all-purpose flour, 1 teaspoon baking powder,** and **½ teaspoon salt** together. Mix in **1 cup cool mashed sweet potato, ⅓ cup melted butter,** and **1 well-beaten egg.** Chill thoroughly. On a lightly floured surface, roll out dough ¼ inch thick and a little larger than baking dish. Proceed as directed in recipe.

Spicy Skillet Chicken

Here's another idea for spicy chicken and fruit, yet with a completely different taste. It gives you protein, some vitamin A, niacin, calcium, and iron.

3 tablespoons butter
4 pounds broiler-fryer chicken pieces (use breasts and legs)
2 tablespoons flour
1 cup condensed chicken consommé
1 can (16 ounces) fruit cocktail (undrained)
¼ teaspoon salt
½ teaspoon turmeric
¼ teaspoon dry mustard
¼ teaspoon ground mace
¼ teaspoon ground cardamom
¼ teaspoon ground ginger
4 shreds saffron
Cooked rice

1. Heat butter in a large heavy skillet. Add chicken pieces and brown on all sides. Remove chicken from skillet.
2. Blend flour into drippings in skillet. Heat until bubbly. Add chicken consommé gradually, stirring constantly. Continue stirring and bring rapidly to boiling. Cook 1 to 2 minutes.
3. Mix in fruit cocktail and liquid. Mix salt, turmeric, dry mustard, mace, cardamom, ginger, and saffron. Return chicken to skillet. Cover; simmer about 30 minutes, or until chicken is tender. Serve with hot fluffy rice.

About 8 servings

Chicken and Dumplings

The fame of this classic chicken dish is richly deserved: as good as it is nutritious, it supplies protein, vitamin A, calcium, and iron.

¼ cup butter or margarine
2 broiler-fryer chickens, cut in serving-size pieces
½ cup chopped onion
¼ cup chopped celery
2 tablespoons chopped celery leaves
1 clove garlic, minced
¼ cup enriched all-purpose flour
4 cups chicken broth
1 teaspoon sugar
2 teaspoons salt

1. Heat butter in a large skillet. Add chicken pieces and brown on all sides. Remove chicken from skillet.
2. Add onion, celery, celery leaves, and garlic to fat in skillet. Cook until vegetables are tender. Sprinkle with flour and mix well. Add chicken broth, sugar, salt, pepper, basil, bay leaves, and parsley; bring to boiling, stirring constantly. Return chicken to skillet and spoon sauce over it; cover.
3. Cook in a 350°F oven 40 minutes.
4. Shortly before cooking time is completed, prepare Basil Dumplings.

¼ teaspoon ground black pepper
1 teaspoon basil leaves
2 bay leaves
¼ cup chopped parsley
Basil Dumplings (see recipe)
2 packages (10 ounces each) frozen green peas

5. Remove skillet from oven and turn control to 425°F. Stir peas into skillet mixture and bring to boiling. Drop dumpling dough onto stew.

6. Return to oven and cook, uncovered, 10 minutes; cover and cook 10 minutes, or until chicken is tender and dumplings are done.

About 8 servings

Basil Dumplings: Combine **2 cups all-purpose biscuit mix** and **1 teaspoon basil leaves** in a bowl. Add **⅔ cup milk** and stir with a fork until a dough is formed. Proceed as directed in recipe.

Chicken Fricassee with Vegetables

This is a little too elegant to be called chicken stew, but it is just as simple to prepare and will earn raves for the cook. It has protein, vitamins A and C, niacin, calcium, and iron.

1 broiler-fryer chicken (about 3 pounds), cut in serving-size pieces
1½ teaspoons salt
1 bay leaf
Water
2 cups sliced carrots
2 onions, quartered
2 crookneck squashes, cut in halves lengthwise
2 pattypan squashes, cut in halves
Green beans (about 6 ounces), tips cut off
1 can (3½ ounces) pitted ripe olives, drained
1 tablespoon cornstarch
2 tablespoons water

1. Place chicken pieces along with salt and bay leaf in a Dutch oven or saucepot. Add enough water to just cover chicken. Bring to boiling; simmer, covered, 25 minutes until chicken is almost tender.

2. Add carrots and onions to cooking liquid; cook, covered, 10 minutes. Add squashes and green beans to cooking liquid; cook, covered, 10 minutes, or until chicken and vegetables are tender. Remove chicken and vegetables to a warm serving dish and add olives; keep hot.

3. Blend cornstarch and 2 tablespoons water; stir into boiling cooking liquid. Boil 2 to 3 minutes. Pour gravy over chicken.

About 4 servings

Chicken Livers and Mushrooms

Chicken-liver lovers will really enjoy this recipe combining mushrooms and oranges with the livers. Rich in nutrients, it provides protein, vitamins A and C, niacin, riboflavin, thiamine, and iron.

2 pounds chicken livers, thawed if frozen
½ cup enriched all-purpose flour
1 teaspoon salt
¼ teaspoon ground white pepper
⅓ cup butter or margarine
1 cup orange sections, cut in halves
1 can (6 ounces) broiled mushrooms
Fresh parsley, snipped

1. Rinse chicken livers and drain on absorbent paper. Mix flour, salt, and pepper; coat chicken livers evenly.
2. Heat butter in a large skillet, add chicken livers, and cook 10 minutes, or until livers are lightly browned and tender. Mix in orange sections; heat.
3. Meanwhile, heat mushrooms in their broth in a small skillet.
4. Arrange cooked chicken livers and heated orange sections on a hot platter. Top with mushrooms and sprinkle with parsley. Serve immediately.

About 6 servings

Country Captain

As pretty to serve as it is good to eat, this crowd-pleasing dish gives you protein, vitamins A and C, niacin, riboflavin, thiamine, calcium, and iron.

1 broiler-fryer chicken (3 to 3½ pounds), cut in serving-size pieces
¼ cup enriched all-purpose flour
½ teaspoon salt
Pinch ground white pepper
3 to 4 tablespoons lard
2 onions, finely chopped
2 medium green peppers, chopped
1 clove garlic, crushed in a garlic press or minced
1½ teaspoons salt

1. Remove skin from chicken. Mix flour, ½ teaspoon salt, and pinch white pepper. Coat chicken pieces.
2. Melt lard in a large heavy skillet; add chicken and brown on all sides. Remove pieces from skillet and keep hot.
3. Cook onions, peppers, and garlic in the same skillet, stirring occasionally until onion is lightly browned. Blend 1½ teaspoons salt, ½ teaspoon white pepper, curry powder, and thyme. Mix into skillet along with parsley and tomatoes.
4. Arrange chicken in a shallow roasting pan and pour tomato mixture over it. (If it does

½ teaspoon ground white
   pepper
1½ teaspoons curry powder
½ teaspoon ground thyme
½ teaspoon snipped parsley
5 cups undrained canned
   tomatoes
2 cups hot cooked rice
¼ cup dried currants
¾ cup roasted blanched
   almonds
   Parsley sprigs

not cover chicken, add a small amount of water to the skillet in which mixture was cooked and pour liquid over chicken.) Place a cover on pan or cover tightly with aluminum foil.

5. Cook in a 350°F oven about 45 minutes, or until chicken is tender.

6. Arrange chicken in center of a large heated platter and pile the hot rice around it. Stir currants into sauce remaining in the pan and pour over the rice. Scatter almonds over top. Garnish with parsley.

About 6 servings

Chicken Mexicana

Two kinds of protein—vegetable and animal—are combined in this south-of-the-border approach to chicken. It's an unusual treat.

3 tablespoons vegetable oil
2 broiler-fryer chickens (2½
   to 3 pounds each), cut in
   serving-size pieces
2 cans (8 ounces each)
   tomato sauce
1 can (13¾ ounces) chicken
   broth
2 tablespoons (½ envelope)
   dry onion soup mix
¾ cup chopped onion
1 clove garlic, minced
6 tablespoons crunchy peanut
   butter
½ cup cream
½ teaspoon chili powder
¼ cup dry sherry
   Cooked rice

1. Heat oil in a large skillet. Add chicken and brown on all sides.

2. Meanwhile, combine tomato sauce, 1 cup chicken broth, soup mix, onion, and garlic in a saucepan. Heat thoroughly, stirring constantly.

3. Pour sauce over chicken in skillet. Simmer, covered, 20 minutes.

4. Put peanut butter into a bowl and blend in cream and remaining chicken broth; stir into skillet along with chili powder and sherry. Heat thoroughly. Serve with hot fluffy rice.

About 6 servings

Chicken with Fruit

Oranges, cherries, and raisins make a wonderful taste contrast to this garlic-browned chicken and contribute to its high nutritional content, which includes protein, vitamins A and C, niacin, calcium, and iron.

1 tablespoon flour
1 teaspoon seasoned salt
¾ teaspoon paprika
3 pounds broiler-fryer chicken pieces (legs, thighs, and breasts)
1½ tablespoons vegetable oil
1½ tablespoons butter or margarine
1 clove garlic, crushed in a garlic press or minced
⅓ cup chicken broth
2 tablespoons cider vinegar
1 tablespoon brown sugar
¼ teaspoon rosemary
1 can (11 ounces) mandarin oranges, drained; reserve syrup
1 jar (4 ounces) maraschino cherries, drained; reserve syrup
1 tablespoon water
1 tablespoon cornstarch
½ cup dark seedless raisins
Cooked rice

1. Mix flour, seasoned salt, and paprika. Coat chicken pieces.
2. Heat oil, butter, and garlic in a large heavy skillet. Add chicken pieces and brown well on all sides.
3. Mix broth, vinegar, brown sugar, rosemary, and reserved syrups. Pour into skillet; cover and cook slowly 25 minutes, or until chicken is tender.
4. Remove chicken pieces to a serving dish and keep warm; skim any excess fat from liquid in skillet. Blend water with cornstarch and stir into liquid in skillet. Add raisins, bring to boiling, stirring constantly, and cook about 5 minutes, or until mixture is thickened and smooth. Mix in orange sections and cherries; heat thoroughly.
5. Pour sauce over chicken and serve with hot fluffy rice.

About 6 servings

Lemon-Broiled Chicken

This tasty dish is easy to prepare and rich in protein, niacin, and iron.

1 broiler-fryer chicken (about 1½ pounds), halved lengthwise
2 tablespoons lemon juice

1. Arrange chicken halves, skin side down, in broiler pan (not on a rack). Bring wing tips onto backs under shoulder joint. Press down.
2. Brush chicken with 1 tablespoon of the

2 tablespoons butter or margarine, melted
1 to 1½ tablespoons sugar
½ teaspoon salt
⅛ teaspoon ground black pepper
½ teaspoon paprika

lemon juice and some of the melted butter. Mix half of sugar, the salt, pepper, and paprika; sprinkle over chicken. Combine remaining sugar, lemon juice, and melted butter; use to brush on chicken while broiling. 3. Place pan under broiler with the surface of chicken 6 to 9 inches from heat. Broil chicken 20 to 25 minutes; turn and broil 15 to 20 minutes. Brush with the lemon butter several times during broiling.

2 servings

Skillet Chicken à l'Orange

Chicken and oranges, another combination of flavors that has stood the test of time, adds a gourmet touch to your meal and protein, vitamins A and C, niacin, and iron to your diet.

3 pounds chicken pieces (legs and breasts)
¼ cup enriched all-purpose flour
1 teaspoon salt
1 teaspoon monosodium glutamate
3 to 4 tablespoons olive oil or vegetable oil
¾ cup chopped onion
½ cup ground almonds
½ teaspoon ground cinnamon
⅛ teaspoon ground cloves
1 cup orange juice
1 cup chicken broth
1 orange, cut in half slices
½ cup golden raisins
1 cup orange segments (about 2 oranges)
Watercress (optional)
Cooked rice or mashed potatoes

1. Coat chicken with a mixture of flour, salt, and monosodium glutamate. Heat oil in a large skillet, add chicken, and brown on all sides. Push chicken to one side of skillet; add onion and cook, stirring occasionally, until just tender (about 5 minutes). If desired, drain off excess fat.
2. Stir into skillet a mixture of the almonds, cinnamon, and cloves. Adding gradually, stir in orange juice and chicken broth. Move chicken pieces through the liquid. Add orange slices and raisins. Cover and cook over low heat 25 to 30 minutes, or until chicken is tender. During final 5 minutes of cooking add orange segments.
3. Remove chicken to a warm serving platter and pour sauce over all. Garnish ends of platter with watercress, if desired. Serve with hot fluffy rice or mashed potatoes.

About 6 servings

Chicken Polynesian Style

If you have leftover chicken, this is a great way to dress it up. The vegetables add vitamin A and calcium to the nutrients found in chicken.

2 cups chicken broth
1 package (10 ounces) frozen mixed vegetables
½ cup diagonally sliced celery
1½ tablespoons cornstarch
1 teaspoon monosodium glutamate
½ teaspoon sugar
½ teaspoon seasoned salt
⅛ teaspoon ground black pepper
½ teaspoon Worcestershire sauce
1 small clove garlic, minced or crushed in a garlic press
1 tablespoon instant minced onion
1 can (6 ounces) ripe olives, drained and cut in wedges
Cooked chicken, cut in 1-inch pieces (about 2 cups)
Chow mein noodles
Salted peanuts
Soy sauce

1. Heat ½ cup chicken broth in a saucepan. Add frozen vegetables and celery; cook, covered, until crisp-tender. Remove vegetables and set aside; reserve any cooking liquid in saucepan.

2. Mix cornstarch, monosodium glutamate, sugar, seasoned salt, and pepper; blend with ¼ cup of the chicken broth. Add remaining broth, Worcestershire sauce, garlic, and onion to the saucepan. Add cornstarch mixture; bring to boiling, stirring constantly. Cook and stir 2 to 3 minutes.

3. Mix in olives, chicken, and reserved vegetables; heat thoroughly, stirring occasionally.

4. Serve over chow mein noodles and top generously with peanuts. Accompany with a cruet of soy sauce.

About 6 servings

Stuffed Roast Capon

When a chicken is too small and a turkey is too big, here's your answer. Protein, B vitamins, and iron are the nutritional benefits of this capon-and-stuffing combination.

½ cup butter or margarine
1½ teaspoons salt

1. For stuffing, melt butter and mix in salt, pepper, thyme, marjoram, and rosemary.

¼ teaspoon ground black
   pepper
¼ teaspoon thyme
¼ teaspoon marjoram
¼ teaspoon rosemary
1½ quarts soft enriched bread
   cubes
½ cup milk
¼ cup chopped celery leaves
¼ cup chopped onion
1 capon (6 to 7 pounds)
   Salt
   Fat, melted

2. Put bread cubes into a large bowl and pour in seasoned butter; lightly toss. Mix in milk, celery leaves, and onion.

3. Rub body and neck cavities of capon with salt. Fill cavities lightly with stuffing; truss bird, using skewers and cord.

4. Place, breast side up, on rack in a shallow roasting pan. Brush skin with melted fat and cover with a fat-moistened cheesecloth.

5. Roast in a 325°F oven 2½ hours, or until a meat thermometer inserted in center of inside thigh muscle registers 180° to 185°F. For easier carving, allow capon to stand about 20 minutes after removing from oven. Serve on a heated platter.

6 to 8 servings

Turkey Spoon Bread

A dish so good-tasting and attractive that you will look forward to making it often. It supplies protein, vitamin A, the B vitamins, and iron.

¾ cup enriched yellow
   cornmeal
2 tablespoons flour
1 teaspoon salt
4 cups turkey broth, cooled*
¼ cup butter or margarine
4 egg yolks
3 cups chopped cooked
   turkey
4 egg whites

* Four cups quick chicken broth (4 chicken bouillon cubes dissolved in 4 cups hot water) may be substituted for turkey broth.

1. Mix cornmeal, flour, and salt in a heavy saucepan. Stirring constantly, gradually add broth and bring to boiling. Continue cooking and stirring until mixture is thickened and smooth. Blend in butter. Turn into a large bowl and set aside to cool.

2. Beat egg yolks until thick and lemon colored; stir into cornmeal mixture. Blend in turkey.

3. Beat egg whites until rounded peaks are formed; gently fold into turkey mixture. Turn into a greased 2-quart shallow baking dish.

4. Bake at 375°F about 40 minutes, or until top is golden brown.

About 8 servings

Roast Turkey with Herbed Stuffing

More and more people are discovering that this classic holiday bird is a year-round treat, and of course it is an excellent source of protein, the B vitamins, and iron.

Cooked Giblets and Broth (see recipe)

4 quarts ½-inch enriched bread cubes

1 cup snipped parsley

2 to 2½ teaspoons salt

2 teaspoons thyme

2 teaspoons rosemary, crushed

2 teaspoons marjoram

1 teaspoon ground sage

1 cup butter or margarine

1 cup coarsely chopped onion

1 cup coarsely chopped celery with leaves

1 turkey (14 to 15 pounds) Fat

3 tablespoons flour

¼ teaspoon salt

⅛ teaspoon ground black pepper

1. Prepare Cooked Giblets and Broth. Measure 1 cup chopped cooked giblets; set the broth aside.

2. Combine bread cubes, reserved giblets, and parsley in a large bowl. Blend salt, thyme, rosemary, marjoram, and sage; add to bread mixture and toss to mix.

3. Heat butter in a skillet. Mix in onion and celery; cook about 5 minutes, stirring occasionally. Toss with the bread mixture.

4. Add 1 to 2 cups broth (depending upon how moist a stuffing is desired), mixing lightly until ingredients are thoroughly blended.

5. Rinse turkey with cold water; pat dry, inside and out, with absorbent paper. Lightly fill body and neck cavities with the stuffing. Fasten neck skin to back with a skewer. Bring wing tips onto back of bird. Push drumsticks under band of skin at tail, if present, or tie to tail with cord.

6. Place turkey, breast side up, on rack in a shallow roasting pan. Brush skin with fat. Insert meat thermometer in the thickest part of the inner thigh muscle, being sure that tip does not touch bone.

7. Roast in a 325°F oven about 5 hours, or until thermometer registers 180° to 185°F. If desired, baste or brush bird occasionally with pan drippings. Place turkey on a heated platter; for easier carving, allow turkey to stand about 30 minutes.

8. Meanwhile, leaving brown residue in roasting pan, pour remaining drippings and fat into a bowl. Allow fat to rise to surface; skim off

fat and measure 3 tablespoons into roasting pan. Blend flour, salt, and pepper with fat. Cook and stir until bubbly. Continue to stir while slowly adding 2 cups reserved liquid (broth and drippings). Cook, stirring constantly, until gravy thickens; scrape pan to blend in brown residue. Cook 1 to 2 minutes. If desired, mix in finely chopped cooked giblets the last few minutes of cooking.

About 25 servings

Cooked Giblets and Broth: Put **turkey neck** and **giblets** (except liver) into a saucepan with **1 large onion**, sliced, **parsley, celery with leaves, 1 medium bay leaf, 2 teaspoons salt,** and **1 quart water.** Cover, bring to boiling, reduce heat, and simmer until giblets are tender (about 2 hours); add the liver the last 15 minutes of cooking. Strain through a colander or sieve; reserve broth for stuffing. Chop giblets; set aside for stuffing and gravy.

Turkey Hash

Here's a quick and easy way to use leftover turkey and provide protein, vitamins A, C, and D, niacin, riboflavin, calcium, and iron all in one dish.

3 tablespoons butter or margarine	1. Heat butter in a saucepan. Mix in mushrooms and onion and cook about 5 minutes.
¾ cup sliced mushrooms	2. Remove from heat and stir in turkey, potatoes, parsley, seasoned salt, and pepper. Gradually add evaporated milk, stirring gently. Heat mixture thoroughly.
½ cup finely chopped onion	
2 cups diced cooked turkey	
2 cups diced cooked potatoes	
1 tablespoon snipped parsley	
1½ teaspoons seasoned salt	
⅛ teaspoon ground black pepper	
⅔ cup (6-ounce can) undiluted evaporated milk	

4 to 6 servings

Curried Turkey Pie

Here's a new turkey pie reflecting the international influence shared by most good cooks today. Protein, vitamin A, niacin, calcium, and iron are the nutritional benefits.

Pastry for a 2-crust 9-inch pie (prepared from a pie crust mix)
¼ **cup firm butter or margarine**
3 **tablespoons flour**
¼ **cup butter or margarine**
1 **cup chopped onion**
3 **apples, pared, cored, and sliced**
4 **cups cubed cooked turkey**
1 **cup cooked green peas**
½ **cup toasted blanched almonds, halved**
¼ **cup golden raisins**
1 **can (3½ ounces) flaked coconut**
1 **can (10½ ounces) condensed chicken noodle soup**
1 **soup can water**
½ **cup milk**
2 **teaspoons curry powder**
2 **tablespoons chutney**
1 **egg, beaten**

1. Prepare pastry following package directions. Chill.
2. Cut ¼ cup firm butter into flour until blended, using a pastry blender or two knives. Set aside.
3. Roll out pastry on a lightly floured surface into a 14 x 11-inch rectangle. Sprinkle butter-flour mixture evenly over half of dough, leaving a 2-inch border. Fold remaining half of dough over butter-flour mixture and roll to about ¼-inch thickness. Fold in thirds and roll out. Repeat rolling and folding three times. Wrap and refrigerate about 30 minutes for easy handling.
4. Meanwhile, heat ¼ cup butter in a large saucepan. Add onion and apples; cook about 3 minutes, stirring occasionally. Mix in turkey, peas, almonds, raisins, and coconut; toss lightly to mix. Turn into a greased shallow 3-quart baking dish. Set aside.
5. Heat soup and water in the saucepan. Cool slightly. Pour half of the soup into an electric blender container and blend, gradually adding remainder of soup and milk, then curry powder and chutney. Blend until smooth. Pour over turkey mixture in baking dish.
6. Roll out pastry a little larger than baking dish, cut several slits in pastry, and fit loosely over top. Turn the pastry overhang under and flute edge. Brush pastry with beaten egg.
7. Bake at 425°F about 25 minutes, or until top is golden.

About 8 servings

Turkey Fiesta with Currant Glaze

Turkey cut into serving pieces and dressed up with a colorful currant glaze makes a festive meal any time of the year. It has protein, vitamins A and C, niacin, calcium, and iron.

4	pounds disjointed turkey
2	teaspoons salt
½	teaspoon paprika
¼	cup butter
2	tablespoons flour
½	teaspoon dry mustard
¼	teaspoon ground ginger
¼	teaspoon ground nutmeg
¾	cup chicken broth (1 bouillon cube dissolved in ¾ cup boiling water)
1	can (6 ounces) frozen orange juice concentrate, thawed
¼	teaspoon Tabasco
2	tablespoons currant jelly
1	tablespoon shredded Parmesan cheese
2	tablespoons currant jelly
2	teaspoons prepared mustard
2	to 3 drops red food coloring

1. Rinse turkey pieces and dry thoroughly by patting with absorbent paper. Sprinkle evenly with salt and paprika.

2. Heat butter in a large heavy skillet over medium heat. Place turkey pieces skin side down in skillet. To brown all sides, turn pieces with tongs or two spoons, as necessary. When turkey is browned, remove from skillet.

3. Blend flour, dry mustard, ginger, and nutmeg. Stir into drippings in skillet. Heat until bubbly, stirring constantly. Add chicken broth gradually, stirring constantly. Blend in orange juice concentrate.

4. Cook rapidly, stirring constantly, until mixture thickens; cook 1 to 2 minutes. Blend in Tabasco, 2 tablespoons currant jelly, and Parmesan cheese. Return turkey pieces to skillet. Cover and simmer about 35 minutes.

5. For glaze, beat remaining currant jelly, prepared mustard, and food coloring together until blended.

6. Remove turkey pieces from sauce and arrange in a large shallow baking pan. Set sauce aside to keep warm. Using a pastry brush, brush each turkey piece generously with glaze.

7. Bake at 325°F about 20 minutes, or until largest pieces of turkey are tender when pierced with a fork; brush with glaze several times. Serve glazed turkey with the sauce.

About 8 servings

Turkey Biscuit Pinwheel with Fresh Mushroom Sauce

Just one cup of chopped turkey goes a long way in this spectacular dish. It's worthy of any occasion, and it gives you protein, the B vitamins, and iron.

1	cup chopped cooked turkey
¼	cup chopped fresh mushrooms
⅓	cup dairy sour cream
¼	cup finely chopped onion
¼	teaspoon salt
⅛	teaspoon ground black pepper
1½	cups all-purpose biscuit mix
½	cup milk
2	tablespoons butter or margarine
½	pound mushrooms, sliced lengthwise
½	cup chopped celery
2	tablespoons flour
¼	teaspoon salt
⅛	teaspoon ground black pepper
1	cup cream

1. Mix turkey, chopped mushrooms, sour cream, onion, ¼ teaspoon salt, and ⅛ teaspoon pepper; set aside.

2. Put biscuit mix into a bowl; add milk and stir until a soft dough is formed. Turn onto a lightly floured surface and knead with the fingertips three or four times. Roll into a rectangle ¼ inch thick and 12 inches long.

3. Spread dough with the turkey mixture to within 1 inch of the edge. Then roll up as for a jelly roll, pressing long edge firmly to seal.

4. Place on a lightly greased cookie sheet, sealed edge down; bring ends of roll together to form a ring. Overlap and press securely.

5. With scissors or sharp knife, cut ring diagonally from outside almost to center, making 12 uniform pieces. Pull out slightly and twist each section so that cut sides rest almost flat on cookie sheet.

6. Bake at 450°F about 20 minutes, or until golden brown.

7. Meanwhile, prepare sauce. Heat butter in a skillet; add sliced mushrooms and celery and cook until mushrooms are lightly browned, stirring occasionally. Remove vegetables with a slotted spoon and set aside. Stir flour and remaining salt and pepper into butter in skillet; heat until bubbly. Add cream gradually, stirring constantly. Bring to boiling and cook 1 to 2 minutes, stirring constantly. Mix in vegetables.

8. Serve sauce hot over servings of biscuit pinwheel.

About 6 servings

Turkey 'n' Dressing Bake

This nutritious whole wheat bread dressing baked with turkey slices supplies protein, the B vitamins, and iron to your diet.

 3 tablespoons butter or margarine
 ½ cup diced celery
 ¼ cup minced onion
 3¼ cups chicken broth (dissolve 4 chicken bouillon cubes in 3¼ cups boiling water)
 5 cups coarse whole wheat bread crumbs; reserve ½ cup crumbs for topping
 ¼ cup snipped parsley
 ½ teaspoon salt
 ¼ teaspoon ground black pepper
 1 egg, slightly beaten
 2 tablespoons flour
 2 eggs, beaten
 ⅛ teaspoon ground black pepper
 ¼ teaspoon crushed leaf sage
 ¼ teaspoon celery salt
   Thin slices of cooked turkey roast (see Note)
 1 tablespoon butter or margarine, melted
   Parsley, snipped

1. Heat 3 tablespoons butter in a large skillet. Mix in celery and onion and cook about 5 minutes. Combine vegetables with 1¾ cups chicken broth, 4½ cups bread crumbs, ¼ cup parsley, salt, ¼ teaspoon pepper, and 1 egg. Mix lightly with a fork. Spoon the mixture over bottom of a shallow 2-quart baking dish; set aside.

2. Mix flour and ¼ cup cool broth in a saucepan until smooth; heat until bubbly. Add remaining broth gradually, stirring constantly. Cook and stir over medium heat until sauce comes to boiling; cook 2 minutes. Remove from heat and gradually add to eggs while beating. Blend in remaining pepper, sage, and celery salt.

3. Arrange the desired amount of turkey over dressing in baking dish. Pour the sauce over all.

4. Toss reserved bread crumbs with melted butter; spoon over top.

5. Bake at 350°F 30 to 40 minutes, or until egg mixture is set. Garnish generously with parsley.

6 servings

Note: Prepare frozen boneless turkey roast, following package directions.

Turkey in Orange Sauce

What to do with leftover turkey need never be a problem again. This combination of turkey and spicy sauce is delicious and also offers protein, vitamins A and C, niacin, calcium, and iron.

1 **can (6 ounces) frozen orange juice concentrate, thawed**
⅓ **cup water**
1 **tablespoon lemon juice**
2 **tablespoons brown sugar**
½ **teaspoon ground ginger**
¼ **teaspoon ground marjoram**
¼ **teaspoon poultry seasoning**
½ **teaspoon salt**
1 **teaspoon cornstarch**
1 **tablespoon cold water**
1 **tablespoon butter or margarine**
White meat of roast turkey, thinly sliced
Parsley sprigs

1. Put orange juice concentrate, ⅓ cup water, and lemon juice into a large skillet. Blend brown sugar, ginger, marjoram, poultry seasoning, and salt; mix with ingredients in skillet. Bring to boiling, reduce heat, and simmer, covered, about 15 minutes, stirring occasionally.
2. Blend cornstarch and water; stir into boiling mixture. Cook, stirring as necessary, 2 to 3 minutes.
3. Add butter and sliced turkey; heat thoroughly.
4. Garnish with parsley.

About 6 servings

Turkey-Oyster Casserole

Truly a New Orleans combination of flavors, turkey and oysters are high in protein, B vitamins, calcium, and iron.

1 **tablespoon butter**
2 **teaspoons grated onion**
4 **ounces mushrooms, sliced lengthwise**
¼ **cup butter**
¼ **cup enriched all-purpose flour**
1 **teaspoon salt**
¼ **teaspoon ground pepper**

1. Heat 1 tablespoon butter with onion in a skillet; add mushrooms and cook over medium heat until lightly browned, stirring occasionally. Set aside.
2. Heat ¼ cup butter in a saucepan over low heat. Stir in flour, salt, pepper, and cayenne; cook until bubbly. Add milk gradually, stirring until well blended. Bring rapidly to boiling and boil 1 to 2 minutes, stirring

Few grains cayenne pepper
2 cups milk
1 egg yolk, slightly beaten
2 tablespoons chopped parsley
¼ teaspoon thyme
2 drops Tabasco
1 pint oysters (with liquor)
2 cups diced cooked turkey
Buttered soft enriched
bread crumbs

constantly.

3. Blend a small amount of the hot sauce into egg yolk and return to remaining sauce, stirring until mixed. Stir in parsley, thyme, and Tabasco.

4. Heat oysters just to boiling; drain. Add oysters, turkey, and the mushrooms to sauce; toss lightly until thoroughly mixed.

5. Turn mixture into a buttered shallow 1½-quart baking dish. Sprinkle with crumbs.

6. Heat in a 400°F oven about 10 minutes, or until mixture is bubbly around edges and crumbs are golden brown.

About 6 servings

Rock Cornish Hens with Fruited Stuffing

One hen is just right for an individual serving, and gives you protein, vitamin A, B vitamins, calcium, and iron.

1½ cups herb-seasoned
    stuffing croutons
½ cup drained canned apricot
    halves, cut in pieces
½ cup quartered seedless
    green grapes
⅓ cup chopped pecans
¼ cup butter or margarine,
    melted
2 tablespoons apricot nectar
1 tablespoon chopped parsley
¼ teaspoon salt
4 Rock Cornish hens (1 to
    1½ pounds each), thawed
    if purchased frozen
    Salt and pepper
⅓ cup apricot nectar
2 teaspoons soy sauce

1. Combine stuffing croutons, apricots, grapes, pecans, 2 tablespoons butter, 2 tablespoons apricot nectar, parsley, and ¼ teaspoon salt in a bowl; mix lightly.

2. Sprinkle cavities of hens with salt and pepper. Fill each hen with about ½ cup stuffing; fasten with skewers and lace with cord.

3. Blend ⅓ cup apricot nectar, soy sauce, and remaining butter. Place hens, breast side up, on a rack in a shallow roasting pan; brush generously with sauce.

4. Roast in a 350°F oven about 1½ hours, or until hens are tender and well browned; baste occasionally with sauce during roasting.

4 servings

Glazed Duckling Gourmet

Here's a treat that could make your reputation as a gourmet cook, so don't tell how simple it is. It has protein, niacin, and iron, plus small amounts of other vitamins and minerals.

2 ducklings (about 4 pounds each), quartered (do not use wings, necks, and backs) and skinned
1½ teaspoons salt
¼ teaspoon ground nutmeg
3 to 4 tablespoons butter
1 clove garlic, minced
1½ teaspoons rosemary, crushed
1½ teaspoons thyme
1½ cups Burgundy
2 teaspoons red wine vinegar
⅓ cup currant jelly
2 teaspoons cornstarch
2 tablespoons cold water
1½ cups halved seedless green grapes
Watercress

1. Remove excess fat from duckling pieces; rinse duckling and pat dry with absorbent paper. Rub pieces with salt and nutmeg.
2. Heat butter and garlic in a large skillet over medium heat; add the duckling pieces and brown well on all sides.
3. Add rosemary, thyme, Burgundy, vinegar, and jelly to skillet. Bring to boiling; cover and simmer over low heat until duckling is tender (about 45 minutes). Remove duckling to a heated platter and keep it warm.
4. Combine cornstarch and water; blend into liquid in skillet; bring to boiling and cook 1 to 2 minutes, stirring constantly. Add grapes and toss them lightly until thoroughly heated.
5. Pour the hot sauce over duckling; garnish platter with watercress.

6 to 8 servings

Roast Goose with Rice-and-Pickle Stuffing

To make a special occasion even more memorable, serve roast stuffed goose. The taste is fabulous, but there's also protein, vitamins A and C, the B vitamins, calcium, and iron.

3 cups cooked rice; or 1 package (6 ounces) seasoned white and wild rice mix, cooked following package directions

1. Combine rice, stuffing croutons, orange sections, onions, cranberries, pickles and liquid, butter, and brown sugar in a large bowl; toss lightly until blended.
2. Rinse goose and remove any large layers of

1 package (7 ounces) herb-
seasoned stuffing croutons

2 medium navel oranges,
pared and sectioned

2 onions, chopped

1 cup cranberries, rinsed,
sorted, and chopped

1 cup sweet mixed pickles,
drained and chopped

¼ cup sweet pickle liquid

½ to ¾ cup butter or
margarine, melted

2 tablespoons brown sugar

1 goose (8 to 10 pounds)

1 tablespoon salt

¼ teaspoon ground black
pepper

2 tablespoons light corn
syrup

1½ cups orange juice

½ cup orange marmalade

fat from the body cavity. Pat dry with absorbent paper. Rub body and neck cavities with salt and pepper.

3. Lightly spoon stuffing into the neck and body cavities. Overlap neck cavity with the skin and skewer to back of goose. Close body cavity with skewers and lace with cord. Loop cord around legs; tighten slightly and tie to a skewer inserted in the back above tail. Rub skin of goose with a little salt, if desired.

4. Put remaining stuffing into a greased casserole and cover; or cook in heavy-duty aluminum foil. Set in oven with goose during final hour of roasting.

5. Place goose, breast side down, on a rack in a large shallow roasting pan.

6. Roast in a 325°F oven 2 hours, removing fat from pan several times during this period.

7. Turn goose, breast side up. Blend corn syrup and 1 cup orange juice. Brush generously over goose. Roast about 1½ hours, or until goose tests done. To test for doneness, move leg gently by grasping end of bone; when done, drumstick-thigh joint moves easily or twists out. Brush frequently during final roasting period with the orange-syrup blend.

8. Transfer goose to a heated serving platter. Spoon 2 tablespoons drippings, the remaining ½ cup orange juice, and marmalade into a small saucepan. Heat thoroughly, stirring to blend. Pour into a serving dish or gravy boat to accompany goose.

6 to 8 servings

Roast Duckling with Orange-Filbert Stuffing

Protein, B vitamins, calcium, and iron are the nutritional benefits derived from these orange-stuffed ducklings, not to mention the gourmet taste.

- **4 cups enriched white bread crumbs**
- **2 cups chopped pared apple**
- **1 cup chopped celery**
- **½ cup chopped onion**
- **2 cups chopped filberts, toasted**
- **2 teaspoons grated orange peel**
- **1½ teaspoons grated lemon peel**
- **2 eggs, beaten**
- **½ cup orange juice**
- **2 to 3 tablespoons lemon juice**
- **¼ cup butter or margarine, melted**
- **1 teaspoon seasoned salt**
- **½ teaspoon ground black pepper**
- **½ teaspoon thyme**
- **¼ teaspoon ground nutmeg**
- **2 ducklings (4 to 6 pounds each)**
- **1 teaspoon salt**
- **2 tablespoons butter or margarine, melted**
- **Watercress or parsley**

1. For stuffing, combine bread crumbs, apple, celery, onion, filberts, orange peel, and lemon peel in a large bowl. Mix eggs, orange juice, lemon juice, ¼ cup butter, seasoned salt, pepper, thyme and nutmeg; add to bread mixture and toss until well mixed.

2. Rub cavities of ducklings with salt. Spoon stuffing into cavities. To close body cavity, skewer and lace with cord. Fasten neck skin to back with skewer. Loop cord around legs, tighten, and then tie; secure wings to body.

3. Place ducklings, breast side up, on a rack in a large shallow roasting pan. Brush with 2 tablespoons butter.

4. Roast in a 325°F oven 2½ to 3 hours.

5. Place ducklings on a heated platter; remove skewers and cord. Garnish with watercress or parsley.

6 to 8 servings

Fish and Shellfish

Trout, perch, shrimp, red snapper, flounder, bass, oysters, scallops—these are only some of the many fish and shellfish we enjoy from our lakes, streams, and oceans. Everyone has a favorite way to prepare these treasures of the lakes and seas, whether it's as a grilled fresh fish, a delicate seafood casserole, or a spicily sauced baked fish.

If you are not a fish lover, you've probably never eaten it properly prepared. Remember, fish is cooked when its flesh becomes opaque and when it flakes easily; overcooking destroys the subtle flavor and fine texture of seafoods. When fish and shellfish are handled delicately in cooking, the results will be delicious. A carefully made *Perch with Parsley and Dill* should convince any doubting Thomases that a simply garnished poached fish can delight the palate. Then try the *Baked Flounder Superb*, with its seasoned scallop stuffing, or the *Broiled Fish Californian*, with its spicy-sweet raisin sauce.

Fish and shellfish deserve to be featured more often at the dinner table because they are some of the most nutritious foods we eat. Generally high in protein and low in fat, fish is an ideal dish for weight watchers and for those who are trying to control their cholesterol level. Seafoods are high in iodine and B vitamins, and if cooked with the bones, they will provide considerable amounts of calcium.

As fish is sold in several forms, here are a few pointers to keep in mind when shopping. *Whole fish* are sold just as they were when they came out of the water; *drawn fish* have been eviscerated (entrails removed). *Dressed fish* have been scaled and eviscerated, and often the head, tail, and fins have been removed. *Fish steaks* are slices of large fish, cut crosswise through the backbone, and *fillets* are the sides of fish. When buying fresh fish, look for springy flesh, bright eyes, shiny scales, reddish gills, and a mild odor. Frozen fish should be solidly frozen and well wrapped.

Browse through this section for some new ideas on fish cookery. You'll find many tempting flavor combinations in the following recipes. Sherry, cider, olives, orange peel, tarragon, nutmeg, cucumber, almonds, sweet pickles, Parmesan cheese—these are only some of the foods and seasonings used with fish to enhance its subtle flavor. The recipes themselves are intriguing to read—when your fish platter reaches the table the real pleasure will begin!

Salmon Bake

Simple to mix and bake, this delicious casserole gives you protein, vitamins A and D, the B vitamins, calcium, and iron.

1 **can (16 ounces) salmon, drained and flaked**
1½ **cups herb-seasoned stuffing croutons**
2 **tablespoons finely snipped parsley**
2 **tablespoons finely chopped onion**
3 **eggs, well beaten**
1 **can (10½ ounces) condensed cream of celery soup**
½ **cup milk**
⅛ **teaspoon ground black pepper**
Lemon, thinly sliced and cut in quarter-slices
Parsley, snipped
Sour cream sauce (prepared from a mix)

1. Toss salmon, stuffing croutons, parsley, and onion together in a bowl. Blend eggs, condensed soup, milk, and pepper; add to salmon mixture and mix thoroughly. Turn into a greased 1½-quart casserole.
2. Bake at 350°F about 50 minutes. Garnish center with overlapping quarter-slices of lemon and parsley.
3. Serve with hot sour cream sauce.

About 6 servings

Savory Salmon Kabobs with Broccoli Sauce

The delectable cheese-and-broccoli sauce makes these salmon patties something special. In addition to the nutrients in the salmon, the kabobs contain protein, vitamins A, C, and D, riboflavin, and calcium.

Broccoli sauce:
2 **tablespoons butter**
2 **tablespoons flour**
½ **teaspoon salt**
1⅔ **cups (14½-ounce can) evaporated milk**

1. For sauce, melt butter in a heavy saucepan. Blend in flour and salt; cook until bubbly. Add evaporated milk gradually, stirring constantly. Return to heat; cook and stir until sauce comes to boiling and is thickened and smooth. Cook 1 to 2 minutes. Stir in cheese, lemon juice,

1 cup (about 4 ounces) shredded Cheddar cheese
1 tablespoon lemon juice
1 teaspoon Worcestershire sauce
1 package (10 ounces) frozen chopped broccoli, cooked and drained

Salmon kabobs:
1 can (16 ounces) salmon, drained and flaked
1 egg, slightly beaten
1 cup (about 4 ounces) shredded Cheddar cheese
½ cup fine dry enriched bread crumbs
¼ cup finely chopped onion
¼ teaspoon Worcestershire sauce
⅛ teaspoon Tabasco
¼ cup butter

Worcestershire sauce, and cooked broccoli. Set aside.
2. For kabobs, mix salmon, egg, cheese, bread crumbs, onion, Worcestershire sauce, and Tabasco in a bowl. Divide mixture into 6 portions and press firmly around wooden skewers.
3. Melt butter over medium heat in a large heavy skillet. Add kabobs and brown evenly, turning frequently. Heat sauce and serve hot over kabobs.

6 servings

Salmon Custard

This lightly spiced custard is perfect for brunch or supper, and it supplies protein, vitamins A and D, niacin, riboflavin, thiamine, and calcium.

2 eggs
½ cup undiluted evaporated milk
1 tablespoon chopped chives
½ teaspoon dry mustard
¼ teaspoon dill weed
¼ teaspoon salt
    Few grains pepper
1 can (7¾ ounces) salmon, drained and flaked
    Paprika

1. Beat eggs slightly in a bowl. Add evaporated milk, chives, dry mustard, dill weed, salt, and pepper; mix well. Stir in salmon. Turn into 2 well-greased individual casseroles. Sprinkle with paprika.
2. Set casseroles in a shallow pan. Pour hot water into pan to a depth of 1 inch.
3. Bake at 350°F 25 to 30 minutes, or until a knife when inserted near center comes out clean. Remove casseroles from water immediately and serve hot.

2 servings

Broiled Salmon

This well-seasoned broiled salmon is so appetizing it is served without a sauce. It provides protein, riboflavin, niacin, vitamin D, and calcium.

6 **salmon steaks, cut ½ inch thick**
1 **cup sauterne**
½ **cup vegetable oil**
2 **tablespoons wine vinegar**
2 **teaspoons soy sauce**
2 **tablespoons chopped green onion**
  Seasoned salt
  Green onion, chopped (optional)
  Pimiento strips (optional)

1. Put salmon steaks into a large shallow dish. Mix sauterne, oil, wine vinegar, soy sauce, and green onion; pour over salmon. Marinate in refrigerator several hours or overnight, turning occasionally.

2. To broil, remove steaks from marinade and place on broiler rack. Set under broiler with top 6 inches from heat. Broil about 5 minutes on each side, brushing generously with marinade several times. About 2 minutes before removing from broiler, sprinkle each steak lightly with seasoned salt and, if desired, top with green onion and pimiento. Serve at once.

6 servings

Cold Poached Salmon with Remoulade Sauce

Here's a sophisticated dish that is suitable for just about any company occasion, and it is generous with protein, riboflavin, niacin, vitamin D, and calcium.

Poached salmon:
1½ **quarts water**
4 **vegetable bouillon cubes**
2 **medium onions, sliced**
1 **carrot, sliced**
1 **lemon, thinly sliced**
1 **teaspoon monosodium glutamate**
1 **teaspoon salt**
10 **peppercorns**
4 **salmon steaks, about ½ pound each**

1. For poached salmon, put water, bouillon cubes, onions, carrot, lemon, monosodium glutamate, salt, and peppercorns into a 4-quart saucepot. Bring to boiling.

2. Meanwhile, put salmon steaks onto a large cheesecloth. Pull up corners of the cheesecloth and tie together. Lower salmon into boiling water. Cover and simmer gently about 15 minutes, or until salmon flakes easily when tested with a fork, but is firm and whole. Uncover and set saucepot with salmon aside until cool (about 1 hour).

Remoulade Sauce:
- 1 cup mayonnaise (low calorie, if desired)
- 2 tablespoons minced green onion
- 1 tablespoon drained capers
- 1 teaspoon Worcestershire sauce
- 1 teaspoon prepared horseradish
- 1 teaspoon finely chopped parsley
- ½ clove garlic, minced
- 1 drop Tabasco
- Leaf lettuce

3. Carefully lift salmon from liquid and set in a pan. Cut away cheesecloth; transfer steaks to an aluminum-foil-lined pan. Carefully peel off skin and discard. Cover tightly with foil and chill thoroughly.

4. For Remoulade Sauce, put mayonnaise into a bowl. Add green onion, capers, Worcestershire sauce, horseradish, parsley, garlic, and Tabasco; blend well. Chill thoroughly before serving.

5. To serve, place leaf lettuce and a chilled salmon steak on each serving plate and accompany with Remoulade Sauce.

4 servings

Salmon Roll-Ups

Just a little bit of effort produces these tempting salmon pastries. They contain protein, the B vitamins, vitamin D, and calcium.

- 1 egg
- 1 teaspoon dry mustard
- 1 teaspoon parsley flakes
- ½ teaspoon instant onion flakes
- 1 can (7¾ ounces) salmon, drained and flaked
- 1 package (10 ounces) fresh dough for parkerhouse dinner rolls
- 2 tablespoons soft butter or margarine

1. Beat egg lightly and set aside 1 tablespoon for later use.

2. Combine remaining beaten egg with dry mustard, parsley flakes, onion flakes, and salmon.

3. Separate dough into pieces. Roll each with a rolling pin into a thin rectangle 3 x 5 inches. Spread rectangles lightly with butter, then with the salmon mixture. Roll up, seal edges, and arrange, sealed edge down, on a cookie sheet. Brush rolls with reserved beaten egg.

4. Bake at 375°F 10 to 12 minutes. Serve hot.

12 roll-ups

Two-Layer Salmon-Rice Loaf

Salmon, rice, and evaporated milk are the ingredients in this hearty loaf that combine to give protein, vitamin A, niacin, riboflavin, thiamine, vitamin D, calcium, and iron.

Salmon layer:
- 1 **can (16 ounces) salmon**
- 2 **cups coarse soft enriched bread crumbs**
- 2 **tablespoons finely chopped onion**
- ½ **cup undiluted evaporated milk**
- 1 **egg, slightly beaten**
- 2 **tablespoons butter or margarine, melted**
- 1 **tablespoon lemon juice**
- 1 **teaspoon salt**

Rice layer:
- 3 **cups cooked enriched rice**
- ¼ **cup finely chopped parsley**
- 2 **eggs, slightly beaten**
- ⅔ **cup undiluted evaporated milk**
- 2 **tablespoons butter or margarine, melted**
- ¼ **teaspoon salt**

Sauce:
- 1 **large onion, quartered and thinly sliced**
- ¾ **cup water**
- 1 **can (10¾ ounces) condensed tomato soup**

1. For salmon layer, drain salmon and remove skin. Flake salmon and put into a bowl. Add bread crumbs, onion, evaporated milk, egg, butter, lemon juice, and salt; mix lightly. Turn into a buttered 9 x 5 x 3-inch loaf pan; press lightly to form a layer.

2. For rice layer, combine rice with parsley, eggs, evaporated milk, butter, and salt. Spoon over salmon layer; press lightly.

3. Set filled loaf pan in a shallow pan. Pour hot water into pan to a depth of 1 inch.

4. Bake at 375°F about 45 minutes. Remove from water immediately.

5. Meanwhile, for sauce, put onion and water into a saucepan. Bring to boiling, reduce heat, and simmer, covered, 10 minutes. Remove onion, if desired. Add condensed soup to saucepan, stir until blended, and bring to boiling.

6. Cut loaf into slices and top servings with tomato sauce.

About 8 servings

Tuna-Bacon Soufflé

Fish and bacon, two flavors not often found together, are combined here with eggs to supply protein, vitamins A and D, niacin, riboflavin, thiamine, calcium, and iron.

8 slices bacon, diced, fried in a skillet, and drained
¼ cup chopped onion
¼ cup chopped celery
⅓ cup butter or margarine
⅓ cup enriched all-purpose flour
½ teaspoon seasoned salt
½ teaspoon basil
⅛ teaspoon ground black pepper
1½ cups milk
6 egg yolks
½ teaspoon Worcestershire sauce
1 can (6½ or 7 ounces) tuna, drained and flaked
⅓ cup drained canned sliced mushrooms
¼ cup snipped parsley
6 egg whites

1. Reserve 2 tablespoons bacon drippings in skillet. Add onion and celery to hot drippings and cook until vegetables are crisp-tender. Set aside.

2. Heat butter in a saucepan. Stir in flour, seasoned salt, basil, and pepper; heat until bubbly. Gradually add milk, stirring to blend. Bring to boiling, stirring constantly, and boil 1 minute. Remove from heat.

3. Meanwhile, beat egg yolks until thick. Spoon in hot sauce, beating thoroughly after each addition. Add Worcestershire sauce, bacon, onion, celery, tuna, mushrooms, and parsley; mix well.

4. Beat egg whites until stiff, not dry, peaks are formed. Spoon tuna sauce over surface of egg whites and carefully fold together until just blended. Gently turn mixture into an ungreased 2-quart soufflé dish (deep straight-sided casserole); spread evenly.

5. Bake at 350°F about 40 minutes, or until a knife comes out clean when inserted in soufflé about halfway between center and edge. Serve immediately.

6 to 8 servings

Tuna à la Philippine

This spicy tuna dish has an unusually tasty sauce, and gives you protein, niacin, riboflavin, thiamine, and iron.

Tuna and rice:
- 1 tablespoon vegetable oil
- 1 cup diagonally sliced celery
- 1 medium onion, sliced
- ½ cup green pepper slivers
- 3 cups cooked enriched rice
- ¼ teaspoon salt
- Few grains pepper
- ¼ teaspoon garlic salt
- ⅛ teaspoon ground ginger
- 2 cans (6½ or 7 ounces each) chunk-style tuna, drained
- ¾ cup water

Sauce:
- ¼ cup firmly packed brown sugar
- 2 teaspoons cornstarch
- ½ teaspoon dry mustard
- ½ cup lemon juice
- ¼ cup water
- 1 tablespoon soy sauce

1. For tuna and rice, heat oil in a large skillet. Mix in celery, onion, and green pepper; cook until crisp-tender. Remove vegetables from skillet and set them aside.

2. Add rice to oil remaining in skillet. Mix salt, pepper, garlic salt, and ginger; sprinkle over rice. Add tuna and stir lightly, keeping tuna pieces as whole as possible. Cook quickly over high heat about 2 minutes, stirring the mixture occasionally.

3. Stir in water and add the reserved vegetables. Cover, bring to boiling, reduce heat, and simmer about 5 minutes to heat thoroughly.

4. Meanwhile, for sauce, mix brown sugar, cornstarch, and dry mustard in a small saucepan. Blend lemon juice, water, and soy sauce; stir in. Bring rapidly to boiling, stirring constantly, and boil 2 to 3 minutes, or until thickened. Pour into a bowl.

5. Turn tuna mixture into a heated serving dish and arrange tuna and vegetables in center. Serve with the sauce.

About 6 servings

Note: If desired, for garnish prepare a thin omelet mixture, cook in a skillet until set, and cut into thin 2- or 3-inch strips.

Gourmet Tuna and Artichoke Casserole

This is not an ordinary casserole, but a real experience in gourmet dining that offers protein, vitamins A and D, the B vitamins, and calcium.

2 cans (6½ or 7 ounces each) chunk-style tuna
  Olive oil
⅓ cup chopped green onion
⅓ cup chopped celery
1 teaspoon seasoned salt
1 teaspoon soy sauce
½ cup enriched all-purpose flour
1 cup cooled chicken broth
2 cups half-and-half
1 tablespoon grated lemon peel
1 tablespoon lemon juice
2 cans (5 ounces each) water chestnuts, drained and sliced
8 ounces fresh mushrooms, sliced
1 package (9 ounces) frozen artichoke hearts, cooked
1½ cups uncooked rice, cooked according to package directions
3 tablespoons butter or margarine
½ cup snipped parsley

1. Drain and reserve oil from tuna. Measure tuna oil; add olive oil to make ⅓ cup. Heat in a large skillet.

2. Add onion and celery and cook until crisp-tender. Stir in seasoned salt, soy sauce, and flour until blended. Add chicken broth and half-and-half gradually, stirring constantly. Cook, stirring until mixture begins to thicken. Boil 1 minute.

3. Stir in lemon peel and juice. Add water chestnuts, mushrooms, and tuna. Mix gently and turn into a 1½-quart casserole; arrange artichoke hearts around edge.

4. Heat in 350°F oven about 20 minutes.

5. Toss cooked rice with butter and parsley; serve with the hot casserole.

6 to 8 servings

Broiled Trout

Here's a slight variation of the classic broiled trout; it offers a new taste combination, together with the protein, niacin, and riboflavin that make this fish so nutritious.

Trout (8- to 10-ounce fish for each serving)
French dressing
Instant minced onion
Salt
Lemon slices
Tomato wedges
Mint sprigs or watercress

1. Remove head and fins from trout, if desired. Rinse trout quickly under running cold water; dry thoroughly. Brush inside of fish with French dressing and sprinkle generously with instant minced onion and salt. Brush outside generously with French dressing.
2. Arrange trout in a greased shallow baking pan or on a broiler rack. Place under broiler with top of fish about 3 inches from heat. Broil 5 to 8 minutes on each side, or until fish flakes easily; brush with dressing during broiling.
3. Remove trout to heated serving platter and garnish with lemon, tomato, and mint.

Trout Amandine with Pineapple

Spiced pineapple adds a little taste surprise to this classic way of preparing fish. Protein, niacin, riboflavin, thiamine, calcium, and iron are the nutrients.

6 whole trout
Lemon juice
Enriched all-purpose flour
6 tablespoons butter or margarine
Salt and pepper
2 tablespoons butter or margarine
½ cup slivered blanched almonds
6 well-drained canned pineapple slices
Paprika
Lemon wedges

1. Rinse trout quickly under running cold water; dry thoroughly. Brush trout inside and out with lemon juice. Coat with flour.
2. Heat 6 tablespoons butter in a large skillet. Add trout and brown on both sides. Season with salt and pepper.
3. Meanwhile, heat 2 tablespoons butter in another skillet over low heat. Add almonds and stir occasionally until golden.
4. Sprinkle pineapple slices with paprika. Place pineapple in skillet with almonds and brown lightly on both sides. Arrange trout on a warm serving platter and top with pineapple slices and almonds. Garnish platter with lemon wedges.

6 servings

Pickle-Baked Trout

The sweet pickles in this dressing will surprise and delight your taste buds. Protein, vitamin A, niacin, riboflavin, and calcium are the nutritional benefits.

2 packages (12 ounces each) frozen trout, thawed, or 4 trout (6 to 8 ounces each)
¼ cup butter or margarine
¼ cup finely chopped celery
1 teaspoon salt
¼ teaspoon ground black pepper
1 tablespoon lemon juice
½ to ¾ cup coarsely chopped sweet mixed pickles

1. Arrange trout on a greased heat-resistant platter or in a greased shallow baking dish.
2. Heat butter in a skillet; add celery and cook until tender. Mix in salt, pepper, lemon juice, and pickles. Spoon into cavity and over trout.
3. Bake at 350°F 20 to 25 minutes, or until fish flakes easily when tested with a fork; baste occasionally. Garnish as desired.

4 servings

Fish Fillets Viennese

Layers of spicy sour cream and crispy bits of bacon dress up these fish fillets so that even the occasional fish fancier will dig in for his share of the protein, vitamin A, niacin, riboflavin, and calcium.

2 packages (16 ounces each) frozen sole fillets
1 teaspoon salt
4 teaspoons lemon juice
1½ cups dairy sour cream
1 tablespoon prepared English mustard
Few grains salt
1 tablespoon flour
6 slices bacon, diced, fried until crisp, and drained
¾ cup diced cucumber
1 tablespoon capers
¼ cup shredded Parmesan cheese

1. Thaw fish fillets, following directions on package. Sprinkle fish evenly with 1 teaspoon salt. Arrange one-third of the fish fillets on bottom of buttered shallow 2-quart casserole. Drizzle evenly with lemon juice.
2. Beat sour cream, prepared mustard, and salt together. Blend in flour.
3. Cover fish fillets with one-third of the sour-cream mixture. Top with one-third of the bacon, ¼ cup of the cucumber, and 1 teaspoon of the capers; repeat layering twice. Top with the Parmesan cheese.
4. Bake at 375°F about 25 minutes, or until fish flakes easily when tested with a fork.

6 to 8 servings

Tuna Tamale Pie

Very south-of-the-border, this pie in a real pastry shell gives big returns—including protein, vitamins A and C, the B vitamins, calcium, and iron—for a minimum amount of effort.

1 unbaked 9-inch pastry shell
3 tablespoons butter or margarine
½ cup chopped green pepper
⅓ cup chopped onion
1 can (16 ounces) tomatoes (undrained)
1 can (12 ounces) vacuum-packed whole kernel corn
1 can (6½ or 7 ounces) tuna, drained and separated in pieces
¼ cup enriched yellow cornmeal
1 tablespoon chili powder
1 teaspoon salt
1½ cups (about 6 ounces) shredded Cheddar cheese
Sliced ripe olives

1. Prepare pastry shell; set aside.
2. Heat butter in a saucepan or skillet; add green pepper and onion and cook until tender, stirring occasionally.
3. Stir in tomatoes with liquid, corn, and tuna. Blend cornmeal, chili powder, and salt; mix in.
4. Turn mixture into the unbaked pastry shell. Form a border with cheese and garnish with olives.
5. Bake at 425°F 15 to 20 minutes, or until crust is golden brown and filling is thoroughly heated. Cool slightly before serving.

6 servings

Tuna Fiesta

Pasta, cheese, and tomatoes spell Italian flavor. Here tuna is added to offer you an interesting casserole that is rich in protein, vitamins A and C, niacin, and calcium.

1 can (6½ or 7 ounces) tuna, drained and separated in large pieces
1 can (16 ounces) stewed tomatoes, drained
1 can (15¼ ounces) spaghetti in tomato sauce with cheese

1. Turn tuna, stewed tomatoes, and spaghetti into a saucepan. Add ketchup, seasoned salt, cheese, and paprika; mix well. Set over medium heat, stirring occasionally, until thoroughly heated (about 8 minutes).
2. Turn into a warm serving dish; garnish with parsley. Serve at once.

About 6 servings

1 tablespoon ketchup
1 teaspoon seasoned salt
½ cup (about 2 ounces)
   shredded sharp Cheddar
   cheese
   Few grains paprika
   Fresh parsley

Note: If desired, reserve cheese and paprika for topping. Mix remaining ingredients and turn into a greased 1-quart casserole. Top with the cheese and paprika. Set in a 350°F oven 20 minutes, or until thoroughly heated. Garnish with parsley.

Tuna-Shrimp Medley

Two favorite seafoods blend to form a delicious gumbolike dish that is served over rice. It contains protein, vitamin A, niacin, calcium, and iron.

2 tablespoons butter or
   margarine
½ cup chopped onion
½ cup chopped celery
1¼ pounds shrimp, rinsed,
   peeled, deveined, and cut in
   halves lengthwise
3 medium (about 1 pound)
   tomatoes, cut in large
   pieces
1 teaspoon sugar
1 cup sliced water chestnuts
½ cup chopped green pepper
½ cup commercial barbecue
   sauce
1 can (6½ or 7 ounces) tuna,
   drained and flaked
1 tablespoon cornstarch
¾ cup water
2 cups packaged enriched
   precooked rice, prepared
   following package
   directions
1 tablespoon butter or
   margarine
2 tablespoons snipped parsley

1. Heat 2 tablespoons butter in a large skillet; mix in onion and celery and cook until soft.

2. Add shrimp and cook about 5 minutes, or until shrimp turns pink.

3. Sprinkle tomatoes with sugar. Stir tomatoes, water chestnuts, green pepper, barbecue sauce, and tuna into the shrimp mixture; cook 5 minutes.

4. Blend cornstarch and water; stir into shrimp mixture and bring to boiling. Reduce heat and simmer 5 minutes, stirring occasionally.

5. Gently toss rice with 1 tablespoon butter and parsley. Spoon the rice around edge of serving dish. Turn tuna-shrimp mixture into center.

6 servings

Walnut-Stuffed Lemon Sole

Crunchy and smooth and spicy and lemony, this baked fish is a tantalizing blend of tastes and textures that abounds in protein, niacin, riboflavin, thiamine, and iron.

6   **sole fillets**
2   **tablespoons butter or margarine**
1½ **cups chopped mushrooms**
2   **tablespoons chopped onion**
½   **cup finely chopped toasted walnuts**
¼   **cup chopped parsley**
¼   **teaspoon salt**
⅛   **teaspoon dill weed**
    Juice of 1 lemon
    Salt and pepper
    Butter or margarine, melted
    Walnut halves

1. Thaw fish if frozen.
2. Heat 2 tablespoons butter in a skillet; add mushrooms and onion. Cook until mushrooms are lightly browned; stir occasionally. Mix in toasted walnuts, parsley, ¼ teaspoon salt, and dill weed.
3. Drizzle sole with lemon juice. Sprinkle with salt and pepper. Place a spoonful of mushroom mixture on the skin side of each fillet and roll up. Place in a greased baking dish. Brush the fish with melted butter.
4. Bake at 350°F 25 to 30 minutes, or until fish flakes easily when tested with a fork. Garnish as desired with walnuts.

6 servings

Sole with Tangerine Sauce

Simple and satisfying, this is an elegant way to provide protein, vitamins A and C, niacin, riboflavin, and calcium.

1   **pound sole fillets**
5   **tablespoons butter or margarine**
2   **teaspoons finely shredded tangerine peel**
½   **cup tangerine juice**
1   **teaspoon lemon juice**
1   **tablespoon finely chopped parsley**
1   **tablespoon finely chopped green onion**
1   **bay leaf**
1   **tangerine, peeled, sectioned,**

1. Thaw fish if frozen.
2. Combine 5 tablespoons butter, tangerine peel and juice, lemon juice, 1 tablespoon parsley, green onion, and bay leaf in a saucepan. Bring to boiling and simmer over low heat until slightly thickened, stirring occasionally. Remove from heat; remove bay leaf and mix in tangerine sections. Keep sauce hot.
3. Mix flour, salt, and pepper; coat fish fillets. Heat 3 tablespoons butter in a skillet. Add fillets and fry until both sides are browned and fish flakes easily when tested with a fork.
4. Arrange fish on a hot platter and pour the

and seeds removed
3 tablespoons flour
½ teaspoon salt
⅛ teaspoon ground black pepper
3 tablespoons butter or margarine
Parsley

hot sauce over it. Garnish with parsley.

About 4 servings

Fish Dinner Flamboyante

If you want your guests to sing your praises, serve this combination that is practically a meal in itself. Nutritionally, it offers two kinds of protein, vitamins A and C, niacin, riboflavin, and calcium.

2 pounds fish fillets (perch, pike, or sole)
1 teaspoon finely crushed tarragon
2 medium onions, thinly sliced
2 firm ripe tomatoes, quartered
1 can (4 ounces) mushroom stems and pieces, drained
1 medium green pepper, cut in strips
4 large pimiento-stuffed olives, sliced
1 package (10 ounces) frozen baby lima beans, cooked and drained
¼ cup butter or margarine
⅛ teaspoon finely crushed oregano
¾ teaspoon salt
¼ teaspoon ground black pepper
Seasoned salt

1. Thaw fish if frozen. Sprinkle fillets with tarragon. Place in a shallow 3-quart baking dish.
2. Layer onion slices evenly over fish. Add tomatoes, mushrooms, half of green pepper strips (reserve other half for garnish), olives, and cooked limas.
3. Mix butter, oregano, salt, and pepper and dot over the fish. Press aluminum foil tightly over the dish.
4. Cook in a 375°F oven 30 to 40 minutes.
5. Before serving, sprinkle with seasoned salt and garnish with the reserved green pepper strips.

6 to 8 servings

Perch Mozzarella

Two kinds of cheese and tomato sauce give a distinctly Italian air to this nutritious dish, which contains protein, vitamins A and C, niacin, riboflavin, and calcium.

6 perch fillets (4 ounces each)
2 eggs, well beaten
1 teaspoon salt
⅛ teaspoon ground white pepper
¾ cup fine dry enriched bread crumbs
6 tablespoons grated Parmesan cheese
½ cup enriched all-purpose flour
⅓ cup butter or margarine
2 cans (8 ounces each) tomato sauce
½ teaspoon basil
½ teaspoon oregano
6 slices (6 ounces) mozzarella cheese

1. Thaw fish if frozen.
2. Mix eggs, salt, and pepper in a shallow dish. Mix bread crumbs and Parmesan cheese on waxed paper. Coat fillets with flour; dip first into egg mixture, then into crumb mixture.
3. Heat butter in a skillet; add fillets and brown on both sides over medium heat.
4. Arrange browned fillets in a 2-quart baking dish. Mix tomato sauce, basil, and oregano; pour over fillets. Top each fillet with a slice of mozzarella cheese.
5. Set in a 350°F oven 15 minutes. Serve immediately.

6 servings

Perch with Parsley and Dill

This delicately seasoned recipe has its own way of saying "Here's the way to serve fish to those who really like the taste of fish." It supplies protein, vitamins A and C, niacin, and riboflavin.

8 medium perch
1 teaspoon salt
½ teaspoon ground black pepper
¼ cup minced parsley
2 tablespoons finely chopped parsley

1. Rinse perch quickly under running cold water; dry thoroughly. Season fish with salt and pepper.
2. Sprinkle minced parsley evenly over bottom of a 1½-quart baking dish. Arrange fish in baking dish. Top with chopped parsley and dill. Pour hot water around the fish.

2 tablespoons chopped fresh dill (or 1 teaspoon dill seed)
¼ cup hot water
Parsley sprigs
Lemon wedges

3. Bake at 350°F 20 to 25 minutes, or until fish flakes easily when tested with a fork.
4. Carefully transfer fish to a warm serving platter and garnish with parsley and lemon.

4 servings

Broiled Fish Californian

A little bit more dressed up, this broiled fish with sauce expands the nutrients to include vitamins A and C, calcium, and iron, as well as protein, niacin, and riboflavin.

Broiled fish:
6 whole fish (such as sea bass, sea or brook trout, or yellow perch), 8 to 10 ounces each
¼ cup lemon juice
1½ teaspoons salt
¼ teaspoon ground black pepper
⅛ teaspoon ground nutmeg
¼ cup butter or margarine, melted

Raisin Sauce:
¼ cup butter or margarine
½ cup firmly packed brown sugar
¼ cup enriched all-purpose flour
1½ teaspoons salt
½ teaspoon grated orange peel
1 cup water
½ cup lemon juice
½ cup orange juice
1 cup golden raisins
Lemon wedges

1. For broiled fish, rinse fish quickly under running cold water. Mix lemon juice, salt, pepper, and nutmeg; brush inside of fish.
2. Arrange fish on a greased broiler rack and brush with half of butter. Place under broiler with top of fish about 3 inches from heat. Broil 5 to 8 minutes (depending on thickness of fish). Turn fish carefully and brush second side with remaining butter. Continue broiling 5 to 8 minutes, or until fish flakes easily.
3. Meanwhile, for Raisin Sauce, melt butter in a saucepan. Blend in brown sugar, flour, salt, and grated orange peel. Heat and stir until thoroughly blended. Remove from heat.
4. Add water, lemon juice, and orange juice gradually, stirring until blended. Cook rapidly, stirring constantly, until sauce thickens. Mix in raisins. Cook about 1 minute.
5. Arrange fish on a heated serving platter. Pour hot sauce over them. Garnish with lemon.

6 servings

Fish Fillets à l'Orange / Walnut-Topped Fish Fillets

This recipe offers a choice of an orangy taste or a crunchy walnut topping. It's delicious either way, providing protein and the B vitamins. The walnuts add more protein and B vitamins, as well as iron, thiamine, and niacin.

1½ **pounds fish fillets (such as whitefish, perch, or pike)**

3 **tablespoons plus 1 teaspoon grated orange peel**

¼ **cup enriched all-purpose flour**

1½ **teaspoons salt**

⅛ **teaspoon ground black pepper**

⅔ **cup fine dry enriched bread crumbs**

1 **egg, slightly beaten**

2 **tablespoons water**

¼ **cup butter or margarine**

2 **tablespoons butter or margarine**

1. Thaw fish if frozen.
2. Prepare grated orange peel.
3. Mix flour, salt, and pepper on waxed paper. Mix 3 tablespoons of grated orange peel and bread crumbs on waxed paper. Combine egg and water in a shallow dish.
4. Heat ¼ cup butter in a large skillet. Coat fish fillets evenly with flour mixture. Dip in egg mixture. Coat evenly with bread-crumb mixture. Add fillets to skillet; cook over medium heat until delicately browned on one side. Turn carefully with wide spatula and brown second side. Cook only until fish flakes easily when pierced with a fork.
5. Place browned fillets on a warm serving platter, scraping loose and removing any bits of fish which may have stuck to skillet.
6. Heat 2 tablespoons butter in same skillet until golden brown. Remove from heat and mix in 1 teaspoon grated orange peel. Immediately pour over fillets.

4 servings

Walnut-Topped Fish Fillets: Follow recipe for Fish Fillets à l'Orange; omit 3 tablespoons grated orange peel. Add ½ **cup coarsely chopped walnuts** to the 2 tablespoons golden brown butter. Spoon over browned fillets and sprinkle with 1 teaspoon grated orange peel.

Fish Fillets Mornay

A cornmeal coating and a luscious cheese sauce combine with these fish fillets to offer protein, vitamin A, and the B vitamins.

Mornay Sauce:
- **3 tablespoons butter or margarine**
- **3 tablespoons flour**
- **¾ cup chicken broth (1 chicken bouillon cube dissolved in ¾ cup boiling water)**
- **¾ cup cream**
- **2 egg yolks, fork beaten**
- **½ cup shredded Parmesan cheese**
- **1 tablespoon butter or margarine**

Cornmeal-coated fish:
- **2 pounds frozen fish fillets, thawed**
- **½ cup enriched yellow cornmeal**
- **1½ teaspoons salt**
- **⅛ teaspoon ground black pepper**
- **Butter or margarine**
- **Toasted blanched almonds**

1. For Mornay Sauce, heat 3 tablespoons butter in the top of a double boiler; blend in flour. Heat until bubbly. Add broth and cream gradually, stirring until smooth. Bring to boiling, stirring constantly; cook 1 to 2 minutes.

2. Stir about ¼ cup of hot sauce into egg yolks. Immediately return to mixture in double boiler. Cook over boiling water about 5 minutes, stirring occasionally.

3. Remove from heat and add cheese and 1 tablespoon butter; stir until cheese is melted. Keep hot.

4. For cornmeal-coated fish, cut fillets into serving-size pieces. Mix cornmeal, salt, and pepper; coat fillets.

5. Heat a small amount of butter in a skillet. Add fillets and brown on both sides.

6. Serve fish on heated platter, top with almonds, and surround with the sauce.

About 6 servings

Fish Fillet Twirls with Celery Stuffing

Baked in a muffin tin, these neatly stuffed fish fillets are easy to serve and are full of protein, vitamins A and D, the B vitamins, calcium, and iron.

2 packages (16 ounces each) frozen fish fillets (6 fillets needed), thawed
Lemon juice
3 tablespoons butter
½ cup diced celery
2 tablespoons chopped green pepper
1 tablespoon finely chopped onion
2 cups soft enriched bread crumbs
2 eggs, beaten
½ cup cream
1 tablespoon minced parsley
½ teaspoon thyme
⅛ teaspoon celery salt
Pinch ground nutmeg
¼ teaspoon salt
Few grains pepper

1. Sprinkle fish fillets with lemon juice. Fit each fillet around the inside of a well-greased muffin-pan well.
2. Heat butter in a large skillet. Mix in celery, green pepper, and onion; cook until celery is tender. Remove from heat.
3. Add bread crumbs to skillet and toss to mix well. Combine eggs, cream, parsley, thyme, celery salt, nutmeg, salt, and pepper; add to bread crumb mixture and stir in. Set over low heat until thoroughly heated, stirring occasionally.
4. Spoon stuffing into fish twirls.
5. Bake at 350°F about 20 minutes, or until fish flakes easily when tested with a fork.
6. Remove fish twirls from wells by running a knife around edges and lifting them out with a spoon. Serve immediately.

6 servings

Baked Fish with Shrimp Stuffing

Shrimp stuffing such as you have probably been served at fine seafood restaurants is easy to make in your own kitchen, and it contains protein, vitamin A, niacin, riboflavin, calcium, and iron.

1 dressed whitefish, bass, or lake trout (2 to 3 pounds)
Salt
1 cup chopped cooked shrimp
1 cup chopped fresh mushrooms
1 cup soft enriched bread crumbs

1. Rinse fish under running cold water; drain well and pat dry with absorbent paper. Sprinkle fish cavity generously with salt.
2. Combine in a bowl the shrimp, mushrooms, bread crumbs, celery, onion, parsley, salt, pepper, and thyme. Pour ¼ cup melted butter gradually over bread mixture, tossing lightly until mixed.

½ cup chopped celery
¼ cup chopped onion
2 tablespoons chopped parsley
¾ teaspoon salt
Few grains black pepper
½ teaspoon thyme
¼ cup butter or margarine, melted
2 to 3 tablespoons apple cider
2 tablespoons butter or margarine, melted
Parsley sprigs

3. Pile stuffing lightly into fish. Fasten with skewers and lace with cord. Place fish in a greased large shallow baking pan. Mix cider and 2 tablespoons melted butter; brush over fish.

4. Bake at 375°F, brushing occasionally with cider mixture, 25 to 30 minutes, or until fish flakes easily when pierced with a fork. If additional browning is desired, place fish under broiler 3 to 5 minutes. Transfer to a heated platter and remove skewers and cord. Garnish platter with parsley.

4 to 6 servings

Anchovy-Stuffed Fish

The B vitamins, calcium, and iron are the benefits you can expect from this flavorful stuffed fish.

1 4-pound dressed fish (such as whitefish, lake trout, bass, haddock, or shad; backbone removed)
1½ cups coarse dry enriched bread crumbs
⅓ cup chopped anchovies (about 24 anchovy fillets)
¼ cup chopped parsley
¼ cup chopped capers
¼ cup chopped green onion
1 egg, beaten
½ cup milk
1 tablespoon salt
1 tablespoon vinegar
½ cup dry enriched bread crumbs
1 teaspoon grated lemon peel
1 egg white, slightly beaten
Butter or margarine, melted

1. Rinse fish thoroughly under running cold water, drain well, and pat dry with absorbent paper.

2. Turn 1½ cups bread crumbs into a large bowl. Mix in anchovies, parsley, capers, and green onion. Blend egg and milk; add to bread-crumb mixture and toss to mix.

3. Rub cavity of fish with 1 teaspoon salt. Lightly spoon stuffing into fish (do not pack). Fasten open edges with skewers and lace if necessary. Mix remaining 2 teaspoons salt and vinegar; rub over fish.

4. Place stuffed fish in a buttered shallow baking dish. Mix ½ cup bread crumbs and lemon peel. Brush fish with egg white. Cover evenly with crumbs.

5. Bake at 350°F about 40 minutes, or until fish flakes easily when pierced with a fork. During baking, drizzle occasionally with melted butter.

8 to 10 servings

Planked Halibut Dinner

A meal in itself, this spread of fish and vegetables makes good eating and good nutrition, too. The vegetables add vitamins A and C and calcium to the nutrients of the fish.

4 **halibut steaks, fresh or thawed frozen (about 2 pounds)**
¼ **cup butter, melted**
2 **tablespoons olive oil**
1 **tablespoon wine vinegar**
2 **teaspoons lemon juice**
1 **clove garlic, minced**
¼ **teaspoon dry mustard**
¼ **teaspoon marjoram**
½ **teaspoon salt**
⅛ **teaspoon ground black pepper**
2 **large zucchini**
1 **package (10 ounces) frozen green peas**
1 **can (8¼ ounces) tiny whole carrots**
Au Gratin Potato Puffs (see recipe)
Butter
Fresh parsley
Lemon wedges

1. Place halibut steaks in an oiled baking pan.
2. Combine butter, olive oil, vinegar, lemon juice, garlic, dry mustard, marjoram, salt, and pepper. Drizzle over halibut.
3. Bake at 450°F 10 to 12 minutes, or until halibut is almost done.
4. Meanwhile, halve zucchini lengthwise and scoop out center portion. Cook in boiling salted water until just tender.
5. Cook peas following directions on package. Heat carrots.
6. Prepare Au Gratin Potato Puffs.
7. Arrange halibut on wooden plank or heated ovenware platter and border with zucchini halves filled with peas, carrots, and potato puffs. Dot peas and carrots with butter.
8. Place platter under broiler to brown potato puffs. Sprinkle carrots with chopped parsley.
9. Garnish with sprigs of parsley and lemon wedges arranged on a skewer.

4 servings

Au Gratin Potato Puffs: Pare **1½ pounds potatoes**; cook and mash potatoes in a saucepan. Add **2 tablespoons butter** and **⅓ cup milk**; whip until fluffy. Add **2 slightly beaten egg yolks, ½ cup shredded sharp Cheddar cheese, 1 teaspoon salt,** and **few grains pepper**; continue whipping. Using a pastry bag with a large star tip, form mounds about 2 inches in diameter on plank. Proceed as directed in recipe.

Halibut au Gratin

Here we have chunky halibut in a rich cheese sauce, baked in individual servings and loaded with protein, vitamins A and D, niacin, riboflavin, and calcium.

Poached halibut:

1½ **pounds frozen halibut, thawed**
   Water
 1 **teaspoon salt**
 5 **peppercorns**
 1 **onion, sliced**
 1 **bay leaf**
 ½ **lemon, sliced**

Cheese Sauce:

 ¼ **cup butter or margarine**
 ¼ **cup enriched all-purpose flour**
 2 **cups milk**
 ½ **teaspoon salt**
 ⅛ **teaspoon ground white pepper**
 ¼ **teaspoon dry mustard**
1½ **cups (about 6 ounces) shredded Cheddar cheese**

Topping:

 ½ **cup buttered bread crumbs**
 1 **tablespoon chopped parsley**
   Paprika

1. For poached halibut, put halibut into a large skillet or saucepot; add enough water to just cover halibut. Add salt, peppercorns, onion, bay leaf, and lemon slices. Bring to boiling, reduce heat, and cover. Simmer until halibut is tender, about 5 minutes. Remove from heat and set aside while preparing sauce.

2. For Cheese Sauce, heat butter in a saucepan; stir in flour. Add milk gradually, stirring constantly. Bring to boiling and cook 1 to 2 minutes, stirring constantly. Blend salt, pepper, and dry mustard; mix in.

3. Remove from heat, add cheese all at one time, and stir until cheese is melted and sauce is smooth.

4. Using 2 forks, divide halibut into chunks. Put equal amounts into 6 buttered individual baking shells or ramekins. Spoon about ⅓ cup cheese sauce into each.

5. Sprinkle with crumbs, parsley, and paprika.

6. Bake at 350°F 20 minutes.

6 servings

Halibut in Herb Sauce

What a sauce this halibut bakes in! You'll love the taste, and you'll appreciate the protein, niacin, riboflavin, and other nutrients the dish supplies.

2 pounds halibut steaks or fillets
2 tablespoons butter or margarine
½ cup fine dry enriched bread crumbs
1 cup vegetable broth (1 vegetable bouillon cube dissolved in 1 cup boiling water)
1 clove garlic, minced or crushed in a garlic press
¼ cup butter or margarine
2 tablespoons minced onion
2 tablespoons ketchup
1 tablespoon minced parsley
1 teaspoon vinegar
½ teaspoon prepared mustard
1 teaspoon salt
Few grains pepper
2 tablespoons cornstarch
2 tablespoons water

1. Thaw fish if frozen.
2. Heat 2 tablespoons butter in a small skillet. Add bread crumbs and mix lightly until crumbs are well coated. Set aside.
3. Pour broth into a saucepan. Add garlic, ¼ cup butter, onion, ketchup, parsley, vinegar, prepared mustard, salt, and pepper. Bring rapidly to boiling.
4. Meanwhile, blend cornstarch and water.
5. Stir cornstarch mixture into boiling seasoned broth. Cook 3 minutes.
6. Arrange halibut steaks in a greased 2-quart baking dish. Pour the sauce over them. Top with the buttered crumbs.
7. Bake at 350°F 30 to 35 minutes, or until fish flakes easily when tested with a fork.

6 servings

Baked Flounder Superb

Neat and delicious in their individual servings, these portions of baked flounder with a cheese-topped sauce offer protein, vitamins A and D, niacin, riboflavin, calcium, and iron.

2 pounds flounder fillets
½ cup fine Melba toast crumbs
¼ cup butter or margarine, melted

1. Thaw fish if frozen; cut fish into 12 pieces.
2. Toss crumbs and melted butter together in a bowl. Add green onion, parsley, poultry seasoning, scallops, and mushrooms; mix well.
3. Place a piece of flounder in the bottom of

2/3 cup minced green onion
2 tablespoons snipped parsley
1/2 teaspoon poultry seasoning
1/2 pound fresh or thawed frozen sea scallops, chopped
1 can (4 ounces) mushroom stems and pieces, drained
2 tablespoons butter or margarine
2 tablespoons flour
1/4 teaspoon salt
Few grains black pepper
1 cup milk
Shredded Parmesan cheese

each of 6 ramekins. Spoon stuffing mixture over flounder and top with remaining flounder pieces.

4. Heat butter in a saucepan. Stir in flour, salt, and pepper and cook until bubbly. Add milk gradually, stirring until smooth. Bring rapidly to boiling; boil 1 to 2 minutes, stirring constantly.

5. Spoon sauce over flounder. Sprinkle with Parmesan cheese.

6. Bake at 350°F 20 to 25 minutes. If desired, set ramekins under broiler with tops about 3 inches from heat until lightly browned; watch carefully to avoid overbrowning.

6 servings

California Style Red Snapper Steaks

Oranges and fish, an unusual taste combination, form a potent combination of nutrients—protein, vitamins A and C, niacin, riboflavin, and calcium.

6 fresh or thawed frozen red snapper steaks (about 2 pounds)
Salt and pepper
1/4 cup butter or margarine, melted
1 tablespoon grated orange peel
1/4 cup orange juice
1 teaspoon lemon juice
Dash nutmeg
Fresh orange sections

1. Arrange red snapper steaks in a single layer in a well-greased baking pan; season with salt and pepper.

2. Combine butter, orange peel and juice, lemon juice, and nutmeg; pour over fish.

3. Bake at 350°F 20 to 25 minutes, or until fish flakes easily when tested with a fork.

4. To serve, put steaks onto a warm platter; spoon sauce in pan over them. Garnish with orange sections.

6 servings

Pastry-Topped Clams and Potatoes

Here's an elegant-looking and satisfying dinner pie that contains protein, vitamin C, and iron. Try it when you need a little lift.

3 tablespoons butter
½ cup chopped onion
2 tablespoons flour
½ teaspoon salt
Few grains black pepper
3 cans (8 ounces each) minced clams, drained (reserve ½ cup liquid)
½ cup milk
1 can (16 ounces) whole cooked potatoes, drained and diced
Pastry (amount needed for a 1-crust 8-inch pie)

1. Heat butter in a large skillet. Add onion and cook until onion is soft, stirring occasionally.
2. Blend in flour, salt, and pepper. Heat until bubbly. Add the reserved clam liquid and milk gradually, stirring constantly. Bring rapidly to boiling, stirring constantly. Cook 1 to 2 minutes.
3. Remove from heat; mix in diced potatoes and minced clams. Turn into an 8-inch pie pan.
4. Prepare pastry and roll out to fit over clam mixture. Cut a design near center of pastry to allow steam to escape during baking. Place pastry on clam mixture and flute edge.
5. Bake at 450°F about 20 minutes, or until pastry is lightly browned.

4 to 6 servings

Crab Cakes

Protein, vitamins A and D, riboflavin, thiamine, calcium, and iron are all crammed into these crispy little crab cakes, and they are easy to make on a moment's notice.

3 tablespoons butter or margarine
¾ cup finely chopped onion
1 cup soft enriched bread crumbs
1 pound crab meat, flaked (bony tissue removed)
3 eggs, beaten
¾ teaspoon salt
1 teaspoon dry mustard
⅛ teaspoon paprika

1. Heat butter in a skillet. Mix in onion, and cook until crisp. Remove from heat and stir in bread crumbs. Mix in crab meat.
2. Combine eggs, salt, dry mustard, paprika, Worcestershire sauce, and parsley; add to crab mixture and blend thoroughly. Mix in enough cream to hold the crab meat mixture together. Shape into twelve 2½-inch cakes. Coat each cake with flour.
3. Heat a ½-inch layer of fat in a deep skillet. Add cakes and fry until golden brown, about

1 teaspoon Worcestershire
sauce
3 tablespoons chopped
parsley
1 to 2 tablespoons cream
Enriched all-purpose flour
(about ½ cup)
Fat or oil for frying
(butter, margarine, or
vegetable oil)
Lemon wedges

3 minutes per side. Drain on absorbent paper, if necessary. Serve with lemon wedges.

4 to 6 servings

Patio Crab Casserole

Here is a relatively easy way to serve a small crowd, and they'll be getting a taste treat as well as protein, vitamin A, and calcium.

¼ cup butter or margarine
2 cups chopped onion
1 pound frozen or 2 cans
(7½ ounces each) Alaska
King crab, drained and
sliced
½ cup snipped parsley
2 tablespoons capers
2 tablespoons snipped chives
2 pimientos, diced
1½ cups corn muffin mix
⅛ teaspoon salt
1 egg, fork beaten
½ cup milk
1 cup cream-style golden
corn
6 drops Tabasco
2 cups dairy sour cream
1½ cups shredded extra sharp
Cheddar cheese

1. Heat butter in a skillet. Add onion and cook until tender. Stir in crab, parsley, capers, chives, and pimientos; heat.
2. Meanwhile, stir corn muffin mix, salt, egg, milk, corn, and Tabasco until just moistened (batter should be lumpy). Turn into a greased shallow 3-quart baking dish and spread evenly to edges.
3. Spoon crab mixture and then sour cream over batter. Sprinkle cheese over all.
4. Bake at 400°F 25 to 30 minutes.
5. To serve, cut into squares.

About 12 servings

Deviled Crab

Once they have tasted these luscious stuffed crabs, your friends will want you to make them again and again. Besides good taste, they give you protein, vitamins A and D, riboflavin, and calcium.

Mustard Sauce:
- 2 tablespoons dry mustard
- 2 tablespoons water
- 2 tablespoons olive oil
- 1 tablespoon ketchup
- ¼ teaspoon salt
- ¼ teaspoon Worcestershire sauce

Crab meat mixture:
- 6 tablespoons butter
- 4 teaspoons finely chopped green pepper
- 2 teaspoons finely chopped onion
- 6 tablespoons flour
- 1 teaspoon salt
- ½ teaspoon dry mustard
- 1½ cups milk
- 1 teaspoon Worcestershire sauce
- 2 egg yolks, slightly beaten
- 1 pound lump crab meat, drained
- 2 teaspoons chopped pimiento
- 2 tablespoons dry sherry
- 1 cup fine dry enriched bread crumbs
  Paprika
  Butter, melted

1. For Mustard Sauce, blend dry mustard, water, olive oil, ketchup, salt, and Worcestershire sauce in a small bowl; set aside.

2. For crab meat mixture, heat butter in a large heavy saucepan. Add green pepper and onion; cook until onion is golden in color.

3. Blend flour, salt, and dry mustard; stir in. Heat until bubbly. Add milk gradually, stirring until smooth. Stir in Worcestershire sauce. Bring rapidly to boiling; cook 1 to 2 minutes.

4. Remove mixture from heat and stir a small amount of hot mixture into the egg yolks; return to saucepan and cook 3 to 5 minutes, stirring constantly.

5. Stir in crab meat and pimiento; heat thoroughly. Remove from heat and blend in sherry and the Mustard Sauce.

6. Spoon into 6 shell-shaped ramekins, allowing about ½ cup mixture for each. Sprinkle top with bread crumbs and paprika; drizzle with melted butter.

7. Set in a 450°F oven about 6 minutes, or until tops are lightly browned and mixture is thoroughly heated. Serve hot.

6 servings

Seafood Rice Medley

Baked and served in individual casseroles, this hearty seafood mixture contains some taste surprises, as well as protein, the B vitamins, calcium, and iron.

1 **pound scallops**
1 **quart boiling water**
1 **teaspoon salt**
1 **large onion, sliced**
2 **cloves garlic, finely chopped**
6 **whole cloves**
12 **peppercorns**
2 **teaspoons caraway seed**
1 **pound small fresh shrimp**
2 **tablespoons butter or margarine**
2 **tablespoons chopped onion**
3 **medium tart red apples, washed, cored, and diced (do not pare)**
¼ **cup lemon juice**
¼ **cup light brown sugar**
3 **cups cooked enriched white rice**
½ **cup salted almonds, coarsely chopped**
1 **can (10½ ounces) condensed cream of celery soup**

1. Rinse scallops under running cold water and put into a saucepan. Pour in 1 quart boiling water and add salt. Cook, covered, over low heat about 6 minutes, or until scallops are just tender. Remove scallops from stock with a slotted spoon. Cut scallops into halves and set aside.

2. Add sliced onion, garlic, cloves, peppercorns, and caraway seed to the stock. Simmer, covered, about 10 minutes.

3. Meanwhile, rinse, shell, and devein shrimp. Bring stock to boiling; add shrimp and simmer, covered, until shrimp are plumped and turn pink (3 to 5 minutes). Drain in a colander; reserve 1⅓ cups of the stock. Remove shrimp with some of the caraway seed adhering to them. Discard spices.

4. Spoon scallops and shrimp equally into 8 buttered individual casseroles. Set aside.

5. Heat butter in a large heavy skillet. Add chopped onion and cook about 3 minutes. Add apples, lemon juice, and brown sugar; toss mixture to blend.

6. Remove from heat; add cooked rice and almonds. Toss lightly with a fork to blend thoroughly. Spoon the mixture into the casseroles.

7. Turn celery soup into a saucepan and blend in reserved stock. Bring to boiling, stirring frequently. Pour the sauce over mixture in individual casseroles.

8. Heat in a 350°F oven about 25 minutes.

8 servings

Scallops Gourmet

Although they are a little time-consuming to prepare, these scallops are sure to impress your dinner guests, as well as giving them protein, vitamins A and C, calcium, and iron.

2 **pounds scallops**
1 **cup boiling water**
1 **teaspoon salt**
3 **to 4 tablespoons lemon juice**
1 **medium onion, sliced**
2 **sprigs parsley**
1 **bay leaf**
¼ **cup butter or margarine**
½ **pound mushrooms, sliced lengthwise**
3 **tomatoes, peeled and diced**
2 **tablespoons butter or margarine**
2 **tablespoons flour**
¼ **teaspoon garlic powder**
8 **patty shells, heated**
 Carrot curls

1. Rinse scallops under running cold water. Put scallops into a saucepan and pour boiling water over them. Stir in salt, lemon juice, onion, parsley, and bay leaf. Cook, covered, over low heat 5 minutes; drain and reserve 1 cup of the stock. If scallops are large, cut into smaller pieces. Set aside.

2. Heat ¼ cup butter in a skillet. Add mushrooms and cook until delicately browned and tender, stirring occasionally. Remove from skillet with slotted spoon; set aside. Add diced tomatoes to skillet and cook 5 minutes. Set aside.

3. Heat 2 tablespoons butter in a saucepan. Blend in flour; heat until bubbly. Add reserved stock gradually, stirring constantly. Continue to stir and bring rapidly to boiling; cook 1 to 2 minutes.

4. Add scallops, mushrooms, tomatoes, and garlic powder to sauce; heat thoroughly.

5. To serve, spoon scallop mixture into patty shells. Garnish with carrot curls.

About 8 servings

Savory Oysters

This easy oyster bake takes only moments of the cook's time, yet gives six to eight servings of healthful protein, the B vitamins, calcium, and iron.

⅓ **cup butter or margarine**
1 **can (4 ounces) sliced mushrooms, drained**
⅓ **cup chopped green pepper**
½ **clove garlic**

1. Heat butter in a large skillet. Add mushrooms, green pepper, and garlic; cook about 5 minutes. Remove skillet from heat; discard garlic. Stir in toasted bread crumbs. Set aside.

2. Mix ¼ cup reserved oyster liquor, cream,

2 cups coarse toasted enriched bread crumbs
1 quart oysters, drained (reserve liquor)
¼ cup cream
1 teaspoon Worcestershire sauce
1 teaspoon salt
1 teaspoon paprika
⅛ teaspoon ground mace
Few grains cayenne pepper

and Worcestershire sauce.

3. Blend salt, paprika, mace, and cayenne.

4. Use about a third of crumb mixture to form a layer in bottom of a greased 2-quart casserole. Arrange about half of oysters and half of seasonings over crumbs. Repeat crumb layer, then oyster and seasoning layers. Pour the liquid mixture over all. Top with remaining crumbs.

5. Bake at 375°F 20 to 30 minutes, or until thoroughly heated and crumbs are golden brown.

6 to 8 servings

Seafood Kabobs

Kabobs again, and you'll skewer yourself a generous portion of protein, calcium, and iron with this mixed seafood version of a favorite dish.

1 lobster tail (8 ounces), cut in 6 pieces
6 scallops
6 shrimp, peeled and deveined
12 large mushroom caps
½ cup olive oil
3 tablespoons soy sauce
1 tablespoon Worcestershire sauce
2 tablespoons white wine vinegar
½ teaspoon grated lemon peel
2 tablespoons lemon juice
½ teaspoon ground pepper
2 teaspoons snipped parsley
18 (4-inch) pieces sliced bacon
12 (1-inch) squares green pepper
6 cherry tomatoes

1. Put lobster pieces, scallops, shrimp, and mushroom caps into a shallow dish.

2. Combine olive oil, soy sauce, Worcestershire sauce, vinegar, lemon peel, lemon juice, pepper, and parsley in a screwtop jar and shake vigorously. Pour the marinade over the seafood and mushroom caps and set aside for at least 2 hours.

3. Drain off marinade and reserve.

4. Wrap each piece of seafood in bacon. Thread pieces on skewers (about 10 inches each) as follows: green pepper, lobster, mushroom, scallop, mushroom, shrimp, and green pepper. Arrange on a broiler rack and brush with marinade.

5. Place under broiler 3 inches from heat. Broil 10 to 12 minutes, turning and brushing frequently with marinade. Add a cherry tomato to each skewer during the last few minutes of broiling.

6 servings

Shrimp Curry on Raisin Toast

Especially good for a leisurely brunch, these individual servings of curried shrimp supply protein, calcium, niacin, and iron.

Quick Raisin Relish (see recipe)
3 tablespoons butter or margarine
1 teaspoon curry powder
2 tablespoons finely chopped green onion with tops
¼ cup finely chopped celery
2 cups deveined cooked shrimp
2 to 3 tablespoons flour
2 cups milk
1 teaspoon seasoned salt
½ teaspoon ground ginger
⅛ teaspoon garlic powder
1 teaspoon lemon juice
12 slices raisin bread, toasted

1. Prepare Quick Raisin Relish; chill.
2. Melt butter with curry powder in a saucepan. Mix in onion, celery, and shrimp. Cook, stirring occasionally, 2 to 3 minutes, or until vegetables are soft. Blend in flour and heat until bubbly. Add milk gradually, stirring constantly. Bring to boiling; stir and cook 1 to 2 minutes. Remove from heat. Blend seasoned salt, ginger, and garlic powder; mix in along with lemon juice.
3. Put 1 slice of toast in each of 6 individual serving dishes. Cover with hot shrimp curry. Cut remaining toast into triangles and place around edge of curry. Top each with a spoonful of the raisin relish.

6 servings

Quick Raisin Relish: Combine 1½ cups dark or golden raisins, 2 tablespoons vinegar, ¼ cup firmly packed brown sugar, 1 tablespoon instant minced onion, and contents of 1 can (8 ounces) crushed pineapple in a saucepan. Cook over low heat 10 minutes, stirring occasionally. Cool and store in covered jar in refrigerator.

About 2 cups relish

Herbed Shrimp Skillet

Here's a skillet-to-table dish you can turn out in a short time, yet it tastes as if hours of preparation went into it. Vitamins A and C, the B vitamins, and calcium are the plusses.

¼ cup butter or margarine
½ cup chopped onion

1. Heat butter in a heavy skillet. Add onion and green pepper and cook until almost

½ cup diced green pepper

3 cups fresh-cut corn (about 5 ears)

2 medium tomatoes, peeled and diced

2 teaspoons sugar

1 teaspoon salt

¼ teaspoon freshly ground black pepper

¼ teaspoon basil

¼ teaspoon crushed thyme

2 cans (4½ ounces each) shrimp, drained and rinsed

tender, about 5 minutes, stirring occasionally to cook evenly.

2. Mix in corn and tomatoes. Blend sugar, salt, pepper, basil, and thyme; stir in. Bring to boiling and cook, covered, about 5 minutes, or until corn is tender.

3. Stir in shrimp and heat thoroughly.

About 6 servings

Shrimp with Tomatoes and Potatoes

Practically a meal in itself, this shrimp-and-vegetable dish serves up protein, vitamins A and C, calcium, and iron.

1½ pounds cooked, shelled shrimp

¼ pound salt pork, diced

1 cup chopped onion

3 medium potatoes, pared and diced (about 2½ cups)

1 clove garlic, minced

1½ teaspoons salt

¼ teaspoon seasoned pepper

¼ teaspoon oregano

2 bay leaves

1½ cups hot water

1 can (28 ounces) Italian-style peeled tomatoes

5 or 6 drops Tabasco

1. Cut shrimp into pieces; set aside.

2. Cook salt pork in a large skillet until lightly browned. Add onion and cook until tender, but not browned.

3. Add potatoes, garlic, salt, seasoned pepper, oregano, bay leaves, and hot water. Bring to boiling, reduce heat, cover, and cook over low heat until potatoes are just tender. Mix in tomatoes, Tabasco, and shrimp.

4. Heat thoroughly, but do not boil. Serve piping hot.

4 to 6 servings

Shrimp Creole

Isn't it good to know that this classic Louisiana dish is as good for you as it is good tasting? Protein, vitamins A and C, calcium, and iron are the benefits.

Cooked shrimp:
- **1 pound fresh shrimp with shells**
- **2 cups water**
- **2 tablespoons lemon juice**
- **2 teaspoons salt**

Sauce:
- **¼ cup fat**
- **¾ cup finely chopped onion**
- **¾ cup minced green pepper**
- **1 can (16 ounces) tomatoes, sieved**
- **1 teaspoon Worcestershire sauce**
- **1 bay leaf**
- **1½ teaspoons salt**
- **¼ teaspoon ground black pepper**
- **½ teaspoon sugar**
- **½ teaspoon oregano**
  Cooked rice

1. For cooked shrimp, rinse shrimp under running cold water.

2. Combine water, lemon juice, and salt in a saucepan and bring to boiling. Drop shrimp into boiling water, reduce heat, and simmer, covered, until pink and tender (about 5 minutes).

3. Drain shrimp immediately and cover with cold water to chill; drain again. Remove tiny legs and peel shells from shrimp. Cut a slit to just below surface along back (curved surface) of shrimp to expose the black vein. With knife point, remove vein. Rinse shrimp quickly in cold water.

4. Reserve about ten whole shrimp for garnish and cut remainder into pieces. Refrigerate until ready to use.

5. For sauce, heat fat in a large heavy skillet. Mix in onion and green pepper and cook until vegetables are tender. Stir in sieved tomatoes, Worcestershire sauce, bay leaf, salt, pepper, sugar, and oregano. Bring mixture to boiling and simmer, uncovered, stirring occasionally. Cook about 15 minutes, or until thickened. Stir in shrimp pieces and heat thoroughly.

6. Serve shrimp mixture on hot fluffy rice and garnish with the whole shrimp.

About 4 servings

Shrimp Kabobs with Seasoned Rice

Everybody likes kabob-style dining, and this shrimp version is bound to be a favorite. You'll be getting protein, vitamin A, niacin, riboflavin, thiamine, calcium, and iron.

2 pounds fresh shrimp, peeled and deveined
1 can (10¾ ounces) condensed tomato soup
2 tablespoons lemon juice
2 tablespoons vegetable oil
2 tablespoons bottled steak sauce
2 teaspoons prepared mustard
½ teaspoon ground black pepper
6 drops Tabasco
2 tablespoons chopped celery
1 clove garlic, minced
Bacon slices, cut in halves
Green peppers, cut in 1-inch squares
Seasoned Rice (see recipe)

1. Put shrimp into a shallow dish.
2. Combine condensed tomato soup, lemon juice, oil, steak sauce, prepared mustard, pepper, Tabasco, celery, and garlic. Beat to blend thoroughly and immediately pour over shrimp. Marinate about 1 hour, turning occasionally. Drain and reserve marinade.
3. Allow four to six shrimp for each skewer (about 9 inches). Alternately thread shrimp, bacon (folded in thirds), and green pepper squares onto skewers. Arrange on broiler rack.
4. Place under broiler about 5 inches from heat and broil about 15 minutes. Turn kabobs often and baste frequently with the marinade. Baste just before serving.
5. Meanwhile, prepare Seasoned Rice.
6. To serve, spoon Seasoned Rice onto a platter and place kabobs on top.

6 servings

Seasoned Rice: Cook **1 cup enriched white rice** following package directions. Meanwhile, heat **2 tablespoons butter or margarine** and **1 clove garlic, minced**, in a saucepan; heat until butter is foamy. Drizzle over cooked rice and toss lightly to coat.

Shrimp Exotica

Shrimp prepared with an exciting combination of other ingredients makes for good nutrition in this unusual dish. Protein, niacin, riboflavin, thiamine, calcium, and iron are the main nutrients.

1½ pounds deveined cooked shrimp

1 can (20 ounces) sliced pineapple, drained; reserve syrup

2 cups water

3 chicken bouillon cubes

1 cup long-grain enriched white rice

¼ cup vegetable oil

1½ cups cubed cooked ham

¼ cup chopped onion

1 clove garlic, crushed in a garlic press or minced

2 tablespoons chopped preserved or crystallized ginger

2 teaspoons soy sauce

2 teaspoons curry powder

½ teaspoon salt

1 medium green pepper, cut in strips

1. Reserve 5 or 6 whole shrimp for garnish. Cut remaining shrimp into pieces. Set aside. Cut 4 pineapple slices into pieces and set aside.
2. Bring water to boiling in a deep saucepan. Add the bouillon cubes, and when dissolved, add the rice gradually, so boiling continues. Cover pan tightly, reduce heat, and simmer 15 to 20 minutes, until a kernel is soft when pressed between fingers.
3. Heat oil in a large skillet. Add ham, onion, and garlic; heat thoroughly, turning with a spoon.
4. Blend ⅔ cup of the reserved pineapple syrup with ginger, soy sauce, curry powder, and salt; add to skillet along with green pepper and heat thoroughly. Add rice and shrimp and remaining pineapple pieces; toss until mixed. Heat thoroughly. Serve on a warm serving platter. Garnish with the pineapple slices and whole shrimp.

About 6 servings

Cereals, Grains, and Pasta

If serving a bowl of rice or spaghetti and meat sauce is the only use you make of the wide variety of grain and pasta products on the market today, read on. Many grain products, such as barley, bulgur, and cornmeal, are staples in the cuisines of other countries, but we Americans are largely unfamiliar with them. Get to know these grains and add variety to your meals. Cracked wheat, or bulgur, for instance, is regularly used in main dishes in North Africa and the Near East. In this chapter, you'll find *Bulgur, Pilaf Style*, made extra flavorful by cooking in chicken bouillon and mixed with onion and other seasonings. Hominy (hulled corn with the germ and bran removed) makes a frequent appearance at meals in our Southern states, but people everywhere will enjoy *Hominy and Bacon*, a delicious casserole topped with a rich tomato sauce. Cornmeal is another versatile grain product. Try *Vegetable Scrapple*, which combines cornmeal, vegetables, and nuts, or *Polenta*, an Italian specialty. You'll find tasty recipes for other grains here, too.

As for pasta, everybody loves it as a filling and flavorful main or side dish, but few people are aware of the many ways there are to serve it. Pasta comes in literally hundreds of shapes and sizes: see what your grocery store has to offer and try out differently shaped pasta products just for fun. Pasta can be topped, baked, or stuffed with many kinds of sauces—a seafood sauce, a spicy meat sauce, a hearty vegetable sauce, or a rich cheese sauce. Or serve it simply tossed with butter or oil and herbs (*Rotini with Almonds and Caraway* is a quick-to-prepare but sophisticated pasta dish).

Rice is as versatile as pasta: its pleasant, mild flavor is well-suited to mixing with other foods and seasonings. Although it may be served plain as a simple accompaniment to a meal, try it dressed up as *Rice Pilaf Deluxe*, or served as a hearty casserole, such as *Spanish Rice au Gratin*. For an occasional change of pace and flavor, cook with brown rice.

Pasta, rice, and other grains are inexpensive (their value as budget-stretchers is well-known) and nutritious. They supply protein, B vitamins, calcium, and iron. Remember to buy enriched pasta and rice—it does make a difference. When pasta or rice is mixed with even small amounts of high-protein foods such as meat or cheese, the nutritional value of the dish increases considerably. Each of the following delicious pasta and grain recipes will let you stay well within your budget and add variety and nutrition to your meals.

Turkey Parmazini

A spaghetti dinner becomes a gourmet treat when served with this sauce containing turkey, ham, fresh mushrooms, and Parmesan cheese. It has protein, vitamin A, the B vitamins, calcium, and iron, as well as taste appeal.

2 tablespoons butter
1¼ cups sliced fresh mushrooms
8 ounces enriched long spaghetti
2 tablespoons butter
¼ cup butter
¼ cup enriched all-purpose flour
¼ teaspoon salt
2 cups milk
1¼ cups cream
2 teaspoons paprika
2 egg yolks, slightly beaten
4 cups julienne cooked turkey
⅔ cup julienne cooked ham
2 cups shredded Parmesan cheese
Paprika

1. Heat 2 tablespoons butter in a small skillet. Add mushrooms and cook over medium heat until mushrooms are lightly browned and tender, stirring occasionally. Remove from heat and set aside to keep warm.

2. Cook spaghetti following package directions; drain. Add 2 tablespoons butter to spaghetti and toss lightly until butter is melted. Set aside to keep warm.

3. Heat ¼ cup butter in a heavy saucepan. Blend in flour and salt. Heat until bubbly, stirring constantly. Add milk gradually, stirring constantly. Bring rapidly to boiling, stirring constantly; cook 1 to 2 minutes. Blend in cream and 2 teaspoons paprika. Heat thoroughly.

4. Stir about 3 tablespoons hot sauce vigorously into egg yolks. Immediately blend with mixture in saucepan. Cook about 3 minutes, stirring constantly. Blend in turkey, ham, mushrooms, and ½ cup Parmesan cheese. Heat thoroughly.

5. Add 1 cup Parmesan cheese to the spaghetti and toss lightly to mix. Turn the spaghetti into a 2½-quart casserole and arrange around edge of casserole. Spoon sauce into center. Sprinkle ½ cup Parmesan cheese over sauce. Sprinkle with paprika.

6. Heat in a 350°F oven about 15 minutes.

6 to 8 servings

Lemony Meat Sauce with Spaghetti

Spicy and lemony, this hearty meat sauce is full of nutrients, including protein (both animal and vegetable), vitamins A and C, the B vitamins, calcium, and iron.

2 pounds ground beef
1½ cups finely chopped onion
1¼ cups chopped green pepper
2 cloves garlic, minced
¼ cup firmly packed brown sugar
1 teaspoon salt
¼ teaspoon ground black pepper
1 teaspoon thyme, crushed
½ teaspoon basil, crushed
2 cups water
2 cans (8 ounces each) tomato sauce
2 cans (6 ounces each) tomato paste
1 can (6 ounces) sliced broiled mushrooms (undrained)
1 tablespoon grated lemon peel
¼ cup lemon juice
1 pound enriched spaghetti
Shredded Parmesan cheese

1. Put meat, onion, green pepper, and garlic into a heated large heavy saucepot or Dutch oven. Cook 10 to 15 minutes, cutting meat apart with fork or spoon.

2. Stir in brown sugar, salt, pepper, thyme, basil, water, tomato sauce, and tomato paste. Cover and simmer 2 to 3 hours, stirring occasionally. About 30 minutes before serving, mix in mushrooms with liquid and lemon peel and juice.

3. Meanwhile, cook spaghetti following package directions; drain.

4. Spoon sauce over hot spaghetti and sprinkle generously with cheese.

10 to 12 servings

Spaghetti à la King Crab

Alaska King crab is combined with tomatoes and spices to make this delicious sauce, which, when poured over enriched spaghetti, offers protein, vitamins A and C, the B vitamins, calcium, and iron.

Parmesan Croutons (see recipe)
2 cans (7½ ounces each) **Alaska King crab** or 1 pound frozen Alaska King crab
2 tablespoons olive oil
½ cup butter or margarine
4 cloves garlic, minced
1 bunch green onions, sliced
2 medium tomatoes, peeled and diced
½ cup chopped parsley
2 tablespoons lemon juice
¼ teaspoon basil
¼ teaspoon thyme
½ teaspoon salt
1 pound enriched spaghetti

1. Prepare Parmesan Croutons; set aside.
2. Drain canned crab and slice. Or, defrost, drain, and slice frozen crab.
3. Heat olive oil, butter, and garlic in a saucepan. Add crab, green onions, tomatoes, parsley, lemon juice, basil, thyme, and salt. Heat gently 8 to 10 minutes.
4. Meanwhile, cook spaghetti following package directions; drain.
5. Toss spaghetti with King crab sauce. Top with Parmesan Croutons. Pass additional grated Parmesan cheese.

About 6 servings

Parmesan Croutons: Put **3 tablespoons butter** into a shallow baking pan. Set in a 350°F oven until butter is melted. Slice **French bread** into small cubes to make about 1 cup. Toss with melted butter. Return to oven until golden (about 6 minutes). Sprinkle with **2 tablespoons grated Parmesan cheese** and toss.

Spaghetti Supreme

The "supreme" part of this recipe is the sauce, rich with cream and herbs. Protein, vitamin A, the B vitamins, calcium, and iron are the benefits when it is poured over a bed of spaghetti and cheese.

8 ounces enriched spaghetti
3 tablespoons olive or vegetable oil
2 tablespoons snipped parsley

1. Cook spaghetti following package directions; drain and keep hot.
2. Meanwhile, heat oil in a skillet. Add parsley, basil, and garlic; cook about 3 minutes, stirring occasionally.

1 teaspoon basil leaves, crushed
3 cloves garlic, minced
2 teaspoons Dijon mustard
1 teaspoon anchovy paste or 3 anchovy fillets, mashed
1/8 teaspoon salt
1/8 teaspoon ground black pepper
1/4 cup water
1/2 cup shredded Parmesan cheese
1/2 cup cream

3. Mix in mustard, anchovy paste, salt, pepper, and water and simmer the sauce about 5 minutes.
4. While sauce is heating, alternate layers of hot spaghetti and cheese on a platter kept in a warm oven.
5. Stir cream into the sauce and heat thoroughly (do not boil); pour over the spaghetti. Serve immediately.

About 4 servings

White Clam Sauce for Linguine

One of the special dishes that Italian restaurants offer with justifiable pride, White Clam Sauce can easily be prepared at home. When combined with linguine, it supplies protein, the B vitamins, and iron.

12 ounces enriched linguine
1/4 cup olive oil
1/2 cup chopped onion
1/4 cup snipped parsley
3 cloves garlic, minced
2 tablespoons flour
1/4 to 1/2 teaspoon salt
    Few grains pepper
3 cans (8 ounces each) minced clams, drained; reserve 1 1/2 cups liquid

1. Cook linguine following package directions; drain and keep hot.
2. Meanwhile, heat oil in a large skillet. Add onion, parsley, and garlic; cook about 3 minutes, stirring occasionally.
3. Mix in flour, salt, and pepper; cook until bubbly. Add reserved clam liquid gradually, while blending thoroughly. Bring rapidly to boiling, stirring constantly, and boil 1 to 2 minutes. Mix in the minced clams and heat; do not boil.
4. Serve clam sauce on the hot linguine.

6 servings

Macaroni 'n' Cheese

In this dish you may discover what macaroni and cheese really ought to taste like. It is rich in protein, vitamin A, the B vitamins, calcium, and iron.

8 ounces (about 2 cups) enriched elbow macaroni
¼ cup butter or margarine
1 teaspoon chopped onion
¼ cup enriched all-purpose flour
1 teaspoon salt
⅛ teaspoon ground black pepper
2 cups milk
2 tablespoons chopped parsley
1 teaspoon basil, crushed
4 teaspoons chopped pimiento
2 cups (about 8 ounces) shredded sharp Cheddar cheese
Parsley sprigs

1. Cook macaroni following package directions; drain.
2. Heat butter in a saucepan. Add onion and cook until lightly browned. Stir in flour, salt, and pepper; cook until bubbly. Add milk gradually, continuing to stir. Bring rapidly to boiling and cook 1 to 2 minutes, stirring constantly to keep mixture cooking evenly.
3. Blend in chopped parsley, basil, and pimiento. Stir in about 1½ cups cheese, reserving remainder for the top. Heat until cheese is melted, stirring constantly.
4. Combine the macaroni and cheese sauce until thoroughly blended. Turn into a buttered 2½-quart baking dish. Sprinkle reserved cheese over top.
5. Set in a 350°F oven 20 to 25 minutes. Garnish with a parsley ball.

About 6 servings

Fiesta Zucchini-Tomato Casserole

Tossed together in a casserole in practically no time at all, this combination of pasta and vegetables adds protein, vitamins A, B, and C, calcium, and iron to your diet.

1½ quarts water
2 packets dry onion soup mix
4 ounces enriched spaghetti, broken
⅓ cup butter or margarine
⅔ cup coarsely chopped onion
1 cup green pepper strips

1. Bring water to boiling in a saucepot. Add onion soup mix and spaghetti to the boiling water. Partially cover and boil gently about 10 minutes, or until spaghetti is tender. Drain and set spaghetti mixture aside; reserve liquid.*
2. Heat butter in a large heavy skillet. Add onion and green pepper and cook about 3 minutes, or until tender. Add zucchini; cover

2 or 3 zucchini (about ¾ pound), washed, ends trimmed, and zucchini cut in about ½-inch slices
4 medium tomatoes, peeled and cut in wedges
¼ cup snipped parsley
1 teaspoon seasoned salt
⅛ teaspoon ground black pepper
⅔ cup shredded Swiss cheese

and cook 5 minutes. Stir in tomatoes, parsley, seasoned salt, and pepper. Cover and cook about 2 minutes, or just until heated.

3. Turn contents of skillet into a 2-quart casserole. Add drained spaghetti and toss gently to mix. Sprinkle cheese over top. If necessary to reheat mixture, set in a 350°F oven until thoroughly heated before placing under broiler.

4. Set under broiler with top about 5 inches from heat until cheese is melted and lightly browned.

6 to 8 servings

* The strained soup may be stored for future use as broth or for cooking vegetables, preparing gravy or sauce, or as desired.

Parmesan Macaroni Casserole

When you serve this luncheon or supper casserole, you'll have a one-dish meal full of protein, vitamin A, the B vitamins, and iron.

4 ounces (about 1 cup) enriched elbow macaroni
1 package (8 ounces) cream cheese
½ teaspoon garlic salt
1 cup milk
½ cup grated Parmesan cheese
1 can (12 ounces) luncheon meat, diced
½ cup sliced celery
¼ cup chopped green pepper
Grated Parmesan cheese

1. Cook macaroni following package directions; drain.

2. Put cream cheese into a heavy saucepan over low heat and soften with a spoon. Add garlic salt and then milk gradually, stirring constantly. Continue to stir and heat thoroughly. Remove from heat. Mix in Parmesan cheese.

3. Turn hot macaroni, luncheon meat, celery, and green pepper into a large bowl. Add and mix in sauce.

4. Turn into a greased 1½-quart casserole. Generously sprinkle top with Parmesan cheese.

5. Set in a 350°F oven until hot and lightly browned (about 25 minutes).

About 6 servings

Peaches-in-Pasta Casserole

This tantalizing combination of flavors can be prepared without much trouble, and is an excellent source of protein, vitamins A, B, and C, and calcium.

8 ounces (about 2 cups) enriched elbow macaroni
¼ cup butter or margarine
¼ cup enriched all-purpose flour
1 tablespoon dry mustard
½ teaspoon salt
1 cup milk
¾ pound sharp Cheddar cheese, shredded
Stewed tomatoes (16-ounce can), cut in pieces
6 to 8 thick (1½-inch) green pepper rings, cooked in boiling water 5 minutes, and drained
1 can (29 ounces) cling peach halves, drained
Grated Parmesan-Romano cheese

1. Cook macaroni following package directions; drain.
2. Heat butter in a large saucepan. Blend in flour, dry mustard, and salt. Heat until bubbly. Add milk gradually, stirring until smooth. Bring to boiling; stir and cook 1 to 2 minutes. Add Cheddar cheese and heat, stirring until melted. Mix in stewed tomatoes and drained macaroni.
3. Turn mixture into a greased shallow 2½-quart baking dish. Press pepper rings into mixture and top each with a peach half, rounded side up. Sprinkle generously with Parmesan-Romano cheese.
4. Set in a 350°F oven until sauce is bubbly (about 25 minutes).

6 to 8 servings

Egg Noodle Bows with Three Cheeses

Here's a three-cheese variation of a world-wide favorite—pasta and cheese. It gives you protein, vitamin A, the B vitamins, calcium, and iron.

Fine dry bread crumbs
4 quarts boiling water
1½ tablespoons salt
12 ounces egg noodle bows (about 6 cups) or 12 ounces medium egg noodles
3 cups Thin White Sauce (see recipe)

1. Coat a buttered 3-quart baking dish with bread crumbs. Set aside.
2. Combine boiling water and salt in a large saucepan or saucepot; add noodles gradually so water continues to boil. Cook uncovered, stirring occasionally, until tender.
3. Meanwhile, prepare Thin White Sauce. Set aside.

2 tablespoons butter or margarine
1 cup freshly grated Parmesan cheese (about 3 ounces)
1 cup diced Swiss cheese (about 4 ounces)
1 cup diced mozzarella cheese (about 4 ounces)

4. Drain noodles and turn into a large bowl. Toss with butter, then Parmesan cheese. Add Swiss and mozzarella cheese; toss lightly.
5. Turn half the noodle mixture into the prepared dish; top with half the white sauce. Repeat layers. If desired, sprinkle grated Parmesan cheese or bread crumbs over top.
6. Heat in a 350°F oven about 25 minutes.

6 servings

Thin White Sauce: Heat **3 tablespoons butter or margarine** in a saucepan; blend in **3 tablespoons flour.** Heat until bubbly. Add **3 cups milk** gradually, stirring constantly. Cook rapidly, stirring constantly, until sauce thickens (2 to 3 minutes). Blend **1½ teaspoons salt, ¼ teaspoon ground black pepper**, and, if desired, **⅛ teaspoon ground nutmeg.** Mix into sauce.

3 cups sauce

Beef-Noodle Casserole

Ripe olives help make this an unusually tasty dish. Quick and easy to prepare, it contains protein, the B vitamins, and iron.

2 cups fine egg noodles
1½ cups Thin White Sauce (one-half recipe)
2 ounces smoked sliced beef, cut in pieces
½ cup shredded Cheddar cheese
¾ cup pitted ripe olives, cut in pieces
¼ cup buttered dry bread crumbs

1. Cook noodles following package directions; drain. Turn into a greased 1½-quart casserole or baking dish.
2. Prepare white sauce and mix in beef, cheese, and olives. Turn sauce onto noodles. Sprinkle buttered bread crumbs over top.
3. Heat in a 350°F oven about 25 minutes, or until top is lightly browned.

4 servings

Delectable Ham-Noodle Casserole

A hint of curry and soy sauce, along with walnuts for a surprise crunch, makes this a truly delectable way to serve ham and noodles. Protein, the B vitamins, and iron are all there, plus a touch of vitamins A and C.

8 ounces (about 4 cups) wide egg noodles
2 tablespoons butter or margarine
3 tablespoons vegetable oil
2 cups diced cooked ham
1 medium onion, sliced
1 green pepper, cut in strips
3 tablespoons sugar
2 tablespoons cornstarch
½ teaspoon salt
⅛ teaspoon ground white pepper
¼ teaspoon curry powder
1 cup chicken broth
1 can (8½ ounces) sliced pineapple, drained and ⅓ cup syrup reserved
½ cup tarragon-flavored white wine vinegar
2 teaspoons soy sauce
½ cup finely chopped walnuts

1. Cook noodles following package directions; drain. Toss with butter; keep warm.
2. Meanwhile, heat oil in a heavy skillet; add ham, onion, and green pepper strips. Cook over low heat until green pepper is crisp-tender; set aside.
3. Thoroughly mix sugar, cornstarch, salt, pepper, and curry powder in a saucepan. Mix broth, pineapple syrup, vinegar, and soy sauce; blend with cornstarch mixture. Cook, stirring constantly, until mixture comes to boiling; boil 3 minutes.
4. Blend sauce with ham mixture in skillet; mix in pineapple slices, cut in halves or quarters. Heat thoroughly.
5. To serve, toss walnuts with buttered noodles and turn into a heated casserole. Spoon ham mixture over noodles.

About 6 servings

Rotini Ratatouille

It takes only thirty minutes to make this unusual vegetable sauce that will supply protein, vitamins A, B, and C, calcium, and iron.

1 medium eggplant
¼ cup olive oil
1 medium onion, thinly sliced

1. Peel eggplant and cut into 3 x 1½-inch strips.
2. Heat oil in a large saucepot, Dutch oven, or large electric skillet or pot. Add onion and

2 cloves garlic, minced
2 medium zucchini, sliced
    ½ inch thick
1 medium green pepper,
    thinly sliced
5 medium tomatoes, peeled
    and quartered or 1 can
    (29 ounces) tomatoes,
    drained
¼ cup chopped parsley
2 teaspoons salt
1 teaspoon basil
½ teaspoon ground black
    pepper
1 pound enriched rotini or
    fusilli
    Grated Parmesan cheese
    (optional)

garlic and cook until almost tender.

3. Add eggplant, zucchini, and green pepper; cook and stir 2 to 3 minutes.

4. Stir in tomatoes, parsley, salt, basil, and pepper; heat to boiling. Reduce heat, cover, and simmer 20 to 25 minutes.

5. Cook rotini following package directions. Drain and put into a heated serving dish. Pour sauce over macaroni.

6. Pass Parmesan cheese, if desired.

6 to 8 servings

Rotini with Almonds and Caraway

There just can't be a simpler dish to prepare than this, or an easier way to provide protein, the B vitamins, calcium, and iron.

8 ounces enriched rotini
¼ cup butter or margarine,
    cut in pieces
½ cup salted toasted sliced
    almonds
1 tablespoon caraway seed,
    toasted
4 teaspoons grated onion

1. Cook rotini following directions on package; drain.

2. Toss cooked rotini with butter, almonds, caraway seed, and onion until well mixed. Serve immediately.

About 6 servings

Note: If desired, substitute medium noodles for rotini.

Pecan-Bacon Brown Rice

Practically every ingredient in this unusual rice recipe has a crisp, crunchy texture, and together they provide an exciting way to serve protein, niacin, riboflavin, thiamine, and iron.

1 **cup brown rice**
6 **slices bacon**
½ **cup coarsely chopped pecans or slivered almonds**
1 **cup thinly sliced mushrooms**
1 **cup thinly sliced celery**
½ **cup sliced green onion**
2 **tablespoons soy sauce**

1. Cook rice following package directions.
2. Cook bacon until crisp in a large skillet; drain well, reserving drippings. Crumble bacon.
3. Put 2 tablespoons drippings into skillet, add pecans and heat until lightly browned (about 5 minutes), stirring frequently. Add cooked rice; cook and stir until lightly browned. Stir in mushrooms, celery, and green onion; cook and stir 1 to 2 minutes, or until vegetables are just crisp-tender. Mix in soy sauce. Top with bacon.

4 to 6 servings

Spicy Raisin Rice / Spicy Raisin Rice with Mushrooms

Raisins and spices dress up this attractive dish, and fresh mushrooms add a festive touch. Niacin, riboflavin, thiamine, calcium, and iron are the nutrients.

¼ **cup butter or margarine**
1 **clove garlic, crushed in a garlic press or minced**
1½ **cups packaged enriched precooked rice**
2½ **cups chicken broth (3 chicken bouillon cubes dissolved in 2½ cups boiling water)**
¼ **cup instant minced onion, or 2 medium onions, finely chopped**

1. Heat butter in a heavy skillet. Stir in garlic and rice; cook over low heat until rice is golden, stirring frequently.
2. Meanwhile, combine broth, onion, and raisins; cover and set aside 5 minutes.
3. Mix salt, paprika, ginger, cinnamon, and allspice and add to rice along with chicken broth mixture; stir to blend. Cover skillet and bring mixture to boiling.
4. Remove from heat immediately and let stand, covered, 5 minutes. Transfer mixture to a warm serving dish. If rice is not to be served

1 cup dark seedless or
   golden raisins
¼ teaspoon salt
½ teaspoon paprika
¼ teaspoon ground ginger
¼ teaspoon ground
   cinnamon
⅛ teaspoon ground allspice

immediately, cover it and set in a warm oven until serving time.

About 6 servings

Spicy Raisin Rice with Mushrooms: Follow recipe for Spicy Raisin Rice. Clean and slice lengthwise ½ **pound mushrooms**. Heat ¼ **cup butter** in skillet. Add mushrooms and cook until lightly browned. Remove from heat and set aside to keep warm while preparing rice mixture. Gently blend in mushrooms before serving.

Hot Green Rice

Don't wait for St. Patrick's Day; serve this one now, and you'll have requests for it all year long. Vitamins A and C, niacin, riboflavin, thiamine, and iron are the nutrients.

1½ cups packaged enriched
    precooked rice
    Chicken broth
½ cup shredded sharp
   Cheddar cheese
¼ cup butter or margarine
⅓ cup finely chopped
   spinach
⅓ cup finely snipped parsley
⅓ cup finely chopped green
   onions with tops
2 eggs, well beaten
1½ cups milk, scalded
    Watercress
    Green pepper strips
    Hard-cooked egg yolk,
    sieved

1. Cook rice in a large saucepan, following package directions; substitute chicken broth for the water and omit salt.
2. Stir in cheese and butter. Add spinach, parsley, and green onions; mix lightly. Stir in beaten eggs and milk, blending lightly but thoroughly.
3. Spoon into heat-resistant individual molds or custard cups or turn into a shallow 2-quart baking dish.
4. Bake at 350°F about 30 minutes, or until set.
5. If rice is baked in molds, unmold and garnish with sprigs of watercress inserted into top of each mold. If baked in a dish, garnish one corner of baking dish with strips of green pepper forming petals of a flower and sieved hard-cooked egg yolk for center of flower.

6 servings

Sweet Potato Rice Skillet

Vitamins A and C, niacin, riboflavin, thiamine, and iron are the chief benefits of this tempting mixture of rice, sweet potatoes, and seasonings.

½ cup butter or margarine
1½ cups coarsely chopped celery
1½ cups chopped onion
 2 cups packaged enriched precooked rice
2½ cups chicken broth (3 chicken bouillon cubes dissolved in 2½ cups boiling water)
 2 tablespoons brown sugar
1¾ teaspoons salt
 ½ teaspoon ground black pepper
 1 teaspoon ground coriander
 ¾ teaspoon crushed rosemary
 ¼ teaspoon ground ginger
 2 eggs, slightly beaten
 1 can (17 ounces) sweet potatoes, drained and cut in ½-inch pieces

1. Heat butter in a large heavy skillet. Mix in celery, onion, and rice and cook until rice is golden, stirring occasionally.

2. Stir in 2 cups of chicken broth. Blend brown sugar, salt, pepper, coriander, rosemary, and ginger; mix in. Bring to boiling and cook, covered, over low heat 15 minutes, or until rice is tender.

3. Mix beaten eggs with remaining ½ cup chicken broth. Blend into the rice mixture. Add sweet potatoes; toss gently. Heat thoroughly before serving.

About 8 servings

Note: If desired, turn into a greased shallow 2-quart casserole. Set in a 325°F oven 20 to 25 minutes, or until thoroughly heated.

Rice Pilaf Deluxe

Rice becomes really elegant here, with raisins, nuts, and onions to add zest, as well as protein, niacin, riboflavin, thiamine, calcium, and iron.

⅓ cup butter
1½ cups uncooked enriched white rice
⅓ cup chopped onion
1½ teaspoons salt
 3 cans (13¾ ounces each) chicken broth
¾ cup golden raisins

1. Heat ⅓ cup butter in a heavy skillet. Add rice and onion and cook until lightly browned, stirring frequently.

2. Add 1½ teaspoons salt, chicken broth, and raisins; cover, bring to boiling, reduce heat, and simmer until rice is tender and liquid is absorbed (20 to 25 minutes).

3. Just before serving, heat 3 tablespoons

3 tablespoons butter
¾ cup coarsely chopped
   pecans
½ teaspoon salt

butter in a small skillet. Add pecans and ½ teaspoon salt; heat 2 to 3 minutes, stirring occasionally.

4. Serve rice topped with salted pecans.

About 8 servings

Yellow Rice Pilaf

Baking makes the difference in this colorful version of rice pilaf, which gives you vitamin A, niacin, riboflavin, thiamine, calcium, and iron.

¼ cup butter or margarine
⅓ cup finely chopped onion
2 cups uncooked enriched
   white rice
4 cups chicken broth
½ teaspoon salt
½ teaspoon ground turmeric

1. Heat butter in a large heavy saucepan. Mix in onion and cook until soft. Add rice, stirring constantly; cook 2 to 3 minutes. Add chicken broth, salt, and turmeric; mix well. Bring mixture rapidly to boiling.

2. Remove from heat and turn into a lightly buttered 1½-quart baking dish. Cover tightly.

3. Bake at 400°F 20 to 25 minutes, or until rice is tender. Remove from oven; uncover and stir rice lightly with a fork to allow steam to escape and to separate kernels. If necessary, cover and keep warm until ready to serve.

6 to 8 servings

Swiss Rice Mold

Tossed and then molded, this dish is easy, yet showy enough for a dinner party. It supplies protein, vitamin A, niacin, riboflavin, calcium, and iron.

3 cups hot cooked enriched
   white rice
2 cups (8 ounces) shredded
   Swiss cheese
¾ cup finely chopped green
   pepper
1 can (4 ounces) Vienna-style
   sausage

1. Toss hot rice, cheese, and green pepper lightly together. Gently pack mixture into a buttered 5- or 6-cup mold.

2. Cut sausages lengthwise into halves and insert at equal intervals around outer edge of rice. Cover with aluminum foil.

3. Heat thoroughly in a 300°F oven about 15 minutes. Unmold onto a heated platter.

About 6 servings

Spanish Rice au Gratin

Cheese, an ingredient you don't normally expect in Spanish rice, makes this dish a special treat. It offers protein, vitamins A and C, niacin, riboflavin, thiamine, calcium, and iron.

½ cup uncooked enriched white rice
1 cup water
½ teaspoon salt
1½ tablespoons butter or margarine
½ cup chopped onion
½ cup chopped celery
⅓ cup chopped green pepper
1 cup canned tomatoes, cut in pieces
½ teaspoon salt
½ teaspoon monosodium glutamate
1 teaspoon sugar
¾ teaspoon chili powder
¼ teaspoon Worcestershire sauce
1 cup (about 4 ounces) shredded Cheddar cheese

1. Combine rice, water, and ½ teaspoon salt in a saucepan. Bring to boiling, reduce heat, and simmer, covered, about 14 minutes.
2. Meanwhile, heat butter in a skillet. Mix in onion, celery, and green pepper. Cook until vegetables are tender. Mix in cooked rice, tomatoes, ½ teaspoon salt, monosodium glutamate, sugar, chili powder, and Worcestershire sauce. Simmer until thick.
3. Turn mixture into a greased baking dish. Top evenly with cheese.
4. Place under broiler 3 to 4 inches from heat until cheese is melted.

3 or 4 servings

Parmesan Rice

A mere toss is all that is necessary to make this delicious cheese-rice combination, which abounds in vitamins A and C, niacin, riboflavin, thiamine, calcium, and iron.

1⅓ cups packaged enriched precooked rice
3 tablespoons butter
3 tablespoons shredded Parmesan cheese
2 tablespoons coarsely chopped pimiento

1. Prepare rice following directions on package.
2. Lightly toss rice with butter, Parmesan cheese, and pimiento. Serve immediately.

About 4 servings

Mushroom-Barley Skillet

Mushrooms and barley make a wonderfully nutritious and flavorful combination, rich in protein and the B vitamins.

6 tablespoons butter or margarine
½ cup minced onion
1 cup regular barley
4 cups boiling chicken or beef broth
Hot water
½ pound mushrooms, sliced
1 teaspoon salt
¼ teaspoon ground black pepper
Pinch garlic salt
2 tablespoons snipped parsley

1. Heat 3 tablespoons butter in a large heavy saucepan. Add onion and cook until soft but not brown.
2. Add barley and cook over medium heat, stirring 3 to 5 minutes, or until barley begins to brown. Add hot broth very slowly to saucepan. Cover and cook over low heat 1 hour, or until barley is almost tender; stir occasionally during cooking and add hot water if more liquid is necessary.
3. Heat remaining 3 tablespoons butter in a skillet. Add mushrooms and cook until almost tender. Season with salt, pepper, and garlic salt. Mix mushrooms with barley; cook 15 minutes, or until barley is tender. Sprinkle with parsley.

4 servings

Fried Cornmeal Mush

This old Southern favorite is as good for you as it is delicious; it contains protein, vitamin A, the B vitamins, and calcium.

1 cup enriched yellow cornmeal
1 teaspoon salt
2¼ cups milk
1½ cups water
Butter or margarine
Syrup or honey

1. Combine cornmeal, salt, and 1 cup milk. Pour remaining milk and water into a saucepan and bring to boiling. Add cornmeal mixture gradually; cook and stir until thickened. Cover and cook over low heat 10 minutes. Pour into a buttered loaf pan, mold, or other container, and chill.
2. Turn out of pan and slice ½ inch thick. Cook on lightly buttered griddle or skillet until crisp and golden, turning once. Serve with butter and syrup or honey.

6 to 8 servings

Vegetable Scrapple

Cornmeal again, dressed up to provide a slightly more sophisticated taste, and supplying protein, vitamin A, the B vitamins, and iron.

3½ cups water
1¼ cups enriched cornmeal
1 tablespoon salt
⅛ teaspoon ground black pepper
½ cup finely chopped onion
½ cup finely chopped carrot
¼ cup finely chopped green pepper
2 tablespoons finely chopped pimiento
1 cup coarsely chopped peanuts

1. Bring water to boiling in a heavy saucepan. Add cornmeal, salt, and pepper gradually, stirring constantly until thick. Stir in onion, carrot, green pepper, and pimiento. Cover and cook over low heat about 15 minutes, stirring occasionally. Mix in peanuts.

2. Turn into a 9 x 5 x 3-inch loaf pan which has been rinsed with cold water. Cool, cover, and refrigerate at least several hours.

3. To serve, cut into ¾-inch slices and brown on both sides on a lightly greased griddle or in a lightly greased skillet.

6 to 8 servings

Polenta

You might think of this as a cornmeal pizza, but whatever its name, it gives you vitamins A and C, the B vitamins, and calcium.

2 tablespoons olive oil
1 clove garlic, crushed
1 can (8 ounces) sliced mushrooms, drained, or 1 pound fresh mushrooms, sliced
1 can (16 ounces) tomatoes (undrained)
⅓ cup tomato paste
1 teaspoon salt
¼ teaspoon ground pepper
3 cups water
1½ teaspoons salt
1 cup enriched cornmeal

1. Heat olive oil and garlic in a skillet. Add mushrooms and cook about 5 minutes, stirring occasionally. When lightly browned, stir in tomatoes with liquid, tomato paste, salt, and pepper. Simmer 15 to 20 minutes.

2. Meanwhile, bring 3 cups water and 1½ teaspoons salt to boiling in a saucepan. Mix cornmeal and 1 cup cold water; stir into boiling water. Continue boiling, stirring constantly to prevent sticking, until mixture is thick. Cover, reduce heat, and cook over low heat 10 minutes or longer.

3. Turn cooked cornmeal onto warm serving platter and top with the tomato-mushroom

1 cup cold water
Grated Parmesan or
Romano cheese

mixture. Sprinkle with grated cheese. Serve at once.

6 to 8 servings

Hominy and Bacon

Serve this to someone who is not a hominy fan, and you're apt to win that person over. At any rate, you'll be providing him with the B vitamins and some protein.

½ pound sliced bacon
1 green pepper, chopped
1 small onion, peeled and chopped
1 can (16 ounces) tomatoes (undrained)
1 tablespoon sugar
1 teaspoon salt
2 cans (16 ounces each) whole hominy, drained

1. Cook bacon in a skillet until lightly browned. Drain bacon on absorbent paper. Reserve 2 tablespoons drippings in skillet. Mix in green pepper and onion and cook until tender. Add tomatoes with liquid, sugar, and salt and simmer 10 minutes.
2. Turn hominy into a greased shallow baking dish; crumble bacon over top and mix with hominy. Pour tomato mixture over all.
3. Heat in a 325°F oven about 45 minutes.

6 to 8 servings

Baked Hominy Grits

Here's another Southern dish just as basic as the protein, vitamins A and D, B vitamins, and calcium it offers.

1 quart milk
½ cup butter or margarine, cut in pieces
1 cup enriched white hominy grits, quick or long-cooking
1 teaspoon salt

1. Heat milk to boiling. Add butter; then add hominy grits gradually, stirring constantly. Bring to boiling and boil 3 minutes, or until mixture becomes thick, stirring constantly. Remove from heat; add salt.
2. Beat mixture at high speed of an electric mixer 5 minutes, or until grits have a creamy appearance. Turn mixture into a greased 1½-quart casserole.
3. Bake at 350°F about 1 hour. Serve hot.

6 to 8 servings

Vegetable-Grits Bake

Vitamin A and the B vitamins are the main nutrients in this easy and rewarding vegetable dish. It offers a tempting way to introduce grits into the diet of those who have yet to discover their good taste.

4 cups boiling water
1 teaspoon salt
1 cup enriched quick white hominy grits (see Note)
1 package (10 ounces) frozen mixed vegetables
¼ pound sharp Cheddar cheese, thinly sliced
½ cup milk
½ cup slightly crushed ready-to-eat cereal flakes

1. Bring water and salt to boiling in a large saucepan. Stir grits slowly into boiling water; return to boiling. Reduce heat; cook 2½ to 5 minutes, stirring occasionally.
2. Meanwhile, cook vegetables following package directions.
3. Alternate layers of cooked grits, cheese, and vegetables in a shallow 1½-quart baking dish. Pour milk over top; sprinkle with crushed cereal.
4. Bake at 325°F about 20 minutes.

About 6 servings

Note: If using regular hominy grits, increase water to 5 cups, cover, and cook slowly 25 to 30 minutes.

Swiss-Style Fruit and Oats

A delicious mixture of fruit and oats, this Swiss dish is sure to become a favorite. And it is loaded with protein, niacin, riboflavin, thiamine, calcium, and iron, too.

2 cups uncooked oats, quick or old-fashioned
1 cup milk
¼ teaspoon salt
1 cup chopped unpared apple
1 cup chopped pecans or walnuts
½ to ⅔ cup golden raisins
½ cup chopped dried figs
½ cup orange juice
¼ cup honey or brown sugar
Milk or cream

1. Combine oats, 1 cup milk, and salt in a bowl. Cover and refrigerate overnight.
2. Before serving, stir in apple, pecans, raisins, dried figs, orange juice, and honey.
3. Serve with milk or cream.

6 to 8 servings

Wheat Berries and Fruit

Although this dish requires planning ahead, it is well worth it. Protein, niacin, riboflavin, thiamine, calcium, and iron are only a part of your reward.

1 **cup whole wheat kernels (berries)**
5 **cups water**
½ **cup chopped dried fruit (apricots, raisins, figs, peaches, or apples)**
¼ **cup honey or brown sugar**
Milk or cream

1. Combine wheat kernels and water in a large saucepan. Bring to boiling and boil 2 minutes. Remove from heat and let stand, covered, 1 hour. (Or soak wheat in water at least 8 hours or overnight.)
2. Bring wheat and liquid to boiling. Simmer, covered, 1½ hours, or until wheat is tender.
3. Drain wheat, reserving ½ cup liquid. Combine reserved liquid, fruit, and honey in saucepan. Bring to boiling; stir in cooked wheat and simmer 10 minutes.
4. Serve warm with milk or cream.

4 to 6 servings

Note: If desired, use sorghum or molasses for sweetening.

Bulgur, Pilaf Style

For a new taste treat, try cracked wheat baked with these special seasonings. It's full of protein, vitamin A, the B vitamins, and iron.

½ **cup butter or margarine**
½ **cup chopped onion**
½ **cup chopped green pepper**
2 **cups bulgur (cracked wheat)**
4 **cups boiling water**
4 **chicken bouillon cubes**
1 **teaspoon salt**
¼ **teaspoon ground black pepper**
1 **cup shredded carrot**

1. Heat butter in a skillet with heat-resistant handle. Mix in onion and green pepper. Cook until onion is tender.
2. Stir in bulgur, cover, reduce heat, and cook 10 minutes over low heat; stir once or twice to prevent sticking.
3. Add boiling water and bouillon cubes; stir until cubes are dissolved; cover tightly.
4. Cook in a 350°F oven 30 minutes. Stir in salt, pepper, and carrot. Continue cooking 15 minutes, or until liquid is absorbed and bulgur is tender.

About 8 servings

Spinach Gnocchi

Don't ask "What's gnocchi?"; you'll discover the answer when the dish is ready. Besides a wonderful taste, it has protein, vitamins A and D, the B vitamins, calcium, and iron.

1½ **cups milk**
1 **tablespoon butter or margarine**
¼ **teaspoon salt**
Few grains nutmeg
¼ **cup farina**
½ **cup well-drained cooked chopped spinach**
1 **egg, well beaten**
1 **tablespoon chopped onion, lightly browned in**
1 **teaspoon butter or margarine**
1½ **cups (about 6 ounces) shredded Swiss cheese**
2 **eggs, well beaten**
¾ **cup milk**
1 **tablespoon flour**
1 **teaspoon salt**
Few grains nutmeg

1. Combine milk, butter, salt, and few grains nutmeg in a saucepan. Bring to boiling and add farina gradually, stirring constantly. Cook over low heat until mixture thickens.

2. Stir in spinach, egg, cooked onion, and 1 cup cheese; blend well. Set aside to cool slightly.

3. Drop mixture by tablespoonfuls close together in a well-greased shallow 9-inch baking dish or casserole. Sprinkle remaining cheese over mounds.

4. For topping, combine eggs, milk, flour, salt, and few grains nutmeg, blending well. Pour over spinach mixture in baking dish.

5. Bake at 350°F 35 to 40 minutes, or until golden brown on top. Serve at once.

4 to 6 servings

Vegetables

Have you ever planned a meal around a vegetable? Try it sometime. Each vegetable has its own unique character, flavor, color, and texture. When cooked to perfection and carefully seasoned or sauced, nothing can compare to garden-fresh vegetables in eye appeal and eating pleasure.

Steam your favorite vegetables, or simmer them in a minimum amount of water, and cook just till tender to preserve their texture, color, and nutrients. Then it takes only minutes to give special treatment to simple vegetable dishes. Toss tender green beans with a blend of curry and sour cream for a delectable accompaniment to a roast. *Tarragon Asparagus Spears* couldn't be easier to prepare, and the hint of herb flavoring will intrigue everyone. Or mix carrots, cauliflower, and green beans with a lemony butter sauce and toasted almonds and you have *Vegetables Amandine*. For slightly more elaborate dishes, try a stuffed vegetable, such as *Cracked Wheat Stuffed Tomatoes*, its filling made extra good with avocado and a touch of mint, or *Ratatouille with Spanish Olives*, a festive dish combining eggplant, tomato, onion, zucchini, and green pepper. Don't pass up those foods you may not be used to serving as vegetables. Celery and green pepper strips, for example, are often served raw or in salads, but served hot with seasonings and sauce they will be a pleasant change of pace at the dinner table.

Vegetables can also be the basis of delicious casseroles and main dishes. *Spinach-Cheese Bake* can take center stage at any meatless meal, and *Brussels Sprouts with Gypsy Rice* or *Cabbage Rolls Paprikash* can be the main attraction at buffet or dinner table. Recipes for some of your favorite foods, such as baked beans and French-fried onion rings, will also be found in the vegetable section.

The nutritional merits of vegetables are well known to us all: vegetables provide essential vitamins and minerals and the roughage necessary for good digestion. Yellow vegetables, such as squash and carrots, are good providers of vitamin A. Green leafy vegetables supply vitamins A and C and calcium. Potatoes and tomatoes are also important sources of vitamin C. And protein is available in dried beans and peas.

Give vegetables the attention they deserve—they'll brighten up any meal and reward you with good nourishment and good taste.

Artichokes with Creamy Dill Sauce

Yogurt is such a good secret ingredient that you may be halfway through dinner before anyone guesses you've used it for the artichokes. Vitamin A, riboflavin, and calcium are the nutrients.

Cooked Artichokes (see recipe)

1 cup creamed cottage cheese

½ cup plain yogurt

1 tablespoon lemon juice

1 teaspoon instant minced onion

1 teaspoon sugar

½ teaspoon dill weed

½ teaspoon salt

Few grains pepper

2 parsley sprigs

1. Prepare desired number of artichokes.
2. Meanwhile, combine cottage cheese, yogurt, lemon juice, onion, sugar, dill weed, salt, pepper, and parsley in an electric blender container. Blend until smooth. Chill.
3. Serve artichokes with sauce for dipping.

About 1½ cups sauce

Cooked Artichokes: Wash **artichokes**. Cut off about 1 inch from tops and bases. Remove and discard lower outside leaves. If desired, snip off tips of remaining leaves. Stand artichokes upright in a deep saucepan large enough to hold them snugly. Add **boiling water** to a depth of 1 inch. Add **salt** (¼ teaspoon for each artichoke). Cover and boil gently 30 to 45 minutes, or until stems can easily be pierced with a fork. Drain artichokes; cut off stems.

Butter-Sauced Asparagus

Fresh asparagus, always a treat, is irresistible when served with this pecan-flavored butter sauce, and it yields vitamins A and C and calcium.

2 pounds fresh asparagus, washed, or 2 packages (10 ounces each) frozen asparagus spears, cooked

¼ cup butter

¼ cup chopped pecans

¼ cup finely chopped celery

1 tablespoon lemon juice

1. Put fresh asparagus into a small amount of boiling salted water in a skillet, bring to boiling, reduce heat, and cook 5 minutes, uncovered; cover and cook 10 minutes, or until just tender.
2. Meanwhile, heat butter in a small saucepan. Add pecans and celery and cook 5 minutes. Stir in lemon juice. Pour over asparagus and serve immediately.

About 6 servings

Tarragon Asparagus Spears / Basil Asparagus Spears

Whether you prefer the taste of tarragon or basil, this recipe is equally delicious with either and offers vitamins A and C, plus calcium.

2 packages (10 ounces each) frozen asparagus spears
¼ cup butter or margarine
½ teaspoon tarragon, crushed

1. Cook asparagus following package directions; drain.
2. Combine butter and tarragon in a large skillet. Heat until butter melts; add the drained cooked asparagus and toss gently to coat evenly. Turn into a serving bowl and serve immediately.

6 to 8 servings

Basil Asparagus Spears: Follow recipe for Tarragon Asparagus Spears; omit tarragon and add **2 teaspoons grated onion** and **¼ teaspoon basil, crushed**, with the butter.

Tangy Green Beans

These spicy, buttery green beans, full of fresh flavor, will add zest to any meal. Vitamin C and calcium are the main nutrients, with some vitamin A and B vitamins thrown in for good measure.

¾ pound fresh green beans, cut crosswise in pieces, or 1 package (9 ounces) frozen cut green beans
½ teaspoon salt
¼ cup butter or margarine
1 medium onion, quartered and thinly sliced
1 tablespoon wine vinegar
¼ teaspoon salt
⅛ teaspoon ground black pepper
¼ teaspoon dill weed
⅛ teaspoon crushed savory

1. Put beans and ½ teaspoon salt into a small amount of boiling water in a saucepan. Bring to boiling and cook, covered, until crisp-tender. Drain and set aside.
2. Heat 3 tablespoons butter in a skillet; add onion and cook 3 to 5 minutes. Mix in beans and cook about 4 minutes, or until thoroughly heated, stirring occasionally. Add remaining butter, wine vinegar, ¼ teaspoon salt, pepper, dill, and savory; toss over low heat until butter is melted.

About 4 servings

Stir-Fry Vegetables and Rice

A bit of Oriental influence is evident in this tasty but quick vegetable dish, which provides protein, vitamins A and C, niacin, riboflavin, thiamine, calcium, and iron.

1 cup brown rice
¼ cup vegetable oil
1 medium onion, thinly sliced
1 cup thinly sliced carrot
1 clove garlic, crushed
1 green pepper, coarsely chopped
1 cup thinly sliced zucchini
1 cup thinly sliced mushrooms
2 cans (16 ounces each) bean sprouts, drained
¼ to ⅓ cup soy sauce

1. Cook rice following package directions; set aside.
2. Heat oil in a large skillet. Add onion, carrot, and garlic; cook and stir over medium high heat about 2 minutes.
3. Add green pepper, zucchini, and mushrooms; cook and stir 2 to 3 minutes.
4. Stir in cooked rice, bean sprouts, and soy sauce. Cook and stir 1 to 2 minutes, or until thoroughly heated.

6 to 8 servings

Buckaroo Beans

Long, slow cooking and several seasonings bring out the flavor and nutritional value of this dish of beans and pork. It offers protein, vitamins A and C, the B vitamins, calcium, and iron.

1 pound dried pinto or red beans
6 cups water
2 medium onions, thinly sliced
2 large cloves garlic, thinly sliced
1 small bay leaf
1 teaspoon salt
½ pound salt pork, slab bacon, or smoked ham

1. Rinse beans and put into a heavy saucepot or kettle. Add water and bring rapidly to boiling; boil 2 minutes and remove from heat. Cover; set aside 1 hour. (If desired, pour the water over the rinsed beans in saucepot, cover, and let stand overnight. Do not drain.)
2. Stir onions, garlic, bay leaf, and 1 teaspoon salt into beans. (If salt pork is used, add salt later.)
3. Wash salt pork thoroughly. Slice through pork or bacon twice each way not quite to the

1 tablespoon butter, margarine, or vegetable oil
1 can (16 ounces) tomatoes (undrained)
½ cup coarsely chopped green pepper
2 tablespoons brown sugar
2 teaspoons chili powder
½ teaspoon dry mustard
¼ teaspoon crushed oregano or cumin
Salt

rind. Cut ham into ½-inch cubes, if used. Add meat to beans and bring rapidly to boiling. Add 1 tablespoon butter to prevent foam from forming. Cover saucepot tightly and cook slowly about 1½ hours.

4. Stir in tomatoes with liquid and green pepper. Blend brown sugar, chili powder, dry mustard, and oregano. Bring rapidly to boiling and reduce heat. Season to taste with salt and simmer, covered, 6 hours or longer; remove cover the last hour of cooking, if desired. If necessary, gently stir beans occasionally to avoid sticking. There should be just enough liquid remaining on beans to resemble a medium-thick sauce.

5. Serve piping hot in soup plates.

About 6 servings

Crunchy Wax Beans

Add a little surprise to canned wax beans with this easy-to-prepare recipe. The B vitamins, vitamin C, some vitamin A, and calcium are the benefits.

2 cans (15½ ounces each) cut wax beans
⅓ cup butter or margarine
2 teaspoons grated onion
2 teaspoons lime or lemon juice
1 cup corn flakes, coarsely crumbled
2 to 3 tablespoons snipped parsley

1. Heat beans as directed on label; drain.
2. Meanwhile, heat butter and onion until butter is browned. Add lime juice and corn flakes and turn to coat. Toss with parsley and hot beans. Serve immediately.

About 8 servings

Lentil-Cheese Supper

It's hard to believe that this delicious blend of vegetables, herbs, and cheese is so easy to prepare. Its nutrients are two kinds of protein, vitamin A, niacin, riboflavin, thiamine, calcium, and iron.

1	**pound lentils**
2	**cups water**
1	**can (16 ounces) tomatoes (undrained)**
1	**cup chopped onion**
2	**cloves garlic, minced**
1	**bay leaf**
2	**teaspoons salt**
$\frac{1}{4}$	**teaspoon ground black pepper**
$\frac{1}{8}$	**teaspoon *each* marjoram, sage, and thyme**
2	**carrots, pared and thinly sliced**
1	**green pepper, chopped**
1	**stalk celery, thinly sliced**
2	**cups (8 ounces) shredded sharp Cheddar cheese**
2	**tablespoons chopped parsley**

1. Rinse lentils and put into a shallow 2- or $2\frac{1}{2}$-quart casserole or baking dish. Add water, tomatoes with liquid, onion, garlic, and bay leaf. Blend salt, pepper, marjoram, sage, and thyme; mix with lentils. Cover.
2. Cook in a 375°F oven 30 minutes.
3. Stir in carrots, green pepper, and celery. Continue cooking 30 minutes.
4. Sprinkle cheese over the top and return to oven until cheese is melted.
5. Sprinkle with parsley.

6 to 8 servings

Flavor-Rich Baked Beans

The classic baked bean is never so delicious as when prepared lovingly at home, and it's full of protein, niacin, riboflavin, thiamine, and iron.

$1\frac{1}{2}$	**quarts water**
1	**pound dried navy beans, rinsed**
$\frac{1}{2}$	**pound salt pork**
$\frac{1}{2}$	**cup chopped celery**
$\frac{1}{2}$	**cup chopped onion**
1	**teaspoon salt**

1. Grease 8 individual casseroles having tight-fitting covers. (A 2-quart casserole with lid may be used.)
2. Heat water to boiling in a large heavy saucepan. Add beans gradually to water so that boiling continues. Boil 2 minutes. Remove from heat and set aside 1 hour.

¼ cup ketchup
¼ cup molasses
2 tablespoons brown sugar
1 teaspoon dry mustard
½ teaspoon ground black pepper
¼ teaspoon ground ginger

3. Remove rind from salt pork and cut into 1-inch chunks; set aside.

4. Add pork chunks to beans with celery, onion, and salt; mix well. Cover tightly and bring mixture to boiling over high heat. Reduce and simmer 45 minutes, stirring once or twice. Drain beans, reserving liquid.

5. Put an equal amount of beans and salt pork chunks into each casserole.

6. Mix one cup of bean liquid, ketchup, molasses, brown sugar, dry mustard, pepper, and ginger in a saucepan. Bring to boiling. Pour an equal amount of sauce over beans in each casserole. Cover casseroles.

7. Bake at 300°F about 2½ hours. If necessary, add more reserved bean liquid to beans during baking. Remove covers and bake ½ hour longer.

8 servings

Barbecued Soy Beans

Here is a crowd pleaser especially good for out-of-doors eating. Protein, niacin, riboflavin, thiamine, calcium, and iron are the nutrients.

1 pound dried soy beans
5 cups water
¼ pound salt pork, diced
1 can (10¾ ounces) condensed tomato soup
½ cup cider vinegar
½ cup chopped onion
½ cup chopped green pepper
1 clove garlic, minced
2 teaspoons Worcestershire sauce
1½ teaspoons dry mustard
1 teaspoon salt
1 teaspoon chili powder
⅛ teaspoon cayenne pepper

1. Rinse soy beans and put into a saucepot or Dutch oven. Pour in water. Bring to boiling and boil 2 minutes. Remove from heat and set aside 1 hour.

2. Add salt pork to beans. Cover and simmer 1 hour, or until beans are almost tender.

3. Add to beans tomato soup, vinegar, onion, green pepper, garlic, and Worcestershire sauce. Blend dry mustard, salt, chili powder, and cayenne; add to beans and mix well. Turn into a bean pot, or 2½- or 3-quart casserole.

4. Bake, uncovered, at 350°F 2 to 2½ hours, or until beans are tender.

6 to 8 servings

Saucy Tomato-Bean Casserole Superb

Three kinds of beans plus Cheddar cheese make this well-seasoned casserole a rich source of protein, niacin, riboflavin, thiamine, vitamin C, calcium, and iron.

3 tablespoons vegetable oil
1 medium onion, chopped
½ cup chopped green pepper
2 cans (8 ounces each) or 1 can (15 ounces) tomato sauce with tomato bits
1 package (1¼ ounces) chili or sloppy joe seasoning mix
1 can (16 or 17 ounces) lima beans, drained
1 can (15½ ounces) red kidney beans, drained
1 can (16 ounces) cut green beans, drained
1 cup (4 ounces) shredded sharp Cheddar cheese

1. Heat oil in a large skillet. Add onion and green pepper; cook, stirring occasionally, until crisp-tender. Mix in tomato sauce, seasoning mix, drained beans, and ½ cup cheese.

2. Turn mixture into a 1½-quart casserole and sprinkle with remaining cheese.

3. Set in a 350°F oven about 35 minutes, or until thoroughly heated.

About 8 servings

Lima Beans New Orleans

Frozen limas have never tasted as good with so little effort as they do here, and of course they're loaded with protein and vitamin C.

1 package (10 ounces) frozen lima beans
1 tablespoon vinegar
2 tablespoons olive oil
½ teaspoon salt
  Dash pepper
2 tablespoons chopped parsley
½ clove garlic, minced
1 teaspoon lemon juice

1. Cook lima beans following package directions; drain if necessary.

2. Add vinegar, olive oil, salt, pepper, parsley, and garlic to limas in saucepan. Heat thoroughly, then mix in lemon juice. Serve immediately.

4 servings

Zesty Beets

Horseradish and mustard add unusual piquancy to this dish of buttered beets, which contains vitamin A and calcium.

1 can or jar (16 ounces) small whole beets
2 tablespoons butter or margarine
2 tablespoons prepared horseradish
½ teaspoon prepared mustard
½ teaspoon seasoned salt

Heat beets in liquid; drain. Add butter, horseradish, prepared mustard, and seasoned salt; stir gently.

About 4 servings

Broccoli with Buttery Lemon Crunch

For those who enjoy a variety of textures as well as flavors, broccoli with a crumb topping is a must, especially since it contains vitamins A and C.

1½ pounds broccoli, washed
¼ cup butter or margarine
½ cup coarse dry enriched bread crumbs
1 tablespoon grated lemon peel
3 tablespoons butter or margarine
1 small clove garlic, crushed in a garlic press or minced
½ teaspoon salt
Few grains black pepper

1. Cook broccoli in a small amount of boiling salted water until just tender. (Cook uncovered 5 minutes, then cover and cook 10 to 15 minutes, or cook, covered, the full time and lift the lid 3 or 4 times during cooking.)
2. Meanwhile, heat ¼ cup butter in a large skillet; add bread crumbs and heat, stirring frequently, until well browned. Remove crumbs from butter with a slotted spoon and mix with the lemon peel.
3. Put 3 tablespoons butter, garlic, salt, and pepper into skillet; heat until butter is lightly browned. Add broccoli and turn gently until well coated with butter.
4. Arrange broccoli in a heated vegetable dish and pour remaining garlic butter over it. Top with the "lemoned" crumbs.

About 6 servings

Brussels Sprouts in Herb Butter

For still another way to serve Brussels sprouts, with an entirely different flavor, try this savory herb sauce. The benefits are vitamin C, some vitamin A, and iron.

2 **pounds fresh Brussels sprouts**
⅓ **cup butter**
1 **tablespoon grated onion**
1 **tablespoon lemon juice**
¾ **teaspoon salt**
¼ **teaspoon thyme**
¼ **teaspoon marjoram**
¼ **teaspoon savory**

1. Cook Brussels sprouts in boiling salted water until just tender.
2. Put butter, onion, lemon juice, salt, thyme, marjoram, and savory into a saucepan. Set over low heat until butter is melted, stirring to blend.
3. When Brussels sprouts are tender, drain thoroughly and turn into a warm serving dish. Pour the seasoned butter mixture over the Brussels sprouts and toss gently to coat sprouts evenly and thoroughly.

About 8 servings

Brussels Sprouts with Gypsy Rice

This casserole provides all the vegetables that any meal needs, as well as vitamins A and C, niacin, riboflavin, thiamine, and iron.

2 **packages (10 ounces each) frozen Brussels sprouts**
½ **cup olive oil**
2 **tablespoons white wine vinegar**
1 **clove garlic, minced**
1 **tablespoon grated lemon peel**
1 **tablespoon lemon juice**
1 **cup uncooked enriched white rice**
1 **teaspoon salt**
1 **small bay leaf**
½ **teaspoon crushed saffron threads**

1. Cook Brussels sprouts following package directions; drain.
2. Mix olive oil, 2 tablespoons wine vinegar, garlic, and lemon peel and juice in a large bowl. Add the hot Brussels sprouts and toss lightly to coat. Set aside, tossing occasionally.
3. Meanwhile, put rice, 1 teaspoon salt, bay leaf, saffron, butter, and water into a large heavy saucepan; stir with a fork. Bring to boiling, stirring occasionally. Reduce heat, cover, and simmer about 30 minutes, or until rice is tender and the cooking liquid is absorbed.
4. Discard bay leaf. Add cooked peas and carrots, olives, eggs, 1 tablespoon wine vinegar,

1   **tablespoon butter or margarine**

2½   **cups cold water**

1   **package (10 ounces) frozen peas and carrots, cooked and drained**

½   **cup sliced pimiento-stuffed olives**

2   **hard-cooked eggs, coarsely chopped**

1   **tablespoon white wine vinegar**

½   **teaspoon salt**

⅛   **teaspoon ground black pepper**

½ teaspoon salt, and pepper; mix lightly.

5. Turn rice mixture into a 2-quart shallow casserole; wreathe with the marinated Brussels sprouts.

6. Set the casserole in a 350°F oven about 20 to 25 minutes, or until thoroughly heated.

About 8 servings

Mama's Company Cabbage

Cabbage prepared like this is good enough for any occasion. You'll know that you are providing vitamins A and C, and calcium, too.

5   **cups finely shredded cabbage**

1   **cup finely shredded carrot**

½   **cup chopped green onion, including some green tops**

½   **teaspoon salt**

⅛   **teaspoon ground black pepper**

1   **beef bouillon cube**

¼   **cup hot water**

¼   **cup butter or margarine**

1   **teaspoon prepared mustard**

⅓   **cup chopped pecans**

¼   **teaspoon paprika**

1. Combine cabbage, carrot, green onion, salt, and pepper in a large heavy saucepan. Dissolve bouillon cube in hot water and add to vegetables in saucepan. Toss with a fork to blend thoroughly. Cover tightly and cook over low heat 5 minutes, moving and turning once during cooking. Drain if necessary; turn into a warm serving dish.

2. Melt butter in a small saucepan over low heat. Stir in prepared mustard and pecans; heat thoroughly and pour over vegetables. Sprinkle with paprika.

About 6 servings

Sweet-Sour Red Cabbage

The red cabbage gets even redder and better when you add red currant syrup and apples, and it is rich in vitamin C and calcium.

1 large head red cabbage
⅓ cup butter or margarine
6 tablespoons cider vinegar
6 tablespoons water
1 teaspoon sugar
½ teaspoon salt
⅔ cup red currant syrup or melted red currant jelly
2 large cooking apples, cored, pared, and sliced

1. Cut cabbage into quarters, cut out core, and remove tough outer leaves. Shred coarsely.
2. Heat butter in a large heavy skillet. Add cabbage; cook about 5 minutes to soften, turning frequently with a spoon.
3. Mix vinegar, water, sugar, and salt and add to cabbage, then stir in syrup and apples. Cover; simmer about 1½ hours, stirring occasionally.

About 8 servings

Cabbage Rolls Paprikash

You can make the filling for these luscious cabbage rolls early in the day and then complete the rolls just before cooking. Protein, vitamins A and C, niacin, riboflavin, calcium, and iron are the nutrients.

8 large cabbage leaves
2½ cups diced cooked chicken
2 tablespoons chopped onion
½ cup finely chopped celery
¼ pound chopped fresh mushrooms
1 small clove garlic, minced
½ teaspoon salt
½ teaspoon thyme leaves
1 egg, beaten
2 tablespoons butter or margarine
6 tablespoons flour
2 cups chicken broth
2 cups dairy sour cream
3 tablespoons paprika

1. Cook cabbage leaves 4 minutes in boiling salted water to cover. Drain and pat dry.
2. Mix chicken, onion, celery, mushrooms, garlic, salt, and thyme; stir in egg.
3. Place ½ cup of the chicken mixture in the center of each cabbage leaf. Fold sides of the cabbage leaf toward center, over filling, and then fold and overlap ends to make a small bundle. Fasten with wooden picks. Place in a 3-quart baking dish.
4. Heat butter in a large skillet. Blend in flour and heat until bubbly. Add chicken broth gradually, stirring until smooth. Blend in sour cream and paprika. Cook over low heat, stirring constantly, until thickened. Pour sauce over cabbage rolls. Cover baking dish.
5. Cook in a 350°F oven 35 minutes.

4 servings

Herbed Carrots and Beans

Two everyday vegetables become very special when combined and seasoned with herbs, and they provide vitamins A and C.

1 cup water
½ teaspoon salt
¼ teaspoon sugar
1 package (9 ounces) frozen cut green beans
4 medium carrots, cut in 2-inch sticks
¼ cup butter or margarine
2 teaspoons grated onion
¼ teaspoon crushed thyme

1. Heat water to boiling in a saucepan. Add salt, sugar, beans, and carrots. Bring water to boiling again, reduce heat, and cook, covered, 7 to 8 minutes, or until just tender; drain.
2. Add butter, onion, and thyme to vegetables; toss to coat well.

About 6 servings

Carrots Lyonnaise

Savory seasonings help you enjoy the flavor and vitamin A of these thinly sliced carrots in an easy-to-prepare dish.

2 tablespoons butter or margarine
3 cups (about 1 pound) thinly sliced carrots
¼ cup chopped onion
1 teaspoon sugar
¼ teaspoon thyme
¼ teaspoon salt
Few grains pepper

Heat butter in a saucepan. Add carrots, onion, sugar, thyme, salt, and pepper. Cover and cook over medium heat about 15 minutes, or until carrots are tender, occasionally moving and turning with a spoon. Serve immediately.

About 4 servings

Glossy Carrots

You may never again be happy with just plain carrots, once you've discovered this delectable way to dress them up and increase their nutritional value. Vitamins A and C and calcium are the main benefits.

24 small whole carrots, pared	1. Cook carrots, covered, in a small amount of boiling water until tender. Drain.
¼ cup butter or margarine	2. Heat butter in a large skillet. Stir in orange juice concentrate, honey, ginger, and salt. Add carrots to skillet set over low heat, turning carrots until well glazed.
¼ cup thawed frozen orange juice concentrate	
2 teaspoons honey	
½ teaspoon ground ginger	
½ teaspoon salt	

About 4 servings

Carrot-Egg Casserole

Here's a casserole made of carrots, cheese, and eggs that is as tasty as it is unusual. Vitamin A and calcium are its outstanding nutrients.

4 cups carrot slices or sticks	1. Cook carrots, covered, in a small amount of boiling salted water until crisp-tender; drain.
¼ cup butter or margarine	2. Meanwhile, heat butter in a small skillet. Mix in onion and cook until crisp-tender.
½ cup chopped onion	3. Combine carrots, onion with butter, cracker crumbs, and cheese; toss to mix well. Spoon one half of the mixture into a greased shallow 1-quart baking dish. Sprinkle with lemon pepper marinade; form a layer of egg slices and sprinkle with additional lemon pepper marinade. Spoon remaining carrot mixture over all.
½ cup finely crushed crumbs from round buttery crackers	
¾ cup (3 ounces) shredded sharp Cheddar cheese Lemon pepper marinade	4. Form a wide border around edge of dish with parsley.
3 hard-cooked eggs, sliced Parsley, minced	5. Set in a 350°F oven until thoroughly heated, about 20 minutes.

About 6 servings

Cauliflower Italiana

An easy-to-stir-up Italian sauce is the winning feature of this cauliflower dish, which provides vitamins A and C and calcium.

2 **packages (10 ounces each) frozen cauliflower**
2 **tablespoons butter or margarine**
½ **clove garlic, minced**
2 **teaspoons flour**
1 **teaspoon salt**
1 **can (16 ounces) tomatoes (undrained)**
1 **small green pepper, coarsely chopped**
¼ **teaspoon oregano**

1. Cook cauliflower following package directions; drain.
2. Meanwhile, heat butter with garlic in a saucepan. Stir in flour and salt and cook until bubbly.
3. Add tomatoes with liquid and bring to boiling, stirring constantly; cook 1 to 2 minutes. Stir in green pepper and oregano.
4. Pour hot sauce over cooked cauliflower.

About 6 servings

Vegetables Amandine

Here's a medley of favorite vegetables served in an herb-flavored, buttery sauce and sprinkled with almonds. Vitamins A and C, calcium, and iron are the nutrients.

6 **medium carrots**
1 **package (10 ounces) frozen cauliflower**
1 **package (9 ounces) frozen cut green beans**
½ **cup blanched almonds, slivered and toasted**
6 **tablespoons butter, melted**
½ **teaspoon lemon juice**
½ **teaspoon crushed rosemary leaves**

1. Wash, pare or scrape, and cut carrots crosswise into ¼-inch slices. Cook carrots, covered, in a small amount of boiling salted water about 10 minutes, or until just tender; drain.
2. Cook cauliflower and green beans following package directions; drain.
3. To serve, arrange vegetables in a serving dish. Sprinkle almonds over top. Mix butter, lemon juice, and rosemary; pour over vegetables.

About 8 servings

Celery Root with Mushrooms and Capers

If you have never tasted celery root, you might be in for a pleasant surprise, especially if you combine it with mushrooms and capers. You will also be getting some protein, niacin, riboflavin, and calcium.

1	celery root (celeriac)
1	lemon, sliced
	Boiling water
¼	cup dry enriched bread crumbs
¼	cup butter or margarine
2	tablespoons butter or margarine
1	cup sliced mushrooms
2	tablespoons capers

1. Wash celery root, cut off ends, and pare. Cut into ½-inch slices.
2. Put slices into a large saucepan; add lemon slices and boiling water to cover. Cover; bring to boiling and cook 30 to 40 minutes, or until tender.
3. Drain celery root, cut into cubes, and pat dry with absorbent paper. Coat cubes with bread crumbs.
4. Heat ¼ cup butter in a skillet. Add celery root and turn pieces frequently to brown all sides.
5. Meanwhile, heat 2 tablespoons butter in a skillet. Add sliced mushrooms and cook over medium heat, stirring occasionally until mushrooms are tender.
6. Mix mushrooms and capers lightly with the browned celery root.

About 6 servings

Celery and Green Pepper au Gratin

You may not believe that celery can become so elegant. Try this recipe, and expect to gain vitamin A, calcium, and some B vitamins.

4	cups diagonally sliced celery
2	green peppers, thinly sliced
¼	cup dry sherry
3	tablespoons butter or margarine, melted

1. Cook celery and green peppers, covered, in a small amount of boiling salted water until crisp-tender (about 5 minutes); drain. Turn vegetables into a shallow 1½-quart baking dish and drizzle with 3 tablespoons sherry.
2. Mix remaining sherry with butter and toss

1 cup soft enriched bread
  crumbs
½ cup crumbled blue cheese

with bread crumbs and blue cheese. Spoon over vegetables.

3. Set under broiler with top 3 to 4 inches from heat. Broil until top is lightly browned.

6 to 8 servings

Corn Custard Fiesta

This corn custard, full of crispy vegetables and topped with cheese, is a perfect way to turn a can of corn into a nutritious treat which offers protein, vitamin A, the B vitamins, calcium, and iron.

1 can (17 ounces) cream-style
  corn
2 eggs, beaten
¼ cup finely shredded carrot
¼ cup chopped green pepper
1 tablespoon chopped celery
1 teaspoon chopped onion
½ teaspoon sugar
½ teaspoon salt
6 drops Tabasco
½ cup crushed soda crackers
¼ cup butter or margarine,
  melted
¼ cup undiluted evaporated
  milk
½ cup shredded Cheddar
  cheese
  Paprika
  Parsley, snipped
  Pimiento-stuffed olive
  slices

1. Turn corn into a bowl. Add eggs, carrot, green pepper, celery, onion, sugar, salt, Tabasco, crushed crackers, butter, and evaporated milk; mix well. Turn into a greased 8 x 8 x 2-inch baking dish, top with cheese, and sprinkle with paprika.

2. Bake at 350°F 30 minutes, or until custard is set and top is golden brown.

3. Remove from oven and mark off servings with lines of parsley. Place an olive slice in center of each piece.

About 6 servings

Creamy Summer Corn and Peas

Sour cream is the surprise ingredient that makes this vegetable combination something special. The nutrients include protein, vitamin A, and calcium.

3 tablespoons butter or margarine
¼ cup finely chopped onion
¼ cup diced celery
1 package (10 ounces) frozen green peas, defrosted to separate
2 cups uncooked fresh corn kernels
1 tablespoon minced parsley
1 teaspoon sugar
1 teaspoon salt
⅛ teaspoon ground black pepper
½ cup dairy sour cream

1. Heat butter in a large skillet. Add onion and celery and cook until crisp-tender.
2. Add peas, corn, parsley, sugar, salt, and pepper; mix well. Cook over low heat 5 minutes, stirring frequently. Stir in sour cream; heat thoroughly but do not boil.

About 6 servings

Corn Spoon Bread

Here is an extranutritious variation of an old Southern favorite. The corn, cornmeal, and milk combine to provide protein, vitamin A, the B vitamins, calcium, and iron.

1 quart milk
1 cup enriched yellow cornmeal
2 tablespoons finely chopped onion
2 tablespoons chopped parsley
4 eggs
2 tablespoons butter or margarine
2 tablespoons prepared baconlike pieces (a soy protein product)

1. Scald milk in top of a double boiler over simmering water.
2. Add cornmeal to scalded milk gradually, stirring constantly. Mix in onion and parsley. Cook over boiling water until thickened, about 10 minutes, stirring frequently and vigorously.
3. Meanwhile, beat eggs in a large bowl until thick and piled softly.
4. Remove double boiler top from water. Stir in butter and baconlike pieces. Blend salt, sugar, baking powder, and seasoned pepper; stir into cornmeal mixture. Add hot mixture

2 teaspoons salt
1 teaspoon sugar
1 teaspoon baking powder
¼ teaspoon seasoned pepper
2 cups corn kernels (fresh, frozen, or canned)

gradually to eggs, beating constantly. Mix in corn. Turn into a buttered 2-quart casserole.
5. Bake at 425°F 40 to 45 minutes, or until top is browned. Serve immediately.

6 to 8 servings

Fresh Corn Vinaigrette

Here's a wonderfully cooling way to serve fresh corn, and since you prepare it ahead of time, it's perfect for company meals or busy days. Vitamins A and C and calcium are the benefits.

4 ears fresh corn
¼ cup vegetable oil
2 tablespoons cider vinegar
¾ teaspoon lemon juice
1½ tablespoons chopped parsley
1 teaspoon salt
½ teaspoon sugar
¼ teaspoon basil
⅛ teaspoon cayenne pepper
1 large tomato, peeled and chopped
¼ cup chopped green pepper
¼ cup chopped green onion
Greens (optional)

1. Husk corn and remove silks. Fill a large kettle half full of water and bring to boiling. Add corn, cover, and return to boiling. Remove from heat and let stand 5 minutes. Drain and set aside to cool.
2. Mix oil, vinegar, lemon juice, parsley, salt, sugar, basil, and cayenne in a large bowl.
3. Cut corn off cob and add to bowl along with tomato, green pepper, and green onion; mix well. Cover and chill several hours.
4. Drain and serve on greens, if desired.

4 to 6 servings

Note: If desired, substitute 1½ cups (12-ounce can, drained, or 10-ounce package frozen, defrosted) whole kernel corn.

Ratatouille with Spanish Olives

Served hot or cold, this eggplant-and-zucchini mixture is perfect for almost any type of meal, and it provides vitamins A and C and calcium.

1   **medium eggplant (about 1½ pounds), pared and cut in 3 x ½-inch strips**
2   **zucchini, cut in ¼-inch slices**
2   **teaspoons salt**
½   **cup olive oil**
2   **onions, thinly sliced**
2   **green peppers, thinly sliced**
2   **cloves garlic, minced**
3   **tomatoes, peeled and cut in strips**
1   **cup sliced pimiento-stuffed olives**
¼   **cup snipped parsley**
¼   **teaspoon ground pepper Parsley, snipped**

1. Toss eggplant and zucchini with 1 teaspoon salt and let stand 30 minutes. Drain and then dry on paper toweling.
2. Heat ¼ cup oil in a large skillet and lightly brown eggplant strips and then zucchini slices. Remove with slotted spoon; set aside.
3. Heat remaining oil in the skillet; cook onions and green peppers until tender. Stir in garlic. Put tomato strips on top; cover and cook 5 minutes. Gently stir in eggplant, zucchini, olives, ¼ cup parsley, remaining salt, and the pepper.
4. Simmer, covered, 20 minutes. Uncover and cook 5 minutes; baste with juices from bottom of skillet. Serve hot or cold, garnished with parsley.

6 to 8 servings

Wheat-Germ-Crusted Eggplant

Thiamine, riboflavin, and iron are the special nutrients provided by this delicious eggplant recipe.

1   **medium eggplant, about 1½ pounds**
2   **eggs, beaten**
½   **teaspoon salt**
1   **cup toasted wheat germ Vegetable oil (about ¾ cup)**

1. Cut eggplant crosswise about 3 inches from stem end. Cut larger piece lengthwise. Slice eggplant into wedges no more than 1 inch wide at the thickest part.
2. Combine eggs with salt in a shallow dish. Coat wedges with egg, then with wheat germ.
3. Heat ¼ cup oil in a large skillet. Add a layer of eggplant and cook over medium heat about 3 minutes per side until eggplant is tender. Continue cooking eggplant a layer at a time, adding oil as needed. Serve hot.

About 6 servings

Note: Be sure to keep heat moderate so that eggplant will be tender when crust is browned.

Lacy French-Fried Onion Rings / Lacy Cornmeal Onion Rings

Whether you use flour or cornmeal, this is a foolproof way to make onion rings, which provide some vitamin A, B vitamins, calcium, and iron.

1 **cup enriched all-purpose flour**
1 **teaspoon baking powder**
1/4 **teaspoon salt**
1 **egg, well beaten**
1 **cup milk**
1 **tablespoon vegetable oil**
4 **sweet Spanish onions**
   Fat for deep frying heated to 375°F
   Salt or garlic salt

1. Blend flour, baking powder, and salt.
2. Combine egg, milk, and oil in a bowl and beat until thoroughly blended. Beat in the dry ingredients until batter is smooth. Cover.
3. Cut off root ends of onions; slip off the loose skins. Slice onions 1/4 inch thick and separate into rings.
4. Using a long-handled two-tined fork, immerse a few onion rings at a time into the batter, lift out and drain over bowl a few seconds before dropping into heated fat. Turn only once as they brown; do not crowd.
5. When rings are golden brown on both sides, lift out and drain on absorbent paper-lined cookie sheet. Sprinkle with salt and serve hot.

About 6 servings

Lacy Cornmeal Onion Rings: Follow recipe for Lacy French-Fried Onion Rings. Substitute **1/2 cup enriched cornmeal** for 2/3 cup flour.

To Freeze French-Fried Onions: Leaving the crisp, tender rings on the absorbent paper-lined cookie sheet on which they were drained, place in freezer and freeze quickly. Then carefully remove rings to moisture-vaporproof containers with layers of absorbent paper between each layer of onions; the rings may overlap some. Cover tightly, label, and freeze.

To Reheat Frozen French-Fried Onions: Removing the desired number of onion rings, arrange them (frozen) in a single layer on a cookie sheet. Heat in a 375°F oven several minutes, or until rings are crisp and hot.

Okra and Corn

Okra contributes its distinctive flavor to this nutritious blend of vegetables rich in vitamins A and C and calcium.

4 slices bacon
1 onion, sliced
1 package (10 ounces) frozen okra, defrosted and cut into ¼-inch thick slices
1 package (10 ounces) frozen corn, defrosted
2 medium tomatoes, peeled and diced (about 1½ cups)
¼ cup diced green pepper
½ teaspoon salt
⅛ teaspoon ground black pepper

1. Fry bacon in a skillet, drain, and crumble; set aside.
2. Put 2 tablespoons bacon fat into skillet and add onion, okra, and corn; cook, stirring frequently 10 minutes.
3. Mix in tomatoes, green pepper, salt, and pepper; cook over low heat about 20 minutes.
4. Turn into a warm serving dish and sprinkle the bacon over top.

About 8 servings

Parsnip Fritters

Plump, tasty little fritters, bursting with vitamin C and calcium, make an appetizing vegetable accompaniment to practically any meal.

4 parsnips (about 1 pound), pared
2 eggs, well beaten
1 tablespoon butter or margarine
½ cup milk
1 teaspoon minced onion
3 tablespoons flour
¼ teaspoon dill weed
¾ teaspoon salt
Few grains black pepper
Fat for deep frying heated to 365°F

1. Cook parsnips, covered, in boiling salted water until tender; drain thoroughly. Mash parsnips, removing any fibrous portions. (There will be about 1¼ cups, mashed.)
2. Add eggs to parsnips and beat well. Beat in butter, milk, and onion. Blend flour, dill weed, salt, and pepper; add to parsnips and mix until thoroughly blended.
3. Drop batter by tablespoonfuls into hot deep fat and fry 2 to 3 minutes, turning several times until fritters are golden brown. Remove with slotted spoon, drain over fat, and place on absorbent paper. Serve hot.

About 4 servings

Herbed Peas

Colorful as well as tasty, this mixture of peas, onions, and pimiento provides a quick way to supply some protein and vitamin A.

$\frac{1}{4}$ **cup butter or margarine**

4 **green onions including tops, thinly sliced**

1 **package (10 ounces) frozen green peas, partially defrosted**

1 **tablespoon minced parsley**

$\frac{1}{2}$ **teaspoon thyme, crushed**

$\frac{1}{4}$ **teaspoon marjoram, crushed**

$\frac{1}{2}$ **teaspoon sugar**

$\frac{1}{4}$ **to $\frac{1}{2}$ teaspoon salt**

1 **tablespoon chopped pimiento**

1. Heat butter in a saucepan or skillet. Add onions and cook about 5 minutes, stirring occasionally.

2. Add peas and parsley to saucepan. Blend thyme, marjoram, sugar, and salt; mix with peas. Cover and cook over low heat until peas are tender, about 7 minutes, stirring occasionally. Stir in the pimiento and turn into a serving dish.

About 4 servings

Fresh Peas with Basil

Fresh peas gain extra flavor when given this special treatment, which enhances their good taste and vitamin A content.

2 **tablespoons butter or margarine**

$\frac{1}{2}$ **cup sliced green onions with tops**

$1\frac{1}{2}$ **cups shelled fresh peas ($1\frac{1}{2}$ pounds)**

$\frac{1}{2}$ **teaspoon sugar**

$\frac{1}{2}$ **teaspoon salt**

$\frac{1}{8}$ **teaspoon ground black pepper**

$\frac{1}{4}$ **teaspoon basil**

1 **tablespoon snipped parsley**

$\frac{1}{2}$ **cup water**

1. Heat butter in a skillet. Add green onions and cook 5 minutes, stirring occasionally. Add peas, sugar, salt, pepper, basil, parsley, and water.

2. Cook, covered, over medium heat 10 minutes, or until peas are tender.

About 4 servings

Note: If desired, use 1 package (10 ounces) frozen green peas and decrease water to $\frac{1}{4}$ cup.

Fried Green Pepper Strips

As a side dish or a hot hors d'oeuvre, these fried green pepper strips make an unusual treat. Vitamins A and C are contained in every crunchy bite.

2 large green peppers
½ cup fine dry enriched bread crumbs
⅓ cup grated Parmesan cheese
1½ teaspoons salt
⅛ teaspoon ground black pepper
1 egg, slightly beaten
2 tablespoons water
Fat or vegetable oil

1. Rinse, cut off tops, remove and discard white fiber and seeds from green peppers. Rinse again and cut into rings ⅛ inch thick. Cut each ring into halves or thirds.

2. Mix bread crumbs, Parmesan cheese, salt, and pepper. Combine egg and water. Coat green pepper strips with crumbs. Then dip into egg, and again coat with crumbs. Refrigerate 1 hour.

3. Heat fat (½-inch depth) in a skillet over medium heat. When oil is hot, fry as many chilled green pepper strips at one time as will float uncrowded one layer deep in fat. Fry about 30 seconds, or until golden brown. Remove strips from fat with fork or slotted spoon. Drain over fat for a few seconds and place on absorbent paper. Serve hot.

About 4 servings

Parsley-Buttered New Potatoes

This classic recipe for preparing delicately flavored new potatoes couldn't be simpler, better tasting, or a more pleasant source of vitamins A and C.

18 small new potatoes
Boiling water
1½ teaspoons salt
2 tablespoons butter
1 tablespoon snipped parsley

Scrub potatoes and put into a saucepan. Pour in boiling water to a 1-inch depth. Add salt; cover and cook about 15 minutes, or until tender. Drain and peel. Return potatoes to saucepan and toss with butter and parsley.

About 6 servings

Note: Snipped chives, grated lemon peel, and lemon juice may be used instead of parsley.

Cheesy Potato Skillet

Protein, vitamin A, riboflavin, and calcium are the nutrients found in this appetizing mixture of potatoes, cheese, and seasonings.

4 large potatoes, washed, pared, and thinly sliced
¼ cup chopped onion
1 tablespoon butter, cut in pieces
½ teaspoon salt
⅛ teaspoon ground pepper
1 tablespoon chopped parsley
1 tablespoon ketchup
½ teaspoon steak sauce
¾ cup (about 4 ounces) finely diced pasteurized process American cheese
1½ cups milk

1. Put potatoes and onion into a large heavy skillet or saucepan. Add butter, salt, pepper, parsley, ketchup, steak sauce, cheese, and milk; stir to mix. Cover skillet.
2. Cook over very low heat until potatoes are tender, about 1 hour.

6 to 8 servings

Note: If desired, cook in an electric skillet.

Potatoes Anna

Nothing could be tastier than this simple recipe, which retains all the goodness of the basic potato flavor, as well as vitamins A and C.

6 to 8 medium potatoes, washed
Salt and pepper
½ cup butter or margarine

1. Pare potatoes and cut into thin crosswise slices. Dry thoroughly with absorbent paper.
2. Arrange even layers of potatoes in a 2-quart buttered casserole, overlapping slices about ¼ inch. Sprinkle each layer with salt and pepper. Dot layers generously with butter.
3. Bake at 425°F 40 to 60 minutes, or until potatoes are golden brown. To remove from casserole for serving, run spatula around edge to loosen. Invert onto warm serving plate.

6 to 8 servings

Potato Pancakes

This German potato classic can be served alone or as an accompaniment to a meat course. Vitamins A and C are its special nutrients.

Butter or margarine (enough, melted, for a ¼-inch layer)

2 tablespoons flour

1½ teaspoons salt

¼ teaspoon baking powder

⅛ teaspoon ground black pepper

6 medium potatoes, washed

2 eggs, well beaten

1 teaspoon grated onion
Applesauce or maple syrup, warmed

1. Heat butter in a heavy skillet over low heat.
2. Combine flour, salt, baking powder, and pepper and set aside.
3. Pare and finely grate potatoes; set aside.
4. Combine flour mixture with eggs and onion.
5. Drain liquid from grated potatoes; add potatoes to egg mixture and beat thoroughly.
6. When butter is hot, spoon batter into skillet, allowing about 2 tablespoonfuls for each pancake and leaving about 1 inch between cakes. Cook over medium heat until golden brown and crisp on one side. Turn carefully and brown on other side. Drain on absorbent paper. Serve with applesauce or maple syrup.

About 20 pancakes

Scalloped Potatoes

This classic potato recipe supplies vitamins A and C, riboflavin, and calcium, so don't overlook it when you are planning a well-balanced meal.

4 to 5 medium (about 1½ pounds) potatoes

2 tablespoons butter or margarine

¼ cup chopped onion (optional)

2 tablespoons flour

¼ teaspoon salt

2 cups milk

1. Wash, pare, and thinly slice potatoes (about 3 cups, sliced). Turn into a 1½-quart casserole.
2. Heat butter in a saucepan. Add onion, if desired, and cook until soft. Mix in flour and salt; heat until bubbly. Add milk gradually, stirring constantly. Bring to boiling and cook until sauce thickens. Pour over potatoes in casserole.
3. Bake at 350°F about 1½ hours, or until potatoes are tender when pierced with a fork.

About 6 servings

AMERICAN SPICE TRADE ASSOCIATION

Parsleyed Oven Pot Roast; Old-Fashioned Cauliflower Pickles

Baked Ripe Olive Minestrone

THE OLIVE ADMINISTRATIVE COMMITTEE

PACIFIC BARTLETT GROWERS, INC.

Whole Wheat Pear Bread

Lamb Crown Roast with Mint Stuffing; Parsley-Buttered New Potatoes; Butter-Sauced Asparagus

AMERICAN DAIRY ASSOCIATION

NATIONAL LIVE STOCK AND MEAT BOARD

Pork Loin Roast; Hash Brown Potatoes au Gratin

Chicken and Dumplings

NATIONAL BROILER COUNCIL

HALIBUT ASSOCIATION OF NORTH AMERICA

Planked Halibut Dinner

ALASKA KING CRAB

Spaghetti à la King Crab

UNITED FRESH FRUIT AND VEGETABLE ASSOCIATION

**Apple-Stuffed Acorn Squash; Stuffed Eggplant Salad; Stuffed Baked
Sweet Potatoes; Cabbage Rolls Paprikash**

Vegetable-Rice Medley

RICE COUNCIL

SPANISH GREEN OLIVE COMMISSION

Mixed Vegetable Salad

Layered Lime-Shrimp Salad

AMERICAN DAIRY ASSOCIATION

DIAMOND WALNUT GROWERS, INC.

Triple-Treat Walnut Bars; Spicy Walnut Diamonds

Clockwise from top left: **Pink Grapefruit Cloud; Orange-Grapefruit Cooler;**
Citrus Fruit Punch; Orange Frappé; Orange Shake

FLORIDA DEPARTMENT OF CITRUS

Swiss Double Bakes

Swiss cheese and yogurt give a distinctive taste to these stuffed baked potatoes, which are rich in vitamins A and C and calcium.

2 **large baking potatoes, scrubbed**
⅓ **cup plain yogurt**
1 **tablespoon butter**
½ **teaspoon salt**
  Few grains pepper
½ **cup shredded Swiss cheese**
1 **tablespoon chopped pimiento**

1. Puncture skins of potatoes with a fork several times. Bake at 375°F about 1¼ hours, or until tender.
2. Cut hot potatoes into halves lengthwise; scoop out potato into a bowl; reserve shells. Mash potato; add yogurt, butter, salt, and pepper and whip thoroughly. Stir in cheese and pimiento. Spoon into potato shells, heaping slightly. Place on a cookie sheet.
3. Return to oven 15 minutes or until thoroughly heated and lightly browned.

4 servings

Springtime Potatoes

A creamy blend of fresh springtime vegetables and potatoes provides vitamins A and C and calcium in a varied combination of flavors.

1 **can (16 ounces) potatoes**
⅓ **cup chopped cucumber, pared**
2 **tablespoons chopped green pepper**
2 **tablespoons sliced radishes**
1½ **tablespoons chopped green onion**
1 **teaspoon salt**
  Few grains pepper
½ **cup dairy sour cream**

1. Heat potatoes in liquid thoroughly in a saucepan; drain.
2. Meanwhile, mix cucumber, green pepper, radishes, green onion, salt, pepper, and sour cream in a saucepan. Heat over low heat, stirring frequently; do not boil.
3. Pour sour-cream mixture over hot potatoes; toss lightly to coat evenly. Serve immediately.

About 4 servings

Hash Brown Potatoes au Gratin

Starting with frozen hash brown potatoes makes it very easy to prepare this hearty and nutritious dish. Vitamins A and C, riboflavin, and calcium are the nutritional benefits.

1 package (2 pounds) frozen chopped hash brown potatoes, partially defrosted
1½ teaspoons salt
Few grains pepper
¼ cup coarsely chopped green pepper
1 jar (2 ounces) sliced pimientos, drained and chopped
2 cups milk
¾ cup fine dry enriched bread crumbs
⅓ cup soft butter
⅔ cup shredded pasteurized process sharp American cheese

1. Turn potatoes into a buttered shallow 2-quart baking dish, separating into pieces. Sprinkle with salt and pepper. Add green pepper and pimientos; mix lightly. Pour milk over potatoes. Cover with aluminum foil.

2. Cook in a 350°F oven 1¼ hours, or until potatoes are fork-tender. Remove foil; stir potatoes gently. Mix bread crumbs, butter, and cheese. Spoon over top of potatoes. Return to oven and heat 15 minutes, or until cheese is melted.

About 6 servings

Sauerkraut with Apples

Quick and easy to prepare, this is a taste-appealing way to introduce vitamin C, calcium, and some vitamin A into any meal.

4 cups drained sauerkraut
2 apples, thinly sliced
½ cup apple cider
1 tablespoon light brown sugar
2 tablespoons butter or margarine
Apple wedges
Parsley sprigs

1. Combine sauerkraut, sliced apples, apple cider, brown sugar, and butter in a saucepan. Cover, bring to boiling, reduce heat, and simmer 5 minutes, or until apples are tender.

2. Garnish with apple wedges and parsley.

About 8 servings

Spinach-Bacon Soufflé

Time the preparation of this unusual soufflé so that you can serve it as soon as it comes from the oven. It's a delightful way to bring vitamins A and C and iron, plus some protein and B vitamins, to the table.

2 cups firmly packed, finely chopped fresh spinach (dry the leaves before chopping)

¼ cup finely chopped green onions with tops

½ pound sliced bacon, cooked, drained, and crumbled

3 tablespoons butter or margarine

¼ cup enriched all-purpose flour

½ teaspoon salt

¼ to ½ teaspoon thyme

1 cup milk

3 egg yolks, well beaten

4 egg whites

2 teaspoons shredded Parmesan cheese

1. Toss the spinach, green onions, and bacon together in a bowl; set aside.

2. Heat butter in a saucepan over low heat. Blend in flour, salt, and thyme. Stirring constantly, heat until bubbly. Add milk gradually, continuing to stir. Bring rapidly to boiling and boil 1 to 2 minutes, stirring constantly.

3. Remove from heat and blend spinach-bacon mixture into the sauce. Stir in the beaten egg yolks; set aside to cool.

4. Meanwhile, beat egg whites until rounded peaks are formed (peaks turn over slightly when beater is slowly lifted upright); do not overbeat.

5. Gently spread spinach-bacon mixture over the beaten egg whites. Carefully fold together until ingredients are just blended.

6. Turn mixture into an ungreased 2-quart soufflé dish (straight-sided casserole); sprinkle top with Parmesan cheese.

7. Bake at 350°F 40 minutes, or until a knife comes out clean when inserted halfway between center and edge of soufflé and top is lightly browned. Serve immediately.

6 servings

Baked Spinach-Stuffed Tomatoes with Tomato-Cheese Sauce

Covered with a rich cheese sauce, each stuffed tomato becomes an individual serving of vitamins A and C, calcium, and iron.

Stuffed tomatoes:
- 6 **firm tomatoes, rinsed**
- ½ **teaspoon salt**
- 1 **pound fresh spinach**
- 2 **tablespoons butter or margarine**
- ¾ **teaspoon salt**
- ⅛ **teaspoon ground pepper**
- 1 **tablespoon minced onion**
- ¼ **cup dry enriched bread crumbs**

Tomato-Cheese Sauce:
- 1 **cup diced tomato pulp**
- 2 **tablespoons minced onion**
- ½ **teaspoon salt**
- ⅛ **teaspoon ground black pepper**
- ½ **cup shredded Cheddar cheese**

1. For stuffed tomatoes, cut a ½-inch slice from the top of each tomato (reserve tops for later use). Seed tomatoes. Scoop out and reserve pulp for the sauce. Sprinkle insides of tomatoes with ½ teaspoon salt.

2. Wash spinach. Put into a saucepan with only the water clinging to the leaves; cover. Cook rapidly about 5 minutes, or until tender. Drain well. Chop spinach finely and mix in butter, ¾ teaspoon salt, pepper, onion, and bread crumbs. Fill tomato shells and replace tops. Place in a greased shallow baking dish.

3. Bake at 350°F 35 minutes.

4. For sauce, put tomato pulp into a saucepan with onion, salt, and pepper. Bring to boiling, reduce heat, and simmer 10 minutes. Stir in cheese and heat only until melted. Serve hot over the baked tomatoes.

6 servings

Creamed Spinach

This tasty dish may please even the spinach-haters, and it will give them valuable nutrients too, including vitamins A and C, riboflavin, calcium, and iron.

- 1 **tablespoon butter**
- 1 **package (10 ounces) frozen chopped spinach, partially defrosted**
- ¾ **teaspoon seasoned salt**
- 1 **teaspoon grated onion**
- 1 **tablespoon flour**
- ½ **cup dairy sour cream**
  Paprika

1. Heat butter in a heavy skillet. Add spinach, seasoned salt, and onion. Cover and cook over high heat 1 to 2 minutes. Reduce heat and cook 5 minutes longer, stirring occasionally.

2. Sprinkle flour over spinach and blend in. Add sour cream in very small amounts, stirring until blended. Heat about 2 minutes but do not boil. Sprinkle with paprika.

About 4 servings

Spinach-Cheese Bake

Eggs and cheese with spinach make an easy and nutritious combination that is full of protein, vitamins A and C, riboflavin, calcium, and iron.

2 packages (10 ounces each) frozen chopped spinach

3 eggs, beaten

¼ cup enriched all-purpose flour

1 teaspoon seasoned salt

¼ teaspoon ground nutmeg

¼ teaspoon ground black pepper

2 cups (16 ounces) creamed cottage cheese

2 cups (8 ounces) shredded Swiss or Cheddar cheese

1. Cook spinach following package directions; drain.
2. Combine eggs, flour, seasoned salt, nutmeg, and pepper in a bowl. Mix in cottage cheese, Swiss cheese, and spinach.
3. Turn into a buttered 1½-quart casserole.
4. Bake at 325°F 50 to 60 minutes.

6 to 8 servings

Whipped Butternut Squash in Shells

Treated with a little imagination, butternut squash becomes both attractive to serve and nutritious to eat. This dish offers vitamins A and C, plus calcium.

2 butternut squash (about 1½ pounds each)

¼ cup butter or margarine

2 teaspoons lemon juice

1½ tablespoons brown sugar

1 teaspoon ground allspice

½ teaspoon salt

Few grains black pepper

¼ cup toasted sliced filberts

1. Wash squash, cut into halves lengthwise, and scoop out seedy centers. Place cut side down in a large shallow baking pan. Pour in boiling water to a ¼-inch depth. Bake at 400°F about 45 minutes, or until tender.
2. Remove from oven and scoop out pulp; reserve shells. Mash pulp and add butter and lemon juice. Blend brown sugar, allspice, salt, and pepper; mix with squash. Spoon mixture into shells. Set on a cookie sheet and cover with aluminum foil.
3. Set in a 400°F oven about 10 minutes, or until heated.
4. Place on serving platter and top with filberts.

About 6 servings

Apple-Stuffed Acorn Squash

Acorn squash, a vegetable that is often overlooked, may become a favorite after you try this recipe. Stuff the squash with apples and reap a harvest of vitamins A and C and calcium.

2　acorn squash
2　tart apples
1½　teaspoons grated fresh lemon peel
1　tablespoon fresh lemon juice
¼　cup butter or margarine, melted
⅓　cup firmly packed brown sugar
　　Salt
　　Cinnamon
　　Apple and lemon slices for garnish (optional)

1. Cut squash into halves lengthwise and scoop out seedy centers. Place cut side down in baking dish and pour in boiling water to a ½-inch depth. Bake at 400°F 20 minutes.
2. Pare, core, and dice apples; mix with lemon peel and juice, 2 tablespoons butter, and brown sugar.
3. Invert squash halves and brush with remaining 2 tablespoons butter; sprinkle with salt and cinnamon.
4. Fill squash halves with apple mixture. Pour boiling water into dish to a ½-inch depth; cover and bake 30 minutes.
5. Before serving, spoon pan juices over squash. If desired, garnish with apple and lemon slices.

4 servings

Stuffed Baked Sweet Potatoes

These double-baked potatoes featuring bananas and pecans will add to your reputation as a gourmet cook. The nutritional rewards are vitamins A and C, and some B vitamins.

4　medium sweet potatoes, washed
1　small ripe banana, peeled
2　tablespoons butter or margarine
⅓　cup fresh orange juice
1　tablespoon brown sugar
1½　teaspoons salt
¼　cup chopped pecans

1. Bake sweet potatoes at 375°F 45 minutes to 1 hour, or until tender when tested with a fork.
2. Cut a lengthwise slice from each potato. Scoop out sweet potatoes into a bowl; reserve shells. Mash banana with potatoes; add butter, orange juice, brown sugar, and salt and beat thoroughly. Spoon mixture into shells. Sprinkle with pecans. Set on a cookie sheet.
3. Return to oven 12 to 15 minutes, or until heated.

4 servings

Scalloped Sweet Potatoes and Apples

Sweet potatoes and apples, baked to piping-hot perfection, make a delicious blend which provides vitamins A and C.

6	medium sweet potatoes, washed
1½	cups apple slices
1	tablespoon lemon juice
½	cup firmly packed brown sugar
¼	cup butter or margarine
½	cup apple juice

1. Cook sweet potatoes in boiling salted water to cover until almost tender; drain. Peel potatoes and cut into crosswise slices, ¼ inch thick.
2. Toss apples with lemon juice. Butter a 1½-quart baking dish. Arrange half of the sweet potatoes in bottom and cover with half of the apple slices. Sprinkle with half of brown sugar. Dot with 2 tablespoons of the butter. Repeat layering. Pour apple juice over all.
3. Bake at 350°F about 45 minutes.

About 6 servings

Versatile Tomato-Celery Stew

This hearty mixture of good foods, containing protein, vitamins A and C, and calcium, is practically a meal in itself.

3	tablespoons butter
½	cup chopped onion
¼	cup chopped green pepper
1	small clove garlic, minced
¾	pound celery, cut diagonally in 1-inch pieces
2	cans (16 ounces each) tomatoes
1	teaspoon sugar
1	teaspoon salt
¼	teaspoon crushed thyme
⅛	teaspoon ground pepper
1	vegetable bouillon cube
2	tablespoons minced parsley
½	cup uncooked enriched rice
¾	to 1 pound canned ham, cut in short strips
	Shredded Parmesan cheese

1. Heat butter in a large saucepan. Add onion, green pepper, and garlic. Cook until onion is soft, about 2 minutes, stirring occasionally.
2. Stir in celery, tomatoes, sugar, salt, thyme, pepper, bouillon cube, and parsley. Bring to boiling.
3. Add rice gradually, stirring with a fork. Simmer, covered, about 50 minutes. Add ham and simmer about 10 minutes, or until ham is thoroughly heated and celery is tender. Sprinkle shredded Parmesan cheese over top before serving. Pass additional cheese.

About 6 servings

Cracked Wheat Stuffed Tomatoes

A hint of mint and the addition of avocado make these stuffed tomatoes an extra-special treat. They provide protein, vitamins A and C, niacin, riboflavin, thiamine, calcium, and iron.

½ cup cracked wheat or bulgur
1½ cups hot water
6 firm medium tomatoes, rinsed
⅛ teaspoon *each* sugar, salt, and pepper
3 tablespoons crushed dried mint
3 tablespoons warm water
1 small ripe avocado
1½ teaspoons salt
½ teaspoon sugar
2 tablespoons lemon juice
⅓ cup olive oil
¼ cup finely chopped green onion
¼ cup snipped parsley

1. Combine cracked wheat and hot water; set aside 30 minutes. Drain cracked wheat thoroughly and set aside.
2. Peel tomatoes. Cut off and discard a ½-inch slice from the top of each. Seed tomatoes. Scoop out pulp, chop it, and turn into a sieve to drain. Invert tomatoes on absorbent paper to drain 30 minutes. Mix ⅛ teaspoon sugar, ⅛ teaspoon salt, and pepper; sprinkle over pulp and insides of tomatoes.
3. Combine dried mint and warm water; set aside 15 minutes. Squeeze dry.
4. Peel avocado; put pulp into a bowl and mash with a fork. Beat in 1½ teaspoons salt, ½ teaspoon sugar, and lemon juice. Add oil in a thin stream, beating constantly. Mix in drained cracked wheat, tomato pulp, mint, green onion, and parsley. Fill tomatoes. Chill.

6 servings

Herb-Topped Tomatoes

Wheat germ and herbs make this simple recipe rewarding in flavor and in nutritional value. Vitamins A and C, riboflavin, thiamine, calcium, and iron are all there.

4 ripe tomatoes, rinsed
¼ cup toasted wheat germ
3 tablespoons butter or margarine, melted
1 teaspoon dried parsley flakes
½ teaspoon salt
⅛ teaspoon basil

1. Slice each tomato into 3 slices.
2. Combine wheat germ, butter, parsley flakes, salt, and basil. Spread about 1 teaspoon mixture on each tomato slice. Arrange on rack of broiler pan.
3. Set under broiler about 5 inches from heat. Broil just until topping is golden. Serve immediately.

6 servings

Turnip Custard

Turnips are so transformed in this unusual custard that you'll hardly recognize them, but you'll appreciate the good taste and the high nutritional value, including vitamins A, C, and D, riboflavin, and calcium.

2 pounds turnips
1 egg, well beaten
¼ cup finely crushed soda crackers
⅔ cup (6-ounce can) undiluted evaporated milk
1 teaspoon salt
   Few grains black pepper
1 cup (about 4 ounces) shredded sharp Cheddar cheese

1. Wash, pare, and cut turnips into pieces. Cook, uncovered, in boiling water to cover until turnips are tender, 15 to 20 minutes; drain. Mash and, if necessary, again drain turnips (about 2 cups mashed turnips).
2. Blend mashed turnips, egg, cracker crumbs, evaporated milk, salt, and pepper. Turn mixture into a buttered 1¼-quart baking dish. Set dish in a pan and pour in boiling water to a 1-inch depth.
3. Bake at 350°F 15 minutes. Sprinkle cheese over top. Bake 5 minutes, or until a knife inserted halfway between center and edge comes out clean. Remove from water immediately.

About 6 servings

Zucchini Boats

Both good nutrition and good taste are the rewards when you prepare this stuffed zucchini that adds vitamins A and C and calcium to your diet.

8 medium zucchini, washed and ends removed
1 medium tomato, cut in small pieces
¼ cup chopped salted almonds
1 tablespoon chopped parsley
1 teaspoon finely chopped onion
½ teaspoon seasoned salt
2 teaspoons butter, melted
¼ cup cracker crumbs

1. Cook zucchini in boiling salted water until crisp-tender, 7 to 10 minutes. Drain; cool.
2. Cut zucchini lengthwise into halves; scoop out and discard centers. Chop 2 shells coarsely; set remaining shells aside. Put chopped zucchini and tomato into a bowl. Add almonds, parsley, onion, and seasoned salt; mix well.
3. Spoon filling into zucchini shells. Mix butter and cracker crumbs. Sprinkle over filling. Set on a cookie sheet.
4. Place under broiler 4 inches from heat. Broil 3 minutes, or until crumbs are golden.

6 servings

Vegetable-Rice Medley

No one would guess that you put this busy-day dinner together in half an hour. It is an excellent source of vitamins A and C, the B vitamins, calcium, and iron.

3 tablespoons butter or margarine
¾ cup chopped onion
1½ pounds zucchini, thinly sliced
1 can (16 ounces) whole kernel golden corn, drained
1 can (16 ounces) tomatoes (undrained)
3 cups cooked enriched white rice
1½ teaspoons salt
¼ teaspoon ground black pepper
¼ teaspoon ground coriander
¼ teaspoon oregano leaves

Heat butter in a large saucepan. Add onion and zucchini; cook until tender, stirring occasionally. Add corn, tomatoes with liquid, cooked rice, salt, pepper, coriander, and oregano; mix well. Cover and bring to boiling; reduce heat and simmer 15 minutes.

About 8 servings

Salads

An attractively arranged bowl of greens or a glistening molded salad can be a real eye-catcher on the dinner table. Serve salads as an appetizing first course, an accompaniment to the entrée, or as the main dish itself.

A tossed salad complements practically any meal, and using a variety of greens will give the salad its special character. There are many types of greens to choose from: crisp iceberg lettuce, buttery Boston lettuce, sweet romaine, dark, pungent escarole, crunchy cabbage, tender watercress, fresh spinach, parsley—all are welcome additions to the salad bowl. Mix and match greens to take advantage of their contrasts in color, flavor, and texture. Brighten up the salad with tomato wedges, thin slices of raw cauliflower, onion rings, pimiento pieces (use your imagination!), toss lightly with a dressing, and it's ready for the table. For something a little different, try the *Parsley-Mint Salad*, an exotic variation of the traditional tossed salad.

Vegetables of all kinds make cool, tempting salads. Beautifully arranged and tastefully garnished, a medley of chilled marinated vegetables will find a place at casual and formal meals alike. Try *Broccoli Vinaigrette with Avocado* for a sophisticated first-course salad. Outdoor get-togethers or family picnics are hardly complete without a hearty bean salad, a satisfying potato salad, or a crunchy coleslaw.

Salads also make wonderful main dishes. For a pleasurable supper on a summer's evening, try the *Chef's Fruit Salad*, with its topping of cheese, slim meat strips, cinnamoned raisins, and tangy dressing. Or let a handsome meat salad, such as the *Greek-Style Lamb-and-Olive Salad* take the lead role at Sunday supper or buffet dinner.

When selecting a salad dressing, keep in mind that it should enhance the flavor and freshness of the salad and not overpower it. Here you'll find a variety of recipes for delicious make-at-home salad dressings, from the simple *Jiffy French Dressing*, always appropriate on a tossed salad, to the unusual *Curry Yogurt Dressing*, a cool creamy topping for a fruit salad.

Salads bring freshness and flavor to meals, and they play an important nutritional role in the diet. The fruits and vegetables used in salads are storehouses of essential vitamins and minerals. Macaroni, rice, and meat salads also provide protein, iron, and B vitamins. Freshness, crispness, and nutritional value—these are the qualities which make salads so popular at meals.

Colorful Coleslaw

This salad is as colorful as confetti and has plenty of substantial food value. Vitamins A and C and calcium are the nutrients.

¼ cup sugar
¼ cup cider vinegar
2½ tablespoons salad oil
¾ teaspoon dry mustard
¾ teaspoon celery seed
¾ teaspoon salt
Few grains pepper
4 cups coarsely shredded cabbage
½ medium red onion, thinly sliced
½ medium green pepper, cut in strips
¼ cup shredded carrot

1. Combine sugar, vinegar, oil, dry mustard, celery seed, salt, and pepper in a saucepan. Heat, stirring until sugar is dissolved.
2. Toss cabbage, onion, green pepper, and carrot in a bowl. Pour hot marinade over vegetables and toss to coat well. Refrigerate about 24 hours.
3. Serve in a bowl or on individual salad plates.

About 6 servings

Lima Bean Salad

Whether you chill this saucy salad for an hour or overnight, it's a good busy-day dish and an excellent way to add vegetable protein and vitamins A and C to your menu.

1 package (10 ounces) frozen lima beans
⅔ cup dairy sour cream
1 tablespoon wine vinegar
2 teaspoons lemon juice
1 teaspoon sugar
¾ teaspoon salt
⅛ teaspoon ground white pepper
1 tablespoon chopped pimiento
1 tablespoon chopped chives

1. Cook lima beans following package directions; drain and set aside.
2. Mix sour cream, vinegar, lemon juice, sugar, salt, and pepper.
3. Lightly toss sour cream mixture with lima beans, pimiento, and chives.
4. Set in refrigerator to chill about 1 hour before serving.

4 to 6 servings

Crispy Caraway Salad / Caraway-Chickpea Salad

Vitamins A and C are the main nutrients found in these two variations of caraway salad. Both will stay crispy and crunchy, even if prepared ahead of time.

¼ cup mayonnaise
2 tablespoons dairy sour cream
1 tablespoon cider vinegar
½ teaspoon salt
½ teaspoon sugar
½ to ¾ teaspoon caraway seed
4 cups thinly sliced cauliflower
½ head lettuce, torn in large chunks
½ cup sliced radishes
Salt
½ cup shredded Swiss cheese

1. Blend mayonnaise, sour cream, vinegar, ½ teaspoon salt, sugar, and caraway seed.
2. Put vegetables into a bowl and sprinkle lightly with salt. Add cheese and dressing; mix lightly. Chill until ready to serve.

8 to 10 servings

Caraway-Chickpea Salad: Drain **1 can (16 ounces) chickpeas (garbanzos)** and blend with **2 tablespoons bottled garlic-French or Italian-type salad dressing;** toss with Crispy Caraway Salad before serving.

Broccoli Vinaigrette with Avocado

This imaginative combination of broccoli, watercress, and avocado gives you vitamins A and C and calcium in a delectable salad.

1 package (10 ounces) frozen broccoli spears
2 tablespoons olive oil
1 tablespoon tarragon vinegar
⅛ teaspoon salt
Few grains pepper
¼ bunch watercress
1 medium ripe avocado
1 tablespoon chopped chives (optional)

1. Cook broccoli following package directions.
2. Combine oil, vinegar, salt, and pepper. Put broccoli into a bowl and pour dressing over it. Chill until ready to serve.
3. Arrange watercress on serving plate or individual salad plates.
4. Peel and slice avocado; arrange on watercress with broccoli. Sprinkle with chives, if desired. Drizzle remaining dressing over salad.

4 servings

Spinach Salad

Fresh spinach is becoming increasingly popular as a salad green; mix it with this homemade dressing and you will understand why. Vitamin A, calcium, and iron are the benefits.

Fresh spinach (about ¾ pound)
⅓ cup salad oil
¼ cup vinegar
1 tablespoon bottled steak sauce
½ teaspoon salt
Few grains pepper
½ teaspoon dry mustard
Prepared baconlike pieces (a soy protein product)

1. Wash spinach, drain, dry, and tear into small pieces. Put into a salad bowl. Chill.
2. Combine oil, vinegar, steak sauce, salt, pepper, and dry mustard in a bottle; cover and shake well. Chill.
3. Just before serving, shake dressing and pour over spinach. Toss until mixed. Top with baconlike pieces.

About 6 servings

Sauerkraut Slaw

You start with canned sauerkraut, but you wind up with a taste treat that seems fresh from the garden. Vitamins A and C and calcium are the nutrients.

2 cups (16-ounce can) sauerkraut, drained and snipped with scissors
1 onion, chopped (about ½ cup)
1 green pepper, sliced (about ¾ cup)
1 unpared red apple, diced (about 1 cup)
⅓ to ½ cup sugar
1 can (16 ounces) sliced tomatoes or tomato wedges, drained
Seasoned pepper

1. Combine sauerkraut, onion, green pepper, apple, and sugar in a serving bowl; toss until well mixed. Cover and refrigerate.
2. Before serving, overlap tomato slices around edge of bowl. Sprinkle slices with seasoned pepper.

8 to 12 servings

Parsley-Mint Salad

Here's an unusual and delectable combination of tomatoes, parsley, and mint, with a special dressing. The salad is rich in vitamins A and C, niacin, riboflavin, thiamine, and calcium.

2 **cups finely chopped parsley**
1/3 **cup finely chopped mint leaves**
1/2 **cup finely chopped onion**
2 **tablespoons olive oil**
4 **teaspoons lemon juice**
1 **tablespoon light corn syrup**
Few grains salt
Few grains freshly ground pepper
2 **medium tomatoes, chilled**
1/4 **cup sesame seed, toasted**

1. Combine parsley, mint, and onion in a salad bowl; cover tightly. Chill thoroughly.
2. Combine oil, lemon juice, corn syrup, salt, and pepper in a jar. Cover jar and shake well. Refrigerate until ready to use.
3. When ready to serve salad, chop the tomatoes. Toss lightly with the parsley mixture. Shake salad dressing well; slowly pour dressing over salad while gently turning and tossing; use only enough to coat ingredients lightly. Sprinkle sesame seed over salad and toss lightly to mix thoroughly.

About 4 servings

Farmer's Chop Suey

In spite of its Chinese name, the ingredients of this refreshing salad are thoroughly American. They will give you vitamins A and C, calcium, and some protein and riboflavin.

1 **large firm cucumber, pared and cut in small cubes**
1 **cup sliced red radishes**
6 **green onions with tops, sliced**
3 **firm ripe tomatoes, cut in chunks**
1/2 **teaspoon salt**
1/8 **teaspoon ground black pepper**
1 **to 1½ cups dairy sour cream**

1. Put cucumber, radishes, green onions, and tomatoes into a large salad bowl. Sprinkle with salt and pepper; toss lightly.
2. Stir sour cream and spoon over all. Serve immediately.

About 6 servings

Marinated Vegetables Salad

Well-chilled and attractively arranged, this piquant vegetable salad will brighten up any meal and add vitamin A, calcium, and some protein, niacin, and riboflavin to your diet.

1	cup vinegar (white wine or cider)
1/3	cup olive oil
1/3	cup finely chopped onion
3	tablespoons chopped parsley
3	small cloves garlic, minced
1 1/2	teaspoons oregano
1 1/2	teaspoons salt
3/4	teaspoon ground black pepper
1/4	pound small fresh mushrooms, cleaned
1	can or jar (8 ounces) artichoke hearts, drained and cut in halves
3/4	cup julienne carrots, cooked crisp-tender
3/4	cup green beans, canned or cooked crisp-tender
3/4	cup sliced raw zucchini
3/4	cup pitted ripe olives
	Lettuce

1. Combine vinegar, oil, onion, parsley, garlic, oregano, salt, and pepper in a saucepan and heat.

2. Put vegetables and olives into a bowl. Pour the heated marinade over them and toss to coat well. Cover bowl tightly. Refrigerate 24 hours; toss several times to mix.

3. To serve, spoon vegetables and olives into a lettuce-lined salad bowl or individual salad bowls or plates. Drizzle with marinade, if desired.

About 8 servings

Stuffed Eggplant Salad

These stuffed eggplants have their own serving bowls, and their taste is every bit as impressive as their dinner-party look. Vitamins A and C and calcium are the benefits.

2	large eggplants
4	medium tomatoes, peeled and diced

1. Wash and dry eggplants; place on a cookie sheet. Bake in a 375°F oven 35 to 45 minutes, or until tender when pierced with a fork.

⅓ cup thinly sliced green onion
⅓ cup olive or salad oil
½ cup fresh lemon juice
¼ cup chopped parsley
1 tablespoon sugar
2½ teaspoons salt
2 teaspoons oregano
¼ teaspoon ground black pepper

Cool.

2. Cut a thin lengthwise slice from the side of each eggplant; carefully spoon out pulp. Chill shells.

3. Dice pulp and put into a bowl. Add tomatoes, green onion, oil, lemon juice, parsley, sugar, salt, oregano, and pepper; toss to mix. Chill.

4. Before serving, drain off excess liquid from salad mixture. Spoon salad into shells.

6 servings

Kidney Bean-Mushroom Salad

Hints of sweet, sour, and hot tastes and a sprinkling of coconut give this unusual mixture of vegetables its unique flavor. It offers protein, niacin, riboflavin, thiamine, and iron.

1 can (about 16 ounces) kidney beans, drained and rinsed
1 can or jar (4 or 4½ ounces) sliced mushrooms, drained
¾ cup thinly sliced celery, cut diagonally
¼ cup golden raisins
2 tablespoons red wine vinegar
1 small clove garlic, minced
2 drops Tabasco
¼ teaspoon ground cardamom
¼ teaspoon curry powder
¼ teaspoon tarragon leaves, crushed
2 tablespoons salad oil
Flaked or shredded coconut

1. Combine beans, mushrooms, celery, and raisins in a large bowl, tossing lightly.

2. Pour vinegar into a bottle or jar; add garlic, Tabasco, cardamom, curry powder, tarragon, and oil. Cover and shake vigorously. Pour over vegetables and toss lightly until well mixed. Chill.

3. Sprinkle coconut over salad before serving.

4 to 6 servings

Tossed Fruit Salad

When you've got a crowd, toss up this mixture of fruits and greens, and top it off with cottage cheese-orange dressing. There's enough protein, vitamin A, vitamin C, riboflavin, and calcium for all.

Cottage Cheese-Orange Dressing:

- 1 cup *each* creamed cottage cheese and plain yogurt
- ¼ cup frozen orange juice concentrate
- 1 tablespoon *each* sugar and mayonnaise
- ¼ teaspoon salt

Salad:

- 2 quarts torn lettuce (bibb, Boston, leaf, romaine)
- ½ pound *each* pitted dark sweet cherries and seedless grapes
- 1 can (13¼ ounces) pineapple tidbits, drained
- 2 oranges, peeled and diced
- 1 apple, pared and diced
- 3 slices cinnamon bread, toasted and cut in small squares

1. For Cottage Cheese-Orange Dressing, put cottage cheese, yogurt, orange juice concentrate, sugar, mayonnaise, and salt into an electric blender container; blend until smooth. Refrigerate until ready to use.

2. Combine lettuce and fruits in a large salad bowl. Add enough dressing to coat lettuce and fruit, tossing gently. Add cinnamon toast squares just before serving.

About 12 servings

Bacon-Bean Salad

Four kinds of beans make this exciting salad a hearty and delicious accompaniment to any meal. Bacon accents the bean flavors and helps provide some of the nutrients, which include protein, niacin, riboflavin, thiamine, vitamin C, calcium, and iron.

- ⅔ cup cider vinegar
- ¾ cup sugar
- 1 teaspoon salt

1. Blend vinegar, sugar, and salt in a small saucepan. Heat until the sugar is dissolved and set aside.

1 **can (16 ounces) cut green beans**
1 **can (16 ounces) cut wax beans**
1 **can (16 ounces) kidney beans, thoroughly rinsed and drained**
1 **medium onion, quartered and finely sliced**
1 **medium green pepper, chopped**
½ **teaspoon freshly ground black pepper**
⅓ **cup salad oil**
1 **pound bacon, cut in 1-inch squares**
  Lettuce (optional)

2. Drain all beans and toss with onion, green pepper, vinegar mixture, and ground pepper. Pour oil over all and toss to coat evenly. Store in a covered container in refrigerator.

3. When ready to serve, fry bacon until crisp; drain on absorbent paper. Toss the bacon with bean mixture. If desired, serve the salad on crisp lettuce.

About 12 servings

Note: If desired, omit bacon.

Serve-Yourself Salad Bowl

This tempting combination of shrimp, marinated vegetables, and salad greens may become a favorite in your home. All to the good, for it provides protein, vitamin C, calcium, and iron.

2 **cups diced cooked potatoes**
2 **cups cooked cut green beans**
2 **cups cooked julienne carrots**
1 **pound cooked and deveined shrimp**
  Lemon French Dressing (page 306)
1½ **quarts mixed salad greens**
½ **cucumber, sliced**
½ **cup sliced radishes**
1 **small onion, sliced**
  Radish roses

1. Put potatoes, green beans, carrots, and shrimp into separate bowls. Pour one-half cup dressing over each and toss gently. Marinate at least 1 hour. Drain, reserving dressing.

2. Before serving, toss salad greens, cucumber, and sliced radishes in a salad bowl. Arrange marinated vegetables and shrimp over greens. Scatter onion rings over beans. Garnish with radish roses. Serve with reserved dressing.

8 to 10 servings

Mixed Vegetable Salad

This recipe, delightful in warm weather, is just as tasty and wholesome with a wintertime meal. It gives you vitamins A and C, some B vitamins, and calcium.

1 cup diced cooked potatoes
1½ cups cooked sliced carrots
1½ cups cooked whole or cut green beans (fresh, frozen, or canned)
1½ cups cooked green peas (fresh, frozen, or canned)
1 cup sliced or diced cooked beets
Bottled Italian-style salad dressing
Lettuce
1 cup sliced celery
1 small onion, chopped
2 hard-cooked eggs, chopped
¾ cup small pimiento-stuffed olives
¾ cup mayonnaise
¼ cup chili sauce
1 teaspoon lemon juice

1. Put potatoes, carrots, beans, peas, and beets into separate bowls. Pour salad dressing over each vegetable; chill thoroughly.
2. To serve, drain vegetables and arrange in a lettuce-lined salad bowl along with celery, onion, eggs, and olives.
3. Blend mayonnaise, chili sauce, and lemon juice. Pass with the salad.

About 8 servings

Fresh Mushroom Salad

As nutritious (vitamins A and C and iron) as it is good to eat, this salad of mushrooms and fresh greens may well become one of your all-time favorites.

½ cup salad oil
1 egg yolk
2 tablespoons lemon juice
1 clove garlic, peeled
¾ teaspoon salt
¼ teaspoon sugar
¼ teaspoon ground black pepper

1. Combine oil, egg yolk, lemon juice, garlic, salt, sugar, pepper, and dry mustard in an electric blender container. Blend until smooth. Chill.
2. Line a salad bowl with outer leaves of romaine.
3. Tear remaining romaine into pieces and put into a large bowl. Add spinach, mushrooms,

⅛ teaspoon dry mustard
1 medium head romaine
¼ pound fresh spinach,
   washed, dried, and torn in
   pieces
¼ pound fresh mushrooms,
   cleaned and sliced
2 tablespoons thinly sliced
   green onion
3 slices bacon, crisp-cooked
   and crumbled

green onion, and bacon. Pour dressing over vegetables; toss gently to coat pieces. Turn into romaine-lined bowl.

6 servings

Greek-Style Lamb-and-Olive Salad

Here's another salad that can be a complete meal, if you choose to serve it that way. It provides protein, vitamins A and C, niacin, riboflavin, thiamine, and calcium.

Greek-Style Salad Dressing:
½ cup olive or salad oil
1 cup red wine vinegar
3 to 4 tablespoons honey
1½ teaspoons salt
⅛ teaspoon dry mustard
2 teaspoons crushed dried
   mint leaves
¼ teaspoon crushed oregano
¼ teaspoon crushed thyme
¼ teaspoon anise seed
Salad:
1½ pounds roast lamb,
   trimmed of fat and cut in
   strips
   Curly endive
1 large cucumber, pared and
   sliced
4 medium tomatoes, sliced
   and quartered
1 cup pitted ripe olives

1. For dressing, mix oil, vinegar, honey, salt, dry mustard, mint, oregano, thyme, and anise.
2. Pour the dressing over cooked lamb in a bowl, cover, and marinate in refrigerator at least 1 hour, or until thoroughly chilled.
3. To serve, arrange curly endive in a large salad bowl. Toss cucumber, tomatoes, and olives with some of the dressing and turn into salad bowl. Spoon meat over vegetables and pour more dressing over all.

6 servings

Chicken Salad

Italian dressing, used as a marinade, adds new interest to chicken salad, which contains protein, niacin, and iron.

1 **envelope Italian salad dressing mix**
2 **cups coarsely chopped cooked chicken**
¼ **cup toasted blanched almonds, chopped**
¼ **cup chopped celery**
2 **teaspoons capers, chopped**
¼ **cup mayonnaise**
1½ **teaspoons lemon juice**
½ **teaspoon salt**
⅛ **teaspoon ground pepper**
  Lettuce cups

1. Prepare salad dressing mix following directions. Pour dressing over chicken and allow to marinate about 1 hour; drain chicken thoroughly.
2. Combine marinated chicken, almonds, celery, and capers in a bowl. Mix mayonnaise, lemon juice, salt, and pepper; add to bowl and toss lightly until thoroughly mixed; chill.
3. To serve, spoon salad into lettuce cups.

About 4 servings

Beef Salad Acapulco

Beef and avocado make a stimulating new taste combination with a Mexican touch. The dish will supply you with protein, vitamins A and C, niacin, riboflavin, and iron.

3 **cups cooked beef strips**
¾ **cup salad oil**
½ **cup red wine vinegar**
1½ **teaspoons salt**
¼ **teaspoon ground pepper**
⅛ **teaspoon cayenne pepper**
1 **tablespoon chili powder**
  Salad greens
  Avocado slices, brushed with marinade
  Onion and green pepper rings
  Tomato wedges
  Ripe olives

1. Put beef strips into a shallow dish. Combine oil, vinegar, salt, pepper, cayenne pepper, and chili powder in a bottle; cover and shake vigorously. Pour over beef strips. Cover; marinate several hours or overnight.
2. Remove beef from marinade and arrange on crisp greens on chilled salad plates. Garnish with avocado slices, onion rings, green pepper rings, tomato wedges, and ripe olives. Serve the marinade as the dressing.

4 to 6 servings

Tossed Supper Salad

Here's a super supper you can toss together from ingredients you probably have on hand (note possible substitutions). You'll be serving protein, vitamins A and C, niacin, calcium, and iron.

Dressing:
- 1 cup salad oil
- ½ cup cider vinegar
- 1 teaspoon salt
- 1 teaspoon sugar
- ½ teaspoon onion salt
- ¼ teaspoon crushed tarragon
- ¼ teaspoon paprika
- ¼ teaspoon dry mustard
- ¼ teaspoon celery salt
- ⅛ teaspoon garlic salt
- ⅛ teaspoon ground black pepper

Salad:
- 2 cans (6½ or 7 ounces each) tuna
- ½ head lettuce
- 1 cup spinach leaves, washed
- 1 cup diced celery
- ¾ cup chopped green pepper
- ½ cup cooked green peas
- 4 sweet pickles, chopped
- 4 radishes, thinly sliced
- 2 hard-cooked eggs, sliced
- 2 tablespoons chopped pimiento
- 2 tomatoes, rinsed and cut in eighths
- 1 teaspoon salt
  Tomato wedges
  Ripe olives

1. For dressing, put oil and vinegar into a jar; mix salt, sugar, and seasonings; add to jar, cover, and shake well. Refrigerate until needed. Shake before using.

2. For salad, drain tuna well and separate into small chunks; put into a bowl. Toss tuna with ½ cup prepared dressing; cover and refrigerate 1 to 2 hours.

3. Tear lettuce and spinach into pieces and put into a large bowl. Add celery, green pepper, peas, pickles, radishes, eggs, and pimiento; add the tuna with its dressing and tomatoes. Sprinkle with salt. Toss lightly until ingredients are mixed and lightly coated with dressing; add more dressing, if desired.

4. Garnish with tomato wedges and ripe olives.

8 to 10 servings

Note: Two cups of diced cooked chicken, turkey, veal, or pork may be substituted for tuna.

Spinach-Beet Salad with Herb Croutons

The dark green of spinach, the deep red of beets, and the gold and white of hard-cooked eggs combine in a delicious salad to give you vitamins A and C, iron, and calcium.

8 ounces fresh spinach, washed and dried
French dressing
2 cups julienne beets
Herb Croutons (see recipe)
Hard-cooked egg slices

1. Tear spinach into pieces and put into a salad bowl; cover and chill.
2. Meanwhile, pour desired amount of French dressing over beets in a bowl; chill.
3. When ready to serve, add marinated beets and Herb Croutons to spinach in bowl; gently toss until greens are evenly coated with dressing. Garnish with hard-cooked egg slices. Serve immediately.

6 to 8 servings

Herb Croutons: Trim crusts from **2 slices toasted white bread** and cut into ¼- to ½-inch cubes. Heat **2 tablespoons butter or margarine** in a small skillet over low heat. Add ¼ **teaspoon thyme**, crushed, ¼ **teaspoon marjoram**, crushed, and bread cubes. Stir until cubes are coated and browned. Remove from heat.

About 2/3 cup croutons

Celery-Pear Salad

Cooked pears and celery in their own lemony sauce make an unusual salad you'll enjoy serving and eating. Vitamin A and calcium are the nutrients you'll gain.

1 cup water
1 cup sugar
¼ **teaspoon vanilla extract**
3 firm ripe pears, halved, pared, and cored
1 cup finely cut Pascal celery
¼ **cup finely chopped onion**
Salt and pepper

1. Mix water and 1 cup sugar in a saucepan. Bring to boiling, stirring until sugar is dissolved. Cover; boil 5 minutes.
2. Add vanilla extract and as many pear halves at a time as will fit in saucepan. Simmer about 5 minutes, or until pears are just tender. Remove pears with slotted spoon and put into a shallow dish.

3 tablespoons salad or
   cooking oil
2 tablespoons lemon juice
½ teaspoon sugar
¼ teaspoon crushed tarragon
   Pinch ground cinnamon
   Salad greens

3. Meanwhile, parboil celery and onion 1 minute in rapidly boiling salted water; drain.
4. Spoon vegetables over pears and sprinkle lightly with salt and pepper.
5. Blend oil, lemon juice, ½ teaspoon sugar, tarragon, and cinnamon; pour over pears and vegetables; chill thoroughly.
6. To serve, put each pear half onto a chilled individual salad plate lined with crisp salad greens. Spoon some of the dressing over each serving.

6 servings

Gourmet Potato Salad

Nobody can resist potato salad, and this gourmet version with its cheese dressing has a subtly different flavor. You'll find it rich in protein, vitamins A and C, riboflavin, thiamine, and calcium.

5 cups cubed cooked potatoes
½ teaspoon salt
⅛ teaspoon ground black
   pepper
4 hard-cooked eggs, chopped
1 cup chopped celery
⅔ cup sliced green onions
   with tops
¼ cup chopped green pepper
1 cup large curd cottage
   cheese
¼ teaspoon dry mustard
½ teaspoon salt
   Few grains black pepper
⅔ cup (6-ounce can) undiluted
   evaporated milk
½ cup crumbled blue cheese
2 tablespoons cider vinegar
   Lettuce

1. Put potatoes into a large bowl and sprinkle with salt and pepper. Add eggs, celery, onions, and green pepper; toss lightly.
2. Put cottage cheese, dry mustard, salt, pepper, evaporated milk, blue cheese, and vinegar into an electric blender container. Blend thoroughly.
3. Pour dressing over mixture in bowl and toss lightly and thoroughly. Chill before serving to blend flavors.
4. Spoon chilled salad into a bowl lined with lettuce. Garnish as desired.

About 8 servings

Potato and Swiss Cheese Salad

Marinated vegetables and bacon-flavored potatoes add exciting new interest to this variation of that old favorite, potato salad. Protein, vitamins A and C, B vitamins, and calcium are the nutrients.

12 slices bacon, diced and fried until crisp (6 tablespoons drippings reserved)

3 medium onions, chopped

1 cup cider vinegar

1½ tablespoons sugar

1½ teaspoons salt

¾ teaspoon monosodium glutamate

¼ teaspoon ground black pepper

6 medium potatoes (about 2 pounds), cooked, peeled, and cubed

¼ cup bottled French dressing

1 tablespoon lemon juice

1 tablespoon prepared mustard

1 teaspoon Worcestershire sauce

1 teaspoon salt

¼ teaspoon paprika

⅛ teaspoon ground black pepper

1 cup dairy sour cream

1 package (10 ounces) frozen green peas, cooked, drained, and cooled

½ cup chopped celery

¼ cup sliced radishes

2 tablespoons chopped chives

4 ounces Swiss cheese, cut in thin strips
Lettuce

1. Heat bacon drippings in skillet. Add onion and cook until tender, stirring occasionally. Mix in vinegar, sugar, 1½ teaspoons salt, monosodium glutamate, and ¼ teaspoon pepper; heat to boiling. Mix in bacon. Pour over potatoes in a bowl and toss lightly to coat evenly. Set aside.

2. Blend French dressing with lemon juice, prepared mustard, Worcestershire sauce, 1 teaspoon salt, paprika, and ⅛ teaspoon pepper. Add gradually, stirring constantly, to sour cream. Put peas, celery, radishes, and chives into a bowl, pour dressing over vegetables, and toss until well coated. Set in refrigerator to marinate.

3. Mix marinated vegetables with seasoned potatoes. Blend well and chill.

4. Before serving, gently toss cheese strips with the salad. Line a chilled platter with lettuce. Mound the potato salad in center.

About 8 servings

Tomato Slices in Roquefort Marinade

Here's a do-ahead that tastes so good you won't believe how easy it is to prepare, and it is a sure way to provide vitamins A and C, plus calcium.

4	firm tomatoes, sliced
2	onions, sliced
1	green pepper, sliced
½	cup salad oil
¼	cup lemon juice
2	tablespoons finely chopped parsley
1	teaspoon salt
½	teaspoon sugar
⅛	teaspoon crushed savory
1¼	ounces Roquefort cheese, crumbled

1. Alternate layers of tomatoes, onions, and green pepper in a large bowl. Blend oil, lemon juice, parsley, salt, sugar, savory, and cheese; pour over the vegetables.
2. Cover bowl and set in refrigerator to marinate about 2 hours.
3. To serve, alternate vegetables on a chilled dish. Spoon some of the marinade over them.

6 servings

Chicken-Fruit Salad

There are a lot of textural variations, from crunchy to creamy, in this chicken-and-fruit combination. It contains generous portions of protein, vitamins A and C, and calcium.

	Creamy Cooked Salad Dressing (page 304)
3	cups cubed cooked chicken Bottled French dressing
½	cup diced celery
1	cup small seedless grapes
½	cup drained crushed pineapple; reserve syrup for dressing
1	orange, sectioned and sections cut in halves
½	cup toasted salted almonds, coarsely chopped
1	tablespoon minced crystallized ginger

1. Prepare Creamy Cooked Salad Dressing; refrigerate.
2. Toss chicken in a bowl with enough French dressing to coat thoroughly; cover and set in refrigerator to marinate about 3 hours, mixing occasionally.
3. Lightly toss together chicken, celery, grapes, pineapple, orange, almonds, and ginger. Pour desired amount of the dressing over chicken mixture and toss gently. Cover and chill thoroughly.
4. To serve, line a salad bowl with chilled crisp greens. Fill bowl with chicken salad.

About 8 servings

Chilled Macaroni Supper Salad

This hearty salad can be a nutritionally sound meal by itself, for it contains two kinds of protein (animal and vegetable), vitamins A and C, B vitamins, and some iron.

8 ounces (2 cups) elbow macaroni, cooked, rinsed, and drained
Italian salad dressing (bottled or prepared from a mix)
1 can (12 ounces) luncheon meat
1 cup mayonnaise
2 tablespoons cider vinegar
1 teaspoon salt
⅛ teaspoon seasoned pepper
1 teaspoon fennel seed
1 can (8½ ounces) green peas, drained
1 canned pimiento, diced
1 can (14½ ounces) asparagus spears, drained

1. Turn macaroni into a large bowl, add Italian dressing, and toss lightly. Set aside.
2. Cut enough thin strips of luncheon meat to alternate with asparagus spears; dice remaining meat and set aside.
3. Mix mayonnaise, vinegar, salt, seasoned pepper, and fennel. Add to macaroni along with diced luncheon meat, peas, and pimiento; toss.
4. Turn salad mixture into a shallow 2-quart dish. Alternate the luncheon meat strips and asparagus spears lengthwise on salad mixture. Brush meat and asparagus generously with additional Italian salad dressing. Chill.

About 6 servings

Watermelon-Pear Salad

Watermelon gives a unique touch to this salad, and adds vitamins A and C to its nutritional content.

Watermelon chunks
Pears (unpared), cut in wedges
Cucumber, pared and cubed
Escarole, torn in pieces
Romaine, torn in pieces
Honey French Dressing (page 302)

1. Chill fruit, cucumber, and greens.
2. Just before serving, combine fruit, cucumber, and greens in a salad bowl, drizzle with desired amount of dressing, and toss until coated.

Chef's Fruit Salad

This version of the classic chef's salad will convince your guests of your culinary genius, even if they are not aware of the protein, vitamin A, niacin, thiamine, calcium, and iron it offers.

Cinnamon-Buttered Raisins:
 1 **tablespoon butter or margarine, melted**
 ½ **cup dark raisins**
 ½ **cup golden raisins**
 ½ **teaspoon ground cinnamon**
Salad:
  Salad greens
 1 **quart shredded salad greens**
 6 **cups mixed fruit**
  Creamy Lemon Celery-Seed Dressing or Celery-Seed Salad Dressing (see recipes)
 1½ **cups Swiss cheese strips**
 1½ **cups cooked ham or turkey strips**

1. For Cinnamon-Buttered Raisins, melt butter in a skillet. Mix in raisins and cinnamon. Set over low heat 5 minutes, stirring frequently. Cool.

2. Line a salad bowl with salad greens. Add shredded greens.

3. Arrange fruit in bowl. Spoon some of the desired dressing over all. Top with cheese and ham strips alternated with Cinnamon-Buttered Raisins. Serve with remaining dressing.

About 6 servings

Creamy Lemon Celery-Seed Dressing: Blend thoroughly **1½ cups mayonnaise, ¼ cup unsweetened pineapple juice, 1 teaspoon grated lemon peel, 1 tablespoon lemon juice, ½ teaspoon celery seed,** and **few drops Tabasco.** Cover and refrigerate at least 1 hour to blend flavors.

About 1½ cups dressing

Celery-Seed Salad Dressing: Combine in a small bowl **¼ cup sugar, ⅓ cup light corn syrup, ¼ cup cider vinegar, 1½ to 2 teaspoons celery seed, 1 teaspoon dry mustard, 1 teaspoon salt, few grains white pepper,** and **1 teaspoon grated onion.** Beat with a rotary beater until mixture is thoroughly blended. Add **1 cup salad oil** very gradually, beating constantly. Continue beating until mixture thickens. Cover and chill thoroughly. Shake before serving.

2 cups dressing

Turnip-Carrot-Cabbage Slaw

Slaw fans will stand up and cheer this triple delight, which is rich in vitamins A and C and calcium.

1   cup shredded white turnip
1   cup shredded carrot
2   cups finely shredded
    cabbage
¼   cup finely chopped onion
¼   cup chopped parsley
3   tablespoons mayonnaise
¼   teaspoon salt
⅛   teaspoon ground black
    pepper

1. Combine turnip, carrot, cabbage, onion, and parsley in a bowl. Blend mayonnaise with salt and pepper; turn onto vegetables. Toss gently until vegetables are evenly coated.
2. Chill, covered, in refrigerator until ready to serve.

About 6 servings

Rice Salad with Assorted Sausages

This salad makes a perfect lunch or snack—filling, flavorful, and nutritious. Protein, niacin, riboflavin, thiamine, and vitamin C are all there for you.

⅓   cup white wine vinegar
1   teaspoon lemon juice
¼   teaspoon French mustard
1   teaspoon salt
¼   teaspoon ground black
    pepper
⅓   cup salad oil
3   cups cooked enriched white
    rice, cooled
3   cups finely shredded red
    cabbage
½   cup raisins
½   cup walnut pieces
    Greens
    Link sausage (such as
    bratwurst, smoky links,
    and frankfurters), cooked

1. Put vinegar into a bottle. Add lemon juice, mustard, salt, and pepper. Cover and shake. Add oil and shake well.
2. Combine rice, cabbage, raisins, and walnuts in a bowl; chill.
3. When ready to serve, shake dressing well and pour over salad; toss until well mixed.
4. Arrange greens on luncheon plates, spoon salad on greens, and accompany with assorted sausages.

6 to 8 servings

Macaroni-Vegetable Salad

Here's another salad that is satisfying enough to make a meal, and is an easy way to add protein, vitamins A and C, and calcium to your diet.

1 **package (7 ounces) enriched macaroni rings**
1 **package (10 ounces) frozen mixed vegetables**
1 **cup diced Cheddar cheese**
1 **cup mayonnaise**
1 **teaspoon salt**
1 **teaspoon onion salt**
½ **teaspoon ground black pepper**
Lettuce
Sliced luncheon meat or sausage (optional)

1. Cook macaroni following package directions. Rinse with cold water; drain. Turn into a bowl.
2. Cook vegetables following package directions; drain. Add vegetables to macaroni along with cheese, mayonnaise, salt, onion salt, and pepper. Chill.
3. Arrange lettuce leaves and, if desired, meat slices on salad plates. Mound salad in center.

6 servings

Garden-Green Salad Mold

Fresh from the garden, the vegetables called for here furnish flavor and nutrients that everyone can enjoy, and will add vitamins A and C and calcium to your diet.

1 **package (3 ounces) lime-flavored gelatin**
¼ **teaspoon salt**
1 **cup boiling water**
1 **cup cold water**
1 **ripe medium avocado**
1 **tablespoon lemon juice**
2 **cups finely shredded cabbage**
½ **cup thinly sliced radishes**
½ **cup thinly sliced green onions with tops**
Crisp greens

1. Put gelatin and salt into a bowl; add boiling water and stir until completely dissolved. Blend in cold water. Chill until slightly thickened.
2. Mash avocado and stir in lemon juice; blend thoroughly with gelatin. Mix in cabbage, radishes, and green onions.
3. Turn into a 1-quart mold or individual molds and chill until firm. Unmold onto chilled serving plate and garnish with salad greens.

About 8 servings

Perfection Salad Deluxe

Finely shredded vegetables embedded in smooth, glistening gelatin is an ideal salad when you want convenience with a touch of elegance. You'll get vitamins A and C.

1 package (3 ounces) lemon-flavored gelatin
1 cup boiling water
¾ cup cold water
½ teaspoon salt
1 tablespoon lemon juice
1 tablespoon white wine vinegar
1 teaspoon grated onion
¼ teaspoon Worcestershire sauce
8 drops Tabasco
1 cup finely shredded cabbage
½ cup finely shredded carrot
¼ cup finely shredded green pepper
¼ cup finely shredded celery
1 tablespoon chopped pimiento
¼ to ½ teaspoon celery seed
Salad greens

1. Put gelatin into a bowl; add boiling water and stir until gelatin is dissolved. Mix in cold water, salt, lemon juice, vinegar, onion, Worcestershire sauce, and Tabasco.

2. Chill until mixture is slightly thicker than consistency of thick unbeaten egg white.

3. Mix cabbage, carrot, green pepper, celery, pimiento, and celery seed into thickened gelatin. Spoon into six ½-cup individual molds. Chill until firm.

4. Unmold onto crisp salad greens on chilled salad plates.

6 servings

Creamy Vegetable Mold

For a creamy vegetable combination bursting with good flavor, try this recipe. The vegetables and dairy products provide protein, vitamins A and C, riboflavin, and calcium.

1½ cups tomato juice
2 packages (3 ounces each) lemon-flavored gelatin
1 tablespoon sugar
½ teaspoon celery salt

1. Heat tomato juice to boiling. Turn gelatin and sugar into a bowl, add tomato juice, and stir until gelatin is dissolved. Stir in celery salt and lemon juice. Chill until slightly thickened.

½ cup lemon juice
1⅔ cups (14½-ounce can) evaporated milk
4 teaspoons instant minced onion
1 cup creamed cottage cheese
1 can (8½ ounces) green peas, drained
1 can (8½ ounces) cut or diagonally sliced green beans, drained
2 tablespoons chopped green pepper
Lettuce

2. Add evaporated milk gradually to the thickened gelatin mixture, stirring constantly to blend thoroughly. Add onion, cottage cheese, peas, beans, and green pepper; mix well.

3. Turn mixture into a 1½-quart ring mold and chill until firm.

4. Unmold onto a chilled serving plate and garnish with crisp lettuce.

About 8 servings

Green Salad Bowl with Tuna

Tuna, always a crowd pleaser, becomes extra special when mixed with vegetables and topped with blue cheese. The nutrients in this salad are protein, vitamin C, niacin, and calcium.

1 package (10 ounces) frozen lima beans
1 package (9 ounces) frozen cut green beans
1 package (9 ounces) frozen artichoke hearts
3 cans (6½ or 7 ounces each) tuna, drained
1 cup oil-and-vinegar-type salad dressing
5 ounces fresh spinach, washed and dried
1 head Boston lettuce
3 green onions including tops, sliced
3 ounces blue cheese, crumbled

1. Cook frozen vegetables following package directions; drain if necessary. Pour dressing over vegetables and tuna. Cool and toss occasionally; cover and chill.

2. Reserve some spinach leaves for lining bowl. Tear spinach and lettuce into pieces and put into a large salad bowl with onions, green beans, and cheese. Line edge of bowl with reserved spinach. Top with lima beans, artichoke hearts, and tuna.

About 8 servings

Stewed Tomato Aspic

A can of stewed tomatoes and a few other common ingredients are all you'll need to make this tasty salad. It's loaded with vitamins A and C.

1 envelope unflavored gelatin
½ cup cold water
1 can (16 ounces) stewed tomatoes
1 tablespoon sugar
¼ teaspoon salt
1 tablespoon cider vinegar
1½ teaspoons prepared horseradish
1½ teaspoons grated onion
¼ teaspoon Worcestershire sauce
2 hard-cooked eggs, cut in quarters
Salad greens

1. Sprinkle gelatin over water to soften.
2. Turn tomatoes into a saucepan and break up any large pieces with a spoon. Stir in sugar, salt, vinegar, horseradish, onion, and Worcestershire sauce and heat to boiling. Add softened gelatin and stir until dissolved.
3. Chill gelatin until slightly thickened.
4. Arrange egg quarters around bottom of a 3- or 4-cup mold. Spoon slightly thickened gelatin mixture into mold. Chill until firm.
5. Unmold and garnish with crisp greens.

4 to 6 servings

Cinnamon Waldorf Molds

This molded version of the Waldorf salad is just as elegant as the original. The nutrients include some protein, niacin, thiamine, and small amounts of vitamin A and calcium.

⅓ cup red cinnamon candies
3 cups water
2 packages (3 ounces each) cherry-flavored gelatin
1 tablespoon lemon juice
2 cups chopped celery
2 cups chopped unpared red apples
1 cup miniature marshmallows
½ cup chopped walnuts
Lettuce

1. Heat cinnamon candies and water to boiling in a saucepan. Remove from heat and add gelatin and lemon juice; stir until gelatin and candies are dissolved.
2. Chill until slightly thickened.
3. Mix in celery, apples, marshmallows, and walnuts. Spoon into 6 to 8 individual fancy molds or turn into a 1½-quart mold. Chill until firm.
4. Unmold onto lettuce.

6 to 8 servings

Blueberry Apricot Nectar Mold

Blueberry fanciers will be delighted with this new idea for a fruit salad. The blue-berries and the apricot nectar supply vitamin A and calcium, as well as small amounts of other vitamins and minerals.

1	**envelope unflavored gelatin**
1	**can (12 ounces) apricot nectar**
1	**tablespoon lemon juice**
¼	**teaspoon salt**
1	**package (3 ounces) cream cheese, softened**
½	**cup dairy sour cream or dairy sour half-and-half**
1½	**cups fresh blueberries Salad greens**

1. Soften gelatin in ¼ cup apricot nectar.
2. Heat remaining nectar to boiling; add gelatin and stir until dissolved.
3. Stir in lemon juice and salt. Chill until slightly thickened.
4. Beat cheese until light; blend in sour cream. Add gelatin mixture gradually, beating until smooth. Chill until slightly thicker. Mix in blueberries.
5. Turn into 3-cup mold or 6 individual molds; chill until firm.
6. Unmold and serve on crisp salad greens.

6 servings

Sparkling Fresh Peach Mold

Fresh peaches and blueberries become a wonderfully tasty salad combination. A secret ingredient—white grape juice—contributes calcium.

2	**envelopes unflavored gelatin**
¼	**cup sugar**
¾	**cup water**
3	**cups white grape juice**
¼	**cup lemon juice**
4	**medium peaches, peeled and sliced**
1½	**cups blueberries Lettuce**

1. Blend gelatin and sugar in a saucepan. Mix in water; stir over low heat until gelatin and sugar are completely dissolved.
2. Remove from heat and stir in the grape juice and lemon juice. Chill until the consistency of unbeaten egg white.
3. Arrange half of the sliced peaches and blueberries in a 1½-quart ring mold. Spoon one-half of the chilled gelatin over fruit. Arrange the remaining fruit in the mold and spoon remaining gelatin over fruit. Chill until firm.
4. Unmold and garnish with crisp lettuce. Serve with desired dressing.

About 8 servings

Raspberry Salad Mold

A raspberry delight, this molded salad is served with sour cream dressing and offers you vitamins A and C, some B vitamins, and calcium.

Sour Cream Dressing (see recipe)
1 package (3 ounces) raspberry-flavored gelatin
1¼ cups boiling water
1 package (10 ounces) frozen raspberries, partially thawed
1 can (8 or 8¼ ounces) crushed pineapple (undrained)
1 large banana, peeled and sliced
½ cup chopped nuts

1. Prepare Sour Cream Dressing and chill overnight.
2. Turn gelatin into a bowl. Add boiling water and stir until gelatin is completely dissolved. Add partially thawed raspberries and stir until berries are completely thawed and separated.
3. Chill in refrigerator or over ice and water until gelatin mixture is slightly thicker than consistency of thick unbeaten egg white.
4. Stir pineapple (with syrup or juice), banana, and nuts into slightly thickened gelatin. Turn into a 1-quart mold and chill until firm.
5. Unmold onto chilled serving plate and serve with Sour Cream Dressing.

6 to 8 servings

Sour Cream Dressing: Mix **1 cup dairy sour cream, 1½ cups miniature marshmallows,** and **1 tablespoon sugar** in a bowl. Add **3 tablespoons lemon juice** gradually, beating until mixture is well blended. Store, covered, in refrigerator overnight.

Broccoli Aspic

Serve your guests this unusual broccoli salad, full of vitamins A and C. It has a party-time look and can easily be prepared well in advance.

2 packages (10 ounces each) frozen broccoli spears
¾ cup oil-and-vinegar French-style salad dressing (from bottle or mix)

1. Cook broccoli following package directions; do not overcook. Drain thoroughly and put into a shallow dish. Pour salad dressing over broccoli and marinate about 1 hour, turning once.

2 envelopes unflavored gelatin
3½ cups water
4 chicken bouillon cubes
1 teaspoon grated onion
½ teaspoon celery salt
1 tablespoon lemon juice
Lettuce
Pimiento strips

2. Meanwhile, soften gelatin in 1 cup water. Dissolve bouillon cubes in 1 cup of the water brought to boiling. Pour over gelatin and stir until dissolved. Add remaining water, onion, celery salt, lemon juice, and 3 tablespoons of the marinade. Chill until slightly thickened.

3. Remove broccoli from marinade and arrange the spears parallel in a single layer in bottom of a lightly oiled 10-inch square pan. Spoon gelatin mixture over broccoli. Chill until firm.

4. To serve, cut into pieces, place on lettuce-lined individual salad plates, and garnish with pimiento strips.

8 servings

Layered Pineapple-Cranberry Salad

All sorts of taste surprises await the unsuspecting diner who is served this two-layer salad mold. The nutrients are vitamins A and C and calcium.

2 packages (3 ounces each)
  orange-flavored gelatin
1¾ cups boiling water
1 can (8 or 8¼ ounces)
  crushed pineapple
  (undrained)
2 tablespoons lemon juice
½ cup finely chopped celery
1 can (16 ounces) whole
  cranberry sauce
½ cup dark seedless raisins
2 tablespoons cider vinegar
1 teaspoon grated orange peel
½ teaspoon grated onion
¼ teaspoon salt
Lettuce

1. Dissolve gelatin in boiling water; divide into two equal portions. Chill in refrigerator or over ice and water until slightly thickened. If gelatin is chilled in refrigerator, stir occasionally; if chilled over ice and water, stir frequently.

2. Mix pineapple (with syrup or juice), lemon juice, and celery into one portion of gelatin. Turn into a 1½-quart mold. Chill until set, but not firm.

3. Stir cranberry sauce, raisins, vinegar, orange peel, onion, and salt into other portion of gelatin. Chill until set, but not firm.

4. Spoon cranberry mixture evenly over pineapple layer in mold. Chill until firm.

5. Unmold and garnish with crisp lettuce.

8 servings

Molded Spinach Cottage Cheese on Platter

Try this molded form of spinach salad—mixed with cottage cheese, sour cream, and other ingredients—if you want good flavor along with protein, vitamins A and C, riboflavin, calcium, and iron.

  1 **package (10 ounces) frozen chopped spinach**
  2 **envelopes unflavored gelatin**
  ¾ **cup water**
  2 **chicken bouillon cubes**
  2 **tablespoons lemon juice**
1½ **cups creamed cottage cheese**
  ½ **cup dairy sour cream**
  ½ **cup sliced celery**
  ⅓ **cup chopped green pepper**
  2 **tablespoons minced green onion**

1. Cook and drain spinach, reserving liquid. Add enough water to liquid to make ½ cup. Set spinach and liquid aside.
2. Soften gelatin in ¾ cup water in a saucepan; add bouillon cubes. Set over low heat; stirring occasionally, until gelatin and bouillon cubes are dissolved. Remove from heat; stir in spinach liquid and lemon juice. Set aside.
3. Beat cottage cheese until fairly smooth with mixer or in electric blender. Blend with sour cream and then gelatin mixture. Stir in spinach, celery, green pepper, and onion. Turn into a 5-cup mold. Chill until firm.
4. Unmold onto a chilled large platter. If desired, arrange slices of summer sausage around the mold.

6 to 8 servings

Dubonnet Chicken Salad Mold

This unusual chicken salad is made in two colorful layers and provides protein, niacin, vitamin C, calcium, and iron.

  2 **envelopes unflavored gelatin**
  1 **cup cranberry juice cocktail**
  1 **cup red Dubonnet**
  1 **cup red currant syrup**
  1 **envelope unflavored gelatin**
  ¾ **cup cold water**
  1 **tablespoon soy sauce**
  1 **cup mayonnaise**

1. Soften 2 envelopes gelatin in cranberry juice in a saucepan; set over low heat and stir until gelatin is dissolved. Remove from heat and stir in Dubonnet and currant syrup.
2. Pour into a 2-quart fancy tubed mold. Chill until set but not firm.
3. Meanwhile, soften 1 envelope gelatin in cold water in a saucepan. Set over low heat

1½ cups finely diced cooked chicken
½ cup finely chopped celery
¼ cup toasted blanched almonds, finely chopped
½ cup whipping cream, whipped
Leaf lettuce
Cucumber slices, scored
Pitted ripe olives

and stir until gelatin is dissolved.

4. Remove from heat and stir in soy sauce and mayonnaise until thoroughly blended. Chill until mixture becomes slightly thicker. Mix in chicken, celery, and almonds. Fold in whipped cream until blended.

5. Spoon mixture into mold over first layer. Chill 8 hours or overnight.

6. Unmold onto a chilled serving plate. Garnish with lettuce, cucumber, and olives.

About 10 servings

Frosty Fruit Salad

Frozen mixed fruit can perk up any meal, and if you follow this recipe, you'll be serving protein, niacin, vitamins A and C, calcium, and iron.

1 cup chopped soft dried prunes
1 cup orange pieces (1 to 2 oranges)
1 can (13¼ ounces) pineapple tidbits, drained; reserve ¼ cup syrup
½ cup sliced maraschino cherries, well drained on absorbent paper
1 envelope unflavored gelatin
⅓ cup cold water
2 cups creamed cottage cheese
1 cup dairy sour cream
1 cup whipping cream, whipped
¾ cup sugar
¾ teaspoon salt
1 large ripe banana, sliced
½ cup chopped salted almonds

1. Prepare fruits and set aside.

2. Soften gelatin in cold water in a small saucepan. Set over low heat and stir until gelatin is dissolved.

3. Sieve cottage cheese into a bowl. Blend in reserved pineapple syrup, sour cream, whipped cream, sugar, and salt; stir in the dissolved gelatin. Add the reserved fruits, banana, and almonds; mix well. Turn into refrigerator trays and freeze.

4. Allow salad to soften slightly at room temperature before serving. To serve, cut into wedges.

About 12 servings

Hearty Bean Salad

Kidney beans, always tasty, are particularly good in salads. Here they form the basis of an unusual mixture of ingredients which supply two types of protein (animal and vegetable), vitamin A, niacin, riboflavin, thiamine, calcium, and iron.

1 **can (15 ounces) kidney beans, drained**
2 **hard-cooked eggs, diced**
¼ **cup chopped onion**
½ **cup diced celery**
⅓ **cup drained sweet pickle relish**
½ **cup shredded sharp Cheddar cheese**
½ **cup dairy sour cream**
Lettuce

1. Mix kidney beans, eggs, onion, celery, relish, and cheese in a large bowl. Add sour cream and toss together lightly; chill.
2. Serve the salad on lettuce.

4 to 6 servings

Ham Mousse Piquant

Two layers, one whipped, the other solid, suggest the contrast of tastes and textures in this flavorful mold, which gives you protein, vitamin A, calcium, and iron.

2 **packages (3 ounces each) lemon-flavored gelatin**
¼ **teaspoon salt**
2 **cups boiling water**
1 **cup cold water**
¼ **cup cider vinegar**
2 **teaspoons grated onion**
¼ **cup water**
⅔ **cup chopped sweet pickle**
¼ **cup diced pimiento**
⅔ **cup mayonnaise or salad dressing**
1 **teaspoon Worcestershire sauce**
1 **cup chilled whipping cream, whipped**

1. Turn gelatin and salt into a bowl. Add boiling water and stir until gelatin is dissolved. Stir in cold water, vinegar, and onion.
2. Remove 2 cups of the mixture and stir in ¼ cup water; chill until mixture thickens slightly.
3. Mix pickle and pimiento into the slightly thickened gelatin. Turn into a ring mold (11 to 12 cups). Chill until just set but not firm.
4. Meanwhile, chill remaining gelatin over ice and water, stirring frequently, until slightly thickened, then whip with rotary beater until fluffy.
5. Blend mayonnaise and Worcestershire sauce; fold into whipped cream. Combine whipped cream mixture, ham, celery, and

4 cups firmly packed coarsely ground cooked ham
1 cup sliced celery
Watercress

whipped gelatin. Turn into mold over pickle layer. Chill until firm.

6. Unmold onto a chilled serving plate. Fill center of mold with watercress.

About 12 servings

Golden Ginger-Peach Salad

Carrots and peaches, both of which furnish vitamin A, make a taste combination that will get a lot of attention in this molded salad.

2 cups sliced peeled peaches (about 3 medium)
¼ cup sugar
¼ cup lemon juice
1 package (3 ounces) lemon-flavored gelatin
1 cup boiling water
½ cup cold water
1 cup finely grated carrot
2 tablespoons chopped crystallized ginger
Salad greens

1. Combine peaches, sugar, and lemon juice. Let stand while preparing gelatin.
2. Turn gelatin into a bowl. Pour in boiling water and stir until dissolved. Stir in cold water. Chill until the consistency of thick unbeaten egg white.
3. Mix in peaches, carrot, and ginger. Spoon into a 5½-cup ring mold. Chill until firm.
4. Unmold and garnish with salad greens.

6 to 8 servings

Orange Juice Mold

Serve this salad mold garnished with crisp greens, and its colorful appearance will rival its tangy taste. Vitamins A and C plus calcium are the nutrients it offers.

2 envelopes unflavored gelatin
1 cup sugar
1¾ cups water
1½ cups strained orange juice
3 tablespoons strained lemon juice
Salad greens

1. Mix gelatin and sugar in a saucepan; stir in water. Set over low heat and stir until gelatin and sugar are dissolved. Remove from heat. Mix in orange and lemon juices.
2. Pour mixture into a 1-quart mold. Chill until firm.
3. Unmold onto a chilled serving plate and garnish with crisp salad greens.

About 6 servings

Cucumber Freeze in Avocado

Ripe avocados are stuffed with a frozen cucumber cream in this unusual salad recipe. It can't fail to get a favorable response, and it will provide vitamins A and C and calcium.

2 **medium cucumbers (unpared)**
1 **cup dairy sour cream**
¼ **cup lime juice**
¼ **cup sugar**
1 **teaspoon salt**
2 **egg whites**
  Ripe avocados
  Salad greens
  Twisted cucumber slices
  Lime wedges

1. Cut cucumbers lengthwise into halves; remove and discard seeds. Grate cucumbers into a bowl.
2. Stir in sour cream, lime juice, sugar, and salt.
3. Beat egg whites until stiff, not dry, peaks are formed. Fold into cucumber mixture. Turn into refrigerator trays.
4. Place in freezer until mixture begins to freeze around edges. Turn into a chilled bowl and beat well. Return to trays and freeze.
5. To serve, cut the desired number of avocados into halves, remove peel, and put cut side up on salad greens. Spoon cucumber freeze into avocado halves. Garnish each with a twisted cucumber slice and a wedge of lime.

About 1 quart cucumber freeze

Grapefruit Ring

Grapefruity and good, this salad mold is rich in vitamins A and C, and makes a refreshing accompaniment to almost any meal.

1½ **cups sugar**
3 **envelopes unflavored gelatin**
1 **cup water**
3 **cups unsweetened grapefruit juice**
1 **cup orange juice**
¼ **cup lemon juice**
  Salad greens (such as curly endive or watercress)

1. Blend sugar and gelatin in a saucepan. Stir in water. Set over low heat, stirring until gelatin and sugar are completely dissolved.
2. Remove from heat and stir in fruit juices. Pour into a 1½-quart ring mold. Chill overnight or until firm.
3. Unmold onto a chilled serving plate. Garnish mold with salad greens.

About 8 servings

Shimmering Strawberry Mold

This recipe calls for a double dose of strawberries—the fresh fruit plus strawberry gelatin—that will please the palates of strawberry lovers everywhere. Vitamin C and some calcium are the nutritional benefits.

2 packages (3 ounces each) strawberry-flavored gelatin
1½ cups boiling water
2 bottles (7 ounces each) lemon-lime carbonated beverage
1 pint fresh ripe strawberries, rinsed and hulled
⅓ cup sugar
Salad greens
Whole strawberries (optional)

1. Turn gelatin into a bowl, add boiling water, and stir until completely dissolved. Mix in carbonated beverage. Stir frequently over ice and water until slightly thicker than consistency of thick unbeaten egg white.
2. Meanwhile, cut berries lengthwise into halves, if large; sprinkle with sugar and set aside.
3. Stir the berries into the slightly thickened gelatin. Spoon into a 2-quart fancy tubed mold (or 10 individual molds). Chill until firm.
4. Unmold onto a chilled serving plate; garnish with crisp salad greens and, if desired, strawberries.

About 10 servings

Note: If desired, nut-coated cream cheese balls may be added to the salad. Soften 1 package (8 ounces) cream cheese; shape into ½-inch balls and roll in finely chopped walnuts (about ¾ cup). Arrange 5 or 6 balls in bottom of 2-quart mold; spoon enough of the slightly thickened gelatin-strawberry mixture into mold to cover cheese balls. Continue layering with remaining balls and gelatin mixture. Chill until firm.

Wilted Cabbage

Very hot dressing is poured over shredded cabbage in this recipe, wilting the cabbage but not diminishing its vitamin C and calcium content.

4 **cups shredded cabbage**	1. Turn cabbage into a bowl.
6 **slices bacon**	2. Cook bacon until crisp in a skillet; drain, reserving ¼ cup drippings. Crumble bacon onto cabbage; set aside.
½ **cup cider vinegar**	
¼ **cup water**	
3 **tablespoons sugar**	3. Put reserved drippings into skillet. Add vinegar, water, sugar, salt, and dry mustard. Heat to boiling, stirring to blend.
½ **teaspoon salt**	
¼ **teaspoon dry mustard**	
	4. Pour dressing over cabbage and bacon; toss lightly to mix.

6 to 8 servings

Layered Lime-Shrimp Salad

Pretty enough for a party, as well as nutritious and quite filling, this molded shrimp salad will fit in with just about any menu you plan, and will contribute protein, vitamin A, riboflavin, calcium, iron, and other nutrients.

Lime Dressing:

½ **teaspoon grated lime peel**
2 **teaspoons lime juice**
½ **teaspoon salt**
1 **cup dairy sour cream**
   Grated lime peel for garnish (optional)

Salad:

1 **can (29 ounces) pear halves**
1 **package (3 ounces) lime-flavored gelatin**
1 **cup boiling water**
1 **package (12 ounces) frozen cooked shrimp, defrosted**
2 **cups creamed cottage cheese**
½ **teaspoon grated lemon peel**

1. For Lime Dressing, gently blend lime peel, juice, and salt into sour cream; chill. Serve garnished with grated lime peel, if desired.

2. Drain pears and reserve syrup.

3. Combine lime gelatin and boiling water in a bowl; stir until dissolved. Stir in ¾ cup of the reserved pear syrup.

4. Pour into a 6½-cup ring mold and chill until slightly thicker than thick unbeaten egg white.

5. Cut 4 pear halves in half and arrange these quarters in sunburst fashion in gelatin. Chill until almost set.

6. Set aside 8 shrimp. Dice remaining shrimp and pear halves. Turn into a bowl. Mix in cottage cheese, lemon peel and juice, and salt.

7. Pour ½ cup of the reserved pear syrup into

1 tablespoon lemon juice
½ teaspoon salt
1 envelope unflavored gelatin
   Crisp salad greens

a saucepan. Sprinkle unflavored gelatin over syrup. Set over low heat and stir until gelatin is dissolved, then stir into cottage cheese mixture.

8. Arrange reserved shrimp around edge of mold. Carefully pour cottage cheese mixture into mold over lime layer. Chill until firm.

9. Unmold onto crisp salad greens on chilled plate. Serve with Lime Dressing.

8 servings

Orange Salad Dressing

With its fresh, orangy taste, this dressing is probably different from anything you've had before. Try it on fruit or vegetables; it gives you vitamins A and C.

½ cup orange juice
¼ cup lemon juice
⅓ cup salad oil
⅓ cup light corn syrup
1 teaspoon seasoned salt
⅛ teaspoon seasoned pepper
½ teaspoon garlic powder
½ teaspoon paprika

1. Pour orange and lemon juices, oil, and corn syrup into a jar. Add seasoned salt and pepper, garlic powder, and paprika; cover and shake well. Chill dressing.

2. Shake dressing well before serving on fruit or vegetable salads.

About 1⅓ cups dressing

Creamy Celery-Seed Dressing

As simple as can be, this creamy dressing will liven up many of your favorite salads, and contribute protein, vitamin A, riboflavin, and calcium as well.

2 teaspoons honey
2 teaspoons vinegar
1 teaspoon celery seed
¼ teaspoon salt
1 cup dairy sour cream

1. Gently fold honey, vinegar, celery seed, and salt into sour cream. Chill several hours to blend flavors.

2. Serve on slices of tomato, cucumber, and avocado.

About 1 cup dressing

Jiffy French Dressing

Here's a good French dressing you can make in a minute; it will turn a simple bowl of greens, rich in vitamin A, into a delectable salad.

1 tablespoon sugar	1. Blend sugar, paprika, dry mustard, salt, and pepper; put into a jar. Add oil and vinegar. Cover jar tightly and shake vigorously to blend. Store in refrigerator.
1 teaspoon paprika	
1 teaspoon dry mustard	
1 teaspoon salt	
⅛ teaspoon ground black pepper	2. Before serving, shake dressing thoroughly.
1 cup salad oil	*1¼ cups dressing*
¼ cup vinegar or lemon juice	

Honey French Dressing

Honey and lemon juice, garnished with poppy or celery seed, make this an interesting variation of traditional French dressing. The lemon juice adds vitamin C to the other nutrients in the salad.

¼ teaspoon grated lemon peel	1. Stir lemon peel, juice, sugar, and salt together. Mix in oil, honey, and celery seed until well blended. Store in a covered container in refrigerator. Mix well before using.
¼ cup lemon juice	
1 tablespoon sugar	
¾ teaspoon salt	
¾ cup salad oil	2. Serve on tossed or molded fruit salads.
½ cup honey	*About 1½ cups dressing*
½ teaspoon celery seed or poppy seed	

Vegetable Medley Salad Dressing Deluxe

Vegetables and seasonings are blended and chilled in this delicious mixture, which adds calcium and vitamins A and C to any salad.

1 cup salad oil	1. Put oil, vinegar, horseradish, sugar, seasonings, vegetables, avocado, and garlic into an
3 tablespoons cider vinegar	

2 tablespoons prepared
horseradish
1 tablespoon sugar
1 teaspoon dry mustard
1 teaspoon paprika
½ teaspoon seasoned salt
¾ teaspoon salt
⅛ teaspoon ground black
pepper
Few grains cayenne pepper
1 medium ripe tomato,
peeled and cut in pieces
1 small onion, peeled and
cut in pieces
½ small cucumber, pared and
cut in pieces
⅓ small ripe avocado, peeled
and cut in pieces
1 large clove garlic, peeled

electric blender container and blend thoroughly. Chill.

2. Serve on a tossed vegetable salad.

About 3½ cups dressing

Cooked Salad Dressing

Protein, vitamins A and D, plus iron are all waiting in this classic cooked dressing which you will want to keep on hand in the refrigerator.

¼ cup sugar
1 tablespoon flour
½ teaspoon dry mustard
½ teaspoon salt
⅛ teaspoon ground pepper
1 cup water
¼ cup cider vinegar
4 egg yolks, fork beaten
2 tablespoons butter or
margarine

1. Blend sugar, flour, dry mustard, salt, and pepper in a heavy saucepan. Add water gradually, stirring constantly. Bring rapidly to boiling; cook and stir mixture 2 minutes. Stir in vinegar.

2. Stir about 3 tablespoons of the hot mixture into the beaten egg yolks. Immediately blend into mixture in saucepan. Cook and stir until slightly thickened.

3. Remove from heat and blend in butter. Cool; chill. Store in a covered jar in refrigerator.

About 1½ cups dressing

Tomato French Dressing

This tasty variation of French dressing adds a spiced tomato flavor to your greens and vitamin A to your diet.

½ cup sugar
1 package powdered fruit pectin
2 teaspoons salt
1 teaspoon dry mustard
1 teaspoon paprika
⅛ teaspoon garlic powder
Few grains white pepper
1½ cups salad oil
1 can (10¾ ounces) condensed tomato soup
⅔ cup cider vinegar
1 teaspoon Worcestershire sauce
1 teaspoon minced onion
3 drops Tabasco

1. Blend sugar, pectin, salt, dry mustard, paprika, garlic powder, and pepper; put into a 1-quart jar. Add oil, condensed soup, vinegar, Worcestershire sauce, onion, and Tabasco. Cover; shake until well blended. Store in refrigerator.
2. Before serving, beat or shake vigorously.

About 1 quart dressing

Note: Dressing may be beaten with an electric mixer on low speed or blended in an electric blender.

Creamy Cooked Salad Dressing

Creamy and smooth, this mild dressing will please the most discriminating of tastes, while it provides vitamin A and calcium.

2 tablespoons sugar
⅛ teaspoon salt
2 tablespoons cider vinegar
2 tablespoons pineapple syrup
3 egg yolks, slightly beaten
1 tablespoon butter or margarine
1 cup chilled whipping cream, whipped

1. Mix sugar and salt in a heavy saucepan. Stir in vinegar and pineapple syrup. Bring to boiling, stirring constantly.
2. Stir about 2 tablespoons of the hot mixture into egg yolks until blended. Immediately blend into mixture in saucepan. Cook and stir until slightly thickened.
3. Remove from heat; blend in butter. Cool and chill.
4. Blend chilled mixture into whipped cream. Cover and refrigerate until ready to use.

About 2 cups dressing

Gourmet French Dressing / Roquefort French Dressing

French dressing is perhaps the salad lover's favorite, and this gourmet version is a special delight when you make it fresh in your own kitchen. For a sophisticated flavor, add Roquefort cheese, and you'll be adding vitamin A and calcium.

¾ cup olive oil
¼ cup vinegar (tarragon or cider)
¼ teaspoon Worcestershire sauce
1 clove garlic, cut in halves
1 teaspoon sugar
½ teaspoon salt
¼ teaspoon paprika
¼ teaspoon dry mustard
⅛ teaspoon ground black pepper
⅛ teaspoon ground thyme

1. Combine oil, vinegar, Worcestershire sauce, garlic, sugar, salt, paprika, dry mustard, pepper, and thyme in a jar; cover and shake well. Chill in refrigerator.
2. Before serving, remove garlic and beat or shake dressing thoroughly.

About 1 cup dressing

Roquefort French Dressing: Follow recipe for Gourmet French Dressing. Blend **3 ounces (about ¾ cup) Roquefort cheese,** crumbled, and **2 teaspoons water** until smooth. Add dressing slowly to cheese, blending well.

No-Oil Salad Dressing

If you love salads but need to avoid the oil in salad dressings, try this low-calorie mixture, which will add to the vitamin A in lettuce and other salad greens.

½ cup water
½ cup white wine vinegar
1 tablespoon cold water
2 teaspoons cornstarch
1 tablespoon sugar
1 tablespoon chopped parsley
1 teaspoon salt
½ teaspoon basil
¼ teaspoon paprika
¼ teaspoon dry mustard
⅛ teaspoon ground white pepper

1. Heat ½ cup water and vinegar to boiling. Blend 1 tablespoon cold water and cornstarch; pour into vinegar mixture, stirring constantly.
2. Cook and stir until slightly thickened. Stir in sugar, parsley, salt, basil, paprika, dry mustard, and pepper. Chill thoroughly.
3. Serve on tossed salad greens.

About 1 cup dressing

Lemon French Dressing

Try this dressing with its hints of garlic and onion on your favorite salad—you'll be getting full flavor and vitamin C.

1⅓ cups salad oil
½ teaspoon dry mustard
½ teaspoon ground black pepper
2 teaspoons minced onion
2 cloves garlic, cut in halves
2 teaspoons sugar
1 teaspoon salt
⅔ cup lemon juice

1. Mix oil, dry mustard, pepper, onion, and garlic. Set aside about 1 hour.
2. Remove garlic pieces. Add sugar, salt, and lemon juice; mix well.
3. Store in covered jar in refrigerator if not using immediately.

About 2 cups dressing

Curry-Yogurt Dressing

Start with a carton of yogurt and in no time you have a mouth-watering salad dressing, just right for your favorite fruit combination. Protein, riboflavin, and calcium are the nutrients.

1 cup (8 ounces) plain yogurt
2 tablespoons honey
½ teaspoon grated orange peel
½ teaspoon grated lemon peel
1 tablespoon orange juice
1 teaspoon lemon juice
1 teaspoon curry powder
⅛ teaspoon salt

1. Turn yogurt into a bowl. Add honey, peels, juices, curry powder, and salt; blend well. Chill.
2. Serve dressing on fruit salad.

About 1 cup dressing

Desserts

Nutritious eating does not mean giving up the pastries and sweets we all love. The fruits, milk products, eggs, and nuts that star in many delicious desserts are wholesome foods that belong in any healthful diet. Many desserts, such as fruit pies and cobblers, milk-based puddings, and ice cream, can count as a serving from one of the Four Food Groups. Sugars and starches used in desserts are not bad in themselves—consumed in moderation they can be included comfortably in the diet. So let desserts play their role, to satisfy a yearning for sweetness and to bring a delightful close to a pleasant meal.

A homemade cake or pie makes any meal a festive occasion and will delight family and guests alike. Cookies are great for mid-afternoon or late-night snacking, for perking up a lunch box, for gift-giving, for entertaining, or as a topper to a heavy dinner. Fruit desserts come in many forms: a light parfait laced with fruit, a more substantial cobbler, a favorite fruit pie. Or simply serve sliced fresh fruit with a whipped topping or a light, lemony sauce. Ice cream and sherbets are perennial favorites. Sherbets couldn't be easier to make—try some of the tempting recipes for cantaloupe-, pineapple-, and watermelon-flavored sherbets. Puddings, too, from the traditional *Rice-Raisin Pudding* to the elegant *Baked Apricot Pudding*, are always welcome.

A dessert should not be just an afterthought to a meal, but rather it should complement it in terms of ingredients, color, flavor, and texture. For instance, if you've served sweet potatoes at dinner, a colorful fruit cobbler or parfait might be a better choice for dessert than pumpkin pie. Follow a hearty meal with a light dessert such as sherbet and cookies or a simple but sophisticated *Cornstarch Blancmange*, topped with crushed, sweetened raspberries. Some desserts seem just right for a summer supper, such as the *Fiesta Melon Mold* or a frosty *Lime Snow*. *Citrus Bundt Cake* or *Torte-Style Cider Pudding* are fitting finales to any winter holiday dinner and are great for that late afternoon warm-up by the fire. Whatever the occasion, whether it's an everyday family meal, a company dinner, or a party, a homemade dessert will make it extra special.

Pie-Pan Apple Dessert

Warm from the oven, this easy-to-make dessert is a satisfying finish to a meal and provides some vitamin A, niacin, thiamine, calcium, and iron.

1 egg
¾ cup firmly packed brown sugar
½ cup enriched all-purpose flour
1 teaspoon baking powder
¼ teaspoon salt
¼ to ½ teaspoon ground nutmeg
1½ cups chopped pared apple
½ cup chopped pecans
Lemon Sauce (see recipe), whipped cream, or ice cream

1. Beat egg until light and fluffy. Beat in brown sugar. Mix flour, baking powder, salt, and nutmeg; add to egg mixture and blend.
2. Stir in apple and pecans. Spread in well-greased 8- or 9-inch pie pan or plate.
3. Bake at 350°F about 30 minutes, or until top is golden brown.
4. Serve warm with Lemon Sauce or desired topping.

About 6 servings

Lemon Sauce: Mix ⅓ cup sugar, 2 teaspoons cornstarch, and a few grains salt in a saucepan. Add 1 cup boiling water gradually, stirring constantly. Continue to stir and bring to boiling; simmer 5 minutes. Remove from heat. Blend in 2 tablespoons butter, ¾ teaspoon grated lemon peel, and 1½ tablespoons lemon juice. Serve warm.

Cinnamon-Banana Roll-Ups

If you've always thought rolls were just bread, here's a new idea for that can of crescent rolls in your refrigerator. This easy dessert offers both A and B vitamins.

2 tablespoons butter or margarine, melted
1 teaspoon grated lemon peel
1 teaspoon sugar
8 wedge-shaped pieces of dough prepared from crescent-style refrigerated rolls or pastry dough
Finely chopped blanched almonds (optional)

1. Combine butter with lemon peel and sugar. Brush lightly over the wedges of dough. If desired, press some chopped almonds into the dough.
2. Roll bananas in one of the butter-cinnamon mixtures. Then, if desired, roll the bananas in coconut or chopped almonds.
3. Place each banana on the long point of the wedge of dough. Roll up and place in an ungreased shallow baking pan.

8 firm small to medium
bananas, peeled
Butter-cinnamon mixture I
or II (see recipes)
Flaked coconut (optional)
Puréed fruit or hot
caramel sauce (optional)

4. Bake at 375°F about 13 minutes, or until rolls are delicately browned.* Serve immediately. If desired, accompany with sauce.

8 banana roll-ups

* For roll-ups using pastry dough, bake at 450°F until pastry is lightly browned.

Butter-cinnamon mixture I: Melt **½ cup butter or margarine** in a saucepan. Stir in **1 tablespoon lemon juice**, **¾ cup sugar**, and **1½ teaspoons ground cinnamon**. Pour mixture into a shallow dish.

Butter-cinnamon mixture II: Melt **½ cup butter or margarine** in a saucepan. Stir in **3 tablespoons brown sugar** and **4 teaspoons ground cinnamon**. Pour into a shallow dish.

Bananas with Royal Pineapple Sauce

Bring the land of the luau to your dinner table with this tangy pineapple-coconut dessert. It has vitamins A and C, also the B vitamins and calcium.

3 tablespoons dark brown
sugar
2 teaspoons cornstarch
1 can (8¼ ounces) crushed
pineapple (undrained)
1 tablespoon butter
⅛ teaspoon almond extract
¼ teaspoon grated lemon
peel
1 tablespoon lemon juice
¼ cup butter
4 firm bananas, peeled
2 tablespoons flaked
coconut

1. Mix sugar and cornstarch in a saucepan. Add pineapple with syrup, 1 tablespoon butter, and almond extract; mix well. Bring to boiling, stirring constantly until thickened.
2. Remove from heat and stir in lemon peel and juice. Set the sauce aside.
3. Heat ¼ cup butter in a heavy skillet. Add bananas; turn them by rolling to cook evenly and brown lightly. (Do not overcook or fruit will lose its shape.)
4. Allowing one-half banana per person, serve at once topped with the warm pineapple sauce. Sprinkle with coconut.

8 servings

Fresh Fruit with Lemon Sauce

There's no need to wait for the blueberry season to serve this colorful fruit medley. You can use either fresh or frozen fruit for this mixture, which contains vitamins A and C.

⅓ cup sugar
1 tablespoon cornstarch
⅛ teaspoon salt
1 cup water
½ teaspoon grated lemon peel
2 tablespoons lemon juice
1 teaspoon vanilla extract
½ cup diced fresh, drained canned, or thawed frozen peaches
½ cup fresh or thawed frozen blueberries
½ cup seeded red grapes, halved, or seedless green grapes

1. Combine sugar, cornstarch, and salt in a saucepan. Blend in water; cook and stir until mixture comes to boiling and is thickened. Remove from heat. Blend in lemon peel and juice and vanilla extract; cool.
2. Mix in fruit, chill, and serve plain or as a topping for cake or pudding.

4 to 6 servings

Peaches 'n' Corn Bread, Shortcake Style

This substantial treat, reminiscent of country living, will satisfy even the heartiest of appetites. Rich in nutrients and taste, this dish contains vitamin A, the B vitamins, and iron.

1 cup sifted enriched all-purpose flour
½ teaspoon baking soda
¼ teaspoon salt
1 cup enriched yellow cornmeal
¾ cup firmly packed light brown sugar
1 egg, beaten
½ cup buttermilk

1. Blend flour, baking soda, salt, cornmeal, and brown sugar in a bowl; set aside.
2. Beat egg, buttermilk, and sour cream until well blended; add to dry ingredients and stir until just smooth (do not overmix).
3. Turn into a greased 11 x 7 x 1½-inch pan and spread batter evenly.
4. Bake at 425°F about 20 minutes.
5. While still warm, cut corn bread into serving-size pieces, remove from pan, and

⅓ **cup dairy sour cream**
Peach Butter Elégante
(see recipe)
Sweetened fresh peach
slices

split into two layers. Spread Peach Butter Elégante generously between layers. Top with peach slices.

9 or 12 servings

Peach Butter Elégante: Thaw **1 package (10 or 12 ounces) frozen sliced peaches.** Drain peaches and cut into pieces; set aside. Put **1 cup firm unsalted butter** or **1 cup margarine** into a small mixing bowl. Beat with electric mixer on high speed just until butter is whipped. Add ½ **cup confectioners' sugar** gradually, beating thoroughly. Add the peaches, about 1 tablespoon at a time, beating thoroughly after each addition. (Do not allow butter to become too soft.) Chill until ready to use.

About 2 cups peach butter

Cornstarch Blancmange

Creamy and cool, this simple dessert is appropriate at the most elegant of dinners. It's delicate in flavor but strong in nutrition, providing protein, vitamins A and D, riboflavin, and calcium.

⅓ **cup sugar**
3 **tablespoons cornstarch**
⅛ **teaspoon salt**
½ **cup cold milk**
1½ **cups milk, heated**
1 **teaspoon vanilla extract**
4 **egg whites**
Fruit sauce

1. Mix sugar, cornstarch, and salt in a saucepan. Stir in cold milk. Add hot milk gradually, stirring constantly. Bring to boiling, stirring constantly; cook 1 minute.
2. Remove from heat. Blend in vanilla extract.
3. Beat egg whites until rounded peaks are formed. Spread over cornstarch mixture and fold together. Turn into a 1-quart mold and chill until firm.
4. Unmold onto a chilled serving plate and serve with desired fruit sauce.

About 6 servings

Spicy Peach Cobbler

Cheese added to a traditional favorite will please some hungry people. The nutrients in this warm dessert are vitamin A, calcium, and some protein.

1 **can (29 ounces) sliced peaches, drained; reserve 1 cup syrup**
½ **cup firmly packed brown sugar**
2 **tablespoons cornstarch**
⅛ **teaspoon salt**
⅛ **teaspoon ground cinnamon**
⅛ **teaspoon ground cloves**
2 **tablespoons cider vinegar**
1 **tablespoon butter or margarine**
1 **cup all-purpose biscuit mix**
½ **cup finely shredded sharp Cheddar cheese**
2 **tablespoons butter or margarine, melted**
¼ **cup milk**

1. Put drained peaches into a shallow 1-quart baking dish. Set aside.
2. Mix brown sugar, cornstarch, salt, cinnamon, and cloves in a saucepan. Blend in reserved peach syrup and vinegar; add 1 tablespoon butter. Bring mixture to boiling, stirring frequently; cook until thickened, about 10 minutes. Pour over peaches and set in a 400°F oven.
3. Combine biscuit mix and cheese. Stir in melted butter and milk to form a soft dough. Remove dish from oven and drop dough by heaping tablespoonfuls on top of hot peaches.
4. Return to oven and bake 20 minutes, or until crust is golden brown. Serve warm.

6 servings

Quick Applesauce Whip

For a light and frothy finish to a Saturday-night supper, try this quick-to-make dessert. Spicy and sweet, it offers some vitamin A and calcium.

1 **can (16 ounces) applesauce**
½ **teaspoon grated lemon peel**
2 **teaspoons lemon juice**
½ **teaspoon ground cinnamon**
3 **egg whites**
⅛ **teaspoon salt**
6 **tablespoons sugar**
Ground nutmeg

1. Combine applesauce, lemon peel, juice, and cinnamon.
2. Beat egg whites and salt until frothy. Add sugar gradually, beating well. Continue beating until rounded peaks are formed. Fold beaten egg whites into applesauce mixture.
3. Spoon immediately into dessert dishes. Sprinkle nutmeg over each serving.

About 6 servings

Purple Plum Crunch

As good as mother's own fresh fruit pies, this juicy dessert is simple to put together and there's no pastry-dough fuss. It's a good source of vitamins A and B, calcium, and iron.

5 cups pitted, quartered
   fresh purple plums
¼ cup firmly packed brown
   sugar
3 tablespoons flour
½ teaspoon ground cinnamon
1 cup enriched all-purpose
   flour
1 cup sugar
1 teaspoon baking powder
¼ teaspoon salt
¼ teaspoon ground mace
1 egg, well beaten
½ cup butter or margarine,
   melted and cooled

1. Put plums into a shallow 2-quart baking dish or casserole.
2. Mix brown sugar, 3 tablespoons flour, and cinnamon; sprinkle over plums and mix gently with a fork.
3. Blend 1 cup flour, sugar, baking powder, salt, and mace thoroughly. Add to beaten egg and stir with a fork until mixture is crumbly. Sprinkle evenly over plums in baking dish. Pour melted butter evenly over the topping.
4. Bake at 375°F 40 to 45 minutes, or until topping is lightly browned. Serve warm.

6 to 8 servings

Note: Other fresh fruits may be substituted for the plums.

Chocolate Peanut Butter Pudding

Combine two favorites like peanut butter and chocolate and you're sure to come up with a winner. This pudding wins nutrition points, too, with its protein, vitamins A and D, niacin, riboflavin, and calcium.

1 small package chocolate
   pudding and pie filling
   (not instant)
1 can (14½ ounces)
   evaporated milk
⅔ cup water
⅓ cup peanut butter
   Slightly sweetened whipped
   cream (optional)
   Chopped salted peanuts
   (optional)

1. Empty pudding mix into a saucepan, then stir in evaporated milk and water.
2. Cook and stir over moderate heat until thickened, about 5 minutes. Remove from heat and stir in peanut butter. Cover and chill.
3. To serve, spoon into dessert dishes. If desired, top with whipped cream and peanuts.

4 to 6 servings

Steamed Pumpkin Pudding

This warm and hearty steamed pudding with its sweet lemon sauce is a great treat on a brisk autumn day. Vitamins A and C and calcium are the nutritional rewards.

Pudding:
1¼ cups fine dry bread crumbs
½ cup enriched all-purpose flour
1 cup firmly packed brown sugar
1 teaspoon baking powder
½ teaspoon baking soda
½ teaspoon salt
½ teaspoon ground cinnamon
½ teaspoon ground cloves
½ cup salad oil
½ cup undiluted evaporated milk
2 eggs
1½ cups canned pumpkin

Lemon Nut Sauce:
½ cup butter or margarine
2 cups confectioners' sugar
¼ teaspoon salt
¼ teaspoon ground ginger
¼ cup lemon juice
½ cup chopped walnuts

1. Blend bread crumbs, flour, brown sugar, baking powder, baking soda, salt, cinnamon, and cloves in a large bowl.

2. Beat oil, evaporated milk, eggs, and pumpkin. Add to dry ingredients; mix until well blended.

3. Turn into a well-greased 2-quart mold. Cover tightly with a greased cover, or tie greased aluminum foil tightly over mold. Place mold on trivet or rack in a steamer or deep kettle with a tight-fitting cover.

4. Pour in boiling water to no more than one half the height of the mold. Cover steamer, bring water to boiling, and keep boiling at all times. If necessary, add more boiling water during cooking period.

5. Steam the pudding 2½ to 3 hours, or until a wooden pick inserted in center comes out clean.

6. For Lemon Nut Sauce, beat butter in a bowl. Blend confectioners' sugar, salt, and ginger; add gradually to butter, beating well. Add lemon juice gradually, continuing to beat until blended. Mix in walnuts.

7. Remove pudding from steamer and unmold onto a serving plate. Serve pudding with Lemon Nut Sauce.

About 12 servings

Note: If pudding is to be stored and served later, unmold onto a rack and cool thoroughly. Wrap in aluminum foil or return to mold and store in a cool place. Before serving, resteam pudding about 3 hours, or until thoroughly heated.

Baked Apricot Pudding

This pudding may be a little more complicated to make than others, but it's well worth the trouble. Vitamin A, niacin, and iron are its nutritional plusses.

1 tablespoon confectioners' sugar
1¼ cups (about 6 ounces) dried apricots
1 cup water
1½ tablespoons butter
1½ tablespoons flour
¾ cup milk
4 egg yolks
½ teaspoon vanilla extract
4 egg whites
6 tablespoons sugar
Whipped cream or whipped dessert topping

1. Lightly butter the bottom of a 1½-quart casserole and sift confectioners' sugar over it.
2. Put apricots and water into a saucepan. Cover; simmer 20 to 30 minutes, or until apricots are plump and tender. Force apricots through a coarse sieve or food mill (makes about ¾ cup purée).
3. Heat butter in a saucepan. Blend in flour. Heat until bubbly. Add milk gradually, stirring constantly. Bring rapidly to boiling, stirring constantly. Cook 1 to 2 minutes. Remove from heat.
4. Beat egg yolks and vanilla extract together until mixture is thick and lemon colored. Spoon sauce gradually into beaten egg yolks while beating vigorously. Thoroughly blend in the apricot purée. Set aside.
5. Using clean beater, beat egg whites until frothy. Add sugar gradually, beating constantly. Continue beating until rounded peaks are formed. Spread apricot mixture gently over beaten egg whites and fold until thoroughly blended. Turn mixture into prepared casserole. Set casserole in a pan of very hot water.
6. Bake at 350°F about 50 minutes, or until a knife inserted halfway between center and edge comes out clean. Cool slightly before serving. Serve with whipped cream.

6 servings

Torte-Style Cider Pudding

Lightly flavored with almonds and lemon and soaked with hot cider, this hearty pudding will be a stunning attraction at the dinner table. Besides its great taste, you'll be getting protein, vitamins A and D, B vitamins, calcium, and iron.

7	**egg yolks**
1½	**cups sugar**
2	**teaspoons grated lemon peel**
4	**cups toasted coarse bread crumbs**
1	**teaspoon ground cinnamon**
1	**cup chopped toasted almonds**
7	**egg whites**
1½	**cups sweet apple cider**
	Whipped cream

1. Beat egg yolks, sugar, and lemon peel together until very thick and lemon colored.
2. Mix bread crumbs, cinnamon, and almonds; fold into the egg-yolk mixture.
3. Beat egg whites until stiff, not dry, peaks are formed. Gently fold into bread-crumb mixture. Turn into a well-greased 9-inch tubed pan.
4. Bake at 350°F about 1 hour, or until top is golden brown. Loosen from sides of pan and then unmold immediately onto a warm serving plate.
5. Heat the cider and pour slowly over the pudding, using just enough to saturate it thoroughly. Serve immediately with whipped cream.

12 to 16 servings

Individual Fruit Puddings

Fruits, nuts, and spices combine to make a richly flavored pudding and to give you vitamins A and C, niacin, thiamine, calcium, and iron. The individual servings become extra special when topped with a tangy orange sauce.

Pudding:

2	**medium oranges**
1½	**cups sifted enriched all-purpose flour**
1	**teaspoon baking soda**
¼	**teaspoon salt**
¼	**teaspoon ground cinnamon**
¼	**teaspoon ground cloves**
¼	**teaspoon ground nutmeg**

1. For pudding, grease eight 5-ounce custard cups. Set aside.
2. Peel oranges; slice into cartwheels, and cut into pieces; reserve juice as it collects.
3. Blend flour, baking soda, salt, cinnamon, cloves, and nutmeg. Set aside.
4. Beat shortening; add brown sugar gradually, beating until fluffy. Add egg and beat thoroughly.

¼ cup shortening
1 cup firmly packed brown sugar
1 egg, well beaten
1 cup dark seedless raisins
½ cup pitted dates, cut in pieces
½ cup walnuts, coarsely chopped

Orange Sauce:
¾ cup sugar
2 tablespoons cornstarch
⅛ teaspoon salt
¾ cup orange juice
½ cup water
1 teaspoon grated orange peel
1 tablespoon butter or margarine

5. Mix in the orange pieces, reserved juice, raisins, dates, and walnuts. Blend in the dry ingredients.

6. Fill custard cups about two-thirds full with mixture; cover tightly with aluminum foil. Set in a pan and fill pan with water to a 1-inch depth. Cover pan with aluminum foil.

7. Cook in a 325°F oven 2 hours.

8. For Orange Sauce, mix sugar, cornstarch, and salt in a saucepan. Add orange juice and water gradually, stirring constantly. Bring to boiling, stirring constantly until thickened; cook over low heat 6 to 8 minutes, stirring occasionally.

9. Remove from heat. Blend in orange peel and butter. Keep warm.

10. Unmold puddings while hot onto dessert plates and spoon sauce over each.

8 servings

Rice-Raisin Pudding

Milk, rice, and raisins—what could be more wholesome? They combine in a traditional rice pudding to give you protein, vitamins A and D, B vitamins, calcium, and iron.

5 cups milk
1 cup uncooked enriched white rice
6 tablespoons sugar
1 teaspoon salt
¾ cup golden raisins
Ground cinnamon

1. Heat milk to boiling in a large saucepan. Add rice, sugar, and salt; stir and bring to boiling. Reduce heat and simmer, covered, 45 minutes. Stir in raisins. Continue cooking about 15 minutes, or until rice is entirely soft when a kernel is pressed between fingers, and mixture is very thick and creamy.

2. Remove from heat. Spoon into individual serving dishes and sprinkle lightly with cinnamon. Serve warm.

About 6 servings

Blueberry-Orange Parfaits

Layers of golden orange custard and brilliant blueberries bring color as well as great flavor to your table. This dessert is rich in vitamins A and C and calcium.

2 tablespoons cornstarch
1 cup sugar
½ teaspoon salt
2 cups orange juice
2 eggs, beaten
½ teaspoon grated lemon peel
2 tablespoons sugar
2 cups fresh blueberries
Whipped cream (optional)

1. Mix cornstarch, 1 cup sugar, and salt in a heavy saucepan. Add a small amount of the orange juice and blend until smooth. Stir in remaining orange juice.
2. Bring mixture to boiling, stirring constantly, and cook 3 to 5 minutes.
3. Stir about 3 tablespoons of the hot mixture into beaten eggs; immediately blend with mixture in saucepan.
4. Cook and stir about 3 minutes. Remove from water and cool. Stir in lemon peel. Chill.
5. Meanwhile, sprinkle 2 tablespoons sugar over blueberries and allow to stand at least 30 minutes. Spoon alternating layers of custard and blueberries in parfait glasses, beginning with a layer of custard and ending with blueberries. Top with whipped cream, if desired.

6 servings

Farina Mold

The whipping cream goes in, not on, this pudding, to make it extra smooth and extra rich. It's served with a bright and colorful fruit topping and supplies protein, vitamins A, C, and D, B vitamins, calcium, and iron.

2½ cups milk
1 teaspoon salt
½ cup enriched farina
1 envelope unflavored gelatin
½ cup milk
2 eggs
½ cup sugar

1. Heat 2½ cups milk in a saucepan. Add salt and farina gradually to milk, stirring constantly to prevent lumping. Bring to boiling and reduce heat; cook and stir 5 minutes.
2. Soften gelatin in ½ cup milk. Set aside.
3. Beat eggs until foamy. Stir sugar and a small amount of hot cereal into eggs. Imme-

1 **cup whipping cream**
1 **teaspoon almond extract**
Berry Sauce (see recipe)

diately blend into cereal in saucepan. Cook over low heat, stirring constantly, 3 minutes. Add gelatin and stir until gelatin is completely dissolved. Cool.

4. Beat whipping cream until soft peaks are formed. Blend in almond extract. Gently fold into the cereal mixture. Turn into a 1½-quart mold and chill until firm. Unmold and serve with Berry Sauce.

About 8 servings

Berry Sauce: Drain **2 packages (10 ounces each) frozen red raspberries,** thawed. Blend raspberry syrup and **1 teaspoon cornstarch** in a saucepan. Bring to boiling, stirring until mixture is thickened; cook 1 minute. Remove from heat and mix in raspberries and **¼ cup strawberry preserves.** Chill thoroughly.

About 2 cups sauce

Honey-Walnut Fruit Dessert

Diners will be refreshed with this unusual chilled dessert containing pineapple, oranges, apples, and cucumber. Vitamins A and C and calcium are the nutrients.

½ **small ripe pineapple**
2 **oranges**
1 **red apple, diced**
1 **medium cucumber, pared and diced**
1 **tablespoon lemon juice**
½ **cup honey**
¼ **cup chopped walnuts**
2 **tablespoons lemon juice**

1. Remove all fruit from pineapple shell. Core and dice fruit. Peel oranges, section, and cut into pieces.

2. Combine orange pieces, pineapple, apple, and cucumber in a bowl. Add 1 tablespoon lemon juice and mix well. Chill.

3. Meanwhile, combine honey, walnuts, and 2 tablespoons lemon juice in a small saucepan. Heat, stirring to blend. Cool; chill.

4. When ready to serve, drain fruit mixture and spoon into dessert dishes. Spoon some honey-walnut mixture over each serving.

About 6 servings

Ginger-Yam Mousse

Ginger and nutmeg give this dessert its tantalizing flavor, and a garnish of whipped topping and toasted almonds give it its elegant appearance. Vitamins A, C, and D, riboflavin, and calcium are all part of it, too.

1½ **cups mashed cooked yams (about 3 medium yams)**
1 **cup sugar**
2 **teaspoons ground ginger**
1 **teaspoon ground nutmeg**
½ **teaspoon ground cinnamon**
   Few grains salt
3 **egg yolks, fork beaten**
2 **cups milk**
½ **teaspoon grated lemon peel**
½ **teaspoon lemon juice**
½ **cup half-and-half**
3 **egg whites**
¼ **cup sugar**
   Whipped dessert topping
   Toasted slivered almonds

1. Put mashed yams into a heavy saucepan. Blend 1 cup sugar, spices, and salt. Mix with yams, then mix in egg yolks and milk. Cook over medium heat, stirring constantly, until mixture is thick. Remove from heat when mixture just comes to boiling.
2. Cool, stirring occasionally. Blend in lemon peel, juice, and half-and-half.
3. Beat egg whites until frothy; add ¼ cup sugar gradually, continuing to beat until stiff peaks are formed. Fold into completely cooled yam mixture.
4. Turn into a 6½-cup ring mold, spreading evenly. Freeze until firm, about 3½ hours.
5. Allow mousse to soften slightly at room temperature before unmolding. Unmold onto a chilled plate. Spoon whipped dessert topping into center and sprinkle with almonds.

6 to 8 servings

Banana-Pineapple Ice Cream

If you don't own an ice cream freezer, beg or borrow one to make this great-flavored ice cream. Besides the fun of making it yourself, you'll be getting vitamins A, C, and D, riboflavin, and calcium.

2 **cups mashed ripe bananas (about 5 medium)**
1 **cup sugar**
1 **teaspoon grated orange peel**
1 **teaspoon grated lemon peel**

1. Crushed ice and rock salt will be needed. Wash and scald cover, container, and dasher of a 3- or 4-quart ice cream freezer. Chill thoroughly.
2. Combine bananas, sugar, orange peel, lemon peel, lemon juice, and lime juice; blend thoroughly. Set aside about 10 minutes.

3 tablespoons lemon juice
2 tablespoons lime juice
1½ cups unsweetened pineapple juice
⅓ cup orange juice
2 cans (14½ ounces each) evaporated milk

3. Stir fruit juices into banana mixture. Add evaporated milk gradually, stirring until well blended.

4. Fill chilled freezer container no more than two-thirds full with ice cream mixture. Cover tightly. Set into freezer tub. (For electric freezer, follow the directions.)

5. Fill tub with alternate layers of crushed ice and rock salt, using 8 parts ice to 1 part salt. Turn handle slowly 5 minutes. Then turn rapidly until handle becomes difficult to turn (about 15 minutes), adding ice and salt as necessary.

6. Wipe cover and remove dasher. Pack down ice cream and cover with waxed paper or plastic wrap. Replace lid. (Plug dasher opening unless freezer has a solid cover.) Repack freezer container in ice, using 4 parts ice to 1 part salt. Cover with heavy paper or cloth. Let ripen 2 hours.

About 2 quarts ice cream

Lime Snow

This dessert couldn't be tastier or easier to make. It's cool and light—perfect for summer evenings—and offers some vitamin C and calcium.

1 package (3 ounces) lime-flavored gelatin
¾ cup boiling water
1 cup unsweetened pine-apple juice
2 tablespoons lemon juice
3 egg whites
¼ cup sugar

1. Turn gelatin into a bowl, pour in boiling water, and stir until gelatin is dissolved. Stir in fruit juices.

2. Chill until mixture is slightly thicker than consistency of thick unbeaten egg white.

3. Beat egg whites until frothy; gradually add sugar, beating well. Continue beating until rounded peaks are formed. Fold into chilled gelatin mixture.

4. Pile mixture into six sherbet glasses and chill until firm, about 2½ hours.

6 servings

Fiesta Melon Mold

A kaleidoscope of colors and flavors, this sparkling gelatin mold will brighten any party buffet and give your delighted guests protein, vitamins A and C, and calcium.

5 teaspoons unflavored gelatin
1 cup orange juice
½ cup water
½ cup sugar
¼ cup lime juice
1¾ cups watermelon juice (press pulp against sides of a fine sieve to extract juice)
¼ teaspoon salt
¾ to 1 cup cantaloupe balls
¾ to 1 cup honeydew melon balls
Frosted green grapes (optional)

1. Soften gelatin in orange juice; set aside.
2. Mix water and sugar in a small saucepan. Place over low heat and stir until sugar is dissolved. Bring rapidly to boiling; boil 3 minutes.
3. Remove from heat; add softened gelatin and stir until gelatin is completely dissolved. Blend in fruit juices and salt.
4. Chill gelatin until slightly thicker than the consistency of thick unbeaten egg white.
5. Mix melon balls into thickened gelatin. Turn mixture into a 1½-quart mold. Chill until firm.
6. To serve, unmold onto a chilled plate and garnish, if desired, with cluster of frosted green grapes.

8 to 10 servings

Lemon Crunch Dessert

A rich, layered dessert with a lemony filling, this can be served soon after coming from the oven, or can be made ahead of time and served chilled. It's packed with vitamins A, C, and D, B vitamins, calcium, and iron.

Lemon mixture:
¾ cup sugar
2 tablespoons flour
⅛ teaspoon salt
1 cup water
2 eggs, well beaten
1 teaspoon grated lemon peel
⅓ cup lemon juice

1. For lemon mixture, mix sugar, flour, and salt in a heavy saucepan; add water gradually, stirring until smooth. Bring mixture to boiling and cook 2 minutes.
2. Stir about 3 tablespoons of hot mixture vigorously into beaten eggs. Immediately blend into mixture in saucepan. Cook and stir about 3 minutes.
3. Remove from heat and stir in lemon peel

Crunch mixture:

½ cup butter or margarine

1 cup firmly packed brown sugar

1 cup enriched all-purpose flour

½ teaspoon salt

1 cup whole wheat flakes, crushed

½ cup finely chopped walnuts

½ cup shredded coconut, finely chopped

and juice. Set aside to cool.

4. For crunch mixture, beat butter until softened; add brown sugar gradually, beating until fluffy. Add flour and salt; mix well. Add wheat flakes, walnuts, and coconut; mix thoroughly.

5. Line bottom of an 8-inch square baking pan with a third of the crunch mixture. Cover with the lemon mixture, spreading to form an even layer. Top with remaining crunch mixture.

6. Bake at 350°F 40 minutes, or until lightly browned. Serve warm or cold.

About 8 servings

Strawberry Gelato

Milk and strawberries are the main ingredients in this pretty, frozen dessert. Together they supply protein, vitamins A, C, and D, and calcium.

5 teaspoons unflavored gelatin

1½ cups sugar

4 cups milk

2 cups instant nonfat dry milk (not reconstituted)

2 packages (10 ounces each) frozen sliced strawberries, thawed

¼ cup kirsch

¼ teaspoon red food coloring

1. Mix gelatin and sugar thoroughly in a large saucepan. Stir in fluid milk and then nonfat dry milk.

2. Stir over low heat until sugar and gelatin are completely dissolved. Set aside to cool.

3. Turn strawberries and kirsch into an electric blender container; blend thoroughly or until smooth. Force the purée through a fine sieve into the cooled milk; add food coloring and stir until blended.

4. Pour into refrigerator trays and freeze until firm, 2 to 3 hours.

5. Spoon the amount of ice cream to be served into a bowl; allow it to soften slightly and whip until smooth, using an electric mixer. Spoon into chilled dessert glasses and serve immediately.

About 2 quarts ice cream

Citrus Bundt Cake

Here's a special dessert to accompany an afternoon cup of coffee or a company dinner. Along with its delicate citrus flavor you'll be enjoying vitamins A and D, B vitamins, calcium, iron, and some protein.

¾ cup butter
2 teaspoons grated lemon peel
2 teaspoons grated orange peel
1¾ cups sugar
3 eggs
3⅓ cups sifted enriched all-purpose flour
1 tablespoon baking powder
½ teaspoon salt
1 cup milk
2 tablespoons lemon juice
2 tablespoons orange juice
⅓ cup sugar
Fruit sauce (optional)

1. Cream butter, grated peels, and 1¾ cups sugar until light and fluffy. Add eggs, one at a time, beating thoroughly after each addition.
2. Blend flour, baking powder, and salt. Mix into creamed mixture alternately with milk. Turn into a generously buttered 10-inch Bundt pan or angel food cake pan.
3. Bake at 325°F 60 to 75 minutes, or until a cake tester comes out clean. Remove from pan immediately and place on wire rack set over a shallow pan.
4. Combine fruit juices and ⅓ cup sugar in a small saucepan. Bring to boiling and boil 3 minutes. Drizzle over warm cake; cool completely before serving.
5. Slice and serve with a fruit sauce, if desired.

One 10-inch Bundt cake

Cranberry Upside-Down Cake

This is a fun-to-make and a fun-to-eat dessert. The cranberries add color, a little tartness, and vitamin C and calcium.

Topping:
¼ cup butter or margarine
⅔ cup sugar
1 tablespoon grated orange peel
½ teaspoon vanilla extract
2 cups fresh cranberries, washed and coarsely chopped
⅓ cup sugar

1. For topping, heat butter in a saucepan. Add ⅔ cup sugar, orange peel, and vanilla extract; blend thoroughly. Spread mixture evenly in an 8 x 8 x 2-inch pan.
2. Combine cranberries and ⅓ cup sugar. Spread over mixture in pan; set aside.
3. For cake, blend flour, baking powder, and salt; set aside.
4. Cream butter with vanilla extract. Add sugar gradually, creaming until fluffy after each addition. Add egg and beat thoroughly.

Cake:

1½ cups sifted enriched cake flour
2 teaspoons baking powder
½ teaspoon salt
½ cup butter or margarine
1 teaspoon vanilla extract
½ cup sugar
1 egg
½ cup milk

5. Beating only until smooth after each addition, alternately add dry ingredients in thirds and milk in halves to creamed mixture. Turn batter over cranberry mixture and spread evenly.

6. Bake at 350°F about 50 minutes.

7. Remove from oven and let stand 1 to 2 minutes in pan on wire rack. To remove from pan, run spatula gently around sides. Cover with a serving plate and invert; allow pan to remain over cake 1 or 2 minutes. Lift pan off. Serve cake warm or cool.

One 8-inch square cake

Wheat-Germ Ice Cream Bars with Peach Sauce

These crunchy ice cream treats are likely to become a favorite in your house, so make the bars and sauce ahead of time to have on hand for a dessert or a snack on a hot afternoon. They'll provide vitamin A, riboflavin, thiamine, calcium, and iron.

1 cup toasted wheat germ
2 tablespoons sugar
¼ teaspoon ground cinnamon
2 tablespoons butter or margarine, melted
2 pint bricks vanilla ice cream
  Peach Sauce (see recipe)

1. For ice cream bars, combine wheat germ, sugar, cinnamon, and butter.

2. Cut each pint of ice cream in thirds crosswise. Roll each piece in wheat-germ mixture to coat and put onto a chilled tray. Store in freezer until ready to serve.

3. Prepare Peach Sauce.

4. To serve, spoon Peach Sauce over ice cream bars.

6 servings

Peach Sauce: Combine ½ **cup sugar, 2 tablespoons cornstarch, ¼ teaspoon ground cinnamon,** and **¼ teaspoon ground nutmeg** in a saucepan; mix well. Add **1 package (10 ounces) frozen sliced peaches,** thawed; stir. Bring to boiling, stirring until sauce is thickened. Cool.

About 1¾ cups sauce

Cantaloupe Sherbet / Pineapple and Watermelon Sherbets

The ingredients are simple and so is the recipe. The result is full fruit flavor in a cool, melt-in-your-mouth sherbet that provides vitamins A and C and calcium.

2 cups ripe cantaloupe pieces
1 egg white
½ cup sugar
2 tablespoons fresh lime juice

1. Put melon pieces, egg white, sugar, and lime juice into an electric blender container. Cover and blend until smooth.
2. Turn into a shallow baking dish. Set in freezer; stir occasionally during freezing.
3. To serve, spoon into chilled dessert dishes.

About 1½ pints sherbet

Pineapple Sherbet: Follow recipe for Cantaloupe Sherbet; substitute **2 cups fresh pineapple pieces** for cantaloupe.

Watermelon Sherbet: Follow recipe for Cantaloupe Sherbet; substitute **2 cups watermelon pieces** for cantaloupe and, if desired, decrease sugar to ¼ cup.

Avocado Ice Cream

Avocado ice cream may sound unusual, but its flavor is wonderful, and it's easy to make. Ask your guests to guess the secret ingredient! They'll be getting vitamins A and C and calcium.

3 ripe avocados
½ cup sugar
⅓ cup lime juice
1 quart vanilla ice cream, slightly softened

1. Halve, pit, and peel avocados. Mash avocado in a bowl. Mix in sugar and lime juice.
2. Spoon ice cream onto avocado mixture and beat until smooth. Turn into refrigerator trays and freeze until firm.
3. To serve, spoon into chilled dessert dishes and serve immediately.

About 2½ pints ice cream

Chocolate Pound Cake Loaf/ Dutch Cocoa Loaf Cake

Although a variation of the traditional recipe, this pound cake can't be beat for appearance and satisfying flavor. It's nutritionally satisfying, too, with vitamins A, C, and D, riboflavin, thiamine, calcium, and iron.

3	cups sifted enriched all-purpose flour
2	teaspoons baking powder
¼	teaspoon salt
½	cup cocoa, sifted
1	cup butter or margarine
½	cup lard
1	tablespoon vanilla extract
½	teaspoon almond extract
3	cups sugar
1	cup eggs (5 or 6)
1¼	cups milk

1. Lightly grease (bottom only) two 9 x 5 x 3-inch loaf pans. Line bottoms with waxed paper; grease paper. Set aside.
2. Combine flour, baking powder, salt, and cocoa and blend thoroughly. Set aside.
3. Cream butter and lard with extracts in a large bowl. Add sugar gradually, creaming thoroughly after each addition. Add eggs, one at a time, beating until fluffy after each addition.
4. Beating only until blended after each addition, alternately add dry ingredients in fourths and milk in thirds to creamed mixture.
5. Turn equal amounts of batter into prepared loaf pans. Spread batter evenly. (Top of baked cakes may have a slight crack down center.) Place pans on center of oven rack so that top of batter will be at center of oven.
6. Bake at 325°F about 65 minutes, or until cake tester inserted in center comes out clean.
7. Cool cakes in pans 15 minutes on wire racks. Loosen sides with a spatula and turn onto rack. Peel off paper, turn right side up, and cool completely.

Two loaf cakes

Dutch Cocoa Loaf Cake: Follow directions for Chocolate Pound Cake Loaf except substitute **⅔ cup Dutch process cocoa** for the ½ cup cocoa and increase butter or margarine to 1½ cups; omit lard.

Date Spice Cake

Sweet dates with an added tang of citrus make this one-layer cake a nutritious treat you will serve time and again. It offers niacin, riboflavin, vitamin D, calcium, iron, and some protein.

2¼ cups sifted enriched all-purpose flour
2 teaspoons baking powder
¼ teaspoon baking soda
½ teaspoon salt
2 teaspoons ground nutmeg
2 teaspoons ground ginger
⅔ cup shortening
1 teaspoon grated orange peel
1 teaspoon grated lemon peel
1 cup sugar
2 eggs
1 cup buttermilk
1 cup chopped dates

1. Grease a 9 x 9 x 2-inch pan. Line with waxed paper cut to fit bottom; grease paper. Set aside.
2. Blend flour, baking powder, baking soda, salt, nutmeg, and ginger.
3. Beat shortening with orange and lemon peels. Add sugar gradually, creaming until fluffy after each addition.
4. Add eggs, one at a time, beating thoroughly after each addition.
5. Beating only until smooth after each addition, alternately add dry ingredients in fourths and buttermilk in thirds to creamed mixture. Mix in dates. Turn batter into prepared pan.
6. Bake at 350°F about 45 minutes.
7. Remove from oven. Cool 5 to 10 minutes in pan on wire rack. Remove cake from pan and peel off paper; cool cake on rack.

One 9-inch square cake

Swiss Chocolate Squares

Chocolaty and rich, these squares will disappear in a hurry when you set them on the table. Your eager-eaters will be getting vitamins A and D, riboflavin, calcium, and iron.

Cake:
1 cup water
½ cup soft margarine
1½ ounces (1½ squares) unsweetened chocolate

1. For cake, combine water, margarine, and chocolate in a saucepan. Set over medium heat and bring to boiling, stirring occasionally. Remove from heat.
2. Blend flour and sugar; stir into the cooked

2 cups enriched all-purpose flour
2 cups sugar
2 eggs
½ cup dairy sour cream
1 teaspoon baking soda
¼ teaspoon salt

Milk Chocolate Frosting:
½ cup soft margarine
6 tablespoons milk
1½ ounces (1½ squares) unsweetened chocolate
4½ cups confectioners' sugar
1 teaspoon vanilla extract
½ cup chopped nuts

chocolate mixture. Beat in eggs and sour cream. Blend baking soda and salt; beat in. Turn into a greased 15 x 10 x 1-inch jelly-roll pan and spread evenly.

3. Bake at 375°F 20 to 25 minutes. Cool on a wire rack.

4. For Milk Chocolate Frosting, combine margarine, milk, and chocolate in a saucepan. Set over medium heat and bring to boiling; boil 1 minute, stirring constantly. Remove from heat.

5. Stir in confectioners' sugar, adding gradually, and beat until smooth. Stir in vanilla extract.

6. Turn frosting onto warm cake and spread evenly. Sprinkle with nuts. Cool completely before cutting into squares.

1½ to 3 dozen cake squares

Salted Peanut Cake

Everyone loves to munch on salted peanuts—add them to a cake and the cake will become a favorite, too. Peanuts are storehouses of protein, B vitamins, and iron.

⅓ cup butter or margarine
1 teaspoon vanilla extract
1 cup sugar
1 egg
1½ cups sifted enriched all-purpose flour
½ teaspoon baking soda
¾ cup buttermilk
1 cup (about 5 ounces) salted peanuts, finely chopped
Confectioners' sugar

1. Cream butter with vanilla extract. Add sugar gradually, creaming until fluffy. Add egg and beat thoroughly.

2. Blend flour and baking soda. Alternately add dry ingredients in fourths and buttermilk in thirds to creamed mixture, beating only until smooth after each addition. Mix in peanuts. Turn into a greased 8 x 8 x 2-inch pan and spread evenly.

3. Bake at 350°F about 50 minutes.

4. Remove pan to wire rack; cool completely. Sift confectioners' sugar evenly over top of cooled cake.

One 8-inch square cake

Carrot Cupcakes

Vegetables aren't as unusual an ingredient in desserts as you might think—pumpkin pie, after all, is a traditional favorite. In these well-flavored cupcakes, carrots add body, moisture, color—and vitamin A and calcium.

1½ **cups sifted enriched all-purpose flour**
  1 **teaspoon baking powder**
  1 **teaspoon baking soda**
  1 **teaspoon ground cinnamon**
 ½ **teaspoon salt**
  1 **cup sugar**
 ¾ **cup vegetable oil**
  2 **eggs**
  1 **cup grated raw carrots**
 ½ **cup chopped nuts**

1. Blend flour, baking powder, baking soda, cinnamon, and salt. Set aside.
2. Combine sugar and oil in a bowl and beat thoroughly. Add eggs, one at a time, beating thoroughly after each addition. Mix in carrots. Add dry ingredients gradually, beating until blended. Mix in nuts.
3. Spoon into paper-baking-cup-lined muffin-pan wells.
4. Bake at 350°F 15 to 20 minutes.

About 16 cupcakes

Frosted Applesauce Cake

Applesauce gives this cake its moistness and its full flavor. Top it with a sugary frosting studded with almonds, and you have a great dessert loaded with niacin, calcium, and iron.

Cake:
  2 **cups sifted enriched cake flour**
  1 **teaspoon baking soda**
  1 **teaspoon ground cinnamon**
 ½ **teaspoon ground cloves**
 ½ **teaspoon salt**
 ½ **cup butter or margarine**
  1 **cup firmly packed brown sugar**
  2 **eggs**
  1 **cup applesauce**
 ⅔ **cup undiluted evaporated milk**

1. For cake, blend cake flour, baking soda, cinnamon, cloves, and salt; set aside.
2. Beat butter until softened. Add brown sugar gradually, creaming until fluffy after each addition. Add eggs, one at a time, beating thoroughly after each addition.
3. Blend applesauce, evaporated milk, and vinegar. Alternately add dry ingredients in fourths and applesauce mixture in thirds to creamed mixture; beat only until smooth after each addition. Stir in raisins. Turn batter into a greased 9-inch square pan and spread evenly.
4. Bake at 350°F about 40 minutes. Set on

2 tablespoons vinegar
¾ cup raisins

Frosting:
2 tablespoons butter or
margarine, softened
½ cup firmly packed brown
sugar
2 tablespoons undiluted
evaporated milk
½ cup toasted blanched
almonds, coarsely chopped

wire rack while preparing frosting.
5. For frosting, cream butter and brown sugar until fluffy; add evaporated milk and beat well. Stir in almonds.
6. Spread frosting lightly over the cake. Place cake under broiler with top of cake about 4 inches from heat. Broil about 1 minute, or until frosting bubbles; watch closely to avoid scorching.

One 9-inch square cake

Banana Sponge Cake

Bananas are readily available in markets today—pick up a couple extra to take advantage of their unique flavor in this light and spongy cake. Bananas provide some vitamin A and the B vitamins.

6 egg yolks
¾ cup sugar
1½ to 3 teaspoons banana
extract
1 teaspoon lemon juice
1½ cups sifted enriched cake
flour
¾ cup sieved ripe banana
6 egg whites
¾ teaspoon salt
¾ cup sugar
Confectioners' sugar icing
(optional)

1. Combine egg yolks, ¾ cup sugar, banana extract, and lemon juice in a bowl. Beat until very thick.
2. Sift about one fourth of the flour at a time over egg yolk mixture, gently folding until blended after each addition. Fold in sieved banana.
3. Beat egg whites and salt until frothy. Add ¾ cup sugar gradually, continuing to beat until stiff peaks are formed.
4. Spread egg yolk mixture over meringue and gently fold together. Turn batter into an ungreased 10-inch tubed pan.
5. Bake at 350°F 45 to 50 minutes. Immediately invert pan and cool cake completely. Remove cake from pan.
6. Drizzle cooled cake with a thin confectioners' sugar icing, if desired.

One 10-inch tubed cake

Fluffy Raspberry Topping/ Fluffy Peach Topping

Make a simple cake glamorous with this luscious topping, or serve it as is for a delectable dessert. Raspberries give you vitamin C and calcium; peaches provide vitamin A.

1 **egg white**
1 **teaspoon lemon juice**
⅛ **teaspoon salt**
¼ **cup sugar**
½ **cup drained crushed red raspberries**
¼ **to ⅓ cup sugar (depending on sweetness of fruit)**

1. Beat egg white, lemon juice, and salt until frothy; add ¼ cup sugar gradually, beating well. Continue beating until rounded peaks are formed.

2. Mix raspberries with desired amount of sugar; add sweetened fruit to meringue and beat until stiff peaks are formed. Chill at least 1 hour before using.

1½ to 2 cups topping

Fluffy Peach Topping: Follow recipe for Fluffy Raspberry Topping; substitute drained crushed **fresh peaches** for the raspberries and **3 or 4 drops almond extract** for the lemon juice.

Triple-Treat Walnut Bars

These walnut delights gain their niacin, thiamine, calcium, iron and even some protein from the whole wheat flour, wheat germ, and walnuts that go into the batter.

½ **cup butter or margarine**
1 **package (3 ounces) cream cheese**
½ **cup firmly packed dark brown sugar**
1 **cup whole wheat flour**
⅓ **cup toasted wheat germ**
1 **package (6 ounces) semisweet chocolate pieces**

1. Cream butter, cheese, and sugar in a bowl until light. Add 1 cup whole wheat flour and wheat germ and mix until smooth. Turn into a greased 13 x 9 x 2-inch pan; spread evenly.

2. Bake at 375°F 15 to 18 minutes, until edges are very lightly browned and top is firm.

3. Remove from oven and sprinkle with chocolate. Let stand about 5 minutes, or until

2 eggs
½ cup honey
⅓ cup whole wheat flour
⅓ cup instant nonfat dry milk
¼ teaspoon salt
¼ teaspoon ground cinnamon
¼ teaspoon ground mace
1½ cups chopped walnuts

chocolate softens, then spread it evenly over baked layer.

4. Combine eggs and honey; beat just until well blended. Add ⅓ cup whole wheat flour, dry milk, salt, cinnamon, mace, and walnuts; mix well. Spoon over the chocolate.

5. Return to oven and bake 18 to 20 minutes, or until top is set. Cool in pan, then cut into bars or diamonds.

About 3 dozen cookies

Quick Banana Frosting

Try this unusual frosting on your favorite citrus-flavored cake or on a rich chocolaty one—everyone will want seconds. The nutrients are vitamin A and some B vitamins and calcium at the same time.

⅓ cup sieved banana
¼ teaspoon lemon juice
 Few grains salt
¼ cup butter or margarine
2½ cups confectioners' sugar

1. Combine banana, lemon juice, and salt.
2. Beat butter until softened. Add confectioners' sugar and sieved banana alternately to the butter, beating until thoroughly blended after each addition.

*Enough to frost sides and tops
of two 8-inch round cake layers*

Choco-Raisin Candy

Raisins and chocolate make such a great combination—and it takes only minutes to mix. Roll the candies in coconut or another trimming and they're ready for the party tray. Raisins contribute not only their special flavor but also niacin, calcium, and iron.

¾ cup dark seedless raisins
½ cup canned chocolate
 frosting
 Finely chopped nuts,
 flaked coconut, cocoa, or
 equal parts confectioners'
 sugar and cocoa

Mix raisins and chocolate frosting. Chill thoroughly. Working quickly, form mixture into 1-inch balls and coat as desired. Refrigerate before serving.

1½ dozen candy balls

Peanut Butter Fudge

Here's another way to use peanut butter, so rich in flavor and full of protein and niacin. Kids will love making this fudge because it's so easy and so tasty.

1 **cup undiluted evaporated milk**
2 **cups sugar**
¼ **cup butter or margarine**
1 **cup miniature marshmallows**
1 **jar (12 ounces) crunchy peanut butter**
1 **teaspoon vanilla extract**

1. Combine evaporated milk, sugar, and butter in a heavy 10-inch skillet. Set over medium heat, bring to boiling, and boil 4 minutes, stirring constantly.
2. Remove from heat and stir in marshmallows, peanut butter, and vanilla extract until evenly blended.
3. Turn into a buttered 8-inch square pan and spread to corners. Chill before cutting into squares.

About 2 pounds fudge

Note: This fudge may be prepared in an electric skillet. Set temperature at 280°F, bring mixture to boiling, and boil about 5 minutes.

Graham Date-Nut Squares with Tangerine Sauce

Graham crackers, dates, and nuts are combined in these delicious cake squares. Top them with a tangerine sauce for an intriguing flavor contrast, and you have a very special dessert that gives you vitamins A, C, and D, B vitamins, calcium, and iron.

Cake:
2⅓ **cups graham cracker crumbs**
1 **teaspoon baking powder**
¼ **teaspoon salt**
3 **eggs**
1 **cup sugar**
1½ **teaspoons vanilla extract**

1. For cake, grease a 9-inch square pan. Line pan with waxed paper cut to fit pan bottom; grease paper. Set aside.
2. Turn graham cracker crumbs into a bowl. Mix in baking powder and salt; set aside.
3. Combine eggs, sugar, vanilla extract, and lemon peel in a bowl. Beat until very thick. Gently fold in graham cracker crumb mixture.

½ teaspoon grated lemon peel
1 cup pitted dates, snipped
1 cup chopped walnuts

Tangerine Sauce:
½ cup sugar
1 tablespoon cornstarch
⅛ teaspoon salt
¾ cup water
¾ cup (6-ounce can) frozen tangerine juice concentrate, defrosted
1 tablespoon butter or margarine
¼ teaspoon grated lemon peel

Mix in dates and walnuts. Turn into the prepared pan and spread to edges.

4. Bake at 350°F 25 to 30 minutes.

5. For Tangerine Sauce, mix sugar, cornstarch, and salt in a saucepan. Add water and mix well. Bring to boiling, stirring constantly until thickened; cook 3 minutes.

6. Remove from heat and blend in tangerine juice concentrate, butter, and lemon peel. Keep sauce warm.

7. Remove cake from oven and cool 5 to 10 minutes in pan on wire rack. Cut into squares and serve warm with the sauce.

16 servings

Spicy Walnut Diamonds

Walnuts not only give us the good taste and delightful crunch that we enjoy so much in cookies; they also provide protein, niacin, thiamine, and iron.

2½ cups sifted all-purpose flour
2 tablespoons cocoa
1½ teaspoons baking powder
1 teaspoon salt
½ teaspoon ground nutmeg
¼ teaspoon ground cloves
2 cups firmly packed brown sugar
3 eggs
½ cup honey
½ cup butter or margarine, melted
1½ cups chopped walnuts (1 cup medium and ½ cup fine)
½ cup confectioners' sugar
2 to 3 teaspoons milk

1. Blend flour, cocoa, baking powder, salt, nutmeg, and cloves.

2. Combine brown sugar and eggs in a large bowl; beat until well blended and light. Add honey, butter, and flour mixture and mix until smooth.

3. Stir in the 1 cup medium walnuts, and spread evenly in a greased 15 x 10 x 1-inch jelly-roll pan. Sprinkle the ½ cup fine walnuts over top.

4. Bake at 375°F about 20 minutes, or just until top springs back when touched lightly in center. Cool in pan.

5. Mix confectioners' sugar and enough milk to make a smooth, thin glaze. Spread over cooled layer. Cut into diamonds or bars.

About 4 dozen cookies

Golden Lemon Squares

Carrots are a surprise ingredient in these lemony squares and add to the nutrients, which include vitamins A and D, riboflavin, calcium, and iron.

2¼ cups sifted enriched all-purpose flour

1 teaspoon baking powder

1 cup butter or margarine, melted and cooled

1½ teaspoons vanilla extract

¾ teaspoon lemon extract

1¼ cups sugar

4 eggs

1 cup mashed cooked carrots, cooled

Lemon Glaze (see recipe)

1. Blend flour and baking powder.
2. Put butter and extracts into bowl of electric mixer and add sugar gradually, beating thoroughly. Add eggs, one at a time, beating well after each addition.
3. Add carrots and flour mixture; beat 1 minute. Turn into a greased 15 x 10 x 1-inch jelly-roll pan.
4. Bake at 350°F about 25 minutes.
5. Cool in pan on wire rack. Spread with glaze; let stand until glaze is set. Cut into squares.

5 to 6 dozen cookies

Lemon Glaze: Beat together 2¼ cups confectioners' sugar, 3 tablespoons lemon juice, and 1 tablespoon water.

Wheat-Flake Bars

These orange-frosted bars are both luscious and nutritious; the whole wheat flakes contribute vitamins A, C, and D, niacin, riboflavin, and thiamine.

2 cups whole wheat cereal flakes

2 cups sifted enriched all-purpose flour

1 teaspoon baking powder

¾ cup firmly packed brown sugar

¾ cup plus 2 tablespoons butter or margarine, chilled

½ cup orange marmalade

1. Mix cereal, flour, baking powder, and brown sugar in a bowl. Cut in butter until crumbly.
2. Press about two-thirds of the mixture in an even layer on the bottom of a 13 x 9 x 2-inch pan. Spread with marmalade; sprinkle remaining cereal mixture over marmalade.
3. Bake at 350°F about 30 minutes. Remove to a wire rack. Cool completely.
4. Frost with Glossy Orange Frosting. Cut

**Glossy Orange Frosting
(see recipe)
Semisweet chocolate pieces**

into 3 x 1-inch bars. Decorate each bar with three semisweet chocolate pieces (points up).

3 dozen cookies

Glossy Orange Frosting: Beat **1 egg white** slightly; beat in **1½ cups confectioners' sugar.** Add **1 tablespoon melted butter or margarine, ⅛ teaspoon salt, 1 teaspoon vanilla extract,** and **¼ teaspoon orange extract;** beat until smooth. Blend in, one drop at a time, orange food coloring (a mixture of about **2 drops of red and 6 drops of yellow**) until frosting is tinted a light orange.

About 1 cup frosting

Prunella Cake

Prunes are rich in vitamin A, niacin, calcium, and iron, and they bring a special flavor and moistness to this lightly spiced cake.

**1 cup soft dried prunes, finely snipped
1⅓ cups sifted enriched all-purpose flour
½ teaspoon baking powder
½ teaspoon baking soda
½ teaspoon salt
½ teaspoon ground cinnamon
½ teaspoon ground nutmeg
½ cup shortening
1 cup sugar
2 eggs
⅔ cup buttermilk
Whipped cream or whipped dessert topping (optional)**

1. Grease a 9 x 9 x 2-inch pan, line with waxed paper cut to fit bottom, and grease paper. Set aside.
2. Put prunes into a bowl. Blend flour, baking powder, baking soda, salt, cinnamon, and nutmeg; add to prunes and set aside.
3. Put shortening into a bowl and gradually add sugar, creaming until fluffy after each addition. Add eggs, one at a time, beating thoroughly after each addition.
4. Beating until smooth after each addition, alternately add dry ingredients in thirds and buttermilk in halves to creamed mixture. Turn into prepared pan.
5. Bake at 350°F 35 to 40 minutes. Cool 5 to 10 minutes in pan on wire rack. Remove cake from pan and peel off paper. Serve cooled cake with whipped cream or whipped dessert topping, if desired.

One 9-inch square cake

Orange-Oatmeal Cookies

Orange flavor makes a delightful variation in that universal favorite, the oatmeal cookie, which gives us protein, niacin, riboflavin, and thiamine.

1¾ **cups enriched all-purpose flour**
4 **teaspoons baking powder**
1 **teaspoon salt**
1 **teaspoon ground nutmeg**
1¼ **cups butter or margarine**
¼ **cup grated orange peel**
2 **cups sugar**
1 **egg**
2 **cups uncooked oats**

1. Blend flour, baking powder, salt, and nutmeg; set aside.
2. Cream butter with orange peel. Add sugar gradually, creaming until fluffy. Add egg and beat thoroughly.
3. Add dry ingredients in thirds to creamed mixture, mixing until blended after each addition. Stir in oats.
4. Drop by teaspoonfuls about 3 inches apart onto lightly greased cookie sheets.
5. Bake at 375°F 12 to 15 minutes.

About 6 dozen cookies

Note: For a more nutritious and an equally delicious cookie, increase the oats to 3 cups.

Date Perfections

Dates and pecans never fail to make a taste-pleasing combination, and they also contain niacin, thiamine, calcium, iron, and some protein.

¾ **cup enriched all-purpose flour**
¾ **teaspoon baking powder**
¼ **teaspoon salt**
2 **eggs**
¾ **cup sugar**
1½ **cups dates, finely chopped**
1 **cup pecans, finely chopped**
¾ **cup confectioners' sugar**
2 **tablespoons lemon juice**

1. Blend flour, baking powder, and salt; set aside.
2. Combine eggs and sugar in a bowl. Beat until mixture is thick and piled softly.
3. Fold in dry ingredients, dates, and pecans until blended. Turn mixture into a greased 11 x 7 x 1½-inch baking pan and spread evenly.
4. Bake at 325°F 30 to 35 minutes.
5. Blend confectioners' sugar and lemon juice. Immediately brush surface of baked layer with the glaze. While warm, cut into squares.

About 2 dozen cookies

Butterscotchies

Nuts, cereal, and coconut combine with other ingredients in a quick-to-make candy that's crunchy and sweet and contains vitamin A, niacin, thiamine, and iron.

½ cup undiluted evaporated milk
¾ cup sugar
¼ teaspoon salt
2 tablespoons butter or margarine
1 package (6 ounces) butterscotch-flavored pieces
1 teaspoon vanilla extract
1 cup flaked coconut
½ cup coarsely chopped walnuts
2 to 2½ cups crisp enriched ready-to-eat cereal

1. Put evaporated milk, sugar, salt, and butter into a heavy 2-quart saucepan. Bring to a full boil, stirring constantly, and boil 2 minutes.
2. Remove from heat. Add butterscotch pieces and vanilla extract; stir until smooth. Add coconut, walnuts, and cereal; toss lightly until well coated.
3. Drop by rounded teaspoonfuls onto a cookie sheet lined with waxed paper or aluminum foil. Allow to stand until set.

About 1½ pounds candy

Lumberjack Cookies

Eat some of these delicious crinkle-top cookies with their calcium and iron content and you'll feel like a lumberjack yourself.

2 cups sifted enriched all-purpose flour
½ teaspoon baking soda
½ teaspoon salt
1 teaspoon ground cinnamon
½ teaspoon ground ginger
½ cup butter or margarine
½ cup sugar
½ cup dark molasses
1 egg
Sugar

1. Blend flour, baking soda, salt, cinnamon, and ginger; set aside.
2. Beat butter until softened. Add ½ cup sugar gradually, creaming until fluffy. Blend in molasses. Add egg and beat thoroughly.
3. Blending well after each addition, add the dry ingredients in fourths to creamed mixture. Chill dough thoroughly.
4. Form chilled dough into balls, using about 2 teaspoons of dough for each. Roll in sugar to coat and transfer to greased cookie sheets.
5. Bake at 350°F about 10 minutes. Cool cookies on wire racks.

About 4 dozen cookies

Peanut Blonde Brownies

There's no chocolate in these blonde brownies, but the peanuts and peanut butter are sources of protein, niacin, riboflavin, thiamine, and iron.

½ cup chunk-style peanut butter
¼ cup butter or margarine
1 teaspoon vanilla extract
1 cup firmly packed light brown sugar
2 eggs
½ cup enriched all-purpose flour
1 cup chopped salted peanuts
Confectioners' sugar

1. Cream peanut butter, butter, and vanilla extract in a bowl. Add brown sugar gradually, beating well after each addition.
2. Add eggs, one at a time, beating thoroughly after each addition until creamy.
3. Add flour in halves, beating until blended after each addition. Stir in peanuts. Turn mixture into a greased 8 x 8 x 2-inch pan and spread evenly.
4. Bake at 350°F 30 to 35 minutes.
5. Remove from oven and cool in pan 5 minutes. Cut into 2-inch squares. Remove from pan and cool on a wire rack. Sift confectioners' sugar over tops.

16 brownies

Peanut Butter Dreams

These two layers of good eating—one containing peanut butter and the other chocolate—are enough to satisfy any sweet tooth. Protein and niacin are the nutrients.

¼ cup butter or margarine
½ cup peanut butter
½ cup firmly packed light brown sugar
1 cup enriched all-purpose flour
2 eggs
1 teaspoon vanilla extract
1 cup firmly packed light brown sugar
⅓ cup enriched all-purpose flour

1. Cream butter and peanut butter thoroughly in a bowl. Add ½ cup brown sugar gradually, creaming until fluffy.
2. Add 1 cup flour in halves to creamed mixture, mixing until well blended after each addition. Press evenly into a greased 9 x 9 x 2-inch pan.
3. Bake at 350°F 10 to 15 minutes, or until layer is lightly browned.
4. Meanwhile, beat eggs, vanilla extract, and 1 cup brown sugar together in a bowl until creamy. Blend ⅓ cup flour and baking pow-

½ teaspoon baking powder
¾ cup flaked coconut
1 package (6 ounces) semisweet chocolate pieces

der; add to egg mixture and beat until well blended.

5. Stir in coconut and chocolate pieces. Spread mixture over the partially baked layer in pan.

6. Return to oven and bake 30 minutes. Cool completely and cut into squares or bars.

About 2 dozen cookies

Tropichocolate Wafers

Thoroughly chilling the dough is the secret of these chocolate-coconut wafers. Vitamin A, the B vitamins, and calcium are the nutrients.

1½ cups sifted enriched all-purpose flour
½ teaspoon baking soda
½ teaspoon salt
½ cup cocoa
½ cup butter or margarine
½ teaspoon vanilla extract
1 cup firmly packed brown sugar
1 egg
¾ cup flaked coconut

1. Blend flour, baking soda, salt, and cocoa. Set aside.

2. Cream butter with vanilla extract. Add brown sugar gradually, creaming until fluffy. Add egg and beat thoroughly.

3. Mixing until well blended after each addition, add dry ingredients in thirds to creamed mixture. Stir in coconut.

4. Chill dough in refrigerator until easy to handle, then shape into 2 rolls about 1½ inches in diameter. Wrap each roll in waxed paper, aluminum foil, or plastic wrap. Chill several hours or overnight.

5. Remove rolls of dough from refrigerator as needed. Cut dough into ⅛-inch slices. Place slices about 1½ inches apart on lightly greased cookie sheets.

6. Bake at 400°F 5 to 8 minutes. Cool cookies on wire racks.

About 5 dozen cookies

Granola Cookies with Raisins

Since granola itself is so full of good things, it's not surprising that granola cookies are both good tasting and rich in B vitamins, calcium, iron, and even contain some protein.

1½ **cups sifted enriched all-purpose flour**
1 **teaspoon baking soda**
1¾ **cups regular granola**
1 **cup firmly packed brown sugar**
½ **cup granulated sugar**
1 **cup butter or margarine (at room temperature)**
1 **teaspoon vanilla extract**
1 **egg**
1 **cup dark or golden raisins**

1. Combine flour and baking soda in a large bowl of electric mixer. Add granola, sugars, soft butter, vanilla extract, and egg. Mix at low speed until blended, then mix at medium speed 2 minutes, scraping bowl occasionally. Stir in raisins.
2. Drop by teaspoonfuls onto greased cookie sheets.
3. Bake at 375°F about 12 minutes. Cool cookies on wire racks.

About 8 dozen cookies

Apricot-Cheese Pie

Apricots and cottage cheese contribute to the good taste of this special pie; protein, vitamin A, niacin, riboflavin, calcium, and iron are its nutrients.

1 **cup dried apricots**
1 **unbaked 9-inch pastry shell**
3 **eggs**
½ **teaspoon grated lemon peel**
1 **teaspoon lemon juice**
¾ **cup sugar**
1 **tablespoon flour**
½ **teaspoon salt**
1½ **cups creamed cottage cheese, sieved**
Sweetened whipped cream

1. Rinse and drain apricots; cut into small pieces and distribute over bottom of pastry shell.
2. Combine eggs, lemon peel, and lemon juice in a bowl; beat slightly. Blend sugar, flour, and salt; add gradually to egg mixture, beating constantly. Add cottage cheese and mix until blended. Pour over apricots in pastry shell.
3. Bake at 375°F about 35 minutes, or until a knife inserted near center comes out clean.
4. Set pie on wire rack to cool before serving.
5. Garnish each serving with a dollop of whipped cream.

One 9-inch pie

Marlborough Pie

This applesauce-custard pie is easy to make and delicious to eat. You'll be serving vitamins A and D, B vitamins, calcium, and iron, too.

1½ cups applesauce
 ¾ cup firmly packed brown sugar
  4 eggs, slightly beaten
 ¼ cup butter or margarine, melted
  1 teaspoon grated lemon peel
  3 tablespoons lemon juice
 ½ teaspoon salt
 ¼ teaspoon ground nutmeg
  1 unbaked 9-inch pastry shell

1. Combine applesauce, brown sugar, eggs, butter, lemon peel and juice, salt, and nutmeg; mix well. Turn into pastry shell.
2. Bake at 450°F 15 minutes. Turn oven control to 300°F and bake 45 to 55 minutes, or until a knife comes out clean when inserted in filling halfway between center and edge. Cool on a wire rack.

One 9-inch pie

Cherry-Rhubarb Pie

To rhubarb lovers, almost nothing can beat the taste of this cherry-rhubarb combination. There's nutritional value, too—vitamin A, calcium, and some vitamin C.

  1 can (16 ounces) pitted tart red cherries (water packed), drained
  1 pound fresh rhubarb, sliced about ⅛ inch thick
1¼ cups sugar
 ¼ cup quick-cooking tapioca
 ⅛ teaspoon baking soda
 ½ teaspoon almond extract
     Few drops red food coloring
     Pastry for a 2-crust 9-inch pie

1. Mix cherries, rhubarb, sugar, tapioca, baking soda, almond extract, and red food coloring; let stand 20 minutes.
2. Prepare pastry. Roll out enough pastry to line a 9-inch pie pan or plate; line pie pan. Roll out remaining pastry for top crust and slit pastry with knife in several places to allow steam to escape during baking.
3. Pour filling into pastry-lined pan; cover with top crust and flute edge.
4. Bake at 450°F 10 minutes. Turn oven control to 350°F and bake 40 to 45 minutes. Remove from oven and set on a wire rack. Serve warm or cooled.

One 9-inch pie

Banana-Butterscotch Pie

Homemade butterscotch pudding and flavorful ripe bananas combine here to make a delicious pie. Every slice contains vitamin A and B vitamins.

¾ cup firmly packed brown sugar
5 tablespoons flour
½ teaspoon salt
2 cups milk
2 egg yolks, slightly beaten
2 tablespoons butter or margarine
1 teaspoon vanilla extract
1 baked 9-inch pastry shell
3 ripe bananas
Whipped cream (optional)

1. Mix brown sugar, flour, and salt in the top of a double boiler. Add milk gradually, stirring until blended. Set over boiling water and cook, stirring constantly until thickened, about 8 minutes. Cover and cook 10 minutes, stirring occasionally.

2. Stir about 3 tablespoons hot mixture vigorously into egg yolks. Immediately blend into mixture in double-boiler top. Cook and stir over boiling water about 5 minutes.

3. Remove from water. Mix in butter and vanilla extract; set aside to cool to lukewarm.

4. Turn half of filling into the baked pastry shell. Cut bananas into crosswise slices and arrange over filling. Turn remaining filling over bananas. Top with whipped cream, if desired.

One 9-inch pie

Lemon-Buttermilk Pie/ Vanilla-Buttermilk Pie

Whichever way you choose to prepare this buttermilk pie, it is a crowd pleaser, rich in protein, riboflavin, vitamin D, and calcium.

3 egg yolks
½ teaspoon grated lemon peel
3 tablespoons lemon juice
½ cup sugar
2 tablespoons flour
¼ teaspoon salt
3 tablespoons butter or margarine, melted

1. Combine egg yolks, lemon peel, and lemon juice in a bowl. Blend ½ cup sugar, flour, and salt. Add to egg-yolk mixture and beat until blended. Mix in melted butter and buttermilk.

2. Beat egg whites until frothy. Add ¼ cup sugar gradually and continue beating until soft peaks are formed. Spread over butter-

1½ cups buttermilk
3 egg whites
¼ cup sugar
1 unbaked 9-inch pastry shell

milk mixture and fold together. Turn into unbaked pastry shell.

3. Bake at 450°F 10 minutes. Turn oven control to 350°F and bake 20 to 25 minutes, or until a knife comes out clean when inserted in filling halfway between center and edge. Cool on a wire rack.

One 9-inch pie

Vanilla-Buttermilk Pie: Follow recipe for Lemon-Buttermilk Pie, omitting lemon peel and juice. Decrease sugar in egg-yolk mixture to 6 or 7 tablespoons, increase buttermilk to 1⅔ cups, and mix in **1½ teaspoons vanilla extract.**

Pear-Meringue Pie

Just about as simple to prepare as a baked pie can be, this meringue treat is also a good source of vitamin A, riboflavin, calcium, and iron.

1 can (29 ounces) pear halves, well drained
1 unbaked 9-inch pastry shell
3 egg yolks
½ cup milk
½ cup firmly packed brown sugar
½ teaspoon grated lemon peel
1 tablespoon lemon juice
¼ teaspoon almond extract
3 egg whites
⅓ cup granulated sugar

1. Arrange pear halves, cut side down, in pastry shell.

2. Beat egg yolks, milk, brown sugar, lemon peel and juice, and almond extract together; pour over pears.

3. Bake at 350°F about 35 minutes.

4. Beat egg whites until frothy; gradually add granulated sugar, beating constantly, until stiff peaks are formed. Swirl meringue over filling. Return to oven and bake 15 to 20 minutes, or until golden brown. Cool on a wire rack.

One 9-inch pie

Pineapple Volcano Chiffon Pie

You might have to use your imagination to see the volcanoes in this pie, but you won't have to imagine the B vitamins, vitamin C, and calcium it contains.

2 envelopes unflavored gelatin
½ cup sugar
¼ teaspoon salt
3 egg yolks, fork beaten
½ cup water
1 can (20 ounces) crushed pineapple (undrained)
¼ teaspoon grated lemon peel
1 tablespoon lemon juice
3 egg whites
 Frozen dessert topping, thawed, or whipped dessert topping
1 baked 9-inch graham cracker crust
1 can (8¼ ounces) crushed pineapple, drained

1. Mix gelatin, ¼ cup sugar, and salt in the top of a double boiler.

2. Beat egg yolks and water together. Stir into gelatin mixture along with undrained pineapple.

3. Set over boiling water. Thoroughly beat mixture and continue cooking 5 minutes to cook egg yolks and dissolve gelatin, stirring constantly.

4. Remove from water; mix in lemon peel and juice. Chill, stirring occasionally until mixture mounds slightly when dropped from a spoon.

5. Beat egg whites until frothy. Gradually add remaining ¼ cup sugar, beating until stiff peaks are formed. Fold into gelatin mixture.

6. Turn filling into crust; chill.

7. Garnish pie with generous mounds of the dessert topping. Spoon on remaining crushed pineapple to resemble "volcanoes."

One 9-inch pie

Beverages

You'll love these refreshing beverages. They're much more flavorful and attractive than a glass of cola—and so much more nutritious.

Whether it's a tangy vegetable cocktail or a flavorful fruit drink, you'll find all these beverages delicious and appealing. Orange, tomato, cranberry, and apricot juices, bananas, cantaloupe, and cucumber are only some of the ingredients that are used in these recipes. Mixed with ginger ale, they make lively, sparkling thirst-quenchers; mixed with ice cream or milk, they become cool and creamy refreshers. Even tea and coffee can be mixed with fruit juices to make delightful drinks.

Here you'll find recipes for tantalizing, nutritious beverages to fit any occasion. You'll enjoy them anytime you want a quick pick-me-up, a between-meal snack, or a friendly appetizer to introduce a meal. All of these beverages and punches are pretty enough for party-time and can complement both casual get-togethers with friends and more formal gatherings the whole year 'round. Serve a frosty cooler with the tart-sweet flavor of citrus, such as *Orange-Grapefruit Cooler*, for a perfect summer afternoon treat or as an appetizer. A fruity milk shake like *Orange Shake* or *Chocolate-Banana Punch*, topped with scoops of ice cream, is a great dessert. For special occasions, serve the lovely *Pink Grapefruit Cloud*, tinted with maraschino cherry syrup and topped with a light meringue. *Hot Buttered Cranberry Punch* can warm you up on a winter afternoon or take the chill off any cool evening.

Garnishes are important final touches that add both flavor and eye-appeal to beverages. Whether it's a sprinkling of nutmeg, a slice of tangy lime, a sprig of mint, or a bright strawberry, a garnish can prove to be the little extra that turns a simple beverage into something special.

A great-looking, great-tasting beverage will delight both family and guests—serve one soon!

Hot Buttered Cranberry Punch

This buttered punch, with its tangy cranberry taste, could easily become everybody's by-the-fire favorite. Vitamin C and calcium will be appreciated, too.

2 cups water
4 cups fresh cranberries, rinsed
1½ cups water
⅔ cup firmly packed brown sugar
½ teaspoon ground cinnamon
¼ teaspoon ground allspice
¼ teaspoon ground cloves
⅛ teaspoon ground nutmeg
⅛ teaspoon salt
1 can (18 ounces) unsweetened pineapple juice
Butter or margarine
Cinnamon sticks (optional)

1. Bring the 2 cups water to boiling in a saucepan. Add cranberries and cook uncovered, without stirring, 5 minutes, or until skins pop.
2. Force cranberries through a food mill or sieve to make a purée (or use an electric blender).
3. Meanwhile, combine 1½ cups water, brown sugar, spices, and salt in a saucepan; bring to boiling.
4. Add the cranberry purée and pineapple juice. Return to heat and simmer 5 minutes. Keep hot over simmering water until serving time.
5. Ladle punch into serving cups or mugs and add dots of butter to each cup. Serve with cinnamon-stick stirrers, if desired.

About 1½ quarts beverage

Pink Grapefruit Cloud

Grapefruit juice, which is rich in vitamin C and calcium, is mixed here with cherry syrup and ginger ale, and topped with meringue for a festive touch.

1 can (6 ounces) frozen grapefruit juice concentrate, reconstituted as directed
½ cup maraschino cherry syrup
1 cup chilled ginger ale
2 egg whites
¼ cup sugar
Ground nutmeg

1. Mix reconstituted grapefruit juice, cherry syrup, and ginger ale; chill.
2. Shortly before serving, beat egg whites until frothy. Add sugar gradually, continuing to beat until stiff peaks are formed.
3. Pour grapefruit mixture into glasses, top with meringue, and sprinkle with nutmeg.

5 cups beverage

Watermelon Punch

Watermelon juice, sweet and cooling, is the basis of this party punch, that will make a special occasion of any event. Vitamins A and C plus calcium are the main nutrients.

2½ cups water
¼ cup lemon juice
1 cup sugar
3 cups watermelon juice*
2 cups orange juice
6 tablespoons lemon juice
Ice
Lemon, lime, and orange slices

1. Combine one-half of the water, ¼ cup lemon juice, and sugar in a saucepan; mix well. Bring to boiling and boil 3 minutes.
2. Mix in remaining water and fruit juices. Chill thoroughly.
3. Pour over ice in a punch bowl. Garnish with fruit slices.

About 2 quarts punch

* To prepare watermelon juice, extract juice from diced watermelon (about 5½ cups) by pressing it against the sides of a fine sieve. If desired, strain juice through cheesecloth.

Cinnamon Hot Chocolate

This spicy variation of the classic hot chocolate recipe provides protein, vitamin A, riboflavin, and calcium.

2 ounces (2 squares) unsweetened chocolate
½ cup strong coffee
½ cup sugar
1 teaspoon ground cinnamon
Few grains ground allspice
Few grains salt
3 cups milk
1½ teaspoons vanilla extract
Whipped cream (optional)

1. Heat chocolate and coffee together in a heavy saucepan, stirring until chocolate is melted and mixture is smooth. Cook 2 minutes, stirring constantly.
2. Mix in sugar, cinnamon, allspice, and salt. Add milk gradually, stirring until blended; heat thoroughly.
3. Remove from heat; blend in vanilla extract. Top each serving with whipped cream, if desired.

About 1 quart beverage

Sparkling Punch

The members of the crowd might never guess what went into the punch bowl in this case, but they are bound to be impressed with the result; they'll be getting vitamin C and calcium.

2½ cups sugar
 1 quart water
 1 cup tea (¼ cup black tea or 4 to 6 tea bags and 1⅓ cups boiling water, following package directions for brewing)
 2 cups lemon juice, chilled
 ½ cup orange juice, chilled
 ½ cup grape juice, chilled
 2 tablespoons chopped fresh mint leaves (or 1 tablespoon dried flakes)
 2 tablespoons chopped cucumber peel
   Few grains cayenne pepper
   Ice
 1 quart ginger ale, chilled
   Hulled ripe whole strawberries
   Sweetened fresh pineapple chunks (or drained canned)

1. Mix sugar and water in a heavy saucepan. Set over low heat and stir until sugar is dissolved. Increase heat, cover, and boil 5 minutes. Cool and chill.

2. When ready to serve, stir tea, juices, mint, cucumber peel, and cayenne into syrup. Pour over ice in a punch bowl. Add ginger ale and stir gently to blend. Garnish with strawberries and pineapple.

About 4 quarts punch

Fruit Medley Punch

A large, ripe banana adds just the right flavor to this mixture of fruit juices and contributes to the nutrients, which include vitamins A and C, calcium, and some protein.

¾ cup sugar
   Few grains salt
 2 cups water
 1 large ripe banana, peeled and cut in pieces

1. Blend sugar, salt, and 2 cups water in a saucepan. Bring to boiling; reduce heat and simmer 2 minutes. Cool; chill.

2. Put banana and orange juice into an electric blender container; cover and blend. Add

½ cup orange juice
¼ cup lemon juice
1 can (12 ounces) apricot nectar
½ cup instant nonfat dry milk
½ cup water

lemon juice and apricot nectar to container and blend thoroughly. Chill.

3. Mix nonfat dry milk and ½ cup water thoroughly; chill.

4. Just before serving, combine chilled syrup, fruit mixture, and milk in chilled pitcher and stir well.

About 1½ quarts beverage

Chocolate-Banana Punch

With or without the ice cream topping, this banana-flavored milk punch is a good source of vitamins A and C, riboflavin, and calcium.

8 ripe bananas
6 cups milk
1 cup instant chocolate-flavored drink mix
1 teaspoon vanilla extract
1½ pints vanilla ice cream
Scoops vanilla ice cream (optional)

1. Cut about one-third of bananas into large pieces and put into an electric blender container. Add one-third of each: milk, drink mix, vanilla extract, and ice cream; blend thoroughly. Pour into a chilled large pitcher. Repeat twice with remaining ingredients.

2. Pour into glasses or a punch bowl and, if desired, top with scoops of ice cream.

About 2 quarts beverage

Icy Nectarine-Plum Whirl

This refreshing fruit-flavored milk mixture gives you the nutrients of milk, plus vitamins A and C supplied by the fruits.

1 or 2 firm ripe nectarines
2 or 3 ripe red plums
½ cup sugar
½ cup milk
3 tablespoons lemon juice
1 cup crushed ice

1. Rinse, cut into halves, remove pits, and cut the nectarines and plums into pieces (enough to yield ½ cup each).

2. Put fruit into an electric blender container with sugar, milk, lemon juice, and ice. Cover; blend until thoroughly mixed. Serve immediately.

About 2½ cups beverage

Four-Fruit Refresher

These four fruit juices with the added fizz of ginger ale make a thirst-quencher that is easy to prepare and full of vitamins A and C and calcium.

2 cups apple juice
1 cup cranberry juice cocktail
1 cup orange juice
2 tablespoons lemon juice
1 teaspoon vanilla extract
2 tablespoons sugar
1 cup chilled ginger ale

1. Blend fruit juices and vanilla extract. Add sugar and stir until completely dissolved. Chill thoroughly.
2. When ready to serve, add ginger ale to fruit-juice mixture; stir to blend.

About 5 cups beverage

Cantaloupe Cooler

Use the blender to turn diced cantaloupe into a liquid nectar which combines with the other ingredients to make a smashing summer drink filled with vitamins A and C and calcium.

4 cups diced ripe cantaloupe
½ cup sugar
Few grains salt
6 tablespoons lime juice
3 cups pineapple-grapefruit juice drink
Crushed ice
Mint sprigs

1. Using an electric blender, liquefy cantaloupe. Pour into a pitcher and add sugar, salt, lime juice, and juice drink; mix well. Chill thoroughly.
2. To serve, stir beverage and pour into glasses half-filled with crushed ice. Garnish with mint.

1½ quarts beverage

Citrus Fruit Punch

Both fruit juices and fruit go into this citrus special which is guaranteed to appeal to all tastes while providing vitamins A and C and calcium.

1 can (6 ounces) frozen orange juice concentrate
1 can (6 ounces) frozen grapefruit juice concentrate

1. Mix orange and grapefruit juice concentrates, water, apricot nectar, and pineapple juice in a pitcher. Chill.
2. Just before serving, alternate strawberries

2¼ cups water
1 can (6 ounces) apricot nectar
¾ cup unsweetened pineapple juice
Whole strawberries and pineapple chunks
3 cups chilled ginger ale

and pineapple chunks on plastic straws to make kabobs. Place in tall glasses with ice. Add ginger ale to fruit juice mixture and pour into glasses.

2 quarts beverage

Hot Spiced Cider

Along with its invigorating warmth, welcome on a winter day, this spiced cider gives you some vitamins and minerals.

2 quarts sweet apple cider
1 teaspoon whole cloves
1 teaspoon whole allspice
2 cinnamon sticks (about 3 inches each)
½ cup firmly packed light brown sugar
Few grains salt
Red apple slices

1. Combine apple cider, cloves, allspice, cinnamon sticks, brown sugar, and salt in a large saucepan. Bring to boiling; simmer, covered, 30 minutes. Remove spices.
2. Serve hot, garnished with apple slices.

About 2 quarts beverage

Orange-Grapefruit Cooler

Almost everyone likes the orange-and-grapefruit combination, and the addition of mint gives it a new twist. Vitamins A and C and calcium are the chief nutrients.

1 can (6 ounces) frozen orange juice concentrate, reconstituted as directed
1 can (6 ounces) frozen grapefruit juice concentrate, reconstituted as directed
Orange wedges
Mint sprigs

1. Pour reconstituted orange juice into an ice cube tray and freeze.
2. Put orange ice cubes into tall glasses and pour cold grapefruit juice over them. Garnish with orange wedges and mint sprigs.

4 servings

Orange Shake

Undiluted frozen orange juice is the key to the rich flavor of this ice cream shake, which provides vitamins A and C, riboflavin, calcium, and some protein.

1 **can (6 ounces) frozen orange juice concentrate, thawed**
1½ **cups vanilla ice cream**
2¼ **cups milk**
4 **scoops vanilla ice cream**
 Maraschino cherries

1. Combine orange juice concentrate, 1½ cups ice cream, and milk in an electric blender container. Cover; process at high speed until smooth.
2. Pour into 4 tall glasses, top with scoops of ice cream, garnish with maraschino cherries, and serve with straws.

4 servings

Note: For a simple orange frappé, pour the orange juice concentrate over shaved or crushed ice in glasses.

Peanut Butter Milk Drink

You have to drink this one to believe it. You know it has protein, and it's also got vitamin A, niacin, riboflavin, vitamin D, and calcium.

¾ **cup cold water**
⅓ **cup instant nonfat dry milk**
1 **tablespoon sugar**
 Few grains salt
2 **tablespoons creamy peanut butter**
⅛ **teaspoon vanilla extract**

Combine water, dry milk, sugar, salt, peanut butter, and vanilla extract in a chilled electric blender container; blend thoroughly.

About 1 cup beverage

Sunshine Cocktail

To enjoy this delicious blend of vegetable and fruit juices, all you need is a good blender. Vitamins A and C are the special nutrients.

1 **cup water**
½ **cup diced carrot**

1. Put water and carrot into an electric blender container and blend until liquefied.

1 piece (about 4 inches)
  celery, cut in pieces
¼ cup diced cucumber
½ cup orange juice
1 tablespoon lime juice
1 slice lemon with peel,
  quartered
1 tablespoon sugar
⅛ teaspoon salt
  Lime wedges

Add celery, cucumber, orange juice, lime juice, lemon, sugar, and salt; blend thoroughly. Chill, if desired.

2. Pour into small glasses and serve with lime wedges.

About 2 cups beverage

Tangy Cocktail

The vegetables and beef in this recipe make a special cocktail that is high in vitamins A and C.

1 can (10½ ounces)
  condensed beef broth
1 can (12 ounces) cocktail
  vegetable juice
1 teaspoon grated onion
1 teaspoon Worcestershire
  sauce
2 drops Tabasco
  Lemon wedges

1. Blend condensed beef broth and vegetable juice. Mix in onion, Worcestershire sauce, and Tabasco. Chill thoroughly.

2. Pour into small glasses and serve with lemon wedges.

About 3 cups beverage

Note: If desired, heat mixture thoroughly and serve hot.

Molasses-Banana Milk Drink

This blend with bananas and milk provides protein, vitamin A, riboflavin, vitamin D, and calcium, and makes an ice-cold summer delight.

2 cups milk
2 medium ripe bananas,
  peeled and cut in pieces
¼ cup light molasses
¼ teaspoon ground ginger
  Ice

1. Combine milk, bananas, molasses, and ginger in an electric blender container; blend until smooth. Chill thoroughly.

2. To serve, pour over ice in glasses.

About 3 cups beverage

Apricot Eggnog

Rich and creamy, this fruity eggnog is laden with vitamin A, calcium, and good taste.

2 eggs, slightly beaten
⅓ cup sugar
⅛ teaspoon salt
1½ cups milk, scalded
1½ cups cold milk
1 teaspoon vanilla extract
¼ teaspoon almond extract
1 can (12 ounces) apricot nectar, chilled
½ cup chilled whipping cream, whipped

1. Combine eggs, sugar, and salt in a bowl. Add the scalded milk gradually, stirring constantly. Pour into a double boiler and cook over simmering water, stirring constantly until mixture begins to coat a spoon.
2. Remove from simmering water and stir in cold milk, vanilla extract, and almond extract; strain. Cool slightly, then chill thoroughly.
3. Blend apricot nectar into chilled custard, then fold in whipped cream.

About 1½ quarts eggnog

Appetite Teaser

See who can guess what's in this unusual combination of orange juice and tomato juice. If they guess right, of course they'll know it's high on vitamins A and C.

1 can (20 ounces) tomato juice
½ cup orange juice
2 tablespoons lemon juice
2 tablespoons chopped onion
1 teaspoon prepared horseradish
1 teaspoon sugar
¼ teaspoon salt
¼ teaspoon paprika
¼ teaspoon celery seed
½ bay leaf
4 whole cloves
Few drops Tabasco

1. Pour juices into a saucepan. Add onion, horseradish, sugar, salt, paprika, celery seed, bay leaf, cloves, and Tabasco; mix well. Set over low heat and bring to boiling. Remove from heat and strain.
2. Chill thoroughly. Serve in small glasses.

About 3 cups beverage

Preserving

Rows of glass jars filled with the jewellike colors of jams, conserves, pickles, relishes, and other homemade preserves are a delight to every homemaker's eye and a ready source for spur-of-the-moment additions of sweetness, spice, and color to meals. Commercial counterparts cannot compare in flavor and variety with homemade products. So try your hand at making your own—you'll be rewarded with delicious jams, jellies, and other condiments that are full of flavor and full of vitamins. Serving possibilities are virtually endless. All-time favorites, such as *Old-Fashioned Cauliflower Pickles* and *Favorite Corn Relish*, will add zest to any meal and spark up a buffet table. Serve fruit or vegetable condiments, such as *Apple-Date Chutney* or *Cucumber-Pepper Relish*, with meat or cheese sandwiches or with rice and meat casseroles. Fruit jams and preserves are delectable on freshly baked bread, but try them also as tasty toppers to ice cream, as fillings in pastries, cakes, and cookies, or as spreads for pancakes and waffles. Fruit conserves, such as *Cranberry-Walnut Conserve*, are delicious accompaniments to meat, poultry, and game. And all of these homemade preserves, sealed in pretty jars and tied with ribbon, make lovely gifts for any occasion.

Making preserves in the home requires a minimum of special equipment. Have on hand a kettle or saucepot, a large spoon, a sieve, a colander, jelly bag, or cheesecloth, fruit jars and caps, and paraffin, and you're all set. Occasionally a candy thermometer is helpful. Select fruits and vegetables of proper ripeness at the height of their season to give optimum color and flavor to home preserves. Follow recipe directions and timings carefully to assure successful jelly-making and preserving

There's plenty of room for imagination in home preserving, too. For example, amounts and types of herbs and spices can be altered to make subtle—or distinctive—changes in flavor. Many jams and conserves are made with two or more fruits; mix and match your favorites for new taste combinations. Store your homemade preserves in a cool place—and serve them often.

Zucchini Pickle Slices

Here is a variation of the classic bread-and-butter pickle. In addition to great flavor, you'll be getting vitamins A and C and calcium.

1	quart cider vinegar
2	cups sugar
½	cup salt
1	tablespoon celery seed
2	teaspoons mustard seed
½	teaspoon ground turmeric
5	pounds zucchini, scrubbed and sliced ¼ inch thick (about 4 quarts)
1½	pounds onions, peeled and very thinly sliced (about 5 cups)

1. Combine vinegar, sugar, salt, celery seed, mustard seed, and turmeric in a kettle. Bring to boiling, stirring until sugar is dissolved. Remove from heat. Stir in sliced zucchini and onions. Cover; let stand 1 hour.

2. Heat zucchini mixture to boiling. Reduce heat; simmer, uncovered, 3 minutes. Remove from heat.

3. With slotted spoon, immediately ladle zucchini and onion slices into hot sterilized jars, completing one jar at a time. Fill with vinegar mixture to within ½ inch of top, covering vegetables completely. Seal jars immediately, following manufacturer's directions. Cool and store.

About 8 pints pickles

Old-Fashioned Cauliflower Pickles

Pickling is so easy and rewarding it's no wonder good cooks everywhere are delighting their families and friends with treats such as this cauliflower classic, which contains vitamins A and C.

3	large heads (2½ to 3 pounds each) cauliflower, rinsed
	Water
1	quart white vinegar
2½	cups sugar
½	cup dried onion flakes
2½	teaspoons salt
2	teaspoons mustard seed
2	teaspoons celery seed
1	teaspoon ground turmeric
10	whole cloves

1. Remove large leaves from cauliflower; break into flowerets.

2. Bring 4 quarts water to boiling in a large saucepot. Add cauliflower. Cover; remove from heat and let stand while preparing the vinegar mixture.

3. Put 1½ quarts water into a large saucepan. Add vinegar, sugar, onion flakes, salt, mustard seed, celery seed, and turmeric. Tie cloves and red pepper in cheesecloth. Add to vinegar mixture. Bring to boiling. Boil, uncovered, 5 minutes.

1 dried red pepper
1 can (4 ounces) pimiento, drained and cut in strips

4. Drain water from cauliflower. Pour hot vinegar mixture over cauliflower. Add pimiento. Return to boiling point and cook about 5 minutes, or until cauliflower is crisp-tender. Remove spice bag.

5. Ladle cauliflower mixture into hot sterilized jars. Seal immediately, following manufacturer's directions. Cool and store.

About 5 quarts pickles

Minted Watermelon Pickles

Everyone loves these wonderful pickles that provide a reminder of summer on a winter day. Watermelon contains vitamins A and C.

Rind of 1 large watermelon (about 12 cups cut rind)
¼ cup salt
7 pints water (14 cups)
8 cups sugar
2 cups cider vinegar
2 lemons, thinly sliced
3 cinnamon sticks (3 inches each)
2 teaspoons whole cloves
2 teaspoons whole allspice
1 tablespoon mint extract
Green food coloring

1. Pare watermelon rind, removing green and pink portions. Cut rind into 1- to 1¼-inch squares. Add salt to 8 cups of water; stir until salt is dissolved. Pour over watermelon rind and let stand overnight. Drain.

2. Cover rind with fresh water and cook, covered, about 1 hour, or until rind is tender. Drain thoroughly.

3. Combine remaining 6 cups water with sugar and vinegar in a 4-quart saucepan; cook over medium heat about 8 minutes.

4. Tie lemon slices and the spices in cheesecloth; add to syrup with the rind. Cook, uncovered, until rind is clear, about 1 hour.

5. Stir in mint extract and several drops food coloring; blend well. Remove rind from syrup with a slotted spoon and pack into hot sterilized jars. Pour syrup over rind, filling to within ½ inch of top. Release air bubbles by running a knife down the side of each jar several times. Seal immediately, following manufacturer's directions. Cool and store.

6 to 7 pints pickles

Annie's Delicious Red Pepper Pickles

Annie was on to a good thing when she put this simple but delicious pickle recipe together. Vitamins A and C are the nutritional benefits.

12 **large sweet red peppers (about 3½ pounds)**
2½ **cups cider vinegar**
1¼ **cups sugar**
1 **cinnamon stick (about 3 inches)**
12 **whole cloves**

1. Wash peppers, quarter lengthwise, remove seeds and white membrane, and cut each quarter into strips about ¾ inch wide.
2. Pour boiling water over peppers in a bowl; cover and set aside about 3 minutes. Drain off the water and immediately cover peppers with icy cold water. Set aside about 10 minutes.
3. Meanwhile, combine vinegar, sugar, cinnamon, and cloves (cloves tied in cheesecloth) in a saucepan. Bring to boiling, stirring until sugar is dissolved. Boil 2 to 3 minutes and remove spices.
4. Put peppers into a colander to drain thoroughly, then pack into hot sterilized jars and pour in the hot pickling liquid. Release air bubbles by running a knife down the side of each jar several times. If necessary, add more hot pickling liquid to fill to within ½ inch of top. Seal jars immediately, following manufacturer's directions. Cool and store.

3 pints pickles

Garden Relish

For a fresh-from-the-garden taste try this crisp combination of salad vegetables. It is uncooked, so all the flavor, vitamins (A and C), and calcium remain intact.

15 **cherry tomatoes, chopped**
¼ **cup chopped celery**
¼ **cup chopped green pepper**
2 **green onions, chopped**
¼ **teaspoon salt**
¼ **teaspoon seasoned salt**
2 **teaspoons prepared mustard**
1 **teaspoon cider vinegar**

1. Combine tomatoes, celery, green pepper, and onions. Drain off any excess liquid that may accumulate after chopping. Combine vegetables with salt, seasoned salt, prepared mustard, and vinegar.
2. Chill thoroughly before serving.

About 1½ cups relish

Curry Pickles

Curry adds a new flavor to the traditional cucumber pickle, which provides vitamin C and calcium.

3	**pounds 5-inch cucumbers (unpared)**
1¾	**cups cider vinegar**
1¼	**cups water**
1	**cup sugar**
2	**tablespoons mustard seed**
2	**tablespoons salt**
1½	**teaspoons curry powder**
1½	**teaspoons celery salt**

1. Wash cucumbers and cut into 1-inch chunks.
2. Combine vinegar, water, sugar, mustard seed, salt, curry powder, and celery salt in a saucepot. Bring to boiling. Add cucumbers and return to boiling. Reduce heat to simmer and ladle mixture into hot sterilized jars. Fill jars to within ⅛ inch of top; be sure the liquid covers cucumbers. Seal jars immediately, following manufacturer's directions. Cool and store.

About 5 pints pickles

Green Tomato Pickles

Several green vegetables are combined in this recipe, making it a storehouse of vitamins A and C plus calcium. You'll like the flavor, too.

5	**unpared cucumbers (5 inches each), thinly sliced**
1½	**pounds green tomatoes, cored and thinly sliced**
1½	**pounds onions, sliced**
4	**green peppers, chopped**
1	**red pepper, chopped**
3	**cups vinegar**
4	**cups sugar**
1	**tablespoon salt**
1	**tablespoon celery seed**
1	**tablespoon mustard seed**

1. Wash and prepare vegetables.
2. Combine vinegar, sugar, salt, celery seed, and mustard seed in a saucepan; bring to boiling. Add vegetables and simmer 10 minutes.
3. Continue simmering and ladle mixture into hot sterilized jars. Fill jars to within ⅛ inch of top; be sure liquid covers vegetables. Seal jars immediately, following manufacturer's directions. Cool and store.

About 5 pints pickles

Cucumber-Pepper Relish

If you relish relishes try this unusual mixture for a new taste sensation. It's easy to prepare, and it provides vitamins A and C plus calcium.

1 **quart coarsely chopped pared cucumber**
2 **cups coarsely chopped green pepper**
1 **cup coarsely chopped red pepper**
1 **cup coarsely chopped onion**
1 **cup chopped ripe tomatoes**
1½ **cups cider vinegar**
¾ **cup sugar**
2 **tablespoons salt**
1 **tablespoon celery seed**
1 **teaspoon ground turmeric**
1 **tablespoon whole allspice**
1 **tablespoon whole cloves**
3 **cinnamon sticks (3 inches each)**

1. Put vegetables into a saucepot. Add vinegar, sugar, salt, celery seed, and turmeric; stir. Tie allspice, cloves, and cinnamon in a 9-inch square of cheesecloth (double thickness). Add spice bag to saucepot. Bring to boiling, stirring until sugar is dissolved. Simmer, uncovered, 30 minutes, stirring occasionally.
2. Immediately fill hot sterilized jars and seal, following manufacturer's directions. Cool and store.

3 pints relish

Favorite Corn Relish

As a flavorful side dish, corn relish adds a distinctive touch to even a simple meal. It also gives you vitamins A and C plus calcium.

1 **quart whole kernel corn (about 8 medium-size fresh corn ears or three 10-ounce packages defrosted frozen kernel corn)**
½ **small head young green cabbage, finely chopped**
2 **medium sweet red peppers, cut in small squares**
½ **bunch celery including heart, edible portion of root, and tender leaves, finely chopped**

1. If using fresh corn, cut kernels from cobs (do not scrape cobs).
2. Combine corn in a large kettle with cabbage, red peppers, celery, onion, garlic, and celery seed. Blend sugar, salt, dry mustard, turmeric, and cayenne; add to kettle. Stir in vinegar.
3. Bring mixture to boiling over medium heat; reduce heat and simmer, uncovered, 15 to 20 minutes. Do not overcook. (Celery should be crisp-tender.)
4. If the consistency of relish is too thin, combine flour with cold water and blend into

1 large onion, finely chopped
1 small clove garlic, minced
1½ teaspoons celery seed
1 cup sugar
1 tablespoon salt
1 tablespoon dry mustard
1 teaspoon ground turmeric
¼ teaspoon ground cayenne pepper
2 cups cider vinegar
2 to 3 tablespoons flour (optional)
½ cup cold water (optional)

the relish. Bring to boiling and continue cooking until the liquid portion is thickened and smooth, stirring constantly.

5. Immediately ladle into hot sterilized jars and seal, following manufacturer's directions. Cool and store.

5 pints relish

Cranberry-Walnut Conserve

This combination of flavors and textures offers a new taste treat when served with a waffle or an English muffin, and it provides niacin, vitamin C, calcium, and iron.

1 orange (unpeeled), finely chopped
2 cups water
1 pound cranberries, rinsed
3 cups sugar
½ cup seedless raisins
½ cup chopped walnuts

1. Combine orange and water in a saucepan. Cook rapidly until peel is tender (about 20 minutes). Add cranberries, sugar, and raisins. Bring to boiling over low heat, stirring occasionally until sugar is dissolved. Increase heat and boil about 8 minutes; as mixture thickens, stir frequently to prevent sticking; add walnuts the last 5 minutes of cooking.

2. Ladle conserve into hot sterilized jars. Seal immediately, following manufacturer's directions.

3. Process 10 to 15 minutes at simmering (180 to 185°F) in a water-bath canner.* Cool and store.

About 4 half-pints conserve

* For a water-bath canner, put a rack in a saucepot and set filled jars on rack. Pour in hot water to cover 1 or 2 inches above jars. Cover saucepot and bring water to simmering before starting the timing.

Apricot Conserve

This recipe is simple and quick to prepare, yet very rewarding to eat. Vitamin A, niacin, and iron are the nutrients.

1½ **pounds dried apricots, cooked and cut in pieces**
1 **tablespoon grated orange peel**
2¼ **cups orange juice**
3 **tablespoons lemon juice**
5 **cups sugar**
1 **cup coarsely chopped walnuts**

1. Combine apricots, peel, juices, and sugar in a large heavy saucepan. Bring mixture to boiling and cook 10 minutes, stirring frequently. Mix in walnuts and cook until thick (about 5 minutes).

2. Ladle conserve into hot sterilized jars. Seal immediately, following manufacturer's directions. Cool and store.

About 8 half-pints conserve

Spiced Peach Jam

Spicy peaches find their way into many good recipes, and here they make a jam that's ideal for breakfast or as a condiment to meat and vegetable dishes. Peaches contain vitamin A.

1½ **pounds fully ripe peaches**
2 **tablespoons lemon juice**
¼ **teaspoon ground nutmeg**
4¼ **cups sugar**
¾ **cup water**
1 **box powdered fruit pectin**

1. Cut into halves, pit, peel, and grind peaches (about 1¾ cups, ground) into a large bowl or pan. Stir in lemon juice and nutmeg. Add sugar, mix well, and set aside.

2. Mix water and fruit pectin in a small saucepan. Bring to boiling and boil 1 minute, stirring constantly. Stir into fruit mixture. Continue stirring about 3 minutes. (There will be a few remaining sugar crystals.) Ladle jam immediately into hot sterilized jars, filling to within ½ inch of top. Cover immediately with lids, following manufacturer's directions. Let stand at room temperature until jam is set.

3. Store in refrigerator if jam is to be used within 2 or 3 weeks, or in freezer for longer storage.

About 3 pints jam

Rosemary Jelly

Delicate and subtle, the sweet-sour taste of this delicious jelly is just right for a bread-and-butter feast. You will also be serving vitamin A, B vitamins, calcium and iron.

2	teaspoons dried rosemary
1½	cups boiling water
3½	cups sugar
2	tablespoons cider vinegar
4	drops red food coloring
½	cup bottled fruit pectin
	Paraffin (optional)

1. Measure rosemary into a small bowl. Add boiling water and set aside 15 minutes.

2. Strain rosemary mixture into 3-quart saucepan and add sugar, vinegar, and food coloring. Set over medium heat and stir until sugar is dissolved. Increase heat and bring mixture to boiling. Immediately add fruit pectin. Boil rapidly 1 minute, stirring constantly. Remove from heat and skim off any foam.

3. Immediately fill hot sterilized glasses or jars and seal with paraffin or lids, following manufacturer's directions. Cool and store.

About 4 half-pints jelly

Strawberry-Lime Jam

Whether you serve this on hot biscuits or on ice cream, you're sure to get requests for more. Be generous with it, for strawberries are loaded with vitamin C.

	Fresh fully ripe strawberries (enough for 1¾ cups crushed fruit)
1	teaspoon grated lime peel
4	cups sugar
2	tablespoons lime juice
½	bottle liquid fruit pectin

1. Rinse, hull, slice, and crush berries. Turn into a large bowl. Stir in lime peel and sugar. Blend lime juice and fruit pectin; stir into fruit. Continue to stir 3 minutes. (A few sugar crystals will remain.)

2. Ladle jam immediately into hot sterilized jars. Seal, following manufacturer's directions. Let stand at room temperature until set, about 24 hours.

3. Store in refrigerator if jam is to be used within 2 or 3 weeks, or in freezer for longer storage.

About 4½ cups jam

Blueberry Jelly

Small amounts of vitamins and minerals, together with large amounts of good fruit flavor, are contained in this real old-fashioned jelly.

1 large lemon, sliced
3 quarts blueberries
3 pounds tart apples
   Sugar (about 4½ cups)
   Paraffin (optional)

1. Pour enough water over lemon slices to just cover (about 1 cup). Cover and refrigerate 12 hours or overnight.
2. Pick over blueberries, discarding blemished berries. Rinse and drain. Turn into a saucepot.
3. Wash apples; remove stems, blossom ends, and blemished portions.
4. Cut apples into quarters, put into a kettle, and cover with water (about 2½ cups). Cook covered, until apples are soft.
5. Drain liquid from lemon slices and stir into blueberries. (Discard lemon peel.) Cook, covered, until berries are soft and juice flows freely.
6. Pour both fruit mixtures into jelly bag* and let drain 6 to 12 hours. (There should be about 6 cups juice.)
7. To make jelly, measure half the juice into a 2-quart saucepan and bring rapidly to boiling. Then to each cup of juice, add ¾ cup sugar and stir until mixture responds to jelly test† or registers a temperature on a candy thermometer which is 8°F higher than boiling temperature of water in your locality. Remove from heat; skim foam from surface. Pour jelly into hot sterilized glasses or jars. Seal jars immediately or cover jelly with melted paraffin.
8. Repeat jelly-making, using remaining juice. Cool and store.

About 7 half-pints jelly

* To make a jelly bag if a commercial bag with frame is not available, cut a double thickness of cheesecloth about 36 inches long and fold in half. Dip cloth in hot water and wring well.

Put a large strainer or colander over a large bowl and lay the cloth in the strainer or colander. Ladle cooked fruit carefully into cheesecloth. Gather together the 4 corners of cloth and tie firmly. Allow juice to drip through cloth into bowl; do not squeeze.

† To test for jelly, dip a small amount of boiling syrup from saucepan with a cool metal spoon and slowly pour it back into saucepan from edge of spoon. Jelly is sufficiently cooked when drops of syrup run together and fall from spoon in a sheet. Remove from heat while testing.

Golden Jelly

Making jelly at home is still fun, as this simple recipe will prove. It will also put vitamins A and C plus calcium on your pantry shelf, ready for your eating pleasure.

4 cups sugar
2 cups orange juice
3 tablespoons lemon juice
2 tablespoons lime juice
½ cup bottled fruit pectin
½ pound paraffin, melted over simmering water

1. Put sugar and fruit juices into a heavy 3-quart saucepan. Bring to boiling, stirring until sugar is completely dissolved. Immediately stir fruit pectin into boiling liquid. Boil rapidly 1 minute, stirring constantly. Remove from heat; skim off any foam.

2. Immediately ladle into hot sterilized jelly glasses, filling to within ½ inch of top. Cover each glass with a layer of melted paraffin about ⅛ thick. Carefully tilt glass to make an even layer and seal paraffin to sides of glass. Prick any air bubbles. Allow to stand until paraffin hardens. Cover with lids. Cool and store.

About 6 half-pints jelly

Note: If using jelly jars, fill to within ⅛ inch of top. Seal immediately, following manufacturer's directions.

Rosy Banana-Peach Jam

Fresh bananas and peaches are combined here to make an unusually tempting jam. Vitamin A and some B vitamins are the nutrients you'll be getting.

1 cup mashed fully ripe bananas (about 3 medium)
3¼ cups mashed fully ripe peaches (about 2 pounds peaches, peeled)
½ cup drained chopped maraschino cherries
2 tablespoons lemon juice
1 box powdered fruit pectin
6 cups sugar

1. Combine prepared fruit and lemon juice in a large saucepan; mix in pectin. Stir and cook over high heat until mixture comes to a full rolling boil. Immediately add and stir in sugar. Bring to a full rolling boil; boil hard 1 minute, stirring constantly.
2. Remove from heat; skim foam with metal spoon and then stir and skim 5 minutes to cool slightly and prevent floating fruit.
3. Ladle jam into hot sterilized jars, filling to within ½ inch of top. Seal jars immediately, following manufacturer's directions. Cool and store.

About 8 half-pints jam

Cherry-Berry Preserves

Vitamins A and C plus calcium are not the only reasons for preserving this fruit combination. Another is its taste, which is a delight to the discriminating palate.

1 pound dark sweet cherries, rinsed, stemmed, pitted, and halved (about 2½ cups)
1 pint strawberries, rinsed, hulled and sliced (about 2 cups)
3 cups sugar
¼ cup water
½ cup lemon juice
¼ teaspoon almond extract

1. Combine cherries, strawberries, sugar, and water in a large saucepan. Set over low heat and stir until sugar is dissolved. Increase heat and bring mixture to boiling; boil 8 minutes. Stir in lemon juice and almond extract; boil 1 minute longer.
2. Remove from heat and skim off any foam.
3. Ladle preserves into hot sterilized jars, filling to within ¼ inch of top. Seal immediately, following manufacturer's directions. Cool and store.

About 4½ cups preserves

Strawberry-Rhubarb Jam

Strawberries and rhubarb are traditionally served together, and not just because they make a great taste combination; they also furnish vitamin C, calcium, and some vitamin A.

3 cups sliced rhubarb
2 cups sliced fresh ripe strawberries
2 tablespoons grated orange peel
1/3 cup orange juice
1 box powdered fruit pectin
5 1/2 cups sugar

1. Combine fruits, orange peel and juice, and pectin in a large saucepan.

2. Bring to a full boil over high heat, stirring constantly. Immediately stir in sugar and bring to a full rolling boil, continuing to stir; boil 1 minute.

3. Remove from heat. Stir the mixture 5 minutes to cool slightly. Ladle jam into hot sterilized jars, filling to within 1/2 inch of top. Seal immediately, following manufacturer's directions. Cool and store.

6 half-pints jam

Apple-Date Chutney

As an accompaniment to a curried dish, or in any number of other ways, chutney provides a delicious and sophisticated touch to your menu, while adding niacin, calcium, iron, and some vitamin A to your diet.

2 pounds tart apples
3 cups cider vinegar
2 cups packed brown sugar
3/4 teaspoon dry mustard
1 teaspoon salt
1 pound dates, chopped
1 large onion, chopped
1/2 cup chopped crystallized ginger

1. Core apples (do not pare) and chop finely. Put apples into a heavy saucepan and add vinegar. Cover tightly and bring to boiling. Reduce heat and cook until apples are tender, about 20 minutes. Add brown sugar, dry mustard, salt, dates, onion, and ginger; mix well. Bring to boiling; cook over low heat about 1 hour; stir frequently to prevent scorching.

2. Immediately ladle chutney into hot sterilized jars and seal, following manufacturer's directions. Cool and store.

6 half-pints chutney

Best-Ever Tomato Preserves

If you still remember grandmother's tomato preserves, this is your chance to recapture the good old days, together with vitamins A and C and calcium.

1 pound tart green apples
4 pounds firm ripe tomatoes
2 lemon slices, each ¼ inch thick
4 cups sugar
Red food coloring (optional)

1. Wash, quarter, core, pare, and cut apples into small cubes (about 3 cups).

2. Wash tomatoes, scald, peel, and cut out around stem ends. Cut tomatoes into small pieces (about 2 quarts).

3. Combine apples, tomatoes, and lemon slices in a large heavy saucepan. Bring to simmering over medium heat and stir in sugar. Boil gently about 1 hour, or until thick and clear; stir occasionally as the mixture begins to thicken. If desired, blend in several drops of red food coloring.

4. Ladle mixture into hot sterilized jars, filling to within ¼ inch of top. Seal immediately, following manufacturer's directions. Cool and store.

About 2 pints preserves

NUTRITIVE VALUES OF FOODS

(Dashes in the columns for nutrients show that no suitable value could be found although there is reason to believe that a measurable amount of the nutrient may be present. The abbreviations used are g for gram(s), mg for milligram(s), cal for calories, and IU for International Units.)

Food	Measure	Weight g	Water %	Cal	Protein g	Fat g	Carbo-hydrate g	Cal-cium mg	Iron mg	Vita-min A IU	Thia-mine mg	Ribo-flavin mg	Niacin mg	Vita-min C mg
Milk Group														
Cheese														
Cheddar	1 oz	28	37	115	7	9	1	213	.3	370	.01	.13	trace	0
cottage, creamed	12 oz	340	78	360	46	14	10	320	1.0	580	.10	.85	.3	0
cream	3 oz	85	51	320	7	32	2	53	.2	1,310	.02	.20	.1	0
Milk														
buttermilk	1 cup	245	90	90	9	trace	12	296	.1	10	.10	.44	.2	2
dry, nonfat, instant	1 cup	68	4	245	24	trace	35	879	.4	20	.24	1.21	.6	5
evaporated, undiluted	1 cup	252	74	345	18	20	24	635	.3	810	.10	.86	.5	3
skim (unfortified)	1 cup	245	90	90	9	trace	12	296	.1	10	.09	.44	.2	2
sweetened condensed, undiluted	1 cup	306	27	980	25	27	166	802	.3	1,100	.24	1.16	.6	3
whole	1 cup	244	87	160	9	9	12	288	.1	350	.07	.41	.2	2
Milk beverage														
cocoa, homemade	1 cup	250	79	245	10	12	27	295	1.0	400	.10	.45	.5	3
Milk desserts														
baked custard	1 cup	265	77	305	14	15	29	297	1.1	930	.11	.50	.3	1
ice cream	1 cup	133	63	255	6	14	28	194	.1	590	.05	.28	.1	1
Yogurt														
made from partially skimmed milk	1 cup	245	89	125	8	4	13	294	.1	170	.10	.44	.2	2
made from whole milk	1 cup	245	88	150	7	8	12	272	.1	340	.07	.39	.2	2
Meat Group														
Fish and Shellfish														
crabmeat, canned	3 oz	85	77	85	15	2	1	38	.7	—	.07	.07	1.6	—
fish sticks, breaded	8 oz pkg.	227	66	400	38	20	15	25	.9	—	.09	.16	3.6	—
flounder, cooked	3.5 oz	100	58	202	30	8	0	23	1.4	—	.07	.08	2.5	2
halibut, cooked	3.5 oz	100	67	171	25	7	0	16	.8	680	.05	.07	8.3	—
salmon, canned	3 oz	85	71	120	17	5	0	167	.7	60	.03	.16	6.8	—
shrimp, canned	3 oz	85	70	100	21	1	1	98	2.6	50	.01	.03	1.5	—
tuna, canned, drained	3 oz	85	61	170	24	7	0	7	1.6	70	.04	.10	10.1	—
Meat														
bacon, broiled or fried crisp	2 slices	15	8	90	5	8	1	2	.5	0	.08	.05	.8	—
beef														
ground, regular, broiled	3 oz	85	54	245	21	17	0	9	2.7	30	.07	.18	4.6	—
pot roast, lean	2.5 oz	72	62	140	22	5	0	10	2.7	10	.04	.16	3.3	—
steak, sirloin, lean only	2 oz	56	59	115	18	4	0	7	2.2	10	.05	.14	3.6	—
ham, roasted, lean and fat	3 oz	85	54	245	18	19	0	8	2.2	0	.40	.16	3.1	—
lamb														
chop, broiled, lean only	2.6 oz	74	62	140	21	6	0	9	1.5	—	.11	.20	4.5	—
leg, roasted, lean only	2.5 oz	71	62	130	20	5	0	9	1.4	—	.12	.21	4.4	—

Food	Measure	Weight g	Water %	Cal	Protein g	Fat g	Carbo-hydrate g	Cal-cium mg	Iron mg	Vita-min A IU	Thia-mine mg	Ribo-flavin mg	Niacin mg	Vita-min C mg
liver, beef, fried	2 oz	57	57	130	15	6	3	6	5.0	30,280	.15	2.37	9.4	15
pork														
chop, cooked, lean only	1.7 oz	48	53	130	15	7	0	7	1.9	0	.54	.16	3.3	—
roast, lean only	2.4 oz	68	55	175	20	10	0	9	2.6	0	.73	.21	4.4	—
sausage														
bologna	(3x⅛ inch) 2 slices	26	56	80	3	7	trace	2	.5	—	.04	.06	.7	—
Braunschweiger	(2x¼ inch) 2 slices	20	53	65	3	5	trace	2	1.2	1,310	.03	.29	1.6	—
frankfurter, heated	1	56	57	170	7	15	1	3	.8	—	.08	.11	1.4	—
veal, roast	3 oz	85	55	230	23	14	0	10	2.9	—	.11	.26	6.6	—
Meat Alternates														
beans														
Great Northern, cooked	1 cup	180	69	210	14	1	38	90	4.9	0	.25	.13	1.3	0
red kidney, canned	1 cup	255	76	230	15	1	42	74	4.6	10	.13	.10	1.5	—
peanuts, roasted, salted	1 cup	144	2	840	37	72	27	107	3.0	—	.46	.19	24.7	0
peanut butter	1 tbsp	16	2	95	4	8	3	9	.3	—	.02	.02	2.4	0
peas, split dry, cooked	1 cup	250	70	290	20	1	52	28	4.2	100	.37	.22	2.2	—
Poultry and Eggs														
chicken														
broiled, boneless	3 oz	85	71	115	20	3	0	8	1.4	80	.05	.16	7.4	—
drumstick, fried, flesh and skin	1.3 oz	38	55	90	12	4	trace	6	.9	50	.03	.15	2.7	—
eggs, whole	1 egg	50	74	80	6	6	trace	27	1.1	590	.05	.15	trace	—
Fruit and Vegetable Group														
Fruits														
apple, raw	1	150	85	70	trace	trace	18	8	.4	50	.04	.02	.1	3
apricots, raw	3	114	85	55	1	trace	14	18	.5	2,890	.03	.04	.7	10
avocado, raw	1 medium	284	74	370	5	37	13	22	1.3	630	.24	.43	3.5	30
banana, raw	1 medium	175	76	100	1	trace	26	10	.8	230	.06	.07	.8	12
blueberries, raw	1 cup	140	83	85	1	1	21	21	1.4	140	.04	.08	.6	20
cantaloupe	½ medium	385	91	60	1	trace	14	27	.8	6,540	.08	.06	1.2	63
dates, pitted, cut	1 cup	178	22	490	4	1	130	105	5.3	90	.16	.17	3.9	0
grapefruit, white	½ medium	241	89	45	1	trace	12	19	.5	10	.05	.02	.2	44
grapes, raw	1 cup	160	81	95	1	trace	25	17	.6	140	.07	.04	.4	6
orange, raw	1 medium	180	86	65	1	trace	16	54	.5	260	.13	.05	.5	66
orange juice, recon-stituted from frozen concentrated	1 cup	249	87	120	2	trace	29	25	.2	550	.22	.02	1.0	120
peach, raw	1 medium	114	89	35	1	trace	10	9	.5	1,320	.02	.05	1.0	7
pear, raw	1 medium	182	83	100	1	1	25	13	.5	30	.04	.07	.2	7
pineapple, raw, diced	1 cup	140	85	75	1	trace	19	24	.7	100	.12	.04	.3	24
plum, raw	1 medium	60	87	25	trace	trace	7	7	.3	140	.02	.02	.3	3
prunes, uncooked	4 medium	32	28	70	1	trace	18	14	1.1	440	.02	.04	.4	1
raisins	(½ oz) 1 pkg.	14	18	40	trace	trace	11	9	.5	trace	.02	.01	.1	trace

Nutritive Values of Foods—*continued*

Food	Measure	Weight g	Water %	Cal	Protein g	Fat g	Carbo-hydrate g	Cal-cium mg	Iron mg	Vita-min A 1U	Thia-mine mg	Ribo-flavin mg	Niacin mg	Vita-min C mg
raspberries, red, raw	1 cup	123	84	70	1	1	17	27	1.1	160	.04	.11	1.1	31
rhubarb, cooked, sugar added	1 cup	272	63	385	1	trace	98	212	1.6	220	.06	.15	.7	17
strawberries, raw, hulled	1 cup	149	90	55	1	1	13	31	1.5	90	.04	.10	1.0	88
tangerine, raw	1 medium	116	87	40	1	trace	10	34	.3	360	.05	.02	.1	27
watermelon, raw	(4x8 inches) 1 wedge	925	93	115	2	1	27	30	2.1	2,510	.13	.13	.7	30
Vegetables asparagus, cooked	4 spears	60	94	10	1	trace	2	13	.4	540	.10	.11	.8	16
beans green, cooked, drained	1 cup	125	92	30	2	trace	7	63	.8	680	.09	.11	.6	15
lima, cooked, drained	1 cup	170	71	190	13	1	34	80	4.3	480	.31	.17	2.2	29
bean sprouts, mung, cooked, drained	1 cup	125	91	35	4	trace	7	21	1.1	30	.11	.13	.9	8
beets, cooked, drained, sliced	1 cup	170	91	55	2	trace	12	24	.9	30	.05	.07	.5	10
broccoli, chopped, cooked, drained	1 cup	155	91	40	5	1	7	136	1.2	3,880	.14	.31	1.2	140
Brussels sprouts, cooked	7–8 per cup	155	88	55	7	1	10	50	1.7	810	.12	.22	1.2	135
cabbage, coarsely shredded	1 cup	70	92	15	1	trace	4	34	.3	90	.04	.04	.2	33
carrots, cooked, diced	1 cup	145	91	45	1	trace	10	48	.9	15,220	.08	.07	.7	9
cauliflower, cooked	1 cup	120	93	25	3	trace	5	25	.8	70	.11	.10	.7	66
celery, raw	1 stalk	40	94	5	trace	trace	2	16	.1	100	.01	.01	.1	4
collard greens, cooked	1 cup	190	91	55	5	1	9	289	1.1	10,260	.27	.37	2.4	87
corn, sweet	1 ear	140	74	70	3	1	16	2	.5	310	.09	.08	1.0	7
cucumber, raw, peeled	6 slices	50	96	5	trace	trace	2	8	.2	trace	.02	.02	.1	6
lettuce, iceberg	1 head	454	96	60	4	trace	13	91	2.3	1,500	.29	.27	1.3	29
onions, cooked	1 cup	210	92	60	3	trace	14	50	.8	80	.06	.06	.4	14
peas, green, cooked	1 cup	160	82	115	9	1	19	37	2.9	860	.44	.17	3.7	33
peppers, green	1 medium	74	93	15	1	trace	4	7	.5	310	.06	.06	.4	94
potato, baked in peel	1 medium	99	75	90	3	trace	21	9	.7	trace	.10	.04	1.7	20
potatoes, french-fried (frozen), heated	10 pieces	57	53	125	2	5	19	5	1.0	trace	.08	.01	1.5	12
spinach, cooked	1 cup	180	92	40	5	1	6	167	4.0	14,580	.13	.25	1.0	50
squash, summer, diced	1 cup	210	96	30	2	trace	7	52	.8	820	.10	.16	1.6	21
squash, winter, baked, mashed	1 cup	205	81	130	4	1	32	57	1.6	8,610	.10	.27	1.4	27
sweet potato, baked in peel	1	110	64	155	2	1	36	44	1.0	8,910	.10	.07	.7	24
tomato, raw	1 medium	200	94	40	2	trace	9	24	.9	1,640	.11	.07	1.3	42
turnips, cooked, diced	1 cup	155	94	35	1	trace	8	54	.6	trace	.06	.08	.5	34
turnip greens, cooked	1 cup	145	94	30	3	trace	5	252	1.5	8,270	.15	.33	.7	68
Bread and Cereal Group Biscuit, homemade (enriched flour)	1	28	27	105	2	5	13	34	.4	trace	.06	.06	.1	trace
Bread cracked wheat	1 slice	25	35	65	2	1	13	22	.3	trace	.03	.02	.3	trace

Nutritive Values of Foods—*continued*

Food	Measure	Weight g	Water %	Cal	Protein g	Fat g	Carbo-hydrate g	Cal-cium mg	Iron mg	Vita-min A IU	Thia-mine mg	Ribo-flavin mg	Niacin mg	Vita-min C mg
raisin	1 slice	25	35	65	2	1	13	18	.3	trace	.01	.02	.2	trace
rye, light	1 slice	25	36	60	2	trace	13	19	.4	0	.05	.02	.4	0
white	1 slice	20	36	55	2	1	10	17	.5	trace	.05	.04	.5	trace
whole wheat	1 slice	28	36	65	3	1	14	24	.8	trace	.09	.03	.8	trace
Farina, quick-cooking, enriched, cooked	1 cup	245	89	105	3	trace	22	147	.7	0	.12	.07	1.0	0
Macaroni, enriched, cooked	1 cup	130	64	190	6	1	39	14	1.4	0	.23	.14	1.8	0
Noodles, enriched, cooked	1 cup	160	70	200	7	2	37	16	1.4	110	.22	.13	1.9	0
Oatmeal, cooked	1 cup	240	87	130	5	2	23	22	1.4	0	.19	.05	.2	0
Rice, enriched, cooked	1 cup	205	73	225	4	trace	50	21	1.8	0	.23	.02	2.1	0
Spaghetti, enriched, cooked	1 cup	140	72	155	5	1	32	11	1.3	0	.20	.11	1.5	0

Source: Adapted from *Nutritive Value of Foods* (Home and Garden Bulletin No. 72).

WEIGHTS, MEASURES, AND COOKING TEMPERATURES

A HANDY METRIC CONVERSION TABLE

To Change	Into	Multiply By	To Changè	Into	Multiply By
inches	centimeters	2.5	centimeters	inches	.4
ounces	grams	28	grams	ounces	.035
pounds	kilograms	.45	kilograms	pounds	2.2
teaspoons	milliliters	5	milliliters	teaspoons	.2
tablespoons	milliliters	15	milliliters	tablespoons	.067
fluid ounces	milliliters	30	milliliters	fluid ounces	.033
cups	liters	.24	liters	cups	4.2
pints	liters	.47	liters	pints	2.1
quarts	liters	.95	liters	quarts	1.06
gallons	liters	3.8	liters	gallons	.26

METRIC EQUIVALENTS FOR U.S. COOKING MEASURES

U.S. Measure		Metric Equivalent	U.S. Measure		Metric Equivalent
¼ teaspoon	=	1.25 milliliters	1 ounce	=	28 grams
½ teaspoon	=	2.5 milliliters	2 ounces	=	56 grams
1 teaspoon	=	5 milliliters	4 ounces	=	113 grams
2 teaspoons	=	10 milliliters	8 ounces	=	226 grams
3 teaspoons	=	15 milliliters	16 ounces	=	452 grams
1 tablespoon	=	15 milliliters	¼ pound	=	.11 kilogram
2 tablespoons	=	30 milliliters	½ pound	=	.23 kilogram
1 fluid ounce	=	30 milliliters	¾ pound	=	.34 kilogram
2 fluid ounces	=	59 milliliters	1 pound	=	.45 kilogram
4 fluid ounces	=	118 milliliters	2 pounds	=	.90 kilogram
8 fluid ounces	=	236 milliliters	4 pounds	=	1.81 kilograms
16 fluid ounces	=	472 milliliters	6 pounds	=	2.72 kilograms
1 cup	=	.24 liter	8 pounds	=	3.62 kilograms
2 cups	=	.47 liter	10 pounds	=	4.54 kilograms

U.S. COOKING MEASURES

3 teaspoons	= 1 tablespoon
2 tablespoons	= 1 fluid ounce
8 fluid ounces	= 1 cup
2 cups	= 1 pint
2 pints	= 1 quart
4 quarts	= 1 gallon
16 ounces	= 1 pound
12 inches	= 1 foot

COOKING TEMPERATURES

Heat	Fahrenheit	Celsius
Very Slow	250–275	121–135
Slow	300–325	149–163
Moderate	350–375	177–191
Hot	400–425	204–218
Very Hot	450–475	232–246
Broil	500–525	260–274

OVEN TEMPERATURES

°F	°C	°F	°C
200	93	375	191
225	107	400	204
250	121	425	218
275	135	450	232
300	149	475	246
325	163	500	260
350	177	525	274

Foods, Nutrients, and Calories
A Glossary

The abbreviations used in this glossary are g for gram(s), mg for milligram(s), oz for ounce(s), and IU for International Units.

Abalone—a shellfish found in California waters.

Acetic acid—the main acid in vinegar.

Acidophilus milk—a cultured milk which has acidophilus bacteria added to it. The product tends to aid digestion much as the more palatable yogurt does.

Acorn squash—a hard-shelled, dark green vegetable with orange or yellow flesh. Baked, mashed, 1 cup (205 g): 130 calories. *Nutrients:* 4 g protein, 1 g fat, 32 g carbohydrate, 8,610 IU vitamin A, 27 mg vitamin C, 57 mg calcium.

Active dry yeast—*see* **Yeast.**

Agar-agar—a vegetable gelatin that comes from a type of seaweed. It is used in the food-processing industry.

A la king—served in a cream sauce with mushrooms, pimiento, and sometimes sherry along with chicken or turkey.

A la mode—literally "in the style," e.g., pie à la mode (with ice cream) or beef à la mode (braised beef with vegetables and gravy).

Albacore—a white-meat tuna.

All-purpose flour—a blend of hard or soft wheat flour that is higher in protein than cake flour. Usually it is enriched with thiamine, riboflavin, niacin, iron, and sometimes calcium and vitamin D.

Allspice—a spice from the dried, small berry of a West Indian tree. Its flavor resembles cinnamon, cloves, and nutmeg combined. Its forms are whole and ground.

Almond—the kernel from the fruit of the almond tree. ½ cup (71 g): 425 calories. *Nutrients:* 13 g protein, 38 g fat, 14 g carbohydrate, 2.5 mg niacin, .17 mg thiamine, 166 mg calcium, 3.3 mg iron.

Ambrosia—a fruit dessert, usually orange, banana, and pineapple mixed with coconut.

American cheese—usually refers to a pasteurized process cheese.

Anchovy—any of various small saltwater fish that are like sardines. 3½ oz (100 g): 176 calories. *Nutrients:* 19 g protein, 10 g fat, trace of carbohydrate, 168 mg calcium.

Animal fats—the fat on and in meat, butterfat from and in whole milk products, and lard.

Animal protein—the protein found in beef, lamb, pork, poultry, fish, shellfish, eggs, and milk.

Anise seed—the small, oval seed that comes from a plant that is a member of the carrot family. It has a licoricelike flavor.

Apple—the edible fruit of a tree in the rose family.

Apple juice or cider, bottled—1 cup (248 g): 120 calories. *Nutrients:* trace of protein, trace of fat, 30 g carbohydrate, 15 mg calcium.

Apple pie (2-crust)—1/16 of 9-inch (159 g): 408 calories. *Nutrients:* 3 g protein, 19 g fat, 59 g carbohydrate.

Apple, raw—1 apple (150 g): 70 calories. *Nutrients:* trace of protein, trace of fat, 18 g carbohydrate, 50 IU vitamin A, 8 mg calcium.

Applesauce, sweetened—1 cup (255 g): 230 calories. *Nutrients:* 1 g protein, trace of fat, 61 g carbohydrate.

Apricot—the yellow to orange fruit of a tree in the rose family. The forms are canned, dried, and fresh.

Apricot nectar, canned—1 cup (251 g): 140 calories. *Nutrients:* 1 g protein, trace of fat, 37 g carbohydrate, 2,380 IU vitamin A, 23 mg calcium.

Apricots, canned, in heavy syrup—1 cup (259 g): 220 calories. *Nutrients:* 2 g protein, trace of fat, 57 g carbohydrate, 4,510 IU vitamin A, 28 mg calcium.

Apricots, dried, uncooked—1 cup (150 g): 390 calories. *Nutrients:* 8 g protein, 1 g fat, 100 g carbohydrate, 16,350 IU vitamin A, 4.9 mg niacin, 100 mg calcium, 8.2 mg iron.

Apricots, fresh—3 (114 g): 55 calories. *Nutrients:* 1 g protein, trace of fat, 14 g carbohydrate, 2,890 IU vitamin A, 18 mg calcium.

Arrowroot—a finely ground starch prepared from the root stalks of the tropical American arrowroot plant. It is used as a thickening for puddings and sauces, especially for children because the starch is nutritious and easily digestible.

Artichoke—a thistlelike plant having an edible head. 2 (100 g): 8 to 44 calories. *Nutrients:* 3 g protein, some fat, 9 g carbohydrate, 51 mg calcium.

Artichoke heart—the tender inner portion of an artichoke; available frozen or canned.

Asparagus—the green or creamy white spears of a perennial in the lily family. 4 green, cooked spears (60 g): 10 calories. *Nutrients:* 1 g protein, trace of fat, 2 g carbohydrate, 540 IU vitamin A, 16 mg vitamin C.

Aspic—a seasoned jelly, usually made of meat stock and added gelatin.

Au gratin—with bread crumbs and/or grated cheese browned in oven or under broiler.

Avocado—a pear-shaped fruit with thin skin that is either green (most of the year) or black (summer). 1 (284 g): 370 calories. *Nutrients:* 5 g protein, 37 g fat, 13 g carbohydrate, 630 IU vitamin A, 30 mg vitamin C, 22 mg calcium.

Bacon—the cured and smoked side of pork that comes in two forms, slab and sliced. 2 crisp-cooked slices (15 g): 90 calories. *Nutrients:* 5 g protein, 8 g fat, 1 g carbohydrate.

Baked beans—the mature dried beans processed in tomato sauce, or brown sugar and molasses, usually with pork, and cooked in an oven. Canned, 1 cup (255 g): 310 calories. *Nutrients:* 16 g protein, 7 g fat, 49 g carbohydrate, 1.5 mg niacin, .2 mg thiamine, 4.6 mg iron.

Banana—the yellowish pulpy fruit of a tropical plant; contains 12 minerals and 6 vitamins and is close to an ideal food. Raw, 1 medium (175 g): 100 calories. *Nutrients:* 1 g protein, trace of fat, 26 g carbohydrate, 12 mg vitamin C, 10 mg calcium.

Barbecue—to roast slowly on gridiron or spit, over coals.

Barley—a whole grain. When the outer and inner husks are removed the grain is polished, thus becoming pearl barley. Pearl, uncooked, 1 cup (200 g): 700 calories. *Nutrients:* 16 g protein, 2 g fat, 158 g carbohydrate, 6.2 mg niacin, 1 mg riboflavin, .24 mg thiamine.

Basil—the leaves and tender stems of an annual of the mint family. This herb has a mild anise flavor and a slight mint aftertaste.

Bavarian cream—a rich custard mixed with gelatin and whipped cream; various flavorings such as fruit juices, wine, chocolate, or rum may be added.

Bay leaf—the dried leaf from the evergreen called sweet-bay or laurel. It is a pungent, aromatic herb.

Bean—the edible seed of various leguminous plants. See also specific kind.

Bean sprout—the sprout or shoot of the soya or mung bean. 1 cup (125 g): 35 calories. *Nutrients:* 4 g protein, trace of fat, 7 g carbohydrate, 21 mg calcium.

Beef—the meat from an adult bovine animal such as a cow, ox, steer, or bull.

Beef broth, condensed—½ cup (120 g): 30 calories. *Nutrients:* 5 g protein, 3 g carbohydrate.

Beef, cooked (braised)—3 oz lean and fat (85 g): 245 calories. *Nutrients:* 23 g protein, 16 g fat, 3.5 mg niacin, .18 mg riboflavin, 2.9 mg iron.

Beef, dried or chipped—2 oz (57 g): 115 calories. *Nutrients:* 19 g protein, 4 g fat, 2.2 mg niacin, .18 mg riboflavin, 2.9 mg iron.

Beef, ground, broiled—3 oz patty (85 g): 245 calories. *Nutrients:* 21 g protein, 17 g fat, 4.6 mg niacin, .18 mg riboflavin, 2.7 mg iron.

Beef heart, lean, braised—3 oz (85 g): 160 calories. *Nutrients:* 27 g protein, 5 g fat, 1 g carbohydrate, 1.04 mg riboflavin, .21 mg thiamine, 5 mg iron.

Beef liver, fried—2 oz (57 g): 130 calories. *Nutrients:* 15 g protein, 6 g fat, 3 g carbohydrate, 30,280 IU vitamin A, 9.4 mg niacin, 2.37 mg riboflavin, .15 mg thiamine, 15 mg vitamin C, 5 mg iron.

Beet—the red edible root of a biennial herb of the crowfoot family. Two 2-inch, cooked (100 g): 30 calories. *Nutrients:* 1 g protein, trace of fat, 7 g carbohydrate, 6 mg vitamin C, 14 mg calcium.

Beet sugar—a sugar processed from the white roots of a variety of garden beet.

Belgian endive—thin, elongated stalks usually bleached while growing. Also known as French endive and Witloof chicory.

Bel paese—an Italian, creamy, soft-ripened cheese with mild to moderately robust flavor.

Bibb lettuce (limestone)—a head similar in shape and size to Boston lettuce. The leaves are deep green with delicate flavor.

Bisque—a thick soup usually made from shell-fish; a rich ice cream containing ground or pulverized nuts or macaroons.

Black-eye peas—small dry beans, oval-shaped and creamy white, with a black spot on one side.

Black strap molasses—a thick, bitter, black syrup remaining after the boiling down of sugar cane juice and the extracting of raw sugar.

Blancmange—a cornstarch and milk pudding usually flavored with vanilla.

Blueberry—a sweet blue or black berry. Raw, 1 cup (140 g): 85 calories. *Nutrients:* 1 g protein, 1 g fat, 21 g carbohydrate, 20 mg vitamin C, 21 mg calcium.

Blue cheese (Roquefort)—a pasty, sometimes crumbly, semisoft, blue-veined cheese of French origin. 1 oz (28 g): 105 calories. *Nutrients:* 6 g protein, 9 g fat, 1 g carbohydrate, 350 IU vitamin A, 89 mg calcium.

Bonito—a saltwater fish related to tuna and mackerel.

Boston lettuce (butterhead)—a loose head lettuce with light green outside leaves and a light yellow heart; lighter in weight and less crisp than iceberg lettuce.

Bouillon—a clear, seasoned stock or broth usually made from browned beef.

Bouquet garni (herb bouquet)—a bunch of aromatic herbs (such as a piece of celery with leaves, a sprig of thyme, 3 or 4 sprigs of parsley, and sometimes a bay leaf) tied neatly together and used to flavor soups and stews.

Bran—the outer protective covering of grain kernels (barley, corn, oats, rice, and wheat) consisting of several thin layers.

Bran cereal, whole—½ cup (28 g): 100 calories. *Nutrients:* 3 g protein, trace of fat, 20 g carbohydrate, 1,333 IU vitamin A, 3.33 mg niacin, .4 mg riboflavin, .33 mg thiamine, 3 mg iron.

Bran flakes, fortified—¾ cup (28 g): 105 calories. *Nutrients:* 2 g protein, trace of fat, 22 g carbohydrate, 1,333 IU vitamin A, 3.33 mg niacin, .4 mg riboflavin, .33 mg thiamine, 10 mg iron.

Bread—a general term for various foods made with flour or meal, salt, liquid, and usually leavening, such as baking powder, eggs, or yeast.

Baking powder biscuits, homemade—2 inch (28 g): 105 calories. *Nutrients:* 2 g protein, 5 g fat, 13 g carbohydrate, 34 g calcium.

Bread crumbs, dry—1 cup (100 g): 390 calories. *Nutrients:* 13 g protein, 5 g fat, 73 g carbohydrate, 3.5 mg niacin, .3 mg riboflavin, .22 mg thiamine, 122 mg calcium.

Muffins, with enriched white flour—1 (40 g): 120 calories. *Nutrients:* 3 g protein, 4 g fat, 17 g carbohydrate, 42 mg calcium.

Rolls, enriched, hard, round or rectangular—1 (50 g): 155 calories. *Nutrients:* 5 g protein, 2 g fat, 30 g carbohydrate, 1.4 mg niacin, .12 mg riboflavin, .13 mg thiamine, 1.2 mg iron.

Rye bread, American, light or pumpernickel—1 slice (25 g): 60 calories. *Nutrients:* 2 g protein, trace of fat, 13 g carbohydrate, .4 mg niacin, .02 mg riboflavin, .05 mg thiamine, .4 mg iron.

White bread, enriched—1 slice (25 g): 70 calories. *Nutrients:* 2 g protein, 1 g fat, 13 g carbohydrate, 6 mg niacin, .05 mg riboflavin, .06 mg thiamine, .6 mg iron.

Whole wheat bread—1 slice (28 g): 65 calories. *Nutrients:* 3 g protein, 1 g fat, 14 g carbohydrate, .8 mg niacin, .03 mg riboflavin, .09 mg thiamine, .8 mg iron.

Brick cheese—a smooth, waxy, semisoft cheese with mild to moderately sharp flavor; United States origin.

Brie—a smooth, runny, soft-ripened, pungent French cheese with mild to pungent flavor.

Broad-leaf endive—*see* **Escarole.**

Broccoli—a vegetable in the cabbage family. The edible portion is made up of loose flower buds, stem, and sometimes a portion of the leaves. Cooked, 1 stalk (180 g): 45 calories. *Nutrients:* 6 g protein, 1 g fat, 8 g carbohydrate, 4,500 IU vitamin A, 162 mg vitamin C, 158 mg calcium.

Broiler-fryer—a young chicken of either sex, 7 to 10 weeks old, that is tender-meated with smooth-textured skin.

Brown sugar—or "soft" sugar consists of extremely fine crystals of white sugar covered with a film of highly refined, dark-colored, cane-flavored syrup. Firmly packed, 1 cup (220 g): 820 calories. *Nutrients:* 212 g carbohydrate, 187 mg calcium, 7.5 mg iron.

Brussels sprouts—a vegetable of the cabbage family. Cooked, ½ cup (77 g): 27 calories. *Nutrients:* 4 g protein, trace of fat, 5 g carbohydrate, 405 IU vitamin A, 67 mg vitamin C, 50 mg calcium.

Buckwheat flour—the finely ground product obtained by sifting buckwheat meal.

Bulgur wheat—an all-wheat food that has been cooked, dried, partly debranned, and cracked into coarse, angular fragments. Canned, seasoned, 1 cup (135 g): 245 calories. *Nutrients:* 8 g protein, 4 g fat, 44 g carbohydrate, 4.1 mg niacin, .05 mg riboflavin, .08 mg thiamine, 27 mg calcium, 1.9 mg iron.

Butter—According to U.S. federal law, butter must have at least 80 percent milkfat. It is made from cream, with or without common salt. 1 tablespoon (14 g): 100 calories. *Nutrients:* trace of protein, 12 g fat, trace of carbohydrate, 470 IU vitamin A, 3 mg calcium.

Butterhead—*see* **Boston lettuce.**

Buttermilk, cultured—made from fresh fluid skim milk. A specially prepared culture of bacteria is added to milk to produce the desirable acidity, body, flavor, and aroma so characteristic of buttermilk. Fluid, cultured, 1 cup (245 g): 90 calories. *Nutrients:* 9 g protein, trace of fat, 12 g carbohydrate, .44 mg riboflavin, 296 mg calcium.

Cabbage—a plain- or curly-leafed vegetable that comes in many varieties, such as early or new, red, Savoy, and celery or Chinese.

Cabbage, cooked—1 cup (145 g): 30 calories. *Nutrients:* 2 g protein, trace of fat, 6 g carbohydrate, 48 mg vitamin C, 64 mg calcium.

Cabbage, raw, chopped—1 cup (90 g): 20 calories. *Nutrients:* 1 g protein, trace of fat, 5 g carbohydrate, 42 mg vitamin C, 44 mg calcium.

Caffeine—a tasteless substance that is a natural constituent of a number of plants including coffee, tea, kola nuts, cocoa beans, and maté.

Calorie—a calorie is a unit of food measurement, with an energy-producing value of one large calorie. One large calorie, also referred to as a kilogram-calorie, is the amount of energy needed to raise the temperature of one kilogram of water from 14.5°C to 15.5°C.

Camembert cheese—a smooth, runny, soft-ripened cheese with a mild to pungent flavor; French origin. 1 wedge (38 g): 115 calories. *Nutrients:* 7 g protein, 9 g fat, 1 g carbohydrate, 380 IU vitamin A, 40 mg calcium.

Canadian style bacon—cured and smoked boneless pork loin. Cooked, 1 slice (21 g): 65 calories. *Nutrients:* 6 g protein, 4 g fat, 3 g carbohydrate, 1.1 mg niacin, .18 mg thiamine.

Canapé—a savory bit of food or highly seasoned spread on a toast round or cracker base.

Cantaloupe—a variety of melon. A ripe cantaloupe should have a slight golden background color under the surface netting and have orange flesh. Raw, ½ melon (385 g): 60 calories. *Nutrients:* 1 g protein, trace of fat, 14 g carbohydrate, 6,540 IU vitamin A, 63 mg vitamin C, 27 mg calcium.

Caper—the flower bud of a Mediterranean caper bush; it is pickled and used for flavoring or as a garnish.

Capon—an unsexed male chicken, usually over 10 months old, weighing 4 pounds or over, with a large proportion of white meat.

Caraway seed—the seed of a biennial plant of the carrot family. This herb has a tangy flavor.

Cardamom—the dried fruit of a plant of the ginger family. The forms of this spice are whole (seed pods) and ground.

Carrot—a long, tapering, orange-colored, edible root.

Carrots, cooked, diced—1 cup (145 g): 45 calories. *Nutrients:* 1 g protein, trace of fat, 10 g carbohydrate, 15,220 IU vitamin A, 48 mg calcium.

Carrots, raw—1 (50 g): 20 calories. *Nutrients:* 1 g protein, trace of fat, 5 g carbohydrate, 5,500 IU vitamin A, 18 mg calcium.

Cashew nut—a kidney-shaped kernel from the fruit of a tropical American evergreen tree. ½ cup (70 g): 392 calories. *Nutrients:* 12 g protein, 32 g fat, 20 g carbohydrate, 1.2 mg niacin, .3 mg thiamine, 2.6 mg iron.

Cauliflower—the creamy white head formed by the young flowers of a plant in the cabbage family. Cooked, 1 cup (120 g): 25 calories. *Nutrients:* 3 g protein, trace of fat, 5 g carbohydrate, 66 mg vitamin C.

Cayenne pepper—a very hot, pungent spice made from capsicum hot peppers; its forms are whole and ground.

Celeriac—*see* **Celery root.**

Celery—an herb with ribbed stalks formed in a bunch. There are two definite types, Golden Heart (white) and Pascal (dark or light green).

Celery, diced—1 cup (100 g): 15 calories. *Nutrients:* 1 g protein, trace of fat, 4 g carbohydrate, 39 mg calcium.

Celery soup, cream of, condensed—⅓ cup (100 g): 81 calories. *Nutrients:* 1 g protein, 5 g fat, 6 g carbohydrate, 45 mg calcium.

Celery cabbage—a long, somewhat loose head of pale green to white leaves. Also called Chinese cabbage. 1 cup (75 g): 10 calories. *Nutrients:* 1 g protein, trace of fat, 2 g carbohydrate, 19 mg vitamin C, 32 mg calcium.

Celery root (celeriac)—a large, tasty root of the celery family.

Celery seed—comes from a member of the parsley family. It has a warm, slightly bitter flavor.

Cereal—a plant of the grass family, which produces a starchy, edible grain, such as wheat, oats, barley, rice, rye, or corn; the grain itself; a breakfast food processed from such a grain.

Chard, Swiss—*see* **Greens.**

Cheddar cheese—a firm, hard-ripened cheese with mild to very sharp flavor; originally from England. 1 oz (28 g): 115 calories. *Nutrients:* 7 g protein, 9 g fat, 1 g carbohydrate, 370 IU vitamin A, 213 mg calcium.

Cheese—a very valuable concentrated food made from the milk of cows, goats, ewes, or camels. It contains most of the food values of milk.

Cherry—a small round or heart-shaped fruit from a tree of the rose family. Canned, red, tart, pitted, water-pack, 1 cup (244 g): 105 calories. *Nutrients:* 2 g protein, trace of fat, 26 g carbohydrate, 1,660 IU vitamin A, 12 mg vitamin C, 37 mg calcium.

Chervil—the leaves of an annual, aromatic, sweet herb whose flavor resembles licorice.

Chestnut—a sweet, starchy, edible nut of the chestnut tree.

Chicken—a domesticated bird whose meat and eggs are an important and popular source of food. Types of chicken available: broiler-fryer, roaster, capon, stewing chicken, and Rock Cornish hen.

Chicken, broiled—3 oz (85 g) flesh only: 115 calories. *Nutrients:* 20 g protein, 3 g fat, 7.4 mg niacin, 1.4 mg iron.

Chicken livers—3½ oz (100 g): 141 calories. *Nutrients:* 22.1 g protein, 4 g fat, 2.6 g carbohydrate, 32,200 IU vitamin A, 11.8 mg niacin, 2.46 mg riboflavin, .2 mg thiamine, 7.4 mg iron.

Chicken noodle soup, condensed—½ cup (100 g): 53 calories. *Nutrients:* 2 g protein, 2 g fat, 6 g carbohydrate.

Chicken soup, cream of, condensed—½ cup (120 g): 95 calories. *Nutrients:* 3 g protein, 6 g fat, 8 g carbohydrate, 410 IU vitamin A, 24 mg calcium.

Chickpea (garbanzo)—a nut-flavored bean that can be used as a main dish vegetable or, pickled in oil and vinegar, in salads. Dried, raw, 3½ oz (100 g): 360 calories. *Nutrients:* 20 g protein, 4 g fat, 61 g carbohydrate, 7 mg iron.

Chicory—*see* **Curly endive.**

Chiffon—a word used to describe a fluffy, light-textured pie or cake.

Chili pepper (chili)—the fruit of an herbaceous plant belonging to the capsicum family. The chili pepper is extremely hot and pungent.

Chili powder—a ground herb and spice blend usually including caraway seed, chili peppers, cumin, garlic powder, onion powder, oregano, black and cayenne peppers.

Chinese cabbage—*see* **Celery cabbage.**

Chive—an all-green herb in the onion family.

Chocolate—the product resulting from the grinding of cocoa nibs (cocoa, or cacao, beans that have been roasted and shelled).

Chocolate pudding, homemade—1 cup (260 g): 385 calories. *Nutrients:* 8 g protein, 12 g fat, 67 g carbohydrate, 390 IU vitamin A, 250 mg calcium.

Chocolate, unsweetened—1 oz (28 g): 145 calories. *Nutrients:* 3 g protein, 15 g fat, 8 g carbohydrate, 22 mg calcium.

Chowder—a thick soup or stew made from vegetables, fish, or shellfish.

Chutney—a condiment made from fruit, spices, and vinegar or lemon juice.

Cider—the unpasteurized juice of apples. Sweet cider is unfermented; hard cider is fermented.

Cider vinegar—the product made by the alcoholic and subsequent acetous fermentations of the juice of apples.

Cinnamon—a sweet, pungent spice available in whole (stick) form or ground.

Citric acid—a crystalline compound obtained from citrus fruits.

Citrus—a genus of plants which includes popular fruits, such as oranges, grapefruits, tangerines, citrons, lemons, and limes.

Clam—a bivalve mollusk found in many parts of the world. Canned (solids and liquid), 3 oz (85 g): 45 calories. *Nutrients:* 7 g protein, 1 g fat, 2 g carbohydrate, 47 mg calcium, 3.5 mg iron.

Clingstone peach—a type of peach having flesh which clings tightly to the pit. It is used chiefly for canning.

Clove—the dried, unopened flower bud of the clove tree. This spice is hot and aromatic.

Coconut—the large, round fruit of the coconut tree. Fresh, shredded, packed, 1 cup (130 g): 450 calories. *Nutrients:* 5 g protein, 46 g fat, 12 g carbohydrate.

Cod—a white-fleshed fish which is usually marketed as frozen fillets, but which may also be sold dried, salted, or fresh.

Cole slaw—a cabbage salad with mayonnaise or vinegar salad dressing.

Collard greens—*see* **Greens.**

Compote—mixed fresh or dried fruit, flavored and served as dessert.

Conserve—a type of preserve containing fruits of several kinds and often nuts.

Consommé—a clear, concentrated stock or broth made from one or several kinds of meat, such as beef, veal, and poultry.

Coriander seed—comes from the dried, ripe fruit of an herb of the parsley family. It has a wild, delicately fragrant aroma.

Corn—a cereal grain; the seeds or kernels are in rows on a long ear or cob.

Corn flakes, fortified—1 cup (25 g): 100 calories. *Nutrients:* 2 g protein, trace of fat, 21 g carbohydrate, .5 mg niacin, .02 mg riboflavin, .11 mg thiamine.

Corn, yellow, sweet, cooked—1 ear (140 g): 70 calories. *Nutrients:* 3 g protein, 1 g fat, 16 g carbohydrate, 310 IU vitamin A, 7 mg vitamin C.

Cornmeal—a meal ground from corn and used to make corn bread, pudding, and mush. Enriched, dry, 1 cup (138 g): 500 calories. *Nutrients:* 11 g protein, 2 g fat, 108 g carbohydrate, 610 IU vitamin A, 4.8 mg niacin, .36 mg riboflavin, .61 mg thiamine.

Corn muffins, homemade—1 (40 g): 125 calories. *Nutrients:* 3 g protein, 4 g fat, 19 g carbohydrate, 42 mg calcium.

Corn oil—a vegetable oil extracted from corn kernels; used in margarine and salad dressing and also in cooking. 1 tablespoon (14 g): 125 calories. *Nutrient:* 14 g fat.

Cornstarch—a white, granular carbohydrate occurring naturally in corn. The refined product is a thickening agent in pie fillings, sauces, and puddings.

Corn syrup—a syrup made from the sugar or glucose of corn. It may be dark, light, or golden.

Cos—*see* **Romaine.**

Cottage cheese—a creamy, unripened cheese made in curds of various sizes. Creamed, 1 cup (245 g): 260 calories. *Nutrients:* 33 g protein, 10 g fat, 7 g carbohydrate, 420 IU vitamin A, .61 mg riboflavin, 230 mg calcium.

Crab—a shellfish in the crustacean group. The main types are blue (includes soft-shelled), Dungeness, and King; may be purchased fresh, frozen, or canned. Crab meat, canned, 3 oz (85 g): 85 calories. *Nutrients:* 15 g protein, 2 g fat, 1 g carbohydrate, 38 mg calcium.

Crabapple—a small colorful apple too sour for eating but used in making jams, jellies, and preserves.

Cranberry—a brilliant red berry grown in marshy land.

Cranberries, raw—⅞ cup (100 g): 46 calories. *Nutrients:* trace of protein, 10 g carbohydrate, 11 mg vitamin C, 14 mg calcium.

Cranberry juice cocktail—1 cup (250 g): 165 calories. *Nutrients:* trace of protein, trace of fat, 42 g carbohydrate, 40 mg vitamin C, 13 mg calcium.

Cream cheese—a rich, mild, creamy, unripened cheese made from cream and milk. 3 oz (85 g): 320 calories. *Nutrients:* 7 g protein, 32 g fat, 2 g carbohydrate, 1,310 IU vitamin A, 53 mg calcium.

Cream (half-and-half)—a mixture of milk and cream with 10 to 12 percent milkfat; frequently homogenized. 1 cup (242 g): 325 calories. *Nutrients:* 8 g protein, 28 g fat, 11 g carbohydrate, 1,160 IU vitamin A, 261 mg calcium.

Crisphead—*see* **Iceberg lettuce.**

Crustacean—any of a group of mostly aquatic animals with crustlike shells, such as crabs, lobsters, and shrimp.

Cucumber—the flavorful fruit of a rough-stemmed trailing vine belonging to the gourd family. Raw, pared, 1 (207 g): 30 calories. *Nutrients:* 1 g protein, trace of fat, 7 g carbohydrate, 23 mg vitamin C, 35 mg calcium.

Cumin seed—an herb resembling parsley; it has a strong, caraway-like flavor.

Curly endive (chicory)—a vegetable with a bunchy head and narrow, ragged-edged, curly leaves; dark green outside, pale yellow heart; pleasantly bitter flavor.

Currant—a fruit that comes in two varieties, fresh and dry. The fresh is a berry of the gooseberry family and the dry is a dried grape.

Curry powder—a spice blend usually including cinnamon, cloves, cumin, fenugreek seed, black and red peppers, and turmeric.

Custard—a flavored, sweetened, egg-and-milk mixture.

Custard, baked—½ cup (132 g): 152 calories. *Nutrients:* 7 g protein, 7 g fat, 14 g carbohydrate, 465 IU vitamin A, 148 mg calcium.

Custard pie (1-crust)—⅙ of 9-inch (151 g): 332 calories. *Nutrients:* 9 g protein, 16 g fat, 35 g carbohydrate, 350 IU vitamin A, 145 mg calcium.

Dairy sour cream—a commercial food product made of cream to which a culture of lactic acid bacteria has been added. It is thick and smooth. 1 cup (230 g): 485 calories. *Nutrients:* 7 g protein, 47 g fat, 10 g carbohydrate, 1,930 IU vitamin A, 235 mg calcium.

Date—the sweet fruit of the tropical date palm. Dates are classified as soft, semidry, and dry. Pitted, cut, 1 cup (178 g): 490 calories. *Nutrients:* 4 g protein, 1 g fat, 130 g carbohydrate, 3.9 mg niacin, 105 mg calcium, 5.3 mg iron.

Dill—an aromatic plant of the parsley family. The fresh leaves or dried seeds are used for flavoring.

Dried fruit—apples, apricots, peaches, figs, prunes, and raisins that are sun-dried or mechanically dehydrated. The moisture content ranges from 15 to 25 percent.

Dried vegetables—vegetables from which the water has been evaporated, thus concentrating the food constituents. In addition to the familiar legumes (lentils, split peas, navy beans), dehydrated mushrooms, onions, potato flakes and granules, parsley flakes, and chive flakes are now available.

Dry milk—the product obtained by removing the water from whole milk. It contains not less than 26 percent milkfat and not more than 4 percent moisture.

Dry mustard—a sharp, hot, pungent, ground spice.

Duchess potatoes—mashed potatoes combined with egg and butter and seasoned with salt, pepper, and nutmeg.

Duck—a web-footed, dark-fleshed bird, either domesticated or wild, that is prized as a great delicacy. A duck about 8 weeks old is called a duckling.

    Duckling—3½ oz (100 g) flesh only: 165 calories. *Nutrients:* 21.4 g protein, 8.2 g fat, 7.7 mg niacin, 1.3 mg iron.

    Duck, wild—3½ oz (100 g) cooked, flesh only: 138 calories. *Nutrients:* 21.3 g protein, 5.2 g fat.

Dumpling—a ball or outer casing of dough, usually boiled but sometimes baked.

Durum wheat—very hard wheat used for making semolina, which in turn is made into macaroni, spaghetti, and other pasta products.

Edam cheese—a hard-ripened, creamy, yellow, Dutch cheese sometimes with a red wax coating. The flavor is mild and nutlike.

Egg—generally refers to the chicken egg, one of our most valuable foods. 1 (50 g): 80 calories. *Nutrients:* 6 g protein, 6 g fat, trace of carbohydrate, 590 IU vitamin A, .15 mg riboflavin, .05 mg thiamine, 27 mg calcium, 1.1 mg iron.

Egg bagel—a hard, doughnut-shaped roll simmered in water before baking. 3-inch (55) g: 165 calories. *Nutrients:* 6 g protein, 2 g fat, 28 g carbohydrate.

Egg chalaza—the twisted, ropelike strands of material on each side of the egg yolk, which anchor the yolk in place. They consist of highly concentrated egg white and are a perfectly wholesome part of the egg.

Egg noodles—a macaroni product that contains 5.5 percent egg solids (fresh, powdered, or frozen). Enriched, cooked, 1 cup (160 g): 200 calories. *Nutrients:* 7 g protein, 2 g fat, 37 g carbohydrate, 1.9 mg niacin, .13 mg riboflavin, .22 mg thiamine, 1.4 mg iron.

Eggplant—the fruit of a plant of the nightshade family, used as a vegetable. The most common variety has dark purple skin and white, spongy flesh. Cooked, 3½ oz (100 g): 19 calories. *Nutrients:* 1 g protein, trace of fat, 4 g carbohydrate, 11 mg calcium.

Emmenthaler cheese—a light yellow cheese from Switzerland which has a smooth texture with large eyes and a sweet, nutlike flavor.

Endive—a type of salad green. It comes in the following varieties: curly endive (chicory), escarole (broad-leaf endive), and Belgian endive (French endive or Witloof chicory).

Enriched—made more nutritious by the restoring, at least in part, of the original nutrients removed during the processing of a product. Some enriched products are bread, cereal, cornmeal, flour, and rice.

Escarole (broad-leaf endive)—a type of salad green with a bunchy head of broad leaves that do not curl at tips; the outer leaves are dark green, the heart pale yellow.

Evaporated milk—unsweetened, canned milk from which about 60 percent of the water has been removed. *See* **Milk** for nutrients.

Farina—a meal or flour obtained from wheat, nuts, potatoes, or Indian corn that is used chiefly as a breakfast cereal. Quick-cooking, enriched, cooked, 1 cup (245 g): 105 calories. *Nutrients:* 3 g protein, trace of fat, 22 g carbohydrate, 1 mg niacin, .07 mg riboflavin, .12 mg thiamine, 147 mg calcium.

Farm cheese—a soft, unripened cheese with a mild, slightly sour flavor and somewhat crumbly texture; American origin.

Fennel—the dried seed of an aromatic herb of the carrot family. It looks like celery and has the flavor and aroma of anise.

Fenugreek seed—the seed of an Asiatic plant of the pea family. Its flavor is pleasantly bitter and its aroma is similar to curry powder.

Fig, dried—the dried fruit from several varieties of fig trees. The color usually is golden brown or black. Dried, 1 large (21 g): 60 calories. *Nutrients:* 1 g protein, trace of fat, 15 g carbohydrate, 26 mg calcium.

Filbert—the cultivated nut of the hazel tree. ½ cup (66 g): 422 calories. *Nutrients:* 8 g

outer covering is removed before further processing. The main forms are whole hominy and grits. Grits, enriched, cooked, 1 cup (245 g): 125 calories. *Nutrients:* 3 g protein, trace of fat, 27 g carbohydrate, 1 mg niacin, .07 mg riboflavin, .1 mg thiamine.

Homogenized milk—pasteurized milk that has been mechanically treated to break up the fat globules.

Honey—the nectar of plants, gathered, modified, stored, and concentrated by honeybees. Its main ingredients are fructose and dextrose.

Honeydew melon—a bluntly oval melon which may vary in size. The flesh is greenish in color and, when ripe, juicy and sweet.

Hors d'oeuvre—a colorful, attractive, bite-size morsel of food often served as an appetizer.

Horseradish—a plant of the cabbage, turnip, and mustard family grown mainly for its root. Its hot taste is from a pungent, highly volatile oil.

Ice—the simplest of frozen desserts made from sugar and water flavored with fruit juice.

Iceberg lettuce (crisphead)—a firm, compact head with medium green outside leaves, pale green heart.

Ice cream—a dessert made from cream, milk, sugar, flavorings, and stabilizers. It must contain at least 10 percent milkfat. ½ cup (66 g): 127 calories. *Nutrients:* 3 g protein, 7 g fat, 14 g carbohydrate, 295 IU vitamin A, 97 mg calcium.

Ice milk—a dessert made from milk, stabilizers, sugar, and flavorings. It contains between 2 and 7 percent milkfat.

Jam—a type of preserve made from whole, small fruits that are either mashed or cooked to a thick pulp with sugar.

Jelly—a type of preserve made by combining fruit juice and sugar in the correct proportions and cooking the mixture until it tests done.

Kale—*see* **Greens.**

Ketchup (catsup)—a smooth, well-seasoned tomato sauce. 1 tablespoon (15 g): 15 calories. *Nutrients:* trace of protein, trace of fat, 4 g carbohydrate, 210 IU vitamin A, 2 mg vitamin C, 3 mg calcium.

Kidney bean—a variety of bean that is large, red, and kidney-shaped. Available either canned or dried. Red, canned, 1 cup (255 g): 230 calories. *Nutrients:* 15 g protein, 1 g fat, 42 g carbohydrate, 1.5 mg niacin, .1 mg riboflavin, .13 mg thiamine, 4.6 mg iron.

King crab—the largest variety of edible crab, with pink to white, delicately flavored meat.

Kohlrabi—the German term for turnip-cabbage.

It is a pale green vegetable which has a globular swelling of the stem. Cooked, 3½ oz (100 g): 24 calories. *Nutrients:* 1 g protein, trace of fat, 5 g carbohydrate, 43 mg vitamin C, 33 mg calcium.

Kumquat—a small, somewhat oval, orange-colored citrus fruit with a thin, sweet, aromatic rind. Raw, 3½ oz (100 g): 65 calories. *Nutrients:* 1 g protein, trace of fat, 17 g carbohydrate, 600 IU vitamin A, 36 mg vitamin C, 63 mg calcium.

Lamb—the meat from a young sheep, especially one that is under a year old.

Lamb chop, with bone, broiled—4.8 oz (137 g): 400 calories. *Nutrients:* 25 g protein, 33 g fat, 5.6 mg niacin, .25 mg riboflavin, .14 mg thiamine.

Lamb kidneys—3½ oz (100 g): 105 calories. *Nutrients:* 16 g protein, 3 g fat, 1 g carbohydrate, 2.42 mg riboflavin, .51 mg thiamine, 7.6 mg iron.

Lard—fat rendered from the fatty tissue of pork.

Leaf lettuce—a variety of lettuce with crisp-textured leaves that branch loosely from its stalk instead of forming a head.

Leek—a type of onion with a slight bulb formation and broad, flat, dark green top.

Legume—the one-celled, two-valved seed pod of certain plants, such as peas, beans, and lentils.

Lemon—an oval citrus fruit with an acid taste. Select firm, heavy lemons with rich yellow color and a reasonably smooth-textured skin with a slight gloss.

Lemon juice—1 cup (244 g): 60 calories. *Nutrients:* 1 g protein, trace of fat, 20 g carbohydrate, 112 mg vitamin C, 17 mg calcium.

Lemon pepper marinade—a ground blend of seasonings usually including coarsely ground black pepper, garlic, dried lemon peel, monosodium glutamate, salt, and sugar.

Lentil—a disc-shaped legume about the size of a pea, used chiefly in soups and stews. Dried, cooked, ½ cup (100 g): 106 calories. *Nutrients:* 8 g protein, 19 g carbohydrate, .6 mg niacin, .06 mg riboflavin, .07 mg thiamine, 2.1 mg iron.

Lettuce—a salad green. The types are iceberg (crisphead), Boston (butterhead), romaine (cos), bibb (limestone), and leaf. Crisphead, 1 head (454 g): 60 calories. *Nutrients:* 4 g protein, trace of fat, 13 g carbohydrate, 1,500 IU vitamin A.

Liederkranz cheese—a soft-ripened, smooth, runny, golden cheese with a hearty, tangy flavor; American origin.

Lima bean—a flat, kidney-shaped bean, light green in color. The smaller sizes are known as butter limas and the larger ones as potato limas. Cooked, ½ cup (85 g): 95 calories. *Nutrients:* 6 g protein, trace of fat, 17 g carbohydrate, 14 mg vitamin C, 40 mg calcium.

Limburger cheese—a soft-ripened, smooth (with holes), off-white cheese with a strong flavor and aroma; Belgian origin.

Lime—a small green citrus fruit. Select limes heavy in weight, with glossy skin.

Lime juice, fresh—1 cup (246 g): 65 calories. *Nutrients:* 1 g protein, trace of fat, 22 g carbohydrate, 79 mg vitamin C, 22 mg calcium.

Limestone lettuce—*see* **Bibb lettuce.**

Liver—a variety meat. Commonly used types are beef, pork, veal, lamb, or baby beef liver.

Lobster—a saltwater crustacean; it is sold fresh, frozen (including rock lobster tails), and canned. Cooked (with 2 tablespoons butter), 1 (334 g): 308 calories. *Nutrients:* 20 g protein, 25 g fat, trace of carbohydrate, 920 IU vitamin A, 2.3 mg niacin, 80 mg calcium.

Lobster tail—usually the tail of the South African rock lobster, which may vary in size from 3 to 16 ounces.

Lox—cured, smoked salmon. 2 oz (56 g): 100 calories. *Nutrients:* 12 g protein, 5 g fat.

Macaroni—a term used to describe macaroni, spaghetti, and egg noodle products.

Macaroni, enriched, cooked until tender—1 cup (140 g): 155 calories. *Nutrients:* 5 g protein, 1 g fat, 32 g carbohydrate, 1.5 mg niacin, .11 mg riboflavin, .2 mg thiamine.

Mace—a spice obtained from the outer covering of the dried fruit seed of the nutmeg tree. It is available either whole (blade) or ground.

Mackerel—a rich-meated saltwater fish related to tuna.

Mandarin oranges—the name given to several zipper-skin oranges including the temple orange, the tangelo, and the tangerine. The satsuma variety is canned.

Mango—the fruit from a tropical and subtropical tree. The fruit is approximately the size of a large avocado. The ripe fruit is red with a juicy, yellow-orange pulp.

Maraschino cherry—a preserved cherry, usually prepared from a sweet cherry. It is artificially colored, with a specially flavored syrup that gives it a distinctive taste.

Marbling—flecks of fat within the lean of a cut of meat which enhance juiciness and flavor.

Margarine—a product made from refined vegetable oils or a combination of animal fats and vegetable oils emulsified with milk. 1 tablespoon (14 g): 100 calories. *Nutrients:* trace of protein, 12 g fat, trace of carbohydrate, 470 IU vitamin A, 3 mg calcium.

Marinate—to allow food, such as meat or fish, to stand in a liquid (usually oil and vinegar) to acquire additional flavor.

Marjoram—a sweet, spicy herb of the mint family. It has a slight mint aftertaste. It is available either whole or ground.

Marmalade—a type of preserve usually made from fruits which have some jellymaking properties, especially citrus fruits.

Mayonnaise—a permanent emulsion of oil droplets in water, stabilized with egg yolk. It is prepared from vegetable oil, vinegar or lemon juice, eggs or egg yolks, and spices. Commercial mayonnaise must contain a minimum of 65 percent vegetable oil. 1 tablespoon (14 g): 100 calories. *Nutrients:* trace of protein, 11 g fat, trace of carbohydrate, 3 mg calcium.

Meat—the edible portion of mammals, such as cattle, swine, and sheep.

Mellow cheese—a cheese (usually Cheddar) that has been cured longer than mild cheese, but not as long as sharp cheese.

Melon—*see* **Cantaloupe; Honeydew melon; and Watermelon.**

Meringue—stiffly beaten egg whites, with or without sugar.

Mild cheese—a cheese (usually Cheddar) that has been cured for less time than mellow or sharp cheese.

Milk—a white, opaque, highly nourishing fluid produced by female mammals for the nourishment of their young.

Milk, evaporated—1 cup, undiluted (252 g): 345 calories. *Nutrients:* 18 g protein, 20 g fat, 24 g carbohydrate, 810 IU vitamin A, .86 mg riboflavin, 635 mg calcium.

Milk, fluid nonfat (skim)—1 cup (245 g): 90 calories. *Nutrients:* 9 g protein, trace of fat, 12 g carbohydrate, .44 mg riboflavin, 296 mg calcium.

Milk, fluid, partly skimmed, 2% (nonfat milk solids added)—1 cup (246 g): 145 calories. *Nutrients:* 10 g protein, 5 g fat, 15 g carbohydrate, 200 IU vitamin A, .52 mg riboflavin, 352 mg calcium.

Milk, fluid whole—1 cup (244 g): 160 calories. *Nutrients:* 9 g protein, 9 g fat, 12 g carbohydrate, 350 IU vitamin A, .41 mg riboflavin, 288 mg calcium.

Milk, instant nonfat dry—1 cup (68 g): 245

calories. *Nutrients:* 24 g protein, trace of fat, 35 g carbohydrate, 20 IU vitamin A (more if fortified), 1.21 mg riboflavin, 879 mg calcium.

Milk, sweetened condensed—1 cup (306 g): 980 calories. *Nutrients:* 25 g protein, 27 g fat, 166 g carbohydrate, 1,100 IU vitamin A, 1.16 mg riboflavin, 802 mg calcium.

Mint—a leaf herb with a strong, sweet aroma and a cool aftertaste.

Molasses—a sweet, thick, dark syrup from sugar cane. It is a natural flavoring agent for candy, baked goods, and ice cream. Light, 1 tablespoon (20 g): 50 calories. *Nutrients:* 13 g carbohydrate, 33 mg calcium, 1 mg iron.

Mollusk—any one of a large group of invertebrate animals with soft, unsegmented bodies enclosed in shells of one or more parts. Clams, mussels, oysters, and snails are mollusks.

Monosodium glutamate—a basic seasoning produced from natural sources and added to foods to enhance their characteristic flavors.

Monterey Jack cheese—a creamy white, smooth, open-textured, mild-flavored cheese; American origin.

Mozzarella cheese—a creamy white, plastic, slightly firm cheese with mild, delicate flavor; Italian origin.

Muenster cheese—a smooth, waxy, creamy white cheese with mild to mellow flavor; German origin.

Mung bean—*see* **Bean sprout.**

Mushroom—a plant without leaves that is a member of the fungi family; classified as a vegetable.

Mushrooms, canned—1 cup, solids and liquid (244 g): 40 calories. *Nutrients:* 5 g protein, trace of fat, 6 g carbohydrate, 4.8 mg niacin, .6 mg riboflavin, 15 mg calcium.

Mushroom soup, cream of, condensed—½ cup (120 g): 135 calories. *Nutrients:* 2 g protein, 10 g fat, 10 g carbohydrate, 41 mg calcium.

Mussel—a form of shellfish belonging to the mollusk family. Mussels are found in all the oceans of the world.

Mustard—a sharp, hot, pungent spice from the seed of an annual of the watercress family. It is available either whole or ground. The term is sometimes used interchangeably with prepared mustard.

Mustard greens—*see* **Greens.**

Natural cheese—cheese processed directly from milk.

Navy beans—a broad term for dried beans that includes Great Northern, pea, flat, and small white beans. Dried, cooked, 1 cup (180 g): 210 calories. *Nutrients:* 14 g protein, 1 g fat, 38 g carbohydrate, 1.3 mg niacin, .13 mg riboflavin, .25 mg thiamine, 4.9 mg iron.

Nectar—the name given to the honey of plants or any delectable beverage, such as apricot nectar.

Nectarine—the fruit of a tree in the rose family. It is related to peaches and almonds and is one of the oldest fruits. 1 small (100 g): 64 calories. *Nutrients:* some protein, trace of fat, 17 g carbohydrate, 1,650 IU vitamin A, 13 mg vitamin C.

Netting—the veinlike network of lines running randomly across the rind of some melons.

Neufchâtel cheese—a soft, unripened, white cheese originally produced in France but now made in the United States as well.

Noodles—flat macaroni products, such as fettuccine, lasaganette, wide lasagne, and egg noodles.

Nut—a dry fruit, the kernel of which is especially edible. See also specific kinds.

Nutmeg—a spice from the dried fruit seed of a tropical evergreen. Its aroma is sweet and delicate. Its forms are whole and ground.

Oatmeal—a meal made from husked, ground or rolled oats. It can be cooked to serve as a cereal, or used as an ingredient in baking. Cooked, 1 cup (240 g): 130 calories. *Nutrients:* 5 g protein, 2 g fat, 23 g carbohydrate, .2 mg niacin, .05 mg riboflavin, .19 mg thiamine.

Oats—the grains of a widely cultivated cereal grass, used both as animal fodder and human food. Rolled oats are oat grains that have been husked, steamed, and flattened by being pressed through rollers.

O'Brien potatoes—a dish made of potatoes cut up and fried with chopped onion, minced green pepper, and pimiento.

Oil—a liquid fat prepared from vegetable, seed, fruit, or bean sources, e.g., corn, cottonseed, olive, peanut, safflower, and soybean. The oil labeled salad, vegetable, cooking, or all-purpose may be a blend of oil from several sources.

Oka cheese—*see* **Port du Salut cheese.**

Okra—the green seed pod of a tall plant of the mallow family used to give thickness and flavor to soups and stews. It can also be served as a vegetable. Cooked, 8 pods (85 g): 25 calories. *Nutrients:* 2 g protein, trace of fat, 5 g carbohydrate, 420 IU vitamin A, 17 mg vitamin C, 78 mg calcium.

Olive, green—the unripe fruit of a tree grown in Mediterranean countries that is pickled in brine and sometimes stuffed with pimiento. 4 medium (16 g): 15 calories. *Nutrients:* trace of protein, 2 g fat, trace of carbohydrate, 8 mg calcium.

Olive oil—oil extracted from olives. It has a distinctive flavor and varies in quality. Virgin olive oil, the oil from the first pressing of the olives, is considered the best.

Olive, ripe—the ripe, black fruit of the olive tree, first harvested and canned (pitted and unpitted) in California in 1901. It has a delicate, unique, nutlike flavor and is an excellent snack food. 3 small (10 g): 15 calories. *Nutrients:* trace of protein, 2 g fat, trace of carbohydrate, 9 mg calcium.

Onion—the edible bulb of a plant of the lily family noted for its pungent odor and taste. It is used as a flavoring and as a vegetable. Mature, dried onions include white, yellow, and red varieties.

Onion, green, without top—6 (50 g): 20 calories. *Nutrients:* 1 g protein, trace of fat, 5 g carbohydrate, 12 mg vitamin C, 20 mg calcium.

Onion, raw—1 (110 g): 40 calories. *Nutrients:* 2 g protein, trace of fat, 10 g carbohydrate, 11 mg vitamin C, 30 mg calcium.

Onion soup (dry mix)—1½ oz (43 g): 150 calories. *Nutrients:* 6 g protein, 5 g fat, 23 g carbohydrate, 42 mg calcium.

Orange—the juicy, edible fruit of an evergreen tree found in tropical climates. Most varieties have a sweet taste. Among the best known varieties are navel, Valencia, Seville, and mandarin (including temple oranges, tangelos, and tangerines).

Orange juice—1 cup (248 g): 110 calories. *Nutrients:* 2 g protein, 1 g fat, 26 g carbohydrate, 500 IU vitamin A, 124 mg vitamin C, 27 mg calcium.

Orange, raw—1 (180 g): 65 calories. *Nutrients:* 1 g protein, trace of fat, 16 g carbohydrate, 66 mg vitamin C, 54 mg calcium.

Oregano (wild marjoram)—a perennial herb of the mint family. It has a strong, slightly bitter flavor. It is available either whole or ground.

Oxtail—the skinned tail of beef cattle. It may be braised with vegetables or used in preparing stew or soup.

Oyster—a marine bivalve mollusk with a rough, irregular shell and grayish flesh that can be eaten raw, cooked, or smoked. There are many varieties, differing in size, plumpness, and taste. Raw, 3 oz (85 g): 53 calories. *Nutrients:*

7 g protein, 1 g fat, 2 g carbohydrate, 2 mg niacin, .14 mg riboflavin, 75 mg calcium, 4.4 mg iron.

Pancake—a quick bread. The cake is made from a batter which is cooked on a griddle or in a skillet. It may be used as a main dish or dessert. Wheat, enriched flour, 4-inch pancake (27 g): 60 calories. *Nutrients:* 2 g protein, 2 g fat, 9 g carbohydrate, 27 mg calcium.

Papaya—the fruit of a tropical American evergreen tree. It has a yellow rind and sweet, juicy, tasty, orange-colored flesh.

Paprika—a sweet to hot ground spice made by grinding dried pods of a variety of red pepper.

Paraffin—a flammable, waxy substance sold in solid form in food stores. It is used for sealing the tops of jam and jelly jars to keep out air and prevent spoilage.

Parfait—a rich ice cream made by pouring a hot, thick syrup over beaten egg whites or beaten egg yolks, adding flavoring, folding in whipped cream, and freezing; also sometimes used to refer to a layered dessert.

Parmesan cheese—a hard-ripened, light yellow, granular, very hard cheese with a sharp, piquant flavor; Italian origin. ¼ cup (35 g): 166 calories. *Nutrients:* 15 g protein, 10 g fat, 1 g carbohydrate, 440 IU vitamin A, 473 mg calcium.

Parsley—an herb with a sweet, spicy flavor; it is available either fresh or dried. Chopped, 1 tablespoon (4 g): trace of calories. *Nutrients:* trace of protein, trace of fat, trace of carbohydrate, 340 IU vitamin A, 7 mg vitamin C.

Parsnip—the white root of a plant in the parsley family. Parsnips have a mild, slightly sweet, nutty flavor. They keep well in both warm and cold temperatures. Cooked, 1 cup (155 g): 100 calories. *Nutrients:* 2 g protein, 1 g fat, 23 g carbohydrate, 16 mg vitamin C, 70 mg calcium.

Pasta—a dough composed chiefly of flour, water, and sometimes eggs, and made into many shapes and sizes, such as spaghetti, macaroni, and noodles.

Pastry—any of several doughs used in making pie crusts, tarts, etc. Pastry is made of flour, fat, liquid, salt, and sometimes sugar.

Pâté—a spiced meat paste such as pâté de foie gras (liver paste).

Pea—the round, green, edible seed of a climbing leguminous plant. Green, cooked, ½ cup (80 g): 57 calories. *Nutrients:* 4 g protein, trace of fat, 9 g carbohydrate, 430 IU vitamin A, 16 mg vitamin C.

Peach—the fruit of a tree in the rose family.

There are many varieties of this yellow fruit and two classifications, clingstone and free-stone. Raw, 1 (114 g): 35 calories. *Nutrients:* 1 g protein, trace of fat, 10 g carbohydrate, 1,320 IU vitamin A.

Peanut—a low-growing plant whose seed pods, containing a leguminous vegetable, develop and mature in the ground; the seed or seed pod of such plant. Roasted, ¼ cup (36 g): 210 calories. *Nutrients:* 9 g protein, 18 g fat, 7 g carbohydrate, 6 mg niacin, .06 mg ribo-flavin, .11 mg thiamine, .7 mg iron.

Peanut butter—a product containing ground kernels of roasted, blanched peanuts, some salt, and a small amount of stabilizer to prevent oil separation. 2 tablespoons (32 g): 190 calories. *Nutrients:* 8 g protein, 16 g fat, 6 g carbohydrate, 4.8 mg niacin.

Peanut oil—a light, tasteless oil processed from chopped, cooked peanuts.

Pear—the fruit of a tree in the rose family. There are summer varieties (e.g., Bartlett and Seckel) and fall or winter varieties (e.g., Anjou, Bosc, and Comice). Raw, 1 (182 g): 100 calories. *Nutrients:* 1 g protein, 1 g fat, 25 g carbohydrate.

Pearl barley—*see* **Barley.**

Pecan—the flavorful, widely used, edible nut of a tree in the hickory family.

Pecan pie (1-crust)—⅙ of 9-inch (137 g): 571 calories. *Nutrients:* 7 g protein, 31 g fat, 70 g carbohydrate, 64 mg calcium, 3.5 mg iron.

Pecans—½ cup (54 g): 370 calories. *Nutrients:* 5 g protein, 38 g fat, 8 g carbohydrate, .5 mg niacin, .46 mg thiamine, 1.3 mg iron.

Pectin—*see* **Fruit pectin.**

Pepper—a pungent spice made from the dried berries of a tropical vine. Black pepper comes from the whole berry, white pepper from the core only.

Pepper, sweet—a mild variety of pepper whose fruit, when unripe and bright green in color, is used as a salad ingredient or as a flavoring in various cooked sauces. Sweet peppers may also be used when mature and bright red in color. 1 pod (74 g): 15 calories. *Nutrients:* 1 g protein, trace of fat, 4 g carbohydrate, 310 IU vitamin A, 94 mg vitamin C.

Perch—any of various spiny-finned, fresh or saltwater food fishes found in both North America and Europe. Yellow, raw, 3 oz (85 g): 78 calories. *Nutrients:* 16 g protein, some fat.

Persimmon—the fruit of two species of persim-mon trees. Both types of persimmon have bright orange skin and flesh and must be soft-ripe before eating. Japanese, 3½ oz (100 g): 77 calories. *Nutrients:* some protein, some fat, 19 g carbohydrate, 2,710 IU vitamin A, 11 mg vitamin C.

Pilaf—a rice dish from the Middle East to which various seasonings, and sometimes meat or poultry, are added.

Pimiento—a variety of sweet, red pepper sold extensively in cans or jars; used as a relish or garnish. Canned, 3 (115 g): 24 calories. *Nutrients:* 1 g protein, trace of fat, 5 g carbo-hydrate, 2,300 IU vitamin A, 130 mg vitamin C, 1.5 mg iron.

Pineapple—the cone-shaped fruit, with a deep green crown, of a tropical or subtropical plant that is grown in Hawaii, Puerto Rico, and Mexico.

Pineapple juice, canned—1 cup (249 g): 135 calories. *Nutrients:* 1 g protein, trace of fat, 34 g carbohydrate, 22 mg vitamin C, 37 mg calcium.

Pineapple, raw, diced—1 cup (140 g): 75 calories. *Nutrients:* 1 g protein, trace of fat, 19 g carbohydrate, 24 mg vitamin C, 24 mg calcium.

Pinenut—the seed of certain pine trees. Pinenuts are usually roasted and salted and served as a snack food.

Pinto bean—a beige-colored, speckled vegetable of the same species as kidney and red beans; used mainly in salads and chili.

Pizza—an open-faced pie consisting of a bread base and topping, usually of tomatoes, cheese, oil, and seasonings and sometimes including anchovies, mushrooms, and sausage.

Pizza, cheese—⅛ of 14-inch (75 g): 185 calories. *Nutrients:* 7 g protein, 6 g fat, 27 g carbohydrate, 107 mg calcium.

Plum—the fruit of a tree in the rose family. The colors of three varieties are purple, blue, and green-yellow (greengage). Raw, 1 (60 g): 25 calories. *Nutrients:* trace of protein, trace of fat, 7 g carbohydrate.

Polenta—the Italian word for cornmeal, corn-meal mush, and dishes made with cornmeal mush.

Pomegranate—the fruit of a shrub or small tree grown in tropical and subtropical areas. It is 2 to 5 inches in diameter with a glossy, deep red or purple rind. The flesh around the seeds is deep crimson.

Popcorn—a variety of corn whose kernels explode when heated. Popular as a snack food.

Poppy seed—a blue-gray or white seed from an

annual of the poppy family. The seed has a nutlike flavor.

Pork—the flesh of a pig used as food. Pork is sold fresh, but it also lends itself particularly well to smoking or salting.

Pork chop, cooked—3.5 oz (98 g): 260 calories. *Nutrients:* 16 g protein, 21 g fat, 3.8 mg niacin, .63 mg thiamine, 2.2 mg iron.

Pork luncheon meat, canned—2 oz (57 g): 165 calories. *Nutrients:* 8 g protein, 14 g fat, 1 g carbohydrate, .18 mg thiamine.

Port du Salut cheese—a semisoft, ripened, creamy yellow cheese with mellow to robust flavor. It was originally made at Port du Salut, a Trappist abbey in France. Other names for this cheese are Port Salut, Trappist cheese, and Oka cheese.

Potato—a vegetable tuber from a plant of the nightshade family. It is classified by shape and skin color. The principal varieties are the Russet Burbank (long russet), the White Rose (long white), the Katahdin (round white), and the Red Pontiac (round red).

Potato, baked—1 (99 g): 90 calories. *Nutrients:* 3 g protein, trace of fat, 21 g carbohydrate, 20 mg vitamin C.

Potato, boiled, pared before boiling—1 (122 g): 80 calories. *Nutrients:* 2 g protein, trace of fat, 18 g carbohydrate, 20 mg vitamin C.

Potato, mashed (milk and butter added)—1 cup (195 g): 185 calories. *Nutrients:* 4 g protein, 8 g fat, 24 g carbohydrate, 330 IU vitamin A, 18 mg vitamin C, 47 mg calcium.

Poultry—includes all domesticated birds used for food: chicken (including capon), turkey, duckling, goose, Rock Cornish hen, squab, and guinea fowl.

Prawn—a shellfish, resembling shrimp, that varies in size from 1 to 8 inches; found in temperate and tropical fresh or salt water.

Preserve—a fruit that has been cooked in heavy syrup until plump and tender.

Process cheese, pasteurized—a blend of fresh and aged natural cheeses which have been mixed and pasteurized, after which no further ripening occurs. American, 1 oz (28 g): 105 calories. *Nutrients:* 7 g protein, 9 g fat, 1 g carbohydrate, 350 IU vitamin A, 198 mg calcium.

Prosciutto—a dry-cured, Italian-style ham that can be eaten without further cooking.

Provençale or **à la Provençale**—a term used to describe a dish containing garlic, olive oil, and usually tomatoes.

Provolone cheese—a hard-ripened, light golden yellow, firm, flaky cheese with mellow to sharp, sometimes smoky, flavor; Italian origin.

Prune—usually refers to the dried fruit of several varieties of plum; the pit is removed after drying. Dried, uncooked, 4 (32 g): 70 calories. *Nutrients:* 1 g protein, trace of fat, 18 g carbohydrate, 440 IU vitamin A, .4 mg niacin, 14 mg calcium, 1.1 mg iron.

Pudding—any of a wide variety of mixtures, savory or sweet, hot or cold, elaborate or simple, usually thickened with cornstarch, flour, arrowroot, or eggs.

Pumpernickel—a dark brown, coarse-textured bread made from unsifted rye flour, or the lighter brown pumpernickel that is made from a mixture of rye and wheat flours.

Pumpkin—the yellow-orange fruit of a coarse, trailing vine belonging to the gourd family. Canned, 1 cup (228 g): 75 calories. *Nutrients:* 2 g protein, 1 g fat, 18 g carbohydrate, 14,590 IU vitamin A, 12 mg vitamin C, 57 mg calcium.

Punch—a hot or cold, alcoholic or nonalcoholic beverage usually served from a large bowl; often fruit-based.

Quick bread—any of various breads which are leavened with baking powder or soda. These include biscuits, muffins, and also sweet breads, such as nut bread and orange bread.

Quince—an acid, applelike, yellow fruit which must be cooked before eating. It is full of pectin and makes flavorful, yet tart, jam or jelly.

Radish—a vegetable belonging to the mustard family. Radishes are round, turnip-shaped, oval, olive-shaped, half-long, or long, and are usually white, red, or black in color. 4 (40 g): 5 calories. *Nutrients:* trace of protein, trace of fat, 1 g carbohydrate, 10 mg vitamin C, 12 mg calcium.

Raisin—a dried grape of varieties grown especially for the raisin industry. Raisins are either seedless or seeded and either dark or golden in color. Seedless, pressed down, 1 cup (165 g): 480 calories. *Nutrients:* 4 g protein, trace of fat, 128 g carbohydrate, .8 mg niacin, 102 mg calcium, 5.8 mg iron.

Raspberry—a fruit of a plant in the rose family. The colors of common varieties are red, black, and purple. Red, frozen, 10-oz pkg. (284 g): 275 calories. *Nutrients:* 2 g protein, 1 g fat, 70 g carbohydrate, 59 mg vitamin C, 37 mg calcium.

Red cabbage—a vegetable whose red leaves are in the shape of a compact head.

Red snapper—a saltwater fish with lean, juicy

meat and a delicate flavor. It is caught in the South Atlantic and the Gulf of Mexico. Raw, 3½ oz (100 g): 93 calories. *Nutrients:* 19 g protein, some fat.

Relish—any of a wide variety of distinctively flavored foods which add special enhancement, e.g., pickles.

Restored cereal—a cereal made from either entire grain or portions of one or more grains to which sufficient amounts of thiamine, niacin, and iron have been added to attain the accepted whole grain levels of these three nutrients found in the original grain(s) from which the cereal is prepared.

Rhubarb—a pink or red vegetable from a perennial plant; only the stalk is edible. It is sweetened and cooked before eating. Cooked, sugar added, 1 cup (272 g): 385 calories. *Nutrients:* 1 g protein, trace of fat, 98 g carbohydrate, 220 IU vitamin A, 17 mg vitamin C, 212 mg calcium.

Rice—a grain from an annual cereal grass. It provides the chief source of food for a great part of the world's population. Polished white rice has the hull and bran removed. Enriched, cooked, 1 cup (205 g): 225 calories. *Nutrients:* 4 g protein, trace of fat, 50 g carbohydrate, 2.1 mg niacin, .02 mg riboflavin, .23 mg thiamine, 1.8 mg iron.

Rice, brown—the whole, unpolished grain of rice with only the outer hull and a small amount of bran removed. It has a nutlike flavor and slightly chewy texture. Raw, ½ cup (50 g): 816 calories. *Nutrients:* 17 g protein, 4 g fat, 175 g carbohydrate, 10 mg niacin, .12 mg riboflavin, .76 mg thiamine, 3.6 mg iron.

Ricotta cheese—a white Italian cheese with moist or dry texture and sweet, nutlike flavor.

Roaster—a young chicken of either sex, usually 3 to 5 months old, that is tender-meated and has soft, smooth-textured skin.

Rock Cornish hen—a type of domestic bird obtained by cross-breeding Cornish with Plymouth Rock chickens. They rarely weigh more than 2 pounds, are tender-meated, and have soft, smooth-textured skin.

Romaine (cos)—type of elongated, green head lettuce with coarser leaves and stronger flavor than iceberg.

Romano cheese—a yellowish-white, granular cheese with sharp, piquant flavor; Italian origin.

Roquefort cheese—*see* **Blue cheese.**

Rosemary—a leaf herb from an evergreen shrub of the mint family. It has a sweet aroma and a piney flavor.

Roux—a blended mixture of flour and fat used to thicken sauces and gravies.

Rutabaga—a large root vegetable of the cabbage family, similar to the turnip. It is yellow in color and has a rather strong taste.

Rye—a hardy annual cereal grass. The seeds are used for bread, flour, whiskey, and feed for poultry and farm animals.

Rye flour—the ground endosperm of the rye kernel. It is low in gluten, and therefore should be used along with wheat flour. Medium, 1¼ cups (100 g): 350 calories. *Nutrients:* 11 g protein, 1 g fat, 74 g carbohydrate, 2.5 mg niacin, .12 mg riboflavin, .3 mg thiamine.

Safflower oil—the edible oil extracted from seeds of the safflower (a yellow herb).

Saffron—the orange-brown dried stigmas of a variety of crocus. The flavor of this spice is pleasantly bitter.

Sage—the leaves of a plant in the mint family. It is a fragrant, slightly bitter herb, available either in leaf form or ground.

Salad dressing—a mayonnaise-type, cooked sauce made of eggs, vinegar, salt, butter, sugar, and various seasonings. 1 tablespoon (15 g): 65 calories. *Nutrients:* trace of protein, 6 g fat, 2 g carbohydrate.

Salad greens—varieties of leafy vegetables used especially for tossed salads. They are cabbage, celery or Chinese cabbage, curly endive, escarole, French endive, lettuce of all types, parsley, Savoy cabbage, spinach, and watercress.

Salmon—any of the various large food fishes that ascend from coastal waters to the headwaters of rivers where they spawn. The pink or red flesh comes in many forms: fresh, frozen, smoked, salted, dried, and canned. Pink, canned, 3 oz (85 g): 120 calories. *Nutrients:* 17 g protein, 5 g fat, 6.8 mg niacin, .16 mg riboflavin, 167 mg calcium.

Salt—sodium chloride, a widely distributed compound found in seawater and in rock salt. Used as a seasoning or preservative.

Saltine—a crisp, salted-top cracker, either square or rectangular. 4 crackers (11 g): 50 calories. *Nutrients:* 1 g protein, 1 g fat, 8 g carbohydrate.

Sapsago cheese—a light green, granular, cone-shaped cheese with a sweet flavor from clover leaves; Swiss origin.

Sardine—a small, immature sea herring packed in oil, mustard, or tomato sauce. Canned in oil, 3 oz (85 g): 175 calories. *Nutrients:* 20 g protein, 9 g fat, 4.6 mg niacin, .17 mg riboflavin, 372 mg calcium, 2.5 mg iron.

Sauce—a liquid or a semiliquid which complements or defines the food it accompanies.

Sauerkraut, canned—shredded cabbage fermented in a brine of its own juice and salt. 1 cup (235 g): 45 calories. *Nutrients:* 2 g protein, trace of fat, 9 g carbohydrate, 33 mg vitamin C, 85 mg calcium.

Sausage—one of a variety of products made with seasoned meat, beef, pork, or veal, and stuffed into casing. The two main classifications are fresh and dry (which may be smoked or unsmoked).

Bologna—2 slices (26 g): 80 calories. *Nutrients:* 3 g protein, 7 g fat, trace of carbohydrate.

Braunschweiger (smoked liver sausage)—2 slices (20 g): 65 calories. *Nutrients:* 3 g protein, 5 g fat, trace of carbohydrate, 1,310 IU vitamin A, .29 mg riboflavin, 1.2 mg iron.

Frankfurter—1 (56 g): 170 calories. *Nutrients:* 7 g protein, 15 g fat, 1 g carbohydrate.

Pork links, cooked—2 links (26 g): 125 calories. *Nutrients:* 5 g protein, 11 g fat, trace of carbohydrate, .21 mg thiamine.

Salami—1 oz (28 g): 130 calories. *Nutrients:* 7 g protein, 11 g fat, trace of carbohydrate, .1 mg thiamine, 1 mg iron.

Vienna, canned—1 sausage (16 g): 40 calories. *Nutrients:* 2 g protein, 3 g fat, trace of carbohydrate.

Savory—an aromatic, pungent leaf herb from an annual plant of the mint family.

Savoy cabbage—a type of cabbage with a round head of yellowish, crimped leaves.

Scallion—the shoot from the white onion that is pulled before the bulb has formed. Both the white stem and green top are eaten raw.

Scallop—a bivalve mollusk whose adductor muscle is used for food. The color of the meat may be creamy white, light tan, orange, or pink. Large sea scallops come from deep waters of the North and Middle Atlantic. Small bay scallops come from mollusks that are found in the inshore bays along the eastern coast of the United States. Cooked, 3½ oz (100 g): 112 calories. *Nutrients:* 23 g protein, 1 g fat, some carbohydrate, 115 mg calcium, 3 mg iron.

Scrapple—a kind of mush made of ground pork, cornmeal, and seasonings, boiled together and then chilled until firm. It is sliced and fried before serving.

Seafood—a general term that refers to any kind of fish from the sea, including shellfish and crustaceans.

Seasoned pepper—a ground blend of coarsely ground black pepper, other spices, dried sweet peppers, and sugar.

Seasoned salt—a blend of ground herbs, monosodium glutamate, salt, and spices.

Semisoft ripened cheese—a cheese which ripens from the inside as well as from the surface. These cheeses contain greater moisture than the firm-ripened varieties.

Semolina—the gritty or grainlike portions of wheat retained in the bolting machines after the fine flour has been sifted through. It is made only from durum wheat and must contain no more than 3 percent flour.

Sesame seed—the seed of the sesame plant, frequently used in baking. The seed has a nutlike flavor and aroma. 1 oz (28 g): 160 calories. *Nutrients:* 5 g protein, 14 g fat, 6 g carbohydrate, 1 mg niacin, .06 mg riboflavin, .28 mg thiamine, 333 mg calcium, 3 mg iron.

Shad—a bony fish often served in the form of fillets. It has delicate, tasty flesh.

Shallot—a vegetable, mild in flavor, belonging to the onion family. It has a small bulb divided into cloves.

Sharp cheese—a cheese (usually Cheddar) cured longer than mild or mellow cheese. Also called aged.

Shellfish—any of the aquatic invertebrate animals which have shells, such as clams, lobsters, mussels, oysters, and shrimp.

Sherbet—water ice (the base of which may be fruit juice or pulp) with beaten egg white or gelatin added; milk sherbet uses milk as part of liquid.

Shish kabob—cubes of boneless lamb usually cut from the shoulder or leg and skewered.

Shrimp—an edible shellfish that is usually dull green but occasionally brown or pink when raw; when cooked, shrimp is pink or pink and white. Canned, 3 oz (85 g): 100 calories. *Nutrients:* 21 g protein, 1 g fat, 1 g carbohydrate, 98 mg calcium, 2.6 mg iron.

Skim milk—milk from which most of the fat has been removed. *See* **Milk** for nutrients.

Soft-ripened cheese—a cheese in which the curing progresses from the outside toward the center. These cheeses contain more moisture than semisoft ripened varieties.

Soft wheat—the wheat milled into cake flour. The protein amount runs from 7 to 10 percent.

Sole—in the United States, the term sole refers to any white fish (generally a type of flounder) that comes in fillets. True sole is imported. Cooked, 3½ oz (100 g): 202 calories. *Nutrients:* 30 g protein, 8 g fat, 2.5 mg niacin.

Sorrel—any of several perennial herbs of the buckwheat family that have green, acid leaves called sour grass.

Soufflé—a light, fluffy baked dish containing a sauce with egg yolks, a flavoring mixture, and beaten egg whites which cause the mixture to puff during baking. Some soufflés contain gelatin and are chilled before serving.

Sour cream—a sweet cream that has been artificially soured by the addition of vinegar or lemon juice. *See* **Dairy sour cream.**

Sour milk—milk soured artificially by the addition of vinegar or lemon juice. It may be substituted for buttermilk.

Soybean—the bean of a leguminous herb, rich in protein, high in fat, and almost starch-free. Soybeans are used extensively as a source of vegetable oil, flour, meal, and other food products. Dried, cooked, ½ cup (125 g): 162 calories. *Nutrients:* 13 g protein, 7 g fat, 13 g carbohydrate, .75 mg niacin, .11 mg riboflavin, .26 mg thiamine, 3.3 mg iron.

Soy sauce—a dark, salty sauce made from soybeans, wheat, yeast, and salt.

Spaghetti—a general term used to designate the solid rod form of a macaroni product.

Spaghetti, enriched, cooked—1 cup (140 g): 155 calories. *Nutrients:* 5 g protein, 1 g fat, 32 g carbohydrate, 1.5 mg niacin, .11 mg riboflavin, .2 mg thiamine, 1.3 mg iron.

Spaghetti in tomato sauce with cheese, canned—1 cup (250 g): 190 calories. *Nutrients:* 6 g protein, 2 g fat, 38 g carbohydrate, 930 IU vitamin A, 10 mg vitamin C, 40 mg calcium.

Spice—a condiment from various plants which usually grow in the tropics. The parts used for seasoning are in these forms: barks, dried leaves, seeds, berries, stigma, and coverings.

Spinach—*see* **Greens.**

Split pea—a dry pea, either green or yellow, with the skin removed; mainly used for split pea soup.

Split pea soup, condensed, prepared with water—1 cup (245 g): 145 calories. *Nutrients:* 9 g protein, 3 g fat, 21 g carbohydrate, 440 IU vitamin A, 29 mg calcium.

Squab—the nestling of a pigeon; usually marketed at about 4 weeks of age when the meat is tender, milky, and delicately flavored.

Squash—the fruit of various vines of the gourd family, eaten as a vegetable, and usually steamed, baked, or fried.

Stew—a thick, souplike dish made with meat or fish, vegetables, and flavoring all cooked together in a liquid or broth in which it is served.

Stewing chicken—a mature hen, usually over 10 months old, with less tender meat than that of a roaster.

Stock—a broth made by slowly simmering trimmings and bones of meat, fish, or poultry, and then skimming and straining the liquid. It is used as a base for soups, sauces, and gravies.

Stone-ground—a term to describe a milling method in which the kernels of grain such as corn, rye, or wheat are coarsely crushed between heavy, slowly rotating millstones.

Strawberry—the juicy, bright red fruit of a trailing plant of the rose family. Raw, 1 cup (149 g): 55 calories. *Nutrients:* 1 g protein, 1 g fat, 13 g carbohydrate, 88 mg vitamin C, 31 mg calcium.

Succotash—a combination of corn and beans (usually lima).

Sugar—a refined product from sugar beets or sugar cane. White granulated sugar is meant if the type of sugar is not specified. White, granulated, 1 cup (200 g): 770 calories. *Nutrient:* 199 g carbohydrate.

Sultana—a variety of seedless grape used in making wine and raisins.

Sweetbreads—the name for the thymus gland of an animal (especially a calf or sometimes a lamb) when it is used as food. Calf sweetbreads, braised, 3½ oz (110 g): 168 calories. *Nutrients:* 32 g protein, 3 g fat, 3 mg niacin, .16 mg riboflavin, .06 mg thiamine.

Sweet potato—the tuberous root of a vine in the morning glory family. It has sweet yellow or orange flesh. Baked, 1 (110 g): 155 calories. *Nutrients:* 2 g protein, 1 g fat, 36 g carbohydrate, 8,910 IU vitamin A, 24 mg vitamin C, 44 mg calcium.

Swiss chard—*see* **Greens.**

Swiss cheese—a firm, pale yellow cheese, with a mild, nutty taste and large holes that form as it ripens. The original Swiss cheese came from Switzerland, but a natural Swiss cheese is also made in America. 1 oz (28 g): 105 calories. *Nutrients:* 8 g protein, 8 g fat, 1 g carbohydrate, 320 IU vitamin A, 262 mg calcium.

Tabasco—a pungent sauce prepared from tabasco peppers.

Tangelo—a citrus fruit of the mandarin orange family. It is a cross between a tangerine and a grapefruit.

Tangerine—a citrus fruit of the mandarin

orange family. It has easily removed, orange-colored skin and a mild, sweet pulp. Raw, 1 (116 g): 40 calories. *Nutrients:* 1 g protein, trace of fat, 10 g carbohydrate, 360 IU vitamin A, 27 mg vitamin C, 34 mg calcium.

Tannin or **tannic acid**—the chemical component of tea that is responsible for both the color and the pungent taste of the brew.

Tapioca—a starchy substance from the cassava root used as a thickening agent or as the main ingredient in certain desserts.

Tapioca cream pudding—½ cup (82 g): 110 calories. *Nutrients:* 4 g protein, 4 g fat, 14 g carbohydrate, 480 IU vitamin A, 86 mg calcium.

Tarragon—the leaves as well as flowering tops of a perennial herb. It has an aromatic, bitter-sweet, aniselike flavor.

Thyme—the leaves of a perennial of the mint family. Its flavor is warm and clovelike. The dried forms are whole and ground.

Tomato—a juicy fruit, red, green, or yellow in color, that is used both raw as a salad ingredient and cooked as a vegetable or a flavoring.

Tomatoes, canned (solids and liquid)—1 cup (241 g): 50 calories. *Nutrients:* 2 g protein, 1 g fat, 10 g carbohydrate, 2,170 IU vitamin A, 41 mg vitamin C, 14 mg calcium.

Tomato, green—1 small (100 g): 24 calories. *Nutrients:* 1 g protein, trace of fat, 5 g carbohydrate, 270 IU vitamin A, 20 mg vitamin C, 13 mg calcium.

Tomato juice—1 cup (243 g): 45 calories. *Nutrients:* 2 g protein, trace of fat, 10 g carbohydrate, 1,940 IU vitamin A, 39 mg vitamin C, 17 mg calcium.

Tomato, red—1 (200 g): 40 calories. *Nutrients:* 2 g protein, trace of fat, 9 g carbohydrate, 1,640 IU vitamin A, 42 mg vitamin C, 24 mg calcium.

Tomato soup, condensed, prepared with water—1 cup (245 g): 90 calories. *Nutrients:* 2 g protein, 3 g fat, 16 g carbohydrate, 1,000 IU vitamin A, 12 mg vitamin C, 15 mg calcium.

Tomato paste—a thick, concentrated tomato purée.

Tomato purée—a concentrated form of canned tomatoes from which most of the water has been removed.

Tomato sauce—puréed tomatoes seasoned with salt, pepper, and often other spices and herbs.

Trappist cheese—*see* **Port du Salut cheese.**

Trout—the name for some varieties of fresh-water fish. Trout vary greatly in color and size. Raw, 3½ oz (100 g): 195 calories. *Nutrients:* 21 g protein, 11 g fat.

Tuna—a saltwater game fish belonging to the mackerel family. Found in all the seas of the temperate and warmer zones of Asia, Africa, and America. Canned in oil, 3 oz (85 g): 170 calories. *Nutrients:* 24 g protein, 7 g fat, 10.1 mg niacin.

Turbot—a large, brown, European, saltwater flatfish of the flounder family whose delicate, delicious flesh is a highly prized food.

Turkey—a domesticated bird very popular for special occasions. Types available: fryer-roaster (under 16 weeks old), young tom (5 to 7 months old), and yearling tom or hen (fully matured, under 15 months old). 3½ oz (100 g) roasted, flesh only: 190 calories. *Nutrients:* 31.5 g protein, 6.1 g fat, 7.7 mg niacin, 1.8 mg iron.

Turmeric—a spice from the root of a plant in the ginger family. It is ground and has a warm, sweet flavor.

Turnip—a white, globe-shaped, purple-capped, smooth root with dark green top. Both turnips and turnip greens are served as vegetables. Cooked, diced, 1 cup (155 g): 35 calories. *Nutrients:* 1 g protein, trace of fat, 8 g carbohydrate, 34 mg vitamin C, 54 mg calcium.

Ugli fruit—a juicy, orangelike fruit that is native to Jamaica. It is about the size of a grapefruit.

Unbleached flour—an all-purpose flour which retains its natural color; no bleaching agent is used.

Unripened cheese—a cheese which does not undergo any curing but is consumed fresh. Soft types have a relatively high moisture content; firm types have a low moisture content and may be kept for several weeks.

Vanilla—a popular flavoring obtained from the beans of a tropical vine in the orchid family. The forms are dried beans and vanilla extract.

Vanilla pudding, homemade—1 cup (255 g): 285 calories. *Nutrients:* 9 g protein, 10 g fat, 41 g carbohydrate, 410 IU vitamin A, 298 mg calcium.

Variety meats—edible animal organs including liver, heart, kidney, tongue, brains, beef tripe, and beef, lamb, and veal sweetbreads.

Veal—the meat from immature cattle, under 3 months of age, containing little fat but a high proportion of connective tissue. Veal cutlet, 3 oz (85 g): 185 calories. *Nutrients:* 23 g protein, 9 g fat, some carbohydrate, 4.6 mg niacin, .21 mg riboflavin, 2.7 mg iron.

Vegetable oil—*see* **Oil.**

Vegetable protein—the protein from vegetable

and plant sources, such as dried beans, peas, and lentils; nuts (especially peanuts); and cereal grains.

Vinegar—an acid liquid used for flavoring and preserving. Most popular types are: cider vinegar, made from apple juice; distilled white vinegar, made from grain alcohol; tarragon vinegar, made from one or more vinegars and flavored with tarragon; and wine vinegar, made from red or white wine.

Waffle—a crisp, flat cake baked in a double griddle marked with a deep pattern, usually of squares. 7-inch waffle, made with enriched flour (75 g): 210 calories. *Nutrients*: 7 g protein, 7 g fat, 28 g carbohydrate, 85 mg calcium.

Walnut—any of several varieties of nuts including the soft-shelled (English) walnut, the hard-shelled (black) walnut, butternuts, and hickory nuts. Soft-shelled, chopped, ½ cup (63 g): 395 calories. *Nutrients*: 13 g protein, 37 g fat, 9 g carbohydrate, .45 mg niacin, .14 mg thiamine, 3.8 mg iron.

Water chestnut—the tuber of a tropical sedge. Water chestnuts have hard, nutlike skins and white flesh which is delicately sweet in flavor and crunchy in texture.

Watercress—an herb of the mustard family with pungent leaves; used as a salad green or as a garnish.

Watermelon—a large, oval or round, edible fruit. The flesh of a fully ripe melon is crisp and juicy, and may be pink or red, depending on the variety. Raw, 1 wedge (925 g): 115 calories. *Nutrients*: 2 g protein, 1 g fat, 27 g carbohydrate, 2,510 IU vitamin A, 30 mg vitamin C, 30 mg calcium.

Wheat—a cereal grain used mostly in making flour and cereals.

Wheat flakes, fortified—1 cup (30 g): 105 calories. *Nutrients:* 3 g protein, trace of fat, 24 mg carbohydrate, 1.5 mg niacin, .04 mg riboflavin, .19 mg thiamine. See package label for additional nutrients.

Wheat flour—the food prepared by milling and sifting cleaned wheat. This flour consists essentially of endosperm and may be bleached or unbleached. All-purpose, enriched, unsifted, 1 cup (125 g): 455 calories. *Nutrients:* 13 g protein, 1 g fat, 95 g carbohydrate, 4.4 mg niacin, .33 mg riboflavin, .55 mg thiamine, 3.6 mg iron.

Wheat germ—the heart of the wheat kernel. Toasted, ¼ cup (28 g): 106 calories. *Nutrients:* 9 g protein, 3 g fat, 12 g carbohydrate, .22 mg riboflavin, .5 mg thiamine, 2.5 mg iron.

Whipped dessert topping—an artificial topping preparation resembling whipped cream and used to decorate desserts. There are several types: whipped topping from an aerosol can; whipped topping prepared from a packaged mix; and frozen whipped topping.

Whipping cream—a product from the fat portion of milk; contains 30 to 40 percent milkfat. Light, 1 cup (239 g): 715 calories. *Nutrients:* 6 g protein, 75 g fat, 9 g carbohydrate, 3,060 IU vitamin A, 203 mg calcium.

Whitefish—a freshwater fish ranging in weight from 2 to 6 pounds; delicious smoked as well as fresh.

White sauce—a basic sauce made with flour, fat, and milk, cream, or a lightly colored broth. Medium, 1 cup (250 g): 405 calories. *Nutrients:* 10 g protein, 31 g fat, 22 g carbohydrate, 1,150 IU vitamin A, 288 mg calcium.

Whole grain cereal—a grain product which has retained the specific nutrients of the whole, unprocessed grain and which contains natural proportions of bran, germ, and endosperm.

Whole wheat flour—a coarse-textured flour ground from the entire wheat kernel. It has a distinctive, nutlike flavor and color. 1 cup (120 g): 400 calories. *Nutrients:* 16 g protein, 2 g fat, 85 g carbohydrate, 5.2 mg niacin, .66 mg thiamine, 49 mg calcium, 4 mg iron.

Whole wheat kernel (berry)—the kernel of wheat with only the chaff removed; requires long, slow cooking before eating. It will be somewhat chewy.

Wild rice—not a true rice but the grain of a tall, aquatic, North American grass. The grains are brownish white and larger than those of ordinary rice. It is prepared like rice but takes longer to cook.

Witloof chicory—*see* **Belgian endive.**

Worcestershire sauce—a pungent, dark-colored liquid usually containing soy sauce, vinegar, garlic, and other seasoning ingredients.

Yam—a moist sweet potato with orange-colored flesh.

Yeast—a microscopic fungus plant which grows by budding or by forming spores, and which is used as a leavening agent. Yeast comes in two forms, compressed and active dry. Compressed yeast is a moist mixture of yeast and starch. It is perishable and must be kept in the refrigerator. Active dry yeast comes in granular form and should be stored in a cool, dry place. Active dry, 1 package (7 g): 20 calories. *Nutrients:* 3 g protein, trace of fat, 3 g carbohydrate, 2.6 mg niacin, .38 mg riboflavin, .16 mg thiamine, 1.1 mg iron.

Yellow or **wax bean**—a yellow, edible-podded vegetable. Cooked, 1 cup (125 g): 30 calories. *Nutrients:* 2 g protein, trace of fat, 6 g carbohydrate, 16 mg vitamin C, 63 mg calcium.

Yogurt—a custardlike product made by fermenting milk with a special culture. It is generally made from homogenized, pasteurized, whole milk, but may be made from skim or partly skimmed milk. From whole milk, 1 cup (245 g): 150 calories. *Nutrients:* 7 g protein, 8 g fat, 12 g carbohydrate, 340 IU vitamin A, .39 mg riboflavin, 272 mg calcium.

Zucchini—a dark green vegetable in the squash family. Cooked, diced, 1 cup (210 g): 30 calories. *Nutrients:* 2 g protein, trace of fat, 7 g carbohydrate, 820 IU vitamin A, 21 mg vitamin C, 52 mg calcium.

REFERENCES

American Heart Association Cookbook, The. Compiled by Ruthe Eshleman and Mary Winston. New York: David McKay, 1973.

Betty Crocker's How to Feed Your Family to Keep Them Fit and Happy . . . No Matter What. New York: Golden Press, 1972.

Deutsch, Ronald M. *The Family Guide to Better Food and Better Health.* Des Moines, Iowa: Meredith, 1971.

Fresh Fruit and Vegetable Cookbook, The. New York: United Fresh Fruit and Vegetable Association, 1973.

Handbook of Food Preparation. 6th ed. Washington, D.C.: American Home Economics Association, 1971.

Jacobson, Michael. *Nutrition Scoreboard.* Washington, D.C.: Center for Science in the Public Interest, 1973.

Lappé, Frances M. *Diet for a Small Planet.* New York: Ballantine, 1971.

Leverton, Ruth. *Food Becomes You.* 3rd ed. Ames, Iowa: Iowa State University Press, 1965.

Margolius, Sidney. *The Great American Food Hoax.* New York: Dell, 1972.

Martin, Ethel A. *Nutrition in Action.* 3rd ed. New York: Holt, Rinehart and Winston, 1971.

Sebrell, William H., Jr., Haggerty, James J., and the Editors of *Life. Food and Nutrition.* Chicago: Time-Life Books, 1967.

Stare, Frederick J. *Eating for Good Health.* New York: Doubleday, 1964.

Tannahill, Reay. *Food in History.* New York: Stein and Day, 1973.

Trager, James. *The Big, Fertile, Rumbling, Cast-Iron, Growling, Aching, Unbuttoned, Bellybook.* New York: Grossman, 1972.

U.S. Department of Agriculture. *Food and Your Weight.* Home and Garden Bulletin No. 74. Washington, D.C., 1973.

————. *Food for Us All: The Yearbook of Agriculture 1969.* Washington, D.C., 1969.

————. *Nutritive Value of Foods.* Home and Garden Bulletin No. 72. Washington, D.C., 1971.

————. *Your Money's Worth in Foods.* Home and Garden Bulletin No. 183. Washington, D.C., 1973.

White, Philip L. and Selvey, Nancy. *Let's Talk About Food.* 3rd rev. ed. Chicago: Publishing Sciences Group, 1974.

FOR ADDITIONAL INFORMATION: Pamphlets and leaflets on food and nutrition are available from the Food and Drug Administration, Region 5, Chicago, Illinois 60604. The Home and Garden Bulletins, published by the U.S. Department of Agriculture (see References), are available from the Superintendent of Documents, Consumer Product Information, Public Documents Distribution Center, Pueblo, Colorado 81009. A Consumer Product Information catalog of federal publications is available from the same address.

Index